RECOLLECTIONS OF EMINENT ECONOMISTS
Volume 2

Recollections of Eminent Economists

Volume 2

Edited by
J. A. Kregel
Professor of International Economics
Associate Director of the Bologna Center
The Johns Hopkins University School of
Advanced International Studies

MACMILLAN

© Banca Nazionale del Lavoro 1989

All rights reserved. No reproduction, copy or transmission of this publication may be made without written permission.

No paragraph of this publication may be reproduced, copied or transmitted save with written permission or in accordance with the provisions of the Copyright Act 1956 (as amended), or under the terms of any licence permitting limited copying issued by the Copyright Licensing Agency, 33–4 Alfred Place, London WC1E 7DP.

Any person who does any unauthorised act in relation to this publication may be liable to criminal prosecution and civil claims for damages.

First published 1989

Published by
THE MACMILLAN PRESS LTD
Houndmills, Basingstoke, Hampshire RG21 2XS
and London
Companies and representatives
throughout the world

Typeset by Wearside Tradespools, Fulwell, Sunderland

Printed in Hong Kong

British Library Cataloguing in Publication Data
Recollections of eminent economists. Vol. 2
1. Economics, 1945–1980—biographies
I. Kregel, J.A. (Jan Allen), *1944–*
330′.092′2
ISBN 0–333–44919–3 Volume 2
ISBN 0–333–46482–6 Two-volume set

Contents

Notes on the Contributors	vii
Acknowledgements	xi
Editor's Introduction	xiii

1. Peregrinations of an Economist and the Choice of his Route   1
   François Perroux

2. My Work on International Monetary Problems   17
   Fritz Machlup

3. Aerial Roots   73
   Paul Streeten

4. An Emigrant from a Developing Country: Autobiographical Notes I   99
   Nicholas Georgescu Roegen

5. Confessions of an Incurable Romantic   129
   Irma Adelman

6. The Life of an Economist   149
   Charles P. Kindleberger

7. Reflections on the Drive to Technological Maturity   163
   W. W. Rostow

8. The Radical Reflections of an Applied Economist   197
   Henry Phelps Brown

9. On the Career of a Microeconomist   209
   William J. Baumol

10. A Fascination with Economics   235
    Karl Brunner

11	Economics as a Public Good *Herbert Giersch*	257
12	Better than Ploughing *James M. Buchanan*	279
13	The Challenge of Macroeconomic Understanding *Edmond Malinvaud*	297

Name Index   317

Notes on the Contributors

Irma Adelman, born in 1930 in Romania, lived in Israel and eventually moved to the US where she completed her PhD at the University of California at Berkeley. After a series of temporary posts she taught at Stanford and Johns Hopkins before being appointed to a chair at Northwestern, which she held from 1966–72. She has also been a Professor at the University of Maryland, 1972–9 and a Senior Economist and consultant to the World Bank. In 1979 she returned to Berkeley as Professor of Economics and Professor of Agricultural and Resource Economics. She is best known for her 'computable general equilibrium models' and her role as an adviser to the Korean government for its export-led growth policy.

William J. Baumol, born in New York in 1922. After postgraduate study and teaching at the London School of Economics he returned to the US to teach at Princeton University. Since 1971 he has held a dual appointment as Professor at both Princeton and New York Universities. In addition to his academic career he has been an active economic consultant, founding Mathematica, a well-known and highly successful consulting firm. After early dissertation work in England on the application of welfare economics to the theory of the state, he turned to the study of economic dynamics, and aspects of applied economics such as environmental economics and the performing arts. Recently his theory of 'contestable markets' has been the subject of wide discussion.

Karl Brunner, born in Switzerland in 1916. A Rockefeller fellowship brought him to the United States in 1949 and to the beginnings of an American academic career at UCLA in 1951 where he achieved the rank of full professor in 1961. In 1966 he took a chair at Ohio State and in 1971 became Fred H. Gowen Professor at Rochester University and Professor at the University of Berne. His early work on money supply analysis led to the formulation of a monetary analysis (with Allen Meltzer) which came to rival Milton Friedman's. Recently his work has extended to the political economy of institutions.

James M. Buchanan, born in 1919 in Tennessee. After directing the Thomas Jefferson Center of Political Economy at the University of Virginia from 1956–68 and founding the Center for the Study of Public Choice at the Virginia Polytechnic Institute in 1969, he moved the Center to George Mason University in 1983. The study of the process of political decision making by means of economic analysis now known as 'Public Choice' theory and of 'constitutional political economy' earned him the Nobel Prize for Economics in 1986.

Nicholas Georgescu Roegen, born in Romania in 1906, studied at a number of institutions in Europe and the US before he returned to an academic and governmental career in his home country where he remained in the post-war period as Secretary General of the Rumanian Armistice Commission. He left Romania in 1948 for Harvard and became Professor at Vanderbilt University the following year and became emeritus professor in 1976. Early study in statistics and business cycles was followed by influential work in consumer theory, dynamic theory and environmental economics. He is perhaps best known for his introduction of the concept of entropy into economic analysis.

Herbert Giersch, born in Germany in 1921, has recently retired as President of the influential Institute of World Economics in Kiel where he was also Professor of Economics. His work in economic growth and planning led to positions in international organisations such as the OECD and membership in the German Federal Republic's Council of Economic Experts (known as the 'wise men') from 1964–70. In 1969 he left his Professorship at the University of the Saar which he had held since 1955 to take up his new posts in Kiel.

Charles P. Kindleberger, born in New York in 1910, spent his early career in the US government and Federal Reserve Board. After active involvement in the Marshall Plan he joined the MIT faculty in 1948 where he was Ford International Professor of Economics until he became emeritus in 1976. He is best known for his development of the interpretation of the post-war role of the US as a Bank providing international intermediation and his 'top country' hypothesis of the hierarchy of the international financial system. His recent work has concentrated on international financial history.

Fritz Machlup, born in Austria, 1902–83. After leaving Austria in the

1930s he was Goodyear Professor at the University of Buffalo, Hutzler Professor of Political Economy at the Johns Hopkins University and in 1960 became Walker Professor of Economics and Finance and Director of the prestigious International Finance Section of Princeton University. After retiring in 1971 he was Professor at New York University until his death in 1983. His substantial contributions to the academic literature were concentrated in the field of international economics, but he also had great influence in methodology and what he called 'economic semantics'.

Edmond Malinvaud, born in France in 1923, has been in government service at the National Institute for Statistics and Economic Studies since 1946 where he has been Professor and Director of its School for Statistics and Economic Management, as an economic adviser to the Minister of Finance from 1972–4 and from 1974 as the Director General of the Institute itself. He has also studied and taught as a visiting Professor in the US at the Cowles Commission and the University of California at Berkeley. He came to international prominence with the publication of his book on *Statistical Methods of Econometrics* and his *Lectures in Microeconomics*. His recent research has produced three books dealing with the discussion of the determination of unemployment within Walrasian and neo-Walrasian general equilibrium models.

François Perroux, born in 1903, played a major role in the post-war development of French national accounts and budget planning as founder and director of the Institute of Applied Economic Science (ISEA) in 1944, which eventually became the Institute of Applied Mathematical and Economic Sciences (ISMEA). Under his guidance for nearly four decades the Institute was the most active and innovative centre of economic research in France. During a university career which started in 1937, he held chairs in Lyon and at the Sorbonne before being elected in 1955 to a chair in the College of France from which he retired in 1975. From 1960–9 he was director of the Institute for the study of the economic and social development (IEDES). In addition to his work on planning and national accounts his work has centred on a criticism of static general equilibrium theory and the formulation of a generalised equilibrium approach based on dynamic modification of the environment.

Henry Phelps Brown, born in England 1906, was a Fellow of New

College, Oxford from 1930–47 and then Professor of Labour Economics at the London School of Economics until retiring in 1968. He is known for his life-long study of the movement of money and real wages and productivity, and the factors which determine them, over long periods and their impact on industrial relations. Among his best-known works are *A Century of Pay* (with M. Browne) 1968, and *The Inequality of Pay*, 1977.

W.W. Rostow, born in New York in 1916, combined economics and history to produce his well-known theory of the 'take-off' in his rendering of the stages of economic development. He has also been an adviser to a number of US governments, serving *inter alia* in the National Security Council and the Department of State in the Kennedy and Johnson administrations from 1961–9. His academic career, which has included teaching at Columbia, Oxford and Cambridge, was spent primarily at MIT. After leaving government service in 1969 he became Rex G. Baker Jr. Professor of Political Economy at the University of Texas in Austin.

Paul Streeten, born in Austria in 1917, has had a career in academic and international institutions in both the United Kingdom and the US since fleeing Austria in the 1930s. He was Fellow of Balliol College from 1948–78, with the exception of a two-year period from 1966–8 when he became Professor of Economics and Acting Director of the Institute of Development Studies in the University of Sussex. In 1968 he returned to Oxford and was Warden of Queen Elizabeth House and Director of the Institute of Commonwealth Studies until 1979. He has also been an adviser on development issues to the British government, the World Bank and the International Labour Organisation. Since 1983 he has been Professor of Economics and Director of the World Development Institute of Boston University.

Acknowledgements

The 'Recollections of Eminent Economists' published in this volume originally appeared in the following numbers of the *Banca Nazionale del Lavoro Quarterly Review*:

François Perroux, no. 133, June 1980, pp. 147–62; Fritz Machlup, no. 133, June 1980, 115–46 and no. 140, March 1982, pp. 3–36; Paul Streeten, no. 157, June 1986, pp. 135–59; Irma Adelman, no. 166, September 1988, pp. 243–62; Nicholas Georgescu Roegen, no. 164, March 1988, pp. 3–32; Charles P. Kindleberger, no. 134, September 1980, pp. 231–45; W. W. Rostow, no. 161, June 1987, pp. 115–46. H. Phelps Brown, no. 132, March 1980, pp. 3–14; William J. Baumol, no. 147, December 1983, 311–35; K. Brunner, no. 135, December 1980, pp. 403–26; H. Giersch, no. 158, September 1986, pp. 251–73; James M. Buchanan, no. 159, December 1986, pp. 359–76; Edmond Malinvaud, no. 162, September 1987, pp. 219–38.

Editor's Introduction

The *Banca Nazionale del Lavoro Quarterly Review* first appeared in 1947, edited by Dott. Luigi Ceriani. It was followed a year later by an Italian-language version, *Moneta e Credito*. The two journals initially dealt with aspects of the Italian economy, but soon enlarged their horizons to the international economy and its component countries.

In 1979 the *Review* asked some of its most frequent contributors, as well as other eminent economists, to contribute recollections and personal reminiscences of their activities and experiences in the process of the development of their research work in economics. No particular constraint or format was placed on these contributions and their form and content varied from extremely personal memoires to more reasoned professional reflections on the development of theory and policy. But they all had one aspect in common, they were the testimony of personal witnesses to the great theory and policy advances made in economics and the rapid growth in the economics profession in the post-war period. Their high quality generated a great deal of interest and discussion and they have been praised in particular for the added contribution which they make to our understanding of economics, as well as the economists who have contributed to it.

In 1988 a first volume of these *Recollections* was published to celebrate the first forty years of the *Banca Nazionale del Lavoro Quarterly Review*. The contents of this second volume, which completes the publication of the remaining *Recollections* which have appeared to date, can also be characterised, as Nerio Nesi, Chairman of the Bank noted in his Preface to the first volume, by the fact that they confirm Allyn Young's statement, quoted by Nicholas Kaldor in his essay in Volume 1: 'Economics is best defined by the particular interests which have prompted its founders – not by its "subject matter" as such.'

As in the first volume, the most difficult task facing the editor of such a collection is the order of presentation, for the authors have varied backgrounds and interests, and as already noted, responded very differently to the open brief given them by the *Review*. The theoretical dialogue over a limited number of basic issues such as the analysis of the cycle, Keynesian economics, imperfect competition which organised the first volume was perhaps too subtle for any but the trained economist to appreciate fully. The lay reader may have been perplexed by the extreme variations in the content and method of treatment adopted by the contributors. This variation is also true of the present set of essays. Some pass in critical review the author's entire scientific contribution to economics, while others deal with more personal details.

The present volume has a much simpler organisation and revolves around people and places; Vienna and Austrian and Romanian political refugees, MIT economic historians and applied microeconomics, to finish with a French non-Walrasian. The volume opens with the recollection of a Frenchman beginning his economics studies in Vienna in the 1930s. Although French, François Perroux exemplifies the 'European' nature of the economics of the period, having studied in most of the major European and American centres of learning, actively involved in the introduction of planning and budgeting in France in the post-war period, and playing a crucial role at the centre of innovation and enquiry in theoretical and applied economics in France. His claim that his real study of the subject began in Vienna gives an idea of the important role played by that city and by Austrian economists in the period which ended with *Anschluss*. The situation was, of course, already changing radically as a result of the depression and the rise of the National-Socialist government in Germany. By the outbreak of the war Austrian economists had been scattered to the four winds and could be found throughout the world, but especially in the US and the UK.

The essays by Fritz Machlup and Paul Streeten give an idea of what Vienna was like as a centre of intellectual ferment and economic ideas. Machlup started in a business career, but maintained his intellectual and research interests outside traditional university employment. Intellectual pursuits and publication at that time did not presuppose either the etiquette of a university position or funding by research grants. But, not being in the direct line of disciples of a university professor, he was unable even to secure a place as an unpaid university lecturer; eventually he emigrated on receipt of an offer in the US of a full professorship. Actively involved in the analysis of international monetary problems in Austria, he eventually went on to succeed Jacob Viner at Princeton University in the most influential chair in international economics in the world.

Paul Streeten's experiences of intellectual life in Vienna are from a more youthful standpoint, but no less interesting having been brought up in a circle including Wilhelm Reich and Karl Popper. He left under rather different circumstances, a clandestine escape to England in the aftermath of *Anschluss*. A university career at Aberdeen University was interrupted by internment and eventual war service, a near fatal wound bringing him back to England where he recovered and commenced a career at Balliol College, Oxford. Like Machlup, he eventually ended in the US, a world renowned expert in economic development.

Georgescu Roegen also came from Mitteleuropa, and his education was as peripatetic as Perroux's, including a PhD from the Sorbonne in statistics, study in London and at Harvard with another of the better known Austrian *émigrés*, Schumpeter, who was instrumental in turning his mathematical genius to the study of economic problems, among which not surprisingly was the cycle. Georgescu, however, felt indebted for the support his education had received from his home country of Romania and gave up Schumpeter's offer to stay at Harvard to make a career in Romania. Only to be forced to flee after the war to the US where after a year he settled at Vanderbilt University in Tennessee. His description of intellectual life in Romania is surprisingly similar to that of Vienna, as are the descriptions of his studies in Paris and London.

Irma Adelman was also a Romanian refugee, but at a much younger age, passing to the United States via Israel. The problem of political discrimination was less important in shaping her career than sexual discrimination, as her difficulty in securing a first post on any but the most temporary basis testifies. But she was also a pioneer in a number of other areas, such as computer simulation of economic models and models of export-led growth. Korea testifies to her qualities as an adviser on development issues. So does the fact that she now warns that this is a policy which may have had its time and that it cannot be applied to all and sundry as a magic formula. Economists need technical expertise, but they cannot be simply technicians.

While the depression and the war were moving 'mitteleuropean' intellectuals towards England and the US, young Americans were being moved in the opposite direction. Both Charles Kindleberger, world expert in international finance, and Walt Whitman Rostow, expert on long-term economic development, were economists who applied economic theory to economic history to produce their special approach to the subject. They also recognised the importance of viewing data in its historical context. Both also studied and taught in Europe, served the US government in the OSS, and took up teaching careers at MIT. Rostow subsequently became an influential US government adviser in the Kennedy and Johnson administrations. Their careers make as interesting a parallel as that of the two Austrian *émigrés*, Machlup and Streeten.

The remainder of the contributions is organised around the general theme of applied economics, and the application of microeconomic theory in particular. Phelps Brown, who had a distinguished career as a student of labour economics, was also involved in government and business advising. His essay raises penetrating questions concerning the relation between modern economics preparation and the requirements for training a good applied economist and policy maker. He finds the two almost completely distinct exercises.

William Baumol's career, on the other hand, presents the strongest of cases for the usefulness of microeconomic theory as the basis of applied work. Baumol's early career provides a parallel to Georgescu Roegen's for he too declined an offer of employment at a foreign university he was visiting (from Lionel Robbins to stay at the London School of Economics) in order to return home where he subsequently was offered a post at Princeton which he has held to this day.

Although Switzerland is well known for the economists who have taught at Lausanne (discussion of the work of Walras and Pareto appears in many of the essays), Swiss economists teaching in Switzerland are not generally internationally known. Karl Brunner's essay suggests why. Similar to the official Austrian academia, closed Swiss academic circles eventually made it easier for Brunner to find the environment he needed to develop his microeconomic approach to monetary analysis in the United States. Brunner's approach to monetary problems, which rivals Milton Friedman's, has always been characterised by its refusal to depart from choice-theoretical analysis even of what are considered to be macro issues.

The belief in the application of microeconomic theory is also the leitmotiv of Herbert Giersch's recollections. He follows Brunner in recognising the importance of a microeconomic analysis of the role of institutions and especially government. This is perhaps due to his experience as a founder member of the German council of economic experts, the so-called 'wise men' who offer independent economic policy advice. As Giersch's essay demonstrates, the problem with independent advice is that the recipient is also independent of having to heed it.

While both Brunner and Giersch give attention to the economic analysis of government and institutions, it has been virtually the life's work of James Buchanan, and he was awarded the Nobel Prize in economics on the basis of it. Buchanan founded the flourishing field of research known as 'public choice' theory. In an era in which English tends to be the dominant means of communication it is interesting to note that major inspiration for his work came from his ability to read untranslated works by Wicksell in German and from studying Italian writers on public finance in the original.

The collection closes, as it started, with a Frenchman who like Perroux, had a background in mathematics and statistics, was trained in the Walrasian framework of general equilibrium and who has moved from fundamentally microeconomic interests to asking fundamental macroeconomic questions via criticism of the Walrasian model. Malinvaud has been one of the leading practitioners of the 'disequilibrium' or neo-Walrasian approach to macroeconomics which has integrated and extended developments in the United States and other European countries. Much like Perroux, Malinvaud now heads an institute which has been at the forefront of innovative work in economic policy and planning. He also shows that even in today's world it is not necessary to have a full-time university position to make fundamental contributions to the subject.

If one were to search for a unifying aspect of the careers of the authors of these essays an obvious candidate would be their extensive experience in government or business. Machlup started as a businessman, Streeten an adviser to the British, Indian and Maltese governments and the World Bank, Georgescu a Romanian government official, Adelman a consultant to the Korean government and the World Bank, Kindleberger at the Federal Reserve and the State department. Rostow as a high government adviser, Phelps Brown as a government adviser, Baumol started his career in the Department of Agriculture, Brunner as an adviser to the European Commission and Swiss trade organisations, Giersch as an OECD official and then one of the Economic 'wise men' and Malinvaud as an employee and then the head of the French government statistical service. It is perhaps ironical that the exception to this generalisation is the economist who has spent his career analysing the behaviour of political decision makers and appears not to have served in any official or unofficial government capacity.

An explanation of this pervasiveness of government service is partially to be found in the fact that many of the authors entered the job market in the depression or just after the Second World War before the expansion of the university system had begun. Government was one of the few outlets for trained economists at the time and judging from the experiences recounted here appears to have offered a fruitful ground for the development of new ideas.

The importance of a stimulating work atmosphere is also one of the themes which runs through the essays. The necessary environment for the fruitful interchange of ideas has been experienced by the authors in Oxford common rooms, the Johns Hopkins University economics department in the mid-1950s, at MIT, and even in prison of war and internment camps!

Obviously, these locations are distributed throughout the world. While some of the authors' changes in locations were not voluntary, it is interesting to note the role played by the Rockefeller Foundation in financing academic travel for visits by European economists to the United States. This was the case of Brunner, Georgescu Roegen, Machlup, Perroux and Malinvaud; in all but the latter two these visits eventually led to emigration to the United States (similar experiences may be noted for a number of the authors of the essays in Volume 1).

Despite their involvement in business and government advising, teaching is a major preoccupation for all the individuals represented. It is interesting to note that at least three of them express the opinion that the best teacher may well be one who confuses rather than clarifies! Indeed, Kindleberger suggests that the success of his MIT students might be due to precisely this fact and Streeten is unable to choose between the formal clarity of Kalecki and the brilliant, if imprecise, intuition of Thomas Balogh as the most important positive influence on his development. On the one hand these considerations refer to the risk that the too formal or polished lecture or argument may hide the real difficulties involved in analysis: if the student thinks he has understood everything when he leaves the lecture hall, the lecture was probably unsatisfactory as a learning device. The real intention, however, is not confusion, but rather the idea that the good lecturer does not necessarily provide pat answers or analysis to every problem, stimulating the student to try to work out answers in a more satisfactory, different way. To teach the student to think for himself. What may appear to be confusion, becomes art.

It is difficult to make generalisations about the theoretical positions of the authors, except to recall that all follow the path of being critical innovators, starting with criticism which eventually displaces the theoretical model which was at the origin of the investigation. It is for this reason that a collection of essays such as this has interest not only at the level of individual contributions, but also as a whole.

For the novice economist they give an idea of how economics is actually done by its best practitioners, while it is a useful antidote for the lay economist or politician who thinks he knows precisely what is needed to set the economy straight, or that his favourite economic guru has the only policy able to cure the ills of the economy. Here we have a group which includes a Nobel Prize-winner and some of the most respected economists who have earned respect in countries which span the globe and in the international economics profession, advisors to governments and powerful business magnates, none of whom would question the fundamental importance to the discipline of economics of the contributions of the others. Yet none are in full agreement with the point of view put forward by the others. As was seen in Volume 1, these economists are representative of the fact that even within broad schools of thought there is no universally accepted truth, rather there are simply points of view, attempts to understand a highly complex and changing amalgam of political, social, natural and economic factors which are more or less convincing and attractive to our curious desire to try to understand and to predict the course of human affairs. As Lord Keynes long ago reminded the readers of the Cambridge Handbook series: 'The Theory of Economics does not furnish a body of settled conclusions immediately applicable to policy. It is a method rather than a doctrine, an apparatus of the mind, a technique of thinking.' These two volumes of recollections show that technique of thinking, the application of that method, by some of the most adept practitioners in the profession.

1 Peregrinations of an Economist and the Choice of His Route

François Perroux

I would be tempted to date my birth certificate as an economist 'Vienna, 1934', when I arrived there as a Rockefeller fellow accompanied by my young wife. But that would be ungrateful to my first French masters.

At the University of Lyons, René Gonnard conferred on the Chair for the History of Economic Doctrines an exceptional lustre, combining a personal approach with an acute analysis of his predecessors. In addition to this homage, I owe him a debt of undying gratitude. Words are powerless to describe a young man's feelings when his intellectual ambitions and capacity are brought out by a mentor who treats him as his son.

Etienne Antonelli took an interest, which was exceptional in those days in France, in Léon Walras' mathematical economics and its sociological setting. He foreshadowed the confrontation between pure economics and socioeconomics which is still proving fruitful.

Thanks to one of the first French mathematicians to be deeply interested in relativity, M. Eyrault, I had the privilege of teaching in an Institute for Financial Science which he directed.

Long before I worked in the French capital (1937–8), I was exchanging views with a great master, Albert Aftalion, who was to become my friend.

I therefore rapidly obtained a grounding in the abstract and rigorous aspects of general theory and was therefore prepared for the refined casuistry of the Viennese.

PEREGRINATIONS AND ACQUISITIONS

There was an ardent pursuit of research in the seminars of Ludwig von Mises whom a certain ostracism kept at a distance from the University.

These meetings, sponsored by the Chamber of Commerce, were thronged by an international audience, attracted by his books and gripped by his lectures. Madame Berger Lieser, an incomparable promoter, organised subtle discussion on the famous foundations of interest, production capital and financial capital, and on the relations between interest rates and wage rates. Philosophers, historians, epistemologists and senior civil servants subjected the constructions of the famous Viennese to a vigilant criticism. Friedrich von Hayek, Joseph Schumpeter, Gottfried von Haberler and Fritz Machlup were already in other countries. Together with von Mises, one could meet R. von Strigl and, on the opposite side, Oskar Morgenstern, who was already fascinated by higher mathematics, closely concerned with economic forecasting (*Wirtschaftsprognose*) and dubious as regards marginal utility and the general interpretation derived from it. With all respect to his memory, I would venture to suggest that Hans Mayer, with his blond Jove-like beard, whose lectures were greatly appreciated and who was mad keen on hunting chamois from peak to peak, was perhaps as an economist content with less elevated pursuits.

As to the complex and profound personality of Othmar Spann, it would call for a lengthy study which, as it happens, has been vigorously carried out by Vallarché. Spann, a sociologist and philosopher, was far removed, thanks to his *Universalismus*, from the prevailing intellectualist positivism. His ardent temperament impelled him to make a thorough study of the relations between social formations and economics. He never succumbed to the temptations of national socialism which was then beginning to ravage the German world. Catholic by upbringing and having drunk at the wellsprings of the old idealistic and romantic Germany, he belonged to a different spiritual universe. Violently attacked by the Viennese liberals, he deserved sympathetic attention which he did not always receive, and he suffered from this isolation. When they invaded Vienna, the national socialists threw him into a concentration camp, where he suffered terribly and almost lost his sight. His memory and his work deserve respect.

Any genuine economic thinking is bound to tackle the equilibrium of interdependence. The Viennese School constructed its theory in a spirit which in many ways was contrary to that of the Lausanne School. It made a distinction, not without justification and using its own analytical instruments, between a halt in the flow of goods and the decisions of economic agents which by their interaction adjust supply and demand. As it took as its starting point the agent (*Wirtschaftssubjekt*) and the subjective theory of marginal utility (*Grenznutzenlehre*), the result could not be otherwise.

The differences between real taxes (*Echttaxen*) and those which are merely apparent, made it possible, with refinements which are still fruitful, to arrive at zones of indeterminateness and at thresholds. This also meant, even when one did not admit it, opening the irritating debate on the *rigorous and meaningful definition of what is called 'normal' profit*. I recall lively discussions between Ludwig von Mises and our common friend, Hugh Gaitskell, who was one day to become Chancellor of the Exchequer and who at that time was modestly pursuing his studies in advanced economics side by side with us.

Whereas von Mises stigmatised the inevitable unemployment caused by the excess of the supply of labour over the demand, or pointed out the long list of disequilibria and compensations which were unavoidable in the abstract, the future leader of the Labour Party stressed the margin for manoeuvre by acting on profit. Even before the great proliferation of analyses of imperfect or monopolistic competition, this kind of discussion could take one very far. 'What can you expect?' insinuated von Mises with a feigned indulgence, the sincerity of which was not quite above reproach. 'He is bent on a socialist career.' The truth was not quite so simple.

It was not just 'naked' economics (utterly opposed to the spirit of the German historical schools) that one learned in Vienna. One was given lessons in an elevated, delicate and all pervading culture. These were the days when it was possible to follow a course by Sigmund Freud whose psychoanalytical explorations were transmuted into a teaching calculated to arouse the earliest burst of enthusiasm. We would listen to the famous city-historian, Dobsch; then, having enjoyed the subtle messages transmitted by the imperial palaces, the Stefankirche, the Votivkirche and the sumptuous galleries of the Kunsthistorisches Museum, sometimes we were privileged to round off a wonderful day of cultural delights by listening to Lotte Lehmann singing *Fidelio* at the Opera.

None of us has forgotten the parties organised by the admirers of Ludwig von Mises at which Felix Kaufman, a living memory with a musical voice, sang in several languages the series of the Lieder of the seminar since its foundation.[1]

'You're leaving for Berlin. So you'll meet Werner Sombart. He's now got to his tenth definition of Socialism.' Such was the viaticum of

Ludwig von Mises. At my first visit to the author of *Der moderne Kapitalismus*, he greeted me with the words: 'You're coming from Vienna. You must have known my enemy von Mises there.'

In Germany at that time, to tell the truth, there was very little to glean. H. von Stackelberg and Erich Schneider came later. It was from Fritz Neumark, my old friend, who gave the best lessons in financial science and general economics and with them that one could immerse oneself in lofty European German culture. I was also interested in the works of Carl Schmitt on the philosophic foundations of politics. I subsequently got to know the profound moral greatness of the man whom I call my friend when he courageously snatched one of my students from the clutches of the Nazi police.

How fruitful was that stay in Rome where I followed some lectures by Luigi Amoroso, and where I became familiar with that extraordinary mathematician, statistician, sociologist and economist, Corrado Gini, and where I also formed irrevocable friendships with Ugo Papi, Giovanni Demaria and later Giuseppe Palomba. I am not forgetting Alberto de Stefani or Lello Gangemi who awakened my interest in special points of public finance, thanks to our joint admiration for De Viti de Marco.

It will be obvious that the assimilation of Pareto's thought via Maffeo Pantaleoni, Barone and their main disciples provides an analytical framework and food for methodological reflection which leaves its mark on whomever benefits from it, especially, perhaps, if he refuses to accept it too docilely.

My wife and I were on the point of steering a course for the United States when war broke out. The 'manoeuvres' in Lorraine and the different diversions of the occupation period had little connection with abstract economics. Since I had to lecture all the same, I took advantage of the opportunity to take up again in detail the Austrian-style equilibrium by preparing a book on *Value*[2] and compare it, in seminars at the Ecole des Hautes Etudes of the Sorbonne, with the versions of equilibrium propounded by Gunnar Myrdal, Knut Wicksell, and of course Léon Walras.

Over and above this, there was the Institut de Sciences Economiques Appliquées, founded in 1944 with the French Resistance and of which one of the first protectors was Lord Keynes himself. These were splendid moments, despite the harshness of the time. We worked there in company with the American doctor Sanders, and the famous Soviet biologist, Serge Chakhotin, a disciple of Pavlov. Pierre Uri and I proceeded to make a detailed study of the Keynes and

White plans, with our eye on the future. I had founded, with François Divisia and René Roy, a Group of Mathematics Applied to Economics, which was assiduously promoted by Maurice Allais, G. Dubourdieu, Jacques Dumontier and G. Lutfalla.

On Liberation, René Pleven gave me the task of studying national accounts in England, and we embarked with some other members of the Institute on a Liberty ship.

At last we were free to enjoy those personal encounters which we had so long yearned for during the terrible years of the occupation.

At Oxford, we were welcomed by Thomas Balogh, Paul Streeten, Burchardt and Steindl; at Cambridge, by Professor Joan Robinson. We were received not far from Manchester, in the gracious dwelling generously thrown open to us by Sir John and Ursula Hicks – in London we worked with Richard Stone. Everywhere in that great country after the glorious trials through which it had passed, we resumed contact with English thought.

Relations were established between the London School of Economics, the famous university cities and our Paris centres where Sir Roy Harrod, Sir John Hicks, Mrs Robinson and Friedrich von Hayek, at that time a professor at the London School, Sir Denis Robertson, and many others expounded their latest works.

Edward Chamberlin from Harvard, after a first visit which followed close on one by Mr Kalecki from Oxford, became a frequent guest and a permanent associate of the ISMEA. It was owing to his friendship and to that of Joseph Schumpeter, to whose work I had devoted a book, that I was invited in 1947, to lecture at Harvard. These lectures are the basis of a long series of my own research efforts and of those which they have inspired.

The first of these dealt with *Economic Spaces* and presented the three concepts which I regard as fundamental, structured space, polarised space and plan space. The other was concerned with *macro units* and *macro decisions*. It contained the seed of complex units and of hierarchised subsets. It was valuable being able at that time to meet, at the Littauer Center, W. Leontief, Walter Isard and Gerschenkron, and, at MIT, Paul Samuelson who submitted to ISMEA the algebraic form of the Hecksher–Ohlin model.

We all knew the potential advances inherent in J.M. Keynes' macroeconomic theory which was gradually adapted, quantified and steered in the direction of the breakdown of aggregates and of mesoeconomics...

To introduce asymmetry into economic theory means going

beyond the static equilibrium of perfect competition and preparing a radical change of perspective in order to understand interdependence.

CHOOSING ONE'S PATH

The recent review in *Les recherches économiques* of Louvain[3] of a *Homage* which was generously devoted to my research[4] credits me with a general concept of economic life in line with the contemporary trend in science and completely different from the 'neo-classic' vision'. It will be noted that this concept admits of an irreversible time, time scales, probabilised spaces, evolutive structuring and disequilibrium analyses. . . .

The choice of my path in fact demanded these substantial interlinking changes '*at the expense of the tranquil certainties of other ages*'[5]. The concepts, particular models, and theorems which I proposed[6] and which 'have stimulated a whole school of researchers to go beyond the mechanics models' flowed from a central intuition and foreshadowed an attempt at the recasting of the theory of interdependence which I undertake in my book on *Active Units and New Mathematics, a Revision of the Theory of Equilibrium*[7] which will be completed by a *Dynamics of Active Units*, the object of my research at the Collège de France for twenty years (1955–75).

PARTIAL APPROACHES TO INTERDEPENDENCE IN A WHOLE

In a course delivered in 1947 at Balliol College in Oxford, 'An outline of a theory of the dominant economy',[8] I concentrated on the asymmetric effects exercised by the United States on world trade. But I was very careful to emphasise that this analytical outline was also in its essence applicable to a firm or an economic subset.

I linked the asymmetry to three parameters: the dimension, the nature of the activities and the negotiating strength. I have not changed my mind. The changes in the state of the world have profoundly transformed the conditions in which they are present and also their consequences, but have not erased their analytical interest.

The word 'domination' was rather clumsy and somewhat sweeping. It gave the impression that one unit completely substitutes its decision for another's. This is precisely the case where the analysis loses its interest, since we are then in the presence of *one and the same unit*. I laboured this distinction, but to absolutely no avail. The unusual terminology chosen in order to *avoid* the confusions inherent in the word 'imperialism' made people think that I accepted the thesis. Although, from the start, I introduced precise distinctions, I had to make the point very strongly and explicitly for people to avoid confusing (a) *influence*, (b) *dominance* and (c) *partial domination*. Since then, a very large number of works have formalised these asymmetries by topological representations and by graphs.

In thorough studies in other countries and in France on general equilibrium, I have often repeated (and appropriated) two affirmations which have been far too little reflected upon. One is by Vilfredo Pareto at a celebration in his honour: 'I saw the concrete aspect and was unable to get through to it! Vedevo la realtà e non potevo coglierla!' The other is by Oskar Morgenstern, to whom we owe so much and who has been so unfairly treated: 'There is no road leading from L. Walras to reality.'

This is something which should make us realise the distance between the determination of a mathematical system and the 'determination' of an observable system, and, no less so, to try to identify the prefabricated obstacles impeding the passage from the conditions on which the famous theorems (of existence, uniqueness, stability and optimality) determine each other[9] to a description of the activity which can simplify it without destroying it.

The critical and fundamental intuition which has since then always guided me has led me to carry out special research which is illuminated by one and the same hypothesis. The conflict-cooperation and the battle-assistance components of any relation between agents – the macro units or complex units, economic spaces, influences, dominances, the effects of propulsion, the real propensities to work and change (innovation), the growth inducing points of training (poles of development, whether spatialised or not), the propellent firms or regions – all these concepts, carefully tried out with the help of numerous observations, will perhaps now be admitted as following from a methodical search for asymmetry in particularised forms and conditions. This same research leads us, in the field of distribution, to take into explicit consideration the social *roles* and *on the other hand* to analyse at the present time the *income discussed* on the levels of primary distribution and redistribution (so inappropriately termed).

A recasting of the theory of interdependence was maturing in the course of this special research. A first overall exposé was presented in my '*Active Units*'. Better than anyone else, I know *all that still has to be done*, and I am doing all I can to fill in the gaps. But it will perhaps be understood after these remarks that I cannot uncritically accept the verdicts which reduce my contribution to a simple criticism or which congratulate me on penetrating views lacking a comprehensive logic, or which in a polemical spirit, decree that my position is not operational. What is not operational, but not in the slightest, is the standard equilibrium, repeated without the subtlety and the scrupulousness of the founders, because it *destroys* the reality of the agent and of his activity on pretext of simplifying it, whether this is expressed uncritically in the current handbooks, or whether it conceals its weaknesses in quantitative models which, be they macro or mesoeconomic, play with *hand-restructured* blocks or sub-blocks which are incompatible with the standard equilibrium if it is interpreted strictly.

FROM EXTRATEMPORAL EQUILIBRIUM TO THE TEMPORARY EXHAUSTION OF THE DRIVE FOR CHANGE

The standard Walraso–Paretian equilibrium, whatever forms it assumes, applies to micro 'doubles' (twins) so 'small' and so numerous in the homogeneous space of perfect competition that none is in a position to oppose the *Diktat* of the price system and to modify the objects and agents surrounding it. Lagrange's mathematics confer on this view a coherence borrowed and indeed plagiarised from classical mechanics. These presuppositions and their consequences are being subjected to a sharp criticism, and one that tends to become general.

We are not going against the stream of advanced research when we start from the agent with an energy capable of transforming his surroundings, an energy which is temporarily exhausted if it reaches its own goal, if it comes up against a physical obstacle or meets with opposition from the partner. By deciding on the goods and services which are at its direct disposal (*space of decision*), it projects and brings into play *operational spaces* (purchases/sales, investment, information).

These spaces are extensible, and under limiting conditions, make it possible to define temporary equilibria in given periods. The whole proposition is amenable to topological formalisation as a prolongation of that of G. Debreu and of K.J. Arrow. The method gives a new lease of life and enriches the current models of monopoly, differentiated competition (R. Triffin), or aggressive or peaceful oligopolies and economic and financial groups. It admits of the representation of subsets articulated hierarchically.

This method is, in one sense, a return to A. Cournot inasmuch as it sees in any economic action a component of free choice and one of power relations and also offers an image of the relations between the *parts* (structured subsets)[10] which 'hold together', to repeat the very words of A. Cournot, in quite a different way from perfect competition prices. In line with the teaching of the general systems, each part, each structured subset has a *dimension*, and receives a *place* in a network of relations and constitutes a locus of actions and of *retroactions*.

The concept of economic space as a whole formed of hierarchically articulated parts has decisive consequences for general equilibrium. Let there be a small number of large units with a structure and given activities; let us call them the Large ones, in trade relations with a large number of the Small ones, also characterised in these two ways. Let the Large and the Small ones be placed in a vertical structure, from the first transformation to the final consumer. The Large ones can impose constraints on the Small ones. The co-satisfaction of the Large ones or the cessation of their oligopolistic struggle to avoid loss may be concomitant, to a large extent, with the dissatisfaction of the Small ones or of a part of them. For reasons of structure, the banking oligopolies, the financial groupings of large businesses, are in a position at a certain time, as a result of the concentration of supply and demand, their superior capacity of information, and their technical superiority, to exercise an asymmetric action on the small units and individuals. In the field of international relations, too, the provocative question can be equally well raised, given the very large concentration of foreign trade: 'Commerce between Big Firms *or* commerce between "nations"?' Between 'nations', that is to say, between sets of small units and of individuals whose behaviour depends on costs and relative prices, and, alone, is the basis of the substitution theorems on which the whole economic logic of the open economy depends.

A number of other cases of asymmetric relations between structured economic areas can be observed and are integrated into the reworked model of *general* interdependence (using 'general' in the sense of 'concerning the whole'), but not a *uniform* one (that is to say, translated by the same reversible relations in each point of the homogeneous economic space).

We have said enough to bring out the opposition between the *fictitious equilibrium* and two *equilibria of observable situations*.

The fictitious equilibrium, as should be repeated again and again, does not describe any 'observable state'; it is a grid for reading off positions, 'a transparent plate with points of reference' through which we can look at economic activity. The grid, the points of reference in the transparent plate, draw attention to the existence, the uniqueness, the stability and the optimality of a *point* of equilibrium, of a *price* for which all the supply is equal to all the demand at the micro- meso- and macroeconomic levels. No doubt. The question remains whether the choice of the form of the grid or of the points of reference of the transparent plate does not conceal the very substance of economic life which is the activity, the action of the agents, who are endowed with memory and plans, differing one from the other and unequal between themselves for given operations in a given period.

There is a radical opposition, *as regards the essence or the substance* of what is observed and constructed, between:

1. the general equilibrium of things (E_c),
2. the general balancing of activities (E_a).

In E_c, goods are moved by the neutral forces of the price system, assimilated to physical forces. Outside time and space, a stoppage of the flow is privileged on the basis of the maximisation theorems linked to perfect competition. If we are to achieve that, the agent 'must be' as if 'he did not exist'. He is reduced to a symbol of passiveness. Supply and demand, are always equal to each other in each case by virtue of *one* price, as *impossible* as the perfectly homogeneous space to which it corresponds and the agent with no activity. This equalisation dictates the cessation of the flow. E_c is the stoppage of the flow of the goods and is translated by recourse to a type of mechanics specific to physical phenomena.

In E_a agents with a drive for change, equipped with units differing in dimension and structure, engage in operations which are or are not compatible with each other. In the whole formed by the articulation of structured parts, the interactions of dissimilar and unequal agents give rise to equilibrations, very real *tâtonnements* (as opposed to the famous Walrasian *tâtonnement*).

The equilibria eventually achieved presuppose, first of all, the intercompatibility of the structures. The equalisation of demand and supply at *one* price has in itself no economic signification except when it is characterised by a relation to the interactions of activities. The temporary exhaustion of the drive for change in the system is characterised by a deceleration of the flow which forces the analysis to define the conditions of metastability, price hierarchy, and levels and degrees of co-satisfaction at the moment at which the *net* energy of the system is approximately equal to zero. Its construction implies methodical borrowings from thermodynamics and recourse to topological forms. It should be obvious that uncertainty, risk, conflict and information are not properties of inert objects, but on the contrary are inherent in man and his activity. Hence, economics fails to function when, in order to 'determine' itself fallaciously, it confines itself to describing the movements of inert objects which a reified man registers passively.

E_a is not, strictly speaking, a generalisation of E_c: it is a balancing of activities (in the sense of a balancing action) different *in kind* from the mechanical equilibrium of objects and exercised in irreversible time. It does not deserve to be called 'encompassing' except as regards the variables which it considers in addition to those of standard equilibrium (the information of the agents) and as regards the types of relations which it admits (equilibrations and regulations).

FROM THE EXHAUSTION OF THE DRIVE FOR CHANGE TO DYNAMISATION

It is the balancing of activities (E_a) which enables us to arrive at a rigorous dynamisation and coherence of the system. This is so for a decisive reason. All economic dynamism has its source in man, i.e. in the agent, and derives its value from the interaction of activities, unfolds in irreversible time and is maintained or eventually gains in intensity and in quality which can only be appreciated in relation to the human being.

The great statistical works on growth, whose merits cannot be overvalued, have sought to find regularities among aggregates and subaggregates, between blocks and sub-blocks of variables supposed to be linked causally by quantitative relations. Working from insufficient materials and statistical mixtures which are in no way analytical quantities, the method was, in advance, exposed to very restrictive limitations. To which must be added those stemming from the moving ten-year averages and from the paradoxical recourse to the Cobb-Douglas function and its constant returns, where evolution has to be described on the basis of modern industrialisation.

In parallel, we have been acquainted with subtly elaborated models of *equilibrium growth* which, as is noted by their creators and competent exponents, add little to what statics tell us.

Research during the last thirty years is thus in sharp contrast to the ambitious, significant and fruitful dynamics of the first 'classics', the Physiocrats, Turgot, Adam Smith and his immediate successors. All of them base their interpretation of long-term evolutions on activities, on the active operations of men and their social groups operating in relations of conflict-cooperation, in ambivalent mixtures of struggles and collaboration.

We are harking back to this impressive tradition if we insert any study of relations between quantified aggregates in such dynamic frameworks where the economic factor finds its coordinates in a social system. Population, technique, the rules of the game, cannot be reduced to relations between prices and quantities. It is as well to consider them, to start with, as exogenous factors, and then be free to see to what extent these groups of variables can be endogenised, inserted in the equations of the 'economic' functioning of the whole.

The typical model of this functioning is the one which links a propulsive subset to a static one, the rate of growth and the change of structure of the latter being a function of these variables for the former. Clearly, qualifications and specifications are essential for the construction of the particular models of propulsive firms, propulsive industries and propulsive regions.[11]

The evolution, when tested against the observable reality, which is studied by this method, puts the cycle and its trend back into the periods of development, distinguishes between cyclical contraction and structural crisis and connects economic dynamics with the dynamism of the social groups.

As it happens, carefully defined mathematics supports the reworking of the dynamics by appropriate formalisations such as Lyupanov's 'stability', R. Thom's point of catastrophe and the models of sequential and organisational games. Thus, we discover the prospects of an integration in the same analytical body of the metastatics of the balancings of active units and of the moving equilibrium of re-elaborated dynamics.

FROM DYNAMISATION TO REGULATION

In the economic whole considered, the decision makers maintain and upvalue the structure of their units, whether simple or complex, and enter in both cases into a conflict-cooperation relation, acting in both cases through regulations and partial equilibrations. In certain conditions, the result is a tendency to the metastability of the *structures* and of the *functioning*, subject to exogenous actions. The degree of this metastability, at various levels, depends on the information and the activity of the agents.

Another point is that history does not record any case of large sets, or 'nations', able to dispense with the *activity* of units called public ones which try to effect a regulation of the whole, with the welfare of the community in mind. It is not on the basis of objects, of collective goods, of merit goods, that this regulation can be correctly interpreted, but as the permanent interaction of *activities* whose plans have neither the same scope nor the same time horizon nor even the same means.

There is not, on the one hand, a 'private' subsystem which can be *completely* isolated under the law of the pure market and, on the other, public agents who engage in sporadic and successive *interventions*. The market is moulded by the society in which it functions and by the evolutive social structures which underlie the overall structures of production, consumption and distribution. Their relatively slow transformation is effected in the conflict-cooperation in the organisational games of the social groups. The latter act to obtain their maximum profit *and* to change to their advantage the rules of the social game.

If this is really so, it is only to be expected that the welfare theories deduced from competitive statics should reveal their weakness. The consumers' surpluses and the Paretian compensations were ill suited, both because they referred back to perfect competition and because they were congenitally linked to statics.

The three famous conditions of economic policy laid down by A.C. Pigou – maximisation of the overall product, reduction of fluctuations, and income equality, have not stood up any better to historical experience. To the first there has been added in recent times the optimum product structure accepted by the population. As to the second, a distinction is made between cycles and structural crises. As for the third, if the reduction of unjustified economic inequalities remains a considerably more fruitful perspective than the general reference to equity, it has become fairly clear that it is the search for a *socially optimal inequality which is really important*.

What is involved is the very form of society, and it is the dynamism of the social promotion of the hierarchised groups which enables us to hope in acceptable approximations to the least inequality. The main means of achieving it is concerted and contractual economics accompanied by through economic information and training of the organised social participants.

It is only in this perspective that we can regard as meaningful both the balance between the three flows – buying and selling, constrained deductions and transfers of solidarity – and, on the other, the first attempts to effect a really collective economic computation which would set out to assess the surpluses and losses imputable to well defined social subsets.

Have I recognised the huge debt which I have contracted towards my predecessors and towards all those who have been for me incomparable fellow researchers? Justified, at least in these few pages, the choice of my path?

I hope so, without being convinced that I have. It is difficult to record in so brief a compass half a century of investigations and to convey to the indulgent reader my sincere regret at not having been able to do better.

At least I can bear witness that economic knowledge, gradually organised, checked and purified by science, economics carried out in a scientific spirit, is worthy, because of the importance of the issues at stake and of its earliest conquests, of the devotion to it of a whole lifetime.

Notes

1. There still echo in my ear the lines:

    When a Frenchman loses his way in Vienna,
    He retains, whatever happens,
    Many a charming memory:
    Noble gardens, distinguished palaces,
    A story of form and line,
    And the graciousness of the moment...

    As regards the Wienerschule,
    Like a knight it arms him
    With the 'Ist es denkbar?' and with the charm
    Of the *a priori* method...

2. *La Valeur* (Paris, PUF, 1943).
3. *Recherches économiques de Louvain*, vol. 44, 1978, n.4.
4. Presses Universitaires, Grenoble, 1978.
5. *Recherches économiques de Louvain (loc. cit.)*.
6. *Recherches économiques de Louvain (loc. cit.)*.
7. Dunod, Paris, 4th quarter 1975. This book tries to formalise the concepts defined in *L'Economie du XXe siècle*, 3e edn. (Paris, PUF, 1969).
8. Cf. Modelski, George (ed.) *Transnational Corporations and World Order*, Readings in International Political Economy. (San Francisco, W.H. Freeman and Co., 1979, pp. 135–54.)
9. Very imperfectly even in the mathematical order.
10. And not the *elements*.
11. Cf. *Le progrès économique, Economies et Sociétiés* (Paris, ISMEA, 1967) and *Prises de vues sur la croissance de l'économie française, 1820–1914* (London, IARIW, 1956).

2 My Work on International Monetary Problems

Fritz Machlup

My first publications were in this field and I am still cultivating it, 55 years later. My first book was on the gold-exchange standard. This book had developed from a seminar paper, done in 1922, and from my doctoral dissertation, completed in 1923. It was published in 1924, with the imprint 1925. Perhaps a brief description of Europe at that time can show how the book fitted in its time.

The Europe of 1914 had ten currencies, all with fixed gold parities and fixed exchange rates. The Europe of 1920 had 27 paper currencies, none with a gold parity, none with fixed exchange rates, and several of them in various stages of inflation or hyperinflation. In Austria–Hungary the circulation of banknotes had increased 14-fold during the four war years; in the three and a half post-war years, from the first half of 1919 to the end of 1922, the paper circulation in the new Austria increased 670-fold. This currency inflation was halted in November 1922 and the price inflation stopped instantaneously. In Germany, the neighbouring country, the wartime currency inflation had been only by a factor of five, but the acceleration of the printing press in the post-war years (chiefly to finance government expenditures in support of the civilian resistance against the French occupation of the Ruhr region) set a record. Banknotes in circulation amounted to 2,014,000,000 mark in May 1914, to 67,485,000,000 mark in March 1921, to 13,092,000,000,000 mark in June 1923, to 28,229,000,000,000 mark in September 1923, and to 496,500,000,000,000,000,000 mark in December 1923.

These were the happenings in the years of my university studies (1920–23). Monetary 'experts' everywhere were raising questions about the best techniques of stabilisation and, possibly, of a return to the gold standard. Austria and The Netherlands had been the only two countries of Europe that before the war had operated gold-exchange standards – fixed gold parities, but no gold coins in circulation and much of the monetary reserves held in pound sterling. What system would most countries of Europe adopt? Would it be the gold-coin, gold-bullion, or gold-exchange standard? Very little was known about the gold standard without gold coins, and when Professor Mises proposed to me to investigate it, historically as well as theoretically, I went to work.[1]

THE GOLD-EXCHANGE STANDARD (1923, 1925)

The German title of my dissertation and book was *Die Goldkernwährung*,[2] in literal translation the 'gold-core standard', a term comprising both gold-bullion standard and gold-exchange standard. A gold-bullion standard, first proposed by Ricardo, had been operated only in England from 1819 to 1821. (England adopted it again in 1925.) The gold-exchange standard had existed in the Dutch-Indies, in India, in the Philippines, in Panama, and in several South American countries, I reported on all these experiences as well as on the major gold-exchange system in Europe, Austria-Hungary.[3]

I began my monetary analysis with the Ricardian dictum 'that the only use of a standard is to regulate the quantity, and by the quantity the value of the currency'.[4] I warned, however, that gold had long since been removed from its previous role as regulator of the quantity of money; domestic credit creation had become responsible for an increasing portion of the nation's money supply (banknotes and deposits). I distinguished the changes in money supply that were accounted for by the 'conversion principle' – the interconvertibility between gold (or foreign exchange) and domestic money – from the changes effected through extension and contraction of domestic credit. With this distinction I hoped to illuminate the continuity of economic thought, to show in particular how the monetary discussion of the nineteenth century, the debate between currency school and banking school, had, apart from confusions, led to insights of enduring value. The currency principle explained monetary expansion through inflows of foreign exchange or gold, while the banking principle explained the extension of domestic credit.

This model of the two origins of new money has been useful to me for over 55 years, as it could have been useful to all monetary analysts. It divides the assets acquired by the central bank or any monetary authorities into foreign and domestic; in the process of acquiring either or both, domestic money is created, but only the foreign assets count as monetary reserves. An acquisition of domestic assets – through the increase in money supply generated by that acquisition and through the associated increase in the demand for goods and services (and the consequent deficit in the payments balance) – is apt to lead to a loss of foreign reserve assets, which brings down the domestic money supply and thereby restores the foreign balance (p. 121).

I also noted that the acquisition of foreign bills of exchange and of balances in foreign banks constituted foreign lending (*Krediterteilung an das Ausland*, p. 141), a theme taken up 40 years later in my Wicksell Lecture of 1965. It was clear to me, back in 1923, that the foreign assets in the possession of the monetary authorities had their chief use as 'interventions fund' (*Interventionsfond*) to keep the domestic currency from depreciating in the foreign-exchange markets (p. 144).

Throughout my book I had a running battle with what was generally called the balance-of-payments theory of currency depreciation. This was an utterly naïve theory which tried to explain the rising prices of foreign currencies by the deficit in the balance of payments, but failed to see that the deficit was determined by an excess of supply of domestic money relative to monetary developments abroad. A chapter on 'Gold-Exchange Standard and Balance of Payments' was devoted entirely to an attempt to straighten out the fallacies – fallacies that have been repeated whenever payments deficits occurred virtually anywhere (pp. 118–39). A (rough) translation from this chapter may be of interest:

> Under a gold standard [including gold-exchange standard] any excess stock of money leads to a deficit in the balance of payments, which in turn leads to an outflow of gold [reserves] and to a concomitant contraction of the money stock, restoring the balance. Under an [inconvertible] paper currency the payments deficit [consequent upon a monetary expansion] leads, not to an outflow of gold [reserves], but instead to a decline in the exchange rate of the currency. With the new ratio between domestic and foreign moneys there is no longer an excess stock of [domestic] money nor a relatively high price level, and the deficit in the balance of payments disappears. [But all this presupposes that domestic credit creation does not recreate the excess money stock and rising prices.] (p. 121)

I repeated this qualification, made in the last sentence in brackets, any number of times, partly because one writer, Otto Heyn, had been busily advocating a policy of offsetting the effects of reserve losses on the domestic money supply, but chiefly because this seemed to be the policy actually pursued by several central banks. I tried to make it clear that these policies of offsetting the contractionary effects of official sales of foreign exchange by expansions of domestic credit were sabotaging the adjustment mechanism. The automatic contraction of the money supply in the course of financing the payments deficit was the very essence of the adjustment process, and to offset this contraction was to prevent the adjustment and to make the deficit chronic (p. 117).

Among the adherents of the naïve balance-of-payments theory of currency depreciation was Professor Spann, the official supervisor of my dissertation. I quoted him as saying that there is no limit to the fall of an exchange rate if the balance of payments is in deficit: 'If, as in any country on the paper standard, no gold is available, the rates of foreign currencies can go on increasing incessantly'.[5] Against this benightedness I had to quote authorities on the purchasing-power-parity theory, not just in the form in which it was expounded by Gustav Cassel, but also in its earlier versions advanced by Ricardo (1812, 1816), George J. Goschen (1861), Ludwig Bamberger (1876) and others. I reminded my readers that 'the domestic price of an import good determines the upper limit to which the importer can go in bidding in the foreign-exchange market' (p. 136). On the other hand, I had to be careful lest my readers forget the role of capital movements and speculation – as so many experts do in our days, 55 years later. I therefore reminded them of the fact that flows of capital funds may, especially in day-to-day balances, play a greater role in international transactions than flows of goods and services (p. 137) and that 'basically, every concrete exchange rate is a speculative rate, a rate that takes account of future developments' (p. 129).

This point – that purchasing-power comparisons are necessarily based on *present* conditions or rather, from a statistical point of view, on *past* records of prices, whereas present expectations necessarily concern *future* developments – is so important that one cannot place too much emphasis on it. Hence, I shall attempt another translation from by book:

Considerations regarding future developments are the reason for why the increase in the prices of foreign currencies may run ahead of that of domestic prices of commodities [i.e. the external depreciation of the currency may be ahead of the internal depreciation, or the reduction of its purchasing power]. The often-heard objection that the general price level, since it rises more slowly than the foreign-exchange rates, can therefore not be accepted as the cause of the rise in rates (and that it must be the other way around, namely, that the price level adjusts itself, with a lag, to the exchange rates) is utterly naive. Just as every economic action is based on the capacity to appraise future utilities . . . and future productivities, so will the formation of prices in the foreign-exchange market anticipate future developments. (pp. 135–6)

I believe I can now, 55 years later, formulate this more felicitously, but I cannot help noting that the essentials of my present theory were all laid down in my first effort. I scoffed then, as I do now, at the officials who 'blamed' the speculators for their disequilibrating sales and purchases of foreign exchange (p. 129). And I subscribe now to what I wrote then: 'A speculative demand for foreign exchange – often called an "illegitimate" demand – is nothing but the reflection of an expectation of a future "legitimate" demand the satisfaction of which is deemed to be uncertain' (p. 145).

There were monetary experts, in the 1920s as later in the 1960s and 1970s, who promised that abolition of gold convertibility would give greater autonomy to monetary authorities in the pursuit of credit policies for domestic objectives. I called this a 'serious error' as long as countries desired stable exchange rates:

> Exchange rates *vis-à-vis* currencies on a gold standard can be kept stable only if the authorities are resigned not to make use of the freedom which they supposedly obtained through the abolition of gold convertibility of the currency. Only an approximately even pace of money creation can make it possible to maintain stable exchange rates. (p. 146)

And likewise:

> A country has the choice either to pursue an independent credit policy and forget about fixed foreign-exchange rates or to maintain fixed exchange rates and forget about independence in its monetary policy . . . The rate of money creation is tied, with the chains of exchange-rate maintenance, to the pace of money creation in the other countries. (p. 160)

Since these formulations may sound like pronouncements of an ultra-monetarist who looks only at the quantity of money and disregards the demand for cash balances, I want to reassure the reader that qualifications regarding changes in the demand for money and in the velocity of circulation were not omitted. But I should admit that these qualifications were far from adequate. While such one-sided emphasis on money supply and insufficient attention to the demand for money holding cannot be justified, it can at least be explained. First of all, the quantitative significance of the two changes was vastly different during these years, with money stocks in nominal terms increasing by a factor of several hundred, almost a thousand, and in Germany much larger. Secondly, the decline in the demand for money holdings was due to expectations which were induced by the extraordinary pace of money creation.

A few additional issues, raised in my 1923–5 book, merit mention in this review. I found it helpful to contrast the internationalism implied in a system of fixed-exchange rates and unrestricted interconvertibility with the nationalism implied in a system of freely-flexible rates and a money supply generated only by domestic credit creation. In the former system an increase in domestic product is shared with other countries, as they can acquire additional goods in exchange for their money; if no new money is created anywhere but money is only transferred from one country to another, any increase in production is distributed among all countries and the world money stock is redistributed. On the other hand, without interconvertibility of national currencies and without foreign or international moneys held as monetary reserves, each country can keep an increase in its production for itself; and, of course, no country possesses any monetary reserves to use for making good a shortfall of its production by incurring a payments deficit. The contrast between nationalism and internationalism becomes even more conspicuous if countries combine the two principles of money creation, the conversion principle and domestic credit expansion. A country pursuing a nationalistic policy can accelerate its domestic money creation whenever its production increases so that it prevents a trade surplus from occurring, and thus it need not share the increase in its output with its trading partners; moreover, when it engages in credit expansion relatively much faster than the expansion abroad, it can produce a deficit in its payments balance and thus capture some of the production of the rest of the world. I characterised this policy as nationalistic because it can succeed in encroaching on other countries' production and in not letting other countries share in its own production. Of course, such a policy results in losses of monetary reserves or in increases in short-term indebtedness, which in the long run is not compatible with the maintenance of fixed exchange rates (pp. 166–7).

A terminological proposal of mine failed to take roots, but the idea did: the idea of a 'standard currency'. I referred to the replacement, in the practical foreign-exchange policies of several countries, of the gold parity by the par of exchange *vis-à-vis* the standard currency. I considered the possibility – 'by no means utopian' or improbable – of 'all countries of a gold-standard community giving up their gold convertibility and taking advantage of the possibility of holding reserves of earning foreign assets in a generalised gold-exchange system' (p. 147). And I considered a development of swap-arrangements that would allow an almost unlimited increase in monetary reserves. I did not recommend such arrangements – which I compared with the notorious malpractice of kite-flying (firms issuing drafts on each other) – but I foresaw this possible development with serious misgivings (p. 148).

The notion of a country with a currency that became the standard for setting exchange values of other currencies led me irresistibly to coining another novel term: the 'dollar-exchange standard' [*Dollarkernwährung*] (pp. 83, 140, 172–7). Besides the dollar-exchange standard I had also occasion to speak of a 'sterling-exchange standard' and 'mark-exchange standard' (pp. 83, 140, and elsewhere).

I had serious misgivings regarding the possible development of a dollar-exchange standard where no currency except the dollar is convertible into gold bullion and all metallic gold reserves are held in the United States:

> It is conceivable that all countries of Europe adopt such a dollar-exchange standard and thus, theoretically speaking, would be a gold-exchange standard without minting a single gold coin [or holding a single gold bar]. In effect, however, one cannot reasonably regard such a dollar-exchange standard as the equivalent of a [genuine] gold-exchange standard. For in such circumstances one can no longer assert that gold functions as a regulator of the value of money. Instead, the monetary policy of the United States has taken over the role as regulator of the real value of gold. When there is only a single large country on a real gold standard – as at

present [1923–5] – the real value of gold depends on the rate of credit creation much more than credit creation depends on [the quantity of] gold. (p. 173)

THE NEW CURRENCIES OF EUROPE (1927)

It was this theme that became a *Leitmotif* in my second book, *Die neuen Währungen in Europa* [The New Currency Systems in Europe].[6] I wrote it, on the invitation of the editors of a monographic series, in 1926. The book appeared early in 1927. The first part was theoretical, the second part described the post-war and post-inflation stabilisation of the currencies of sixteen countries, beginning with Latvia in 1922 and ending with Belgium in 1926. (France was still struggling with inflation and succeeded only in 1927 in stabilising the franc; also several other countries, including Italy, were still working on their monetary problems when I prepared my survey.) Only four of the sixteen countries provided that the monetary reserves for banknotes were to be held in gold; and only one, The Netherlands, prescribed (for a few years) gold reserves also for the deposit liabilities of the central bank. The other twelve countries allowed parts or all of their monetary reserves to be in the form of foreign exchange. Thus they had adopted the gold-exchange standard.

One may be tempted to stress the contrast with the pre-1914 conditions in the matter of gold coins: now [1926] only one of the sixteen countries, Sweden, provided for the redemption of banknotes in gold coins; and only one, Great Britain, for the redemption in gold bullion. In none of the sixteen countries did gold coins come back into circulation. Thus the gold-coin standard had not survived the First World War, but I doubt that one could reasonably regard it as a 'war victim'. Gold circulation had not been of real significance even before 1914. The new gold-exchange standard, during the first years of operation in the 1920s, used chiefly the US dollar as reserve asset; and for a few years, between 1927 and 1931, the pound sterling became the major reserve asset of the Netherlands. All in all, the situation which I had anticipated in my first book had materialised. The dollar-exchange standard had arrived. And with the United States as the only country buying and selling gold at a fixed dollar price, the value of gold in terms of commodities was now dependent on the credit policy of the Federal Reserve System.

Most of the theoretical pronouncements of Part I were improved reformulations of those made in the earlier book.

I want to select a few of the problems, examined in my 1927 book, for closer inspection in this survey. I raised the question to what extent gold can fulfil the function of determining the quantity of money or, at least, of restraining its increase. The case of the strict 'full-bodied' gold standard was, of course, merely an imagined 'ideal type'; the real question was how to control the issue of money that was neither gold coin nor gold certificate. One method of control was the imposition of legal limits, either absolute beyond a gold reserve or relative, a multiple of a gold reserve. If the gold reserve consisted of real gold, not just of claims on foreign currency convertible into gold, and if the authorities in charge of creating domestic money conscientiously obeyed the reserve requirements, there would be some ground for believing that the gold cover, or the rules for a 'gold backing' however arbitrary, could really serve the purpose of preventing excessive money creation (p. 17). In actual fact, these rules of thumb limit the issue of banknotes and bank deposits only as long as the authorities are willing to be restrained. If they are willing, any other rule of thumb, not at all related to gold or gold reserves, can work just as well; if they are not willing, if they believe that they have a strong reason for creating more money, the barrier will be lifted, and any rule, golden or not, will be suspended or abolished. And if the so-called backing consists only of gold-exchange, of claims on countries with gold-convertible currencies, the reserves are no longer scarce, indeed, with credit policies internationally coordinated and with easily arranged swap arrangements, reserves have become augmentable *ad libitum* (p. 20).

The second method of control was the conversion principle, the principle of satisfying any demand for foreign exchange by a standing offer to convert any amount of domestic money into gold or gold-convertible foreign currencies at fixed rates and without restrictions. Since any excessive creation of domestic money would lead to a demand for foreign exchange, and since the sale of the demanded gold or foreign exchange would syphon out, or mop up, the excess money, this operated as an automatic control of the stock of domestic money. If, however, 'cooperation or cartelisation of the central banks' (p. 18) succeeds in obtaining parallel monetary expansion and parallel upward movements of prices, outflows of gold, losses of reserves, and consequent contractions of money supplies will be avoided. 'Under a cartel system of central banks things work differently. If all countries try to keep interest rates low, no international gold movements will dictate recourse to tighter discount policies' (p. 19). Although these formulations anticipate not only the substance but also the form of statements heard in the late 1970s, I must admit that the words 'locomotive theory' and 'convoy theory' did not occur to me in 1927.

The policy recommendations which I derived, as an unqualified anti-inflationist, from my theoretical arguments, were patently opposite to the dominant thinking of the time. Since the gold-exchange standard increased the gross reserves of the participating countries and allowed practically unlimited expansions of monetary reserves, I urged that the reserves be kept exclusively in gold metal. If these gold stocks were held abroad they ought to be earmarked as the stocks of the owner, not to be comingled with the stocks of the country in which they are held (p. 22). The practice of most countries to hold their reserves chiefly in the form of claims on the United States must stop if the gold standard is to survive (p. 23). The monetary system of the United States was a 'manipulated' [managed] currency (p. 24) and the international monetary system was the dollar-exchange standard (p. 25), a 'situation that cannot last' (p. 25).

One brief phrase from the historical part of the book should be quoted, because it shows that what was almost self-evident to me, as to almost all of my contemporaries, is so little understood today, 52 years later. I mentioned that the internal depreciation (price inflation) of the Austrian currency, which had, 'as it is the rule in advanced phases of an inflation, been running ahead' of the increase in the quantity of money, came to a halt in September 1922, two months before the currency inflation was stopped (p. 40). Every informed student of economics at that time knew without any doubt that, when inflation accelerates, exchange rates increase faster than domestic commodity prices, and prices increase faster than the monetary expansion, even though that expansion was the necessary condition in the whole process.

THE TRANSFER PROBLEM (1928 AND 1930)

Germany had succeeded in 1924 in establishing a new currency, the new Reichsmark, worth 1,000,000,000,000 inflated old mark – a trillion, in the American way of counting. The new currency was stable both in domestic purchasing power and in terms of the US dollar. After the Dawes Plan of 1924 had stipulated the size of reparations to be paid to the victorious nations, the transfer problem became a hotly debated issue. The question was how Germany could convert the tax revenues collected in German Reichsmark into gold or foreign currencies to pay the reparations. Hjalmar Schacht, the same man who had been in charge of stopping the money-printing presses and had maintained fixed exchange rates – at times by means of a 'ruthless' stop of all bank lending – now warned against borrowing from abroad, because repayment of foreign debts in addition to payment of reparations could not be managed. The country could not succeed in turning around its trade balance and achieving an export surplus sufficient to yield the foreign exchange required.[7]

Schacht was right in pointing to the excessive borrowing by the German governments (national, state and local) and public agencies through bond issues abroad and loans from American banks; he was right also in warning of future difficulties in servicing and repaying these debts, particularly since they had been incurred for financing unproductive public projects which yielded no returns. Schacht was wrong, however, in much of his economic theorising about the adjustment mechanism. Since his views were shared and strongly supported by many official and academic experts, I wrote an article to explain the adjustment process and, in particular, the relation between the budgetary problem of raising the funds through domestic tax collection and the transfer problem of achieving export surpluses adequate to obtain the foreign exchange needed for the payments. My article was published in the late summer of 1928 in the journal of the Austrian Bankers' Association.[8]

Schacht was not ignorant of the adjustment mechanism under the gold standard, or gold-exchange standard; he knew that contraction of the domestic money supply could produce an export surplus with stable exchange rates, but he feared that the contraction might be intolerable. Today I would concede this point, but in 1928 I did not. Having lived through the post-war inflations and having observed that with strong political will one can stop inflation (and even engineer absolute contractions), and that the pains from such measures are (or, at least, were in the historical cases) small compared with the injuries suffered through hyperinflation, I was a fanatic anti-inflationist, almost insensitive to the costs of deflation. (After all, these costs would be relatively small if wage rates and prices were sufficiently flexible.) My harsh criticism of Schacht's fear of deflation was due to my inexperience with deflation and downward rigidity of wage rates.

I now admit this bias, but I do not repudiate the analysis contained in my 1928 essay. I still believe it to be useful, especially the exposition of the adjustment process under fixed exchange rates which uses three sequence-models of the adjustment process, for capital imports, debt repayments, and reparations payments. I showed first the sequences for 'one-shot' transactions and then the differences for the case of serial movements, that is, for continuing flows of capital or reparations (anticipating some features of period analysis in multiplier theory, published sixteen years later).

The single-shot sequence for capital imports begins with the receipt of foreign funds and the purchase of these funds by the central bank; it continues with the associated expansion of the domestic money stock and consequent increases in incomes and prices, with a resulting stimulation of imports; it ends with the use of the accumulated foreign-exchange reserves for paying for the imports, the associated reduction in the money stock and the return of incomes and prices to the previous levels.

The single-shot sequence for debts repayments by private debtors begins with the accumulation of cash balances by the debtors in preparation for the payment and with the consequent reduction in the active circulation of domestic money; it continues with corresponding reductions of incomes and prices, leading to a decline in imports and an encouragement of exports; the receipt of foreign currency paid for the export surplus and its sale to the central bank raise domestic circulation and restore incomes and prices to previous levels; finally the foreign exchange acquired by the central bank is now available for converting the domestic balances accumulated for paying the foreign creditors.

The single-shot sequence for reparations payments is much the same as the sequence for debt payments except that the domestic balances are accumulated, not by private debtors, but by the tax payers, the tax collectors (the internal-revenue service) and the agent in charge of collecting domestic balances for later conversion into foreign exchange.

The model sequences for serial flows of funds do not end with restoring domestic money stocks, incomes, and prices to the previous levels. For, before this phase in the sequence is reached, the next instalment repeats the early steps of the preceding instalment, so that money stocks, incomes, and prices remain at the higher or lower level to which inflow or outflow of funds has moved them. In all cases, it is essential that the authorities abstain from offsetting policies. Regarding the process for outpayments I quote from the English version: If

> a soft-hearted central-bank policy undertakes to replace by domestic credit expansion the purchasing power withheld, then the effective circulation and the cash balances of would-be buyers are not reduced and there will be no pressure upon incomes and prices, no tightening of the money market, no increase in exports, no reduction in imports – and no transfer. (p. 411)

Again, with regard to reparations, 'the transfer problem is solved once the budgetary problem – the problem of raising the domestic funds without resort to credit creation – is solved' (p. 412). The qualifications which I added to this apodictic statement were, I must admit, not adequate, because I had argued on the basis of strong assumptions regarding flexibility of wage rates and ability to pay taxes (pp. 415–16), German original, pp. 207–8).

On one important point history has proved me right. I contended that trade balances were quite flexible and could turn around under the pressure of capital flows and appropriate monetary adjustments. This is what I wrote:

> This is completely missed and misunderstood by all those economists who consider themselves certified balance-of-payments accountants but naively believe that one can project a balance of payments into the future or infer from the present state what the future state of the balance of payments will be. They all stare, as if hypnotized, at the large import surplus of today [1928], without which, they believe, the German economy cannot live. And then they raise the rhetorical question how, with such a deficit in the balance of payments, the nation can be expected to pay debts or reparations. Needless to say, if one takes the import surplus that has actually resulted from the receipt of foreign loans as given and unalterable, one can come to no other conclusion but that the repayment of the loans or the payment of reparations will be impossible. Only a handful of economists have seen the logical snare. The fallacy of the autonomy or independence of the balance of trade constitutes the fundamental defect in the naive balance-of-payments theory. (p. 408)

These lines were written in 1928, half a year before Keynes argued the contrary, referring to the trade balance as 'a sticky mass with strong internal resistances'.[9] Germany's trade balance in 1927 showed a deficit of RM 2847 million; in 1928 the deficit had declined to RM 1230 million; in 1929 it had vanished and given place to a small surplus of RM 36 million; in 1930 the surplus increased to RM 1642 million, and in 1931 to RM 2872 million. These figures show what can be done in a very short time (though it was surely painful); they also show the risk of relying on the 'latest' statistical data, as Keynes had based his argument on the trade statistic for 1927 with the large deficit – which no longer existed in 1929. Also he argued that Germany could not possibly do with smaller imports; in fact, imports fell by almost 23 per cent from 1929 to 1930; and by another 35 per cent from 1930 to 1931.

In 1930 I published another article, 'Transfer and Price Effects', in reply to Gottfried Haberler's article with the same title and referring also to the debate between Keynes and Bertil Ohlin in the pages of the *Economic Journal*.[10] I discussed first the limiting cases, where price and income elasticities of demand were zero and made a transfer impossible no matter how much price relations were changing; and, on the other hand, where income elasticities alone could achieve a transfer without any price changing at all. I proceeded to examine the arguments which led Keynes to his conclusion that the transfer problem might be insoluble (or practically insoluble) even where the budgetary problem has been solved. I concluded that Keynes had exaggerated the difficulties; and I pleaded for a clarification of the meaning of 'transfer difficulties'. Just what was meant? An adverse change in the terms of trade? An increase in real transfer obligations because of lower prices? Budget troubles (tax rates, tax revenues)? Wage disputes and strikes? Unemployment because of wage rigidity despite reduced effective demand? Losses of gold and exchange reserves and severe shortages of foreign exchange, endangering the maintenance of fixed exchange rates? Reduction in the standards of living? (My appeal was not heeded. I myself tried this clarification 33 years later, in an essay written in 1963 and published as Chapter XIX in the volume on *International Payments, Debts, and Gold*.)

In a postscript to the 1964 English translation of my 1930 article I admitted 'to some embarrassment about the excessive orthodoxy in my analysis' of 1928 and 1930. I added:

A few of my transgressions along these lines have been omitted or mitigated in my translation for the present volume, but I have allowed enough of them to stand in order to avoid false pretensions regarding my performance of earlier years. By too much retouching, stressing the correct predictions or anticipations, and glossing over the wrong ones, a 'reproduction' of old writings may give an exaggerated impression of the writer's wisdom or prescience. There is more justification for reproducing old articles in order to show the development of ideas over time than there is to establish priorities or prove precocity. (p. 424)

The excessive orthodoxy related, as I have said before, to the inadequate recognition of the evils of deflation in times of 'pressure-resistance wage rates' (p. 424).

FLIGHT OF CAPITAL (1932)

During the 1920s and early 1930s the problem of capital movements inspired by fear had become increasingly serious. The fears that motivated the flight of capital from an unsafe to a safer country were chiefly of imposition of stricter controls of transfers and conversions, of confiscation of property, and of political suppression. The dangers of communism or national socialism in Germany made capital flight from Germany a timely subject of discussion. In a lecture at Frankfurt in the Spring of 1932, I presented my 'Theory of Flight of Capital'.[11]

I began with distinctions of the sources of the funds used for remittance abroad and of the techniques employed in converting them into assets held abroad. The theoretical analysis consisted chiefly in combining different sources with different techniques. The sources were (1) existing liquid balances, (2) new saving, (3) amortisation of fixed capital and liquidation of working capital, (4) sales of property, (5) collection of claims, and (6) new borrowing. The techniques of conversion were (a) taking domestic money abroad and selling it there; (b) buying foreign money on the domestic foreign-exchange market or from the central bank; (c) exporting commodities or services and leaving a part of the proceeds abroad; and (d) acquiring foreign assets or balances from other residents of the home country (pp. 514–16). I described also some other techniques employed to circumvent various foreign-exchange restrictions, but found that they could be fitted under one of the four headings. I showed that 'technique (d) involved no net exportation of capital but merely a transfer of ownership of capital previously exported (p. 520). One case could not easily be fitted into the scheme: when the exporter of capital exchanges his domestic money against the foreign money offered by an importer of capital. It seems that the two parties merely trade places as holders of domestic and foreign assets, but the question is whether the capital import was induced by the terms of the exchange or whether it was autonomous in the sense that it would have taken place also in absence of the capital export. In the latter case the supply of capital in the home country is reduced, as it is in most of the other cases discussed (pp. 520–1).

I examined various consequences of capital flight: the resulting interest differentials (Germany 7 per cent, Switzerland 2 per cent), the liquidity position of the banks (when induced imports of short-term foreign capital 'replace' the potential long-term capital that flees abroad), the liquidity crisis of the banking system, or threat of insolvency, when the foreign funds are suddenly withdrawn, the probability of a transfer problem arising from capital flight, etc. I found that there were 'natural' limits to the possible flight of capital – except if the central bank permits an expansion of domestic credit and thereby finances the capital exports (p. 527). In this case the central bank provides or replenishes the domestic funds that seek conversion into foreign currencies and furnished also these currencies, with the result that no net capital export takes place (since the loss of monetary reserves constitutes an official capital import) and, of course, no real transfer of resources takes place:

> Whereas otherwise [in cases without domestic credit creation] the flight of capital produces its own offsetting item in the balance of payments (in the form of additional exports) [or reduced imports], in the case of a counter-deflationary credit policy the central bank has to furnish the offsetting item (in the form of a loss in its foreign-exchange reserves). (p. 428)

This article has never been translated into English. I did not want it included in any of the collections of my essays, chiefly because of its implied policy recommendation for central banks never to come to the aid of commercial banks confronted with sudden withdrawals of foreign loans. Such a tough position may have been justified in the case of Austrian banks which, for all I knew, had been insolvent, not merely illiquid, and were saved by the monetary authorities by means of new central-bank credits coupled with foreign-exchange controls prohibiting repayments of foreign loans. As a general principle, however, my 1932 position appears unduly dogmatic and insensitive to the painful consequences of bank failures on many sectors of the economy.

OFFICIAL MEMORANDA AND ARTICLES IN NEWSPAPERS (1931–4)

Early in 1932 I was invited to submit a memorandum to the Economic Committee of the League of Nations on the monetary and financial crisis. I wrote it in German; it was distributed in French (perhaps also in English, though I have seen only the French version) in June 1932.[12] The German original was published in 1933 in *Schmollers Jahrbuch*.[13]

I wrote another brief memorandum for the League upon invitation of the division or section concerned with Austrian financial management and the internationally guaranteed loan to Austria. After the collapse of the Austrian Creditanstalt in 1931, Austria had introduced strict foreign-exchange controls, and the imposition of a general transfer moratorium was proposed. A new economic advisor to the Austrian government, Maurice Frère (later Governor of the Bank of Belgium) was about to assume his duties in Vienna. The officials in Geneva believed that a position paper on the Austrian system of exchange controls would be helpful at that juncture. This brief paper was distributed in French.[14] Maurice Frère remembered many years later how much he appreciated this introduction to his new functions. The paper argued that the credit expansion in connection with the support of the Creditanstalt had made the official foreign-exchange rates untenable. To maintain the fictitious rates by means of payments restrictions and costly controls of all international transactions was injurious to many sectors of the economy. Many export industries had already been given exemptions in the form of permission of 'private clearing arrangements' under which exporters sold their foreign proceeds to Austrian importers at premiums up to 30 per cent of the official rates. With some 80 per cent of foreign trade already being transacted at free-market exchange rates, there was no danger that liberalisation of the remaining part would lead to higher commodity prices, provided that further credit expansion was avoided. The proposed transfer moratorium was not needed and not desirable. At the right exchange rates there would be no shortage of foreign exchange; freeing of the markets might even reduce the discount of the Austrian currency relative to its official (fictitious) parity. I finally proposed that exporters be generally permitted to sell abroad for payment in Austrian currency; this practice would strengthen the Austrian schilling in foreign markets.

It was not enough to help national, foreign, and international officials obtain a better understanding of the economic situation; it was necessary to educate the public to comprehend that regulations, bureaucratic controls and restrictions were not the right way to cope with the crisis. The influence of the daily press on public opinion was recognised by a small group of economists, who agreed to supply the newspapers with a flow of easily understandable articles. Ludwig Mises, Gottfried Haberler, Oskar Morgenstern, and myself, plus a few others, met periodically in the home of Julius Meinl, large importer of coffee and other foodstuffs, to discuss what themes would be important to discuss in articles submitted to the editors of the daily papers. In the period between September 1931 and May 1934 I had 148 articles published in Austrian newspapers, most of them in the *Neues Wiener Tagblatt*, where I started a weekly column under the heading 'Two Minute Economics' [*Zwei Minuten Volkswirtschaft*]. The column as well as the majority of my articles were published without my by-line, though some articles were 'by an industrialist', 'by a financial expert', 'by an economist', 'by an exporter', and so forth, all of which was quite truthful.

While my friends who knew of this activity of mine understood its educational value and gave me every encouragement, at least one academic economist used my journalistic enterprise as one of his several arguments against my appointment as a lecturer [*Privatdozent*] at the university. Professor Hans Mayer evidently thought that the Academic Senate would agree with him in considering popular writing for newspapers as undignified, disreputable, or at least unbecoming a scholar at the University of Vienna. (My candidacy was kept pending for two years; I withdrew it in 1935 when I was appointed full professor at the University of Buffalo in the United States.) I have thought this experience worth telling as an interesting side-light.

THE THEORY OF FOREIGN EXCHANGE (1939–40)

From October 1933 to January 1935 I had a fellowship of the Rockefeller Foundation, which I spent in the United States, chiefly at Columbia, Harvard, Chicago, and Stanford Universities, doing research on subjects other than international monetary economics. During the spring term of 1935 I taught at Harvard as visiting professor, substituting for Professor John Williams, who went on leave to the Federal Reserve Bank of New York. I resumed my Rockefeller Fellowship in the autumn of 1935 and spent the period October 1935 to January 1936 in England, chiefly at Cambridge, where Keynes had just completed his *General Theory*, and at the London School of Economics, where I enjoyed stimulating discussions with Robbins, Hayek, Lerner, and many others. In February 1936 I started teaching at the University of Buffalo. My publications during these and the next few years were in a variety of fields; it was not before 1938 that I returned to the field of international monetary economics. During the summer session at Northwestern University I began to write my essay on the 'Theory of Foreign Exchange'.[15]

I once described this essay as 'essentially an analysis of market equilibrium, dissecting both supply and demand in the market for foreign currency, first with flexible, then with fixed, exchange rates' (p. 2). This statement, together with the stated objective 'to show how the simple curve analysis can be used to advantage in the theory of foreign exchanges' (p. 7), may seem to give support to those who interpret my essay as the prototype of the 'elasticity approach' to foreign-exchange and balance-of-payments analysis. I submit that this interpretation is wrong. Movements *along* the curves are described in terms of price elasticities, but movements (shifts) *of* the curves are not. Such shifts of supply and demand curves depicting conditions in the foreign-exchange market may be caused by monetary changes. As I said on the first page of the article, 'Another objective of the article is to incorporate into the theory of foreign exchanges relevant results of recent work in monetary economics' (p. 7). For example, an excess supply of domestic money, caused by a rise in the stock of money or a decline in the demand for it, would shift the demand curve for foreign exchange to the right, and perhaps also the supply curve to the left. Hence the curve analysis which I proposed may also be used in an exposition of the monetary approach to exchange-rate and balance-of-payments analysis.

I submit that the elasticity approach is relevant as long as the assumption of unchanged incomes is pertinent, but loses some of its relevance when monetary changes lead to significant changes in incomes. It is a mistake, however, to regard the elasticity approach and monetary approach as rivals; each has its applications. Even if it seems that in our days of rapid changes of money stocks we may be better served by a monetary approach, a good pedagogue will not be so naïve as to stop teaching the implications of 'unrealistic' assumptions. He will continue to teach movements along curves even if he believes that the effects of shifts of curves are more important in the explanation of particular changes. He will perhaps find satisfaction in his students' fascination when they learn that an adjustment process following a given event, say, an inflow of foreign capital in a certain amount, may produce very similar changes in the balance of trade with freely flexible exchange rates and unchanged money stocks, on the one hand, and with fixed exchange rates and correspondingly increased money stocks, on the other. The didactic value of such teaching much exceeds that of trying to teach only what may happen when all assumptions conform with what one believes to be the 'actual' conditions of the month or year in which we live.

I have offered these observations before discussing the essay under review because I am seriously disturbed by the interpretations offered by some recent 'surveyors' of the theories in question. But I may also remark how pleased I have been with a recent reconsideration of the validity and relevance of the elasticity approach in Chipman's chapter in Dreyer's volume.[16] This reconsideration is based on such erudition and mathematical sophistication that I find myself overwhelmed. I could not possibly, no matter how hard I tried, reproduce Chipman's arguments in support of my own arguments. But, hoping that the younger generation of economists is better equipped to do so, I may recommend to them to study what Chipman has to say on these issues.

Now to my essay. It proceeded methodically from assumptions where curves are given and unchanged to assumptions where they shift in more or less determinate directions, and finally to assumptions where one can hardly know anything about either the shapes or the shifts of the curves, and, hence, about the most likely outcomes of specified changes and possible repercussions and adjustments. I made it clear from the outset that I was not talking about the statistical balance of trade, which reflects only the past; an ex ante theory, linking exchange rates with trade, has to get the time dimensions right. In order to synchronise transactions in the exchange and commodities markets, I assumed that all contracts are for future delivery, that is, that all sales and purchases of foreign exchange occur in the forward market and all contracts for exports and imports are immediately covered (pp. 9–10). This avoids working with awkward problems of leads and lags. Also I made it clear that one cannot get around the problem of adjustment periods in the commodities market except by assuming different shapes (elasticities) of the supply and demand curves for products in the short, medium-long, and long run. To work with only one set of curves – instead of different curves for different reaction periods – is a simplification for the sake of teaching purposes, but not permissible for explanations of the past or predictions of the future (pp. 10–11).

I first assumed that all offers and bids in the foreign-exchange markets were exclusively those of commodity traders, the exporters offering foreign currency for sale, the importers bidding for foreign currency, and no one selling from and adding to his stocks of foreign or domestic money, no one making or receiving gifts to or from foreigners, no one making, taking, repaying, or collecting a foreign loan, no one selling or buying fixed assets or securities to or from residents of foreign countries, and no one, least of all the central bank, selling or buying gold. On these assumptions a surplus or deficit in the balance of trade is logically impossible and complete adjustment is achieved instantaneously, without the possibility of a time lag (p. 11). If incomes are given and unchanged, the elasticities of the supply and demand curves in the exchange market are indispensable variables in the analysis of the effects of changes in tastes, production costs, tariffs and other trade barriers, etc. The first task was to explain, following Haberler's earlier analysis, how these elasticities were derived from the elasticities in the markets for exports and imports, and these in turn from the elasticities in the markets for exportables and importables (pp. 12–19).

The next step was to introduce long-term capital movements and unilateral transfers. The other assumptions were maintained, especially the exclusion of changes in stocks of foreign and domestic money, and in short-term lending and borrowing. The effects of the newly admitted payments and receipts, either unrequited or for long-term securities, are unambiguous and instantaneous. By logical necessity, dictated by the assumptions, the new price of foreign currency and the new balance of trade is determined by the direction and size of the assumed noncommodity transactions and the elasticities of the 'given' market curves. Despite all tautological reasoning and implicit theorising, the simple exercise elucidates the very important but often neglected possibility

> that in consequence of [a] capital export, commodity imports may show an increase in terms of dollars but a decrease in terms of foreign currency. Statisticians, trying to 'verify' a fall in imports due to increased capital exports, should beware of the trap. (p. 22)

They rarely do, I am sorry to say.

The next step admits 'invisible trade' or the sales and purchases of services to and from foreign residents. There are different things to say regarding different services – say, freight and shipping, tourism, and income from foreign securities and direct investment – and I have often tried, unfortunately in vain, to persuade the statisticians to separate the data. Because of substitutabilities and complementarities between various goods and services the assumption of given elasticities of supply and demand in the foreign-exchange market has to be relaxed, but as long as changes in the money supply are excluded the curves will shift only modestly as a result of the other changes admitted to the model (pp. 25–7). At this juncture I made some observations about the limitations of the purchasing-power-parity theory, altogether in line with what I had said in my earlier publications (p. 27).

In the subsequent section I introduced movements of gold and foreign balances under the gold standard or any system with pegged exchange rates. With this step the applicability of the elasticity approach has come to an end, which should be obvious to any reader for, if the price of gold or foreign currency is maintained by official sales and purchases, the elasticities of supply and demand beyond the gold points or outside the narrow band of permitted flexibility are irrelevant. What matters instead are the changes in the money supply associated with the official interventions, and the corresponding shifts in the curves due to the increase or reduction of income and effective demand. Thus, the monetary approach becomes relevant. Of course, the changes in the stock of money operate through incomes and prices; and relative incomes and prices are therefore the factors that determine the international flows of goods and services. (This is why, many years later, I preferred to speak of relative prices rather than elasticities: relative prices remain significant when money stocks change, while elasticities of 'given' supply and demand curves do not.) The question is whether changes in the stock of money should be taken as independent variables or as dependent variables determined by fixed behaviour rules of the monetary authorities. The gold standard or the system of fixed exchange rates prescribe rules of the game; if these rules are observed, and if no discretionary restrictions are imposed on trade and payments, the authorities, in purchasing all foreign currency offered and in selling all foreign currency demanded at the set exchange rates, create the domestic money they pay and destroy the domestic money they collect for the foreign exchange.

The resulting shifts in the supply and demand curves for foreign exchange cannot be read off any given diagram – unless one assumes unchanging ratios of central-bank money to the total money stock, unchanging relationships between changes in money stocks and changes in real incomes, and unchanging relationships between changes in real incomes and changes in the effective demand for imports. For the fun of playing monetary theory, it is legitimate to make all these assumptions; but for purposes of predicting actual developments, it would be unwise to do so. However, one can without such strong assumptions explain and predict with sufficient accuracy the course of events that constitute adjustment. All that is needed is to assume that the monetary authorities continue to abide by the rules and not violate them by offsetting the changes in money stock that are associated with the changes in gold or exchange reserves. As long as the supply and demand curves have not shifted enough to intersect at the level of the fixed exchange and within the band that surrounds it, there will be an excess supply which the authorities have to absorb or an excess demand which they have to satisfy. In the process they will create or destroy money and this will go on until the adjustment is complete. The flow of gold or foreign exchange corresponds to what in later years came to be called 'financing the imbalance of payments'; but the associated changes in the money stock, if not offset by domestic credit policy, will eventually restore balance (p. 31). The process takes time, whereas it is instantaneous under freely flexible rates and unchanged money stock.

I proceeded to analyse the working of various institutional changes of the gold-standard system. An Exchange Stabilisation Fund may hold both foreign and domestic balances for its interventions in the market; alternatively, it may borrow (repay) domestic money from (to) the central bank; in another variant, it may borrow (repay) in the open money market. Depending on these circumstances, the effects may differ; indeed, even the borrowing in the money market may have different consequences depending on whether the loans come from non-banks, from commercial banks with ample excess reserves, or from banks without much excess liquidity (pp. 34–5). A capital import from abroad may then, in a system of fixed exchange rates, lead to a stiffening of the money market, and not to an increase in the money stock, if the foreign currency received from the foreign lenders or investors is acquired by the Exchange Stabilisation Fund with domestic balances borrowed from non-banks or loaned-up commercial banks. The increase in domestic interest rates in this process may, however, lead to some activation of hitherto idle balances (p. 36). The parts of my essay exemplified by these considerations received very little attention in the literature, as far as I know. They surely cannot be characterised as an instance of the 'elasticity approach'.

The final section of the essay (pp. 39–50) dealt with 'exchange speculation and interest rates'. In this section I dropped the assumption of organised exchange stabilisation, but warned that this was 'not equivalent to returning to the assumption of [freely] flexible exchange rates or, still less, to the assumption of independent currencies' (p. 40). The point was that commercial banks and specialised foreign-exchange dealers, confident regarding the authorities' latent dedication to principles of monetary stability, would engage in voluntary, informal pegging activities, at least for a short time. I incorporated these attitudes of buying and selling into the graphical representation of the foreign-exchange market, but felt compelled to state reservations which I find worth repeating:

> The graph is . . . open to objections on methodological grounds. Firstly, the assumptions concerning expectations of future exchange-rate changes [or absence of changes] are of one type in the case of the exporters' and importers' supply and demand, and of a totally different type in the case of the dealers' supply and demand . . . Secondly, the exporters' and importers' supply and demand refer to a *flow* of foreign exchange . . . whereas the dealers' supply and demand refer to a *stock* of foreign exchange . . . The combination of all these curves and parts of curves in one graph is, I believe, legitimate for a short period (e.g., for the *period* of one month if the other curves represent *rates* per month). (p. 41)

The monetary consequences of private purchases and sales of foreign exchange for and from stocks of currencies held were shown to depend on such circumstances as 'the flexibility of the banks' ratios between reserves and deposits, and on the flexibility of their "borrowed reserves"; second, on whether foreign balances are counted among the reserves' (p. 42). These conditions differed from country to country and from time to time. In the United States, at the time of writing [1938] such private purchases and sales of exchange were likely to have expansionary and contractionary effects except where non-bank dealers had to seek the required funds in the open market from non-bank sources (p. 43).

I then proceeded to a discussion of the reaction of interest rates in the money market to an increased supply of foreign exchange that is not absorbed by the central bank, and to an increased demand for foreign exchange that is not satisfied by the central bank (pp. 46–7).

With this analysis I anticipated, as far as I understand it, much of what the portfolio-adjustment approach suggested – about thirty years later. I mention this chiefly in order to re-emphasise the fact that several of the approaches regarded as rivalling one another are actually complementary, and their applicability depends on the prevailing situation: the elasticity approach is appropriate when changes in monetary variables are insignificant; the monetary approach, when central banks substantially vary the money supply; the portfolio approach, when commercial banks and non-bank holders of monetary assets are actively engaged in financing foreign transactions.

In the last pages of the article I discussed the effects of speculation 'based on definite expectations', on the one hand, and of more 'erratic' speculation, on the other, both by foreign-exchange dealers and by commodity traders (p. 48). I concluded that

> short-run analysis becomes ... impossible if rapid, erratic and unpredictable changes in expectations make almost everybody a speculator.[17] Theoretical analysis is then more or less confined to the long period, and it loses, of course, some of its significance: its immediate applicability to currently observable facts is gone. (p. 49)

This view I still hold, forty-one years after I put it into words. But I would add today that my scepticism is even greater concerning short-run empirical-statistical analysis. Most of the attempts to use for econometric analysis of exchange rates and payments balances, daily, monthly, quarterly, or even annual series of statistical data from periods, with ongoing inflationary processes, erratic changes in expectations, and substantial speculative transactions, seem futile. We must not rely on 'findings' from such analyses and venture predictions based on the estimated coefficients.

This view may easily be misinterpreted as an attack on empirical research. The fact that I pointed to the impossibility of short-run *theory* of 'erratic and unpredictable changes in expectations' should save both the reader and me from an interpretation prejudicial only to *empirical* analysis. When transactors in the foreign-exchange market are buffeted by contradictory news and rumours several times during a day or week, no one can reasonably expect much regularity in the recorded observations. In the absence of regularities, neither theoretical nor empirical analysis can produce valuable insights.

EIGHT QUESTIONS ON GOLD (1940–1)

At the annual meeting of the American Economic Association in December 1940 Hans Neisser and Charles O. Hardy presented papers on the past and current gold policy of the United States. I was invited to be one of the discussion speakers. My comments under the title 'Eight Questions on Gold' were published in the volume of proceedings in February 1941.[18] Since I agreed with what Neisser and Hardy had presented, I chose to formulate eight questions and to answer them in a deliberately provocative way. I shall restate the eight answers, hoping that it will be clear what the questions were:

1. Raising the price of gold in 1934, from $20.67 to $35.00 per ounce, was a mistake; the chief motives were fallacious, some other objectives could have been achieved by better methods, and some indirect effects were quite undesirable (p. 31).

2. Reducing the price of gold at this time (1940) would be a mistake; it would not be beneficial to the United States and would definitely harm the British, who were financing their purchases of airplanes and other urgently needed war materiel through sales of gold (p. 32).

3. The large purchases of gold by the United States during recent years (1934–40) did not involve heavy real costs for the United States; considering the large unemployment and excess capacity, the opportunity costs of the exports sold in exchange for the gold were rather low (p. 33).

4. 'The United States need not be much concerned that other nations after the war may repudiate gold as long as the United States itself does not repudiate it' (p. 34).

5. 'Unless gold production becomes as exuberant as silver production once did, it is not likely that gold will lose value in terms of foreign currencies while we maintain its dollar value ... The commodity value of gold is much more a function of government spending and credit expansion than a function of the gold supply' (p. 35).

6. To readmit gold into domestic circulation by minting new gold coins would not be a good idea, though it would do no harm either; but there is 'no advantage in our committing ourselves to a definitive gold price at this moment when everything is in flux and nobody knows how the world will look in a few months' (p. 36).

7. The idea to use the large gold stocks of the Treasury to reduce the government debt is quite silly, apart from the fact that gold certificates have been issued against the gold; the former owners of government securities would not want to hold the proceeds in gold but would immediately resell it to the government in exchange for dollars in order to purchase earning assets; to print paper money to redeem the government debt would be no more inflationary, and much simpler, than using gold for this purpose (p. 37).

8. Possession of the large gold reserve is not, and will hardly ever be, an advantage to the United States; the other countries will need loans after the war, but will hardly have enough exports to buy back the gold (p. 37).

I was wrong on the eighth question. The gold holdings of the United States increased still further after 1940, and on balance no gold was used (lost) until 1949. But from then on, gold was gradually redistributed among several (chiefly European) countries, and after 1960 the United States engaged in all sorts of policies designed to avoid losing more of its gold at a fast rate. I had qualified my answer in 1940 by saying that 'in a serious inflation [in the United States] fast rising prices might create and permit an import surplus and in payment for ... [it], as well as in a flight of capital, we might lose a portion of our gold stock'. But I added that these were 'rather improbable possibilities' (p. 37). In this I was mistaken.

THE FOREIGN-TRADE MULTIPLIER (1941–3)

In 1939 I had started to work on multiplier analysis and made a polite bow to the 'leakage' from the investment-generated income flow due to larger imports induced by the increased income.[19] I then turned to the analysis of export-generated incomes. In other words, from the analysis of the home-investment multiplier I proceeded to the foreign-trade multiplier; the resulting multiple reflected, besides the positive income-generating effects of autonomous increases in exports, the negative effects of income-induced increases in imports and the positive or negative effects of the changes in exports induced by income changes abroad. I lectured on these problems in 1941 and published a book, *International Trade and the National Income Multiplier*, in 1943 with the Blakiston Company.[20]

As I said in the preface of the book,

I have tried to improve the multiplier technique by discarding the idea of the instantaneous or timeless multiplier and introducing time as an important variable. I believe that period analysis, showing the step-by-step adjustments of incomes, imports and exports as sequences in time is best adapted to the . . . purposes. And . . . [it] constitutes really 'dynamic economics'. (p. vii)

The book contained thirty tables of arithmetic illustrations of various model sequences, besides simple algebraic expositions of the models. (The algebra was indispensable, not an exercise in sophistication.) I considered the primitive arithmetic sequences necessary for students' full understanding of the models and, after all these years, I still do. Students who have gone only through the albegra rarely develop the intuitive comprehension of the significance of some of the relations involved, especially of the lapse of time in processes approaching 'income equilibrium' at the level of the 'full' multiplier, which could be reached only after an infinite length of time (p. 49). In order to reduce the full multiplier to a somewhat less impossible construct, I provided formulas for the computation of time-specific multipliers ('the multiplier as a function of time') and a tabulation showing 'the time necessary for the income increase to reach 90 per cent of the full multiple' (p. 51). [One purpose was, of course, to disabuse students from the erroneous belief that it could ever be possible that nothing else would change on the way approaching equilibrium and hence, that the 'neighborhood of equilibrium' could actually be reached.]

The arithmetic sequences disclosed something that algebraic formulas of the full-multiplier values might have left concealed: the existence of waves in the series of income increases and of changes in trade balances as adjustment proceeds from period to period. Indeed, I found that, where such 'wavelike movements in the changes in income occur, the respective figures may once pass through the 10 per cent neighborhood of equilibrium and then leave this zone again in order to return there only on the way back' (p. 89). These waves had puzzled me at first sight, but then I found algebraic and verbal explanations that gave me the satisfaction of a discoverer, although the matter was relatively simple. [The interested reader can find the answer on pp. 83–4 of the book.]

Most of the problems analysed in the book related to the effects which certain changes, occurring at home or abroad, would over time have upon national income and the trade balance. The disequilibrating changes could be divided into four major groups: (1) autonomous changes in exports or imports (where 'autonomous' stands for 'not induced by changes in income'), (2) changes in exports induced by changes in incomes abroad, (3) opposite changes in investments (which stands for 'primary disbursements') at home and abroad, and (4) parallel changes in investments at home and abroad. Included in the third and fourth of these groups are problems of international movements of capital and unilateral payments, which comprise the income effects (in contra-distinction to the price effects) of the mechanism involved in the transfer problem.

Just as the multiplier mechanism implies that changes in foreign trade may be regarded as either autonomous or induced, changes in capital movements may likewise be disequilibrating or equilibrating; the former pair of adjectives, however, would be inappropriate in connection with capital movements because it was defined as independent of or induced by changes in *income*. I proposed to distinguish 'spontaneous' movements of capital from 'accommodating' ones. For example, every system of fixed exchange rates 'implies the preparedness to accommodate the exporters [of merchandise], who offer foreign claims or balances, by taking these assets off their hands and holding them for the time being ... Behind this foreign·lending is *not a spontaneous demand for foreign claims or securities* but rather a latent preparedness to accommodate those who come to dispose of foreign balances'. Not that the accommodation is 'done out of sheer kindness or as a service to customers ... All except the monetary authorities engage in these transactions strictly for business reasons', in the expectation of gaining through slight differentials between foreign and domestic interest rates or between spot and forward exchange rates, or through small changes in spot rates, etc. The accommodating buyers and sellers of foreign exchange from and to exporters and importers may be banks, dealers, speculators, and monetary authorities (pp. 134–5).

The newly coined term – accommodating capital flows – won wide acceptance, particularly after James Meade adopted it for his book *Balance of Payments*. It served me well in the analysis of the old controversy whether changes in the trade balance caused changes in the capital balance, or the other way around. I was able to show that the chain of causation could not be seen at all unless 'net capital movements' were divided into spontaneous and accommodating ones (pp. 139–43).

The last chapter of my book was given to 'Apologies and Confessions'. I confessed that the theory of the multiplier was only in most exceptional circumstances applicable to real-world situations. And I apologised for having offered detailed models and exact formulas for inapplicable theories. To be sure, the 'fundamental' assumptions of most theories are counterfactual and surely unrealistic, but as a rule the weakening of such assumptions and the recognition of their 'as if' function does not make the inferences from the theories completely irrelevant. In the case of multiplier theory, however, the conclusions deduced from the assumptions prove inapplicable to most historical situations. The chief merit of its careful exposition and examination is that in the process one learns why the theory rarely applies.

I remember with a mixture of pride and embarrassment the praise which Jacob Viner (who preceded me as Walker Professor of Economics and International Finance at Princeton University) gave to that last chapter of my book. For he added sarcastically: 'If you had placed this chapter at the beginning rather than at the end of the book, the readers would learn that they do not have to spend their time going through the rest of the book'. It was precisely because I had realised this possibility that I deferred the denouement until the end of the book. For I firmly believe that even theories without practical significance should be fully understood; indeed, only such understanding helps us see that these theories cannot be accepted in support of policy recommendations (p. 218).

We may never 'have the information enabling us to substitute real numbers in our formulas'; we may have no ground for assuming that any of the variables, even if we knew the value it had yesterday, would have the same value tomorrow; we may be convinced that none of the other necessary conditions holds in reality; still the formulas serve a purpose.

Their purpose is to exhibit certain relationships between independent and dependent variables, to show whether they are positively or negatively correlated, to tell whether it is their magnitudes or their proportions which matter, to indicate which ones are more important and which less, and, last but not least, to warn us about the things which we are to find out before we try to make general statements, not to speak of predictions'. (pp. 199–200)

I may, to keep this account of my work more personal, insert that I spent the years from 1942 to 1946 in Washington, the first year at the Brookings Institution, the other three years in a government position. In 1947 I left the University of Buffalo to accept a professorship at the Johns Hopkins University in Baltimore. The next thirteen years at Hopkins were the years of my greatest productivity as a teacher. I had the most extraordinary group of graduate students working for the PhD degree, attracted by high stipends and a unique programme of instruction and research.

DOLLAR SHORTAGE, SO-CALLED (1949–54)

From the end of the 1940s to the early 1960s the discussion of international monetary problems was plagued by a misunderstanding, widespread among official experts and journalists, and aided and abetted by some respected economists: the idea of dollar shortage in non-dollar countries. What ailed these countries were two conditions: one, they were trying to maintain the foreign-exchange rates of their currencies at levels that overvalued them relative to domestic prices and incomes, partly in consequence of excessive expansions of credit; and second, with capital stocks depleted in the war and post-war period, they had not yet been able to build up adequate monetary reserves. The first problem was a problem of the 'flow supply' of foreign exchange, inadequate because they were paying too little for it; the other was a problem of the 'stock supply' of foreign exchange, inadequate because it takes time to accumulate reserves even after the inflow has responded to appropriate adjustment measures. The dollar-shortage theorists, however, like the balance-of-payments theorists after the First World War, did not understand that monetary policy and disaligned exchange rates were the strategic variables. They looked for some 'structural' explanations of a supposedly 'chronic' dollar shortage. With these two adjectives, structural and chronic, they meant to dismiss the relevance of monetary factors in the situation.

The situation was similar to that after the First World War, and the same theoretical fallacies reappeared. Thus, my attempts to clear up the misunderstandings were, in a way, repeat performances after twenty-five years, though perhaps on a somewhat higher level of theoretical craftsmanship, reflecting the advances of economic theory and the greater competence of the exponents of the erroneous view. I wrote three articles on the subject; two were published in 1950 and the third in 1954.

The first article examined the arguments of those who opposed the judgement that higher prices for foreign currencies would reduce or eliminate the excess demand for, or the shortage of, foreign exchange. Many of these arguments rested on the belief that a depreciation or devaluation of the currency would not lead to an improvement of the trade balance, because the price elasticities of supply and demand in international trade were too low. I coined the term 'elasticity pessimism' to denote this position, and titled my article 'Elasticity Pessimism in International Trade'.[21] The term has been widely adopted.

'*Moderate* elasticity pessimism pervades [the thinking of] those who warn of miserable terms of trade or an intolerable distribution of income. *Hopeless* elasticity pessimism pervades those who warn of perverse elasticities making the disequilibrium in the exchange market incurable.' My article dealt with the severe cases of elasticity pessimism; I attempted to show that this view tended 'to overestimate the magnitudes of the elasticities which are required if exchange depreciation is to have remedial effects and, second . . . to underestimate the actual magnitudes of the elasticities' (p. 52).

The overestimation of the *required* elasticities is most explicit in the Lerner formula,[22] which concentrates on elasticities of demand for foreign goods, that is, on the sum of the price elasticity of domestic demand for imports and the price elasticity of foreign demand for exports of the country that lets its currency depreciate in the foreign-exchange market. The 'critical values' of these elasticities are those at which a depreciation of the currency will neither reduce nor increase the excess demand for foreign exchange. According to that formula, the sum of the absolute values of the two elasticities of demand for commodities (absolute, that is, disregarding the minus signs for demand elasticities) has to be 1 (unity); if it is smaller than unity, the excess demand for foreign currency will increase when its price is increased. This theorem rests on two assumptions: (1) that the price elasticities of supply of commodities are zero, that is, that the domestic prices of exportable and importable commodities remain unchanged in the countries' own currencies, regardless of the quantities demanded; and (2) that the initial position is one of balance, that is, that the values of exports and imports are equal (pp. 54–5). If, contrary to these assumptions, the elasticities of supply are greater than zero or the value of imports initially exceeds the value of exports, the sum of the demand elasticities may be well below unity without causing a perverse result (pp. 55–8).

The underestimation of *actual* elasticities was a matter of statistical and econometric research. I showed that the attempts at measuring the price elasticities of the demand for imports were beset by conceptual as well as statistical problems, which made the findings suspect of being biased in a downward direction. The major conceptual problem lies in the fact that the 'statistical demand curve' in these cases relates not to a single commodity but to a 'non-homogeneous aggregate of many commodities' with very different observations of past price-quantity changes. Investigators did not calculate weighted averages of the elasticities for all commodities in the bundle, but instead resorted to working with indices of total physical imports and of average price changes of import goods (p. 61). I offered illustrations to show that, depending on what changes in prices and quantities were observed, 'the elasticity of demand for [a] bundle of two commodities seems to be far below the elasticity of demand for any one of the commodities' (p. 62), which of course is a ridiculous result. I also reported on research by Arnold Harberger and Guy Orcutt that proved biases inherent in index-number techniques, curve-fitting techniques, and arbitrary (though customary) choices of assumptions (pp. 62–8).

The second article of this triad was a conceptual discourse designed to disentangle a hodge-podge of concepts that had been given the same name: 'balance of payments'. Since dollars shortage had been described as a chronic deficit in the balance of payments, I thought it would help if the equivocation inherent in this term could be made transparent. My article, 'Three Concepts of the Balance of Payments and the So-Called Dollar Shortage',[23] was widely quoted, but I doubt that it persuaded many economists to be more careful in stating what they meant when they spoke of a deficit in the balance of payments.

The three basic concepts are the market balance of payments, a balance of supply and demand; the programme balance of payments, a balance of hopes and desires; and the accounting balance of payments, a balance of credits and debits (p. 69). Each of the three types of balance allows for an indefinite number of subtypes. The *market* balance is purely hypothetical and essentially *ex ante*; for example, it is addressed to the following kind of question: 'how would the quantity of foreign currency offered for sale increase or decrease if the price of foreign currency were 5 per cent higher, with no expectations being entertained regarding a further rise or subsequent reduction in that price, and with no change occurring in the domestic money supply and in national income?'. The *programme* balance may be part of a formal national plan, a forecast consistent with national targets, a projection of past experiences adjusted for expected or desired changes, an estimate of hoped-for sources of foreign funds and their preferred uses – all affected by judgements of political 'realities' or perhaps wishful thinking; needless, to say, it is *ex ante*, but the hypotheses are less in the nature of micro- and macroeconomic theorising than in the nature of national planning. The *accounting* balance is an arrangement of statistical data derived *ex post* from records, reports, and estimates, organised by conventional categories and with all items operationally defined. (The statistical balances of goods and services, balances on current account, balances on current and long-term capital account, balances on liquidity basis, and balances on official-settlements basis are subtypes of the accounting balance.)

The three major types of balance serve altogether different purposes. The market balance is an analytical tool of the economic theorist who reasons about shifts of supply and demand curves, and about movements along these curves, consequent upon a variety of hypothetical changes. The programme balance is a kind of budget made by an appointed or self-appointed national planner who thinks about the next year or a longer planning period; it may also be a programme made by a forecaster who takes political 'necessities and possibilities' as given. The accounting balance is the compilation of empirical data for a past period by a statistician who uses conventional or otherwise defined procedures of organising the accounts.

In each of these types of balance the notion of a deficit varies with the purpose; 'there is no necessary relationship between these deficits; indeed a deficit in one of the three senses may be compatible with a simultaneous surplus in one of the other senses' (p. 89). 'In discussions of the equivocal "dollar shortage" we should insist on full identification of the concept employed' (p. 92). I am afraid, few economists have insisted and still fewer have complied.

The third article was on 'Dollar Shortage and Disparities in the Growth of Productivity'.[24] It differed from the earlier two articles in that it was directed at one specific structural explanation of dollar shortage – growth disparities – and at three proponents of that explanation: Thomas Balogh, John H. Williams. and John R. Hicks. The expositions by Balogh and Williams in 1946 and 1952, respectively, had not been sufficiently clear to allow a well-focused critical analysis. The argument presented by Hicks is straightforward, pointed, and subject to clear-cut dissection. Hicks distinguished:

> between barter effects and monetary effects. Barter effects are those which persist whatever the course of money incomes. Monetary effects are those which arise out of difficulties in the adjustment of money incomes. If a difficulty is purely monetary, people ought to find a means of doing something about it; but nothing can be done about a 'real' difficulty, one inherent in a barter effect. (p. 100)

What effects can be expected from an increase in productivity in country A, with no change in productivity in B? Hicks proposed three different answers, depending on the sectors in which productivity improves. If productivity in A increases uniformly in all industries, there may be pleasant barter effects but unpleasant monetary effects for B. Difficulties can be avoided by an appropriate monetary policy of A, allowing incomes in A to rise. In the second case, 'if improvements are concentrated on A's export industries, and B can thus get more imports for the same money, no monetary troubles and only a real boon for B may result from this kind of development' (p. 101). In the case of 'import-biased improvements', however, Hicks sees trouble for B. The demand for B's exports will be reduced when A's efficiency in making import substitutes increases; and no monetary arrangements can be devised to avoid a loss for B. Hicks believed that most of the progress of productivity in the twentieth century had been in North America and was of the import biased variety, causing continuing dollar shortage in Britain (p. 102).

My criticism of Hicks' explanation fastened on several points of alleged but not substantiated facts. They related to Britain's terms of trade (which for some periods were rather favourable), America's monetary expansion (which often exceeded that of Britain), and British per capita real income (which increased during most of the time, whereas it should have declined if the theory were both valid and applicable to the British case). The main point, however, was a point of theory. Hicks' explanation of dollar shortage in Britain was based on an absolute loss of real income due to steadily deteriorating barter terms of trade. If in fact, however, real income in Britain increased, a worsening of the terms of trade could have, at worst, slowed down the increase. To be sure, if British labour costs were raised at the gross rate of productivity increase without taking any account of the deduction due to adverse changes in the terms of trade, one would have to expect unemployment or price inflation and dollar shortage. But the same result would have arisen if wage rates had increased faster than productivity – without any deterioration of Britain's terms of trade, without any differences in the growth of productivity, and without any import bias in the productivity growth of Britain's trading partners. Hence, growth disparities and adverse terms of trade are neither necessary nor sufficient conditions of dollar shortage (p. 106).

If a nation has a dollar shortage while its plane of living is rising, the shortage should not be explained as the consequence of structural obstacles to a faster increase in national income; it is satisfactorily explained by the economic policies adopted. (p. 109)

RELATIVE PRICES AND AGGREGATE SPENDING (1955–6)

Whether and under what conditions the trade balance of a country would be improved by a depreciation or devaluation of its currency in the foreign-exchange market had been debated with reference to elasticities and/or to relative monetary expansion. As I have said before, elasticities are relevant if one discusses given conditions of supply and demand, particularly given and unchanged money stocks and incomes; otherwise monetary variables have the leading roles. When the elasticity pessimists contended that 'actual' elasticities were too low to promise any improvements in the trade balance, I attempted to show why their pessimism was not justified. When balance-of-payments theorists disregarded or downgraded the role of monetary policy, I attempted to show that the role of money in the play of market forces was strategic. In 1952 an article was published proposing an altogether new approach, doing away with the elasticities approach and glossing over the monetary approach. The proponent, Sidney Alexander, called it the 'income-absorption approach'.[25]

I examined the new approach in two articles published in 1955 and 1956: 'Relative Prices and Aggregate Spending in the Analysis of Devaluation'[26] and 'The Terms-of-Trade Effects of Devaluation upon Real Income and the Balance of Payments'.[27] In the first of these articles I gave a streamlined exposition of Alexander's argument. At its core is the truism that a country can have an export surplus only if it absorbs (for consumption and domestic investment) less output than it produces, and an import surplus if it absorbs more than it produces. It follows that a country, by letting its currency depreciate, will improve its trade balance only if its income [output] 'increases while absorption increases less or stays unchanged or falls; or if absorption decreases while income decreases less or stays unchanged' (p. 175). There is nothing wrong with this argument; it is important and unexceptional. What is needed, however, is a theory which satisfactorily explains the relationships between changes in foreign-exchange rates and changes in domestic production and absorption. [I usually make a distinction between devaluation and depreciation, but in this discussion I did not want to complicate matters and used the two terms as equivalents.]

I examined all the links between an exchange-rate change and changes in income and absorption which Alexander had suggested, and found that they actually presupposed elasticities or monetary changes or both. The 'idle-resources effect' presupposes a response of exports to the higher price of foreign currencies (elastic foreign demand for exports and elastic domestic supply of exports), an increase in domestic money incomes (expansion of the money stock or its velocity when the foreign-exchange proceeds of exports are acquired by domestic banks), and increased spending out of increased incomes (marginal propensity to spend, or income elasticity of demand). The 'terms-of-trade effect' presupposes changes in the ratio of export prices to import prices (which depend on a complex set of elasticities of supply and demand, abroad and at home). The 'cash-balance effect' – the effect on domestic absorption due to the decline in the purchasing power of nominal cash balances that is associated with a rise in the price level consequent upon higher prices of traded goods – presupposes both given elasticities (for example, of the demand for cash balances) and specified monetary-policy reactions (p. 179). The 'income-redistribution effect', that is, the differential impact of higher prices on groups with different propensities to spend (implying shifts of real incomes from fixed-income recipients to others, from wage earners to profit earners, and from tax payers to governments) presupposes given marginal propensities (or income elasticities of demand). The 'money-illusion effect', that is, the effect on real absorption (and on saving) which one may expect when income recipients disregard a decline in the real value of their money income, presupposes ongoing price increases, for which monetary expansion is evidently a necessary condition (p. 180).

I mentioned three other direct effects on absorption which Alexander had included but not named. I called them the 'price-expectation effect', the 'high-cost-of-investment effect', and the 'high-cost-of-imports effect'. Then I added, what Alexander had failed to include, the 'resource-reallocation effect', that is, the possible increase in output due to a more efficient allocation of resources when misaligned exchange rates are corrected (pp. 181–2). That such reallocation again presupposes a set of price elasticities of supply and demand needs no elaboration.

I emphasised the common fallacy implied in reasoning from definitional identities. Just as the trade balance can be seen as the difference between income and absorption, one may see absorption as the difference between income and the trade balance, or income as the sum of absorption and trade balance. To regard the trade balance as the residual, determined by the two other aggregates, may be seriously misleading (pp. 186–8). The possibility of a logical snare becomes most apparent when one remembers that one country's trade deficit is another country's (or all other countries') trade surplus. If one believes that the effects of devaluation on a country's trade balance can be deduced from the effects on its own national income and its own absorption, how can this be reconciled with the same claim of causation in the other country or countries? Assuming only two countries trading with each other, should one assume that the improvement in one country's trade balance imposes a deterioration on the other country's balance and that this 'dictates' or 'enforces' changes in that country's income and absorption? Or, if the same theory is to hold for both countries, so that in each country the effects on income and the direct and indirect effects on absorption determine the net effect on the trade balance, is the balance not clearly overdetermined? What forces will reshape the two balances to become equal in magnitude and opposite in sign? These questions showed clearly that Alexander's first version of the income-absorption approach was untenable.

In the second article I concentrated on the terms-of-trade effects of the devaluation. Although most writers on the subject, including Alexander, have used the 'commodity terms of trade' in their arguments, and although Dennis Robertson had found that the 'double-factor terms of trade' were the 'most relevant to discussion of relative national standards of living, or of equilibrium rates of exchange', I came out in favour of using the 'single-factor terms of trade'. My reasons were that changes of the relative national incomes are irrelevant for positive economics – relevant are only the effects on the income of the devaluing country – and that the commodity terms of trade would not tell us anything about these effects if productivity in that country were increased, as it well might when devaluation results in a reallocation of resources (pp. 198–201).

Alexander had reasoned that devaluation would most likely worsen the commodity terms of trade, and that this would imply a reduction of national income and also an 'initial' deterioration of the trade balance by the same amount (partially abated later by the indirect effects of the income reduction upon domestic absorption). I found this reasoning faulty on several grounds: (1) the commodity terms of trade need not always deteriorate as a result of devaluation; (2) even when they do deteriorate, the single-factor terms of trade may improve and, hence, national income may rise instead of falling; and (3) even if national income falls, the trade balance need not deteriorate, either by the same amount or at all. Alexander's contention was that the fall in national income would cause an equal and simultaneous deterioration in the trade balance, evidently because people would 'initially' import unchanged quantities of goods at increased prices. One might with equal justification argue that people would 'initially' refuse to spend more of their income on imported goods and would instead reduce their real absorption accordingly. Both these suppositions are extreme, and some middle position looks more likely (p. 204). However, if the country has no exchange reserves left, or does not want to deplete them any further, and if it cannot increase its foreign borrowing, the second extreme will be the only possible outcome. This indeed constitutes the 'immediate adjustment' under freely flexible exchange rates when neither domestic nor foreign financing is forthcoming (p. 204).

Having distinguished three possible effects of currency devaluation upon national income, I found that they may be interrelated. Thus, a positive idle-resources effect or a positive resource-reallocation effect may be the consequence of a negative terms-of-trade effect in the sense that the positive effects can be had only if export prices were lowered enough to induce the increase in exports. In such instances, attempts to isolate the terms-of-trade effect may obstruct the understanding of the relationship (p. 205).

The meanings of 'changes in national income' and 'changes in absorption' in this and similar analyses have usually been assumed to be clear and not subject to challenge. That there are substantial differences between various operational definitions would not vitiate theoretical arguments, but differences between fundamental constructs may be stultifying. For our immediate purposes we should distinguish three theoretically relevant constructs:

(1) changes in the total domestic production of finished [read: final] goods and services valued at constant prices ('real domestic output'), (2) changes in the total domestic use, for consumption and investment, of goods and services valued at constant prices ('real intake'), and (3) changes in the total amount of income received or earned, with goods and services valued at constant prices, and with [international] income transfers, capital earnings, and all changes in foreign assets and liabilities accounted for insofar as they arise from current transactions ('real income').

The names used for the triad, 'output, intake, and income' combine simple prepositions – out, in – with short verbs – put, take, come. The concept of real intake is an equivalent of what Alexander called absorption, and what other writers have designated with half a dozen other names. My hope that the term 'intake' would be adopted by the professional literature has not been fulfilled.

The difference between output and income is important for several arguments. A frequent example is the case of international unilateral transfers, such as donations or reparations payments; but for the problem before us, it is the effect of price changes on foreign claims and liabilities that is of major significance. 'We can imagine a situation in which there is absolutely no change in physical output, physical intake, physical exports, and physical imports, but where the foreign prices of exports are reduced and/or the foreign prices of imports increased. A loss in foreign assets or increase in foreign debt would occur as a result. Hence, real income would be reduced although domestic output at constant prices was not changed' (p. 216). The proposed definition of real income takes account only of changes in assets and liabilities 'as they arise from current transactions'. It disregards therefore changes in the value of old assets and liabilities. Take, for example, the changes in the commodity values of existing foreign claims or debts. Does a reduction of the foreign purchasing power of foreign-exchange reserves held by the monetary authorities reduce the national income, either in the year when the change occurs or in the years when the reserves are used? What does an increase in the price of gold do to the real income of a nation that holds large stocks of gold? Most theorists have decided to close their eyes to such problems; they are satisfied to overlook differences between output and the numerous variants of income by denoting all of these by the letter Y and solving the simultaneous equation as if Y were identical with Y.

EQUILIBRIUM AND DISEQUILIBRIUM (1958)

In the discussions of dollar shortage, payments balance, trade balance, exchange rates, and so forth, the terms equilibrium and disequilibrium were being bandied about as if these were simple household words. Most non-economists innocently believed that disequilibrium was 'a bad thing', and equilibrium 'a good thing'; many thought that there could be 'chronic' disequilibrium; and virtually all were convinced that one could 'see' or 'observe' an equilibrium if one looked at some data. To disabuse students of such views, I felt it necesarry to write an article on 'Equilibrium and Disequilibrium: Misplaced Concreteness and Disguised Politics'. I began writing it in 1955; it was published in 1958.[28]

'The chief purpose of the essay [was] to show the dangers to clear analysis that may arise from the failure to notice the differences between analytical, descriptive, and evaluative equilibrium concepts' (p. 112). But it went beyond making such distinctions and attempted to show that in descriptions of factual situations and in judgements of positive and negative values the pair of terms was redundant, confusing, or both, whereas in abstract economic analysis it was an important methodological device, a mental tool helpful in suggesting 'a causal nexus between different events or changes' (p. 113). The nexus can be shown in form of four mental steps: (1) the initial position, or 'equilibrium'; (2) the disequilibrating change, or 'new datum'; (3) the adjusting (equilibrating) changes, or 'reactions'; and (4) the final position, or 'new equilibrium'. This scheme serves as:

> a mental experiment in which the first and last steps, the assumption of initial and final equilibria, are methodological devices to secure that Step 2 is the sole cause and Step 3 contains the complete sequence of effects. The function of the initial equilibrium is to assure us that 'nothing but 2' causes the changes under Step 3; the function of the final equilibrium is to assure us that 'nothing but 3' is to be expected as an effect of the change under Step 2 (although the 'completeness' of the list of effects will always be merely relative to the set of variables included in the equilibrium. (p. 115)

It is essential to understand that all equilibria are relative, because there is a wide choice of variables, and of relations among variables, to be included. In 'equilibrium in international trade' we may choose either to include or to disregard such variables as expectations of future changes, the size of monetary reserves, the liquidity of the banking system, and so forth. For the sake of quick comprehension, especially for teaching purposes, one will prefer the simplest possible model with only a few variables, but of course one will avoid using such a model as the basis for policy recommendations. The heuristic value of a theoretical model (algebraic, geometric, or verbal):

> is not impaired if an important factor is left out, provided the omission is not inadvertent. Indeed, the importance of any factor can be demonstrated only by leaving it out of account and then showing the difference it makes when it is reinstated as one of the variables in the equilibrium system. (p. 117)

I defined equilibrium in economic analysis:

> as *a constellation of selected interrelated variables so adjusted to one another that no inherent tendency to change prevails in the model which they constitute*. The model as well as the equilibria are, of course, mental constructions (based on abstraction and invention). (p. 119)

As an alternative but equivalent definition of equilibrium I proposed 'mutual compatibility of a selected set of interrelated variables of particular magnitudes'; the assumed interrelationships may be behavioural, technological, psychological, institutional, or merely definitional. But

> the crux of the matter is that the addition of another variable, somehow related to one or more of the others, would change the picture . . . One cannot overemphasize this *relativity* of compatibility and incompatibility regarding extra variables included in, or excluded from, the selected set. (p. 120)

To characterize a concrete [historical] situation 'observed' in reality as one of 'equilibrium' is to commit the fallacy of misplaced concreteness . . . , first, because of the general fallacy involved in jumping the distance between a useful fiction and particular data of observation and, second, because of the fallacy involved in forgetting the relativity of equilibrium with respect to variables and relations selected. (p. 122)

Apart from misplaced concreteness, there was also the matter of value judgements, and several respected economists have indulged not only in mixing evaluation with analysis – which is all right as long as it is explicit – but also in hiding value judgements in the concept of equilibrium:

> By imputing a value judgement, a political philosophy or programme, or a rejection of a programme or policy, into the concept of equilibrium designed for economic analysis, the analyst commits the fallacy of implicit evaluation or disguised politics. (p. 124)

I proceeded to examine the writings of several distinguished economists on the theory of international trade and finance. I found full awareness of the relativity of equilibrium (Joan Robinson), built-in politics and simulated stability (Ragnar Nurkse), openly embraced political criteria (Paul Ellsworth and Charles Kindleberger), explicit criticism of persuasive definitions of equilibrium (Paul Streeten), and vacillation between explicit relativity with value neutrality in some parts and implied value judgements in others (James Meade). Positive analysis was sometimes 'sabotaged' by the use of value-laden equilibrium concepts; this occurred, for example, when the adjustment or 'equilibration' was leading to a final position that did not meet the political criteria stipulated for 'equilibrium' – say, full employment (pp. 125–35).

In view of the layman's idea that a trade deficit is always a 'disequilibrium' of the balance of payments, it is important to comprehend that explaining the deficit means to show it as an adjustment, or equilibrating change, following an antecedent disequilibrating change, for example, increased government spending, expansionary monetary policy, devaluation of a trading partner's currency, receipt of foreign investment, etc. This, incidentally, was one of the main theses which I had proclaimed, as early as 1923, and hoped to impress on the reader (*Goldkernwährung*, pp. 137–9).

PROPOSAL TO REDUCE THE PRICE OF GOLD (1960–1)

Two things happened in the second half of 1960, one to me, the other to the US dollar; but both had much to do with my continuing concern with international finance. I left the Johns Hopkins University, where I had been for thirteen years, and moved to Princeton University to become Walker Professor of Economics and International Finance and also Director of the International Finance Section. This meant that I devoted more time than previously to international monetary problems, in teaching, research, and editing various series of publications. The Princeton Essays in International Finance, together with the Studies and Special Papers, became my responsibility, and I took it very seriously; I solicited, suggested, and commissioned manuscripts on timely topics and I did much editing to make the essays more readable.

The other thing that happened was the first flight from the dollar into gold. In 1958 the dollar shortage had been transformed into a dollar glut, not by any drastic change in the balance of payments of the United States, but by the simple realisation on the part of the central banks that they had accumulated all the dollars they wanted. There had been several proposals that the dollar price of gold be raised – doubled, according to some – and many Europeans acted on the expectation that these proposals would be adopted. This caused a large demand for gold in the London market and elsewhere; the price of gold in London climbed temporarily to $40 an ounce, or more than 13 per cent over the official parity.

This episode caused me to make a 'Proposal to Reduce the Price of Gold'.[29] At the annual meeting of the economic associations, I was one of the discussion speakers in a session of the American Finance Association, where Frank Southard and Ralph Wood read papers. I used this occasion to make my strange proposal – which shocked a good many people.

My proposal was for reducing the price of gold in several small steps. 'This would reverse historical experience, and those who persist in holding gold would lose money' (p. 240). To inflict such losses on gold hoarders was, however, not my purpose. Indeed, since the reduction would be announced several months in advance, speculators and hoarders could gain by selling gold before the reduction and, if they distrusted the authorities, buying back afterwards. After a few reductions, many people might decide to stay out of the market. The real purpose of my plan was discourage further gold purchases by private investors or speculators and thus to avoid further losses of official gold reserves. The one-way expectations – due to rumors, recommendations, and pressures for a large raise in the official price of gold, but never a hint of reduction – had made 'long' positions, speculation for a rise, almost riskless. A series of small reductions, perhaps every three months, with the monetary authorities prepared to sell and buy unlimited quantities of gold, could redress this situation. It might lead to a net dishoarding of gold, an increase in official gold reserves, and a considerable easing of the money markets with lower interest rates.

I ended my paper with a warning: 'While I regard my proposal as more than a "gadget" or "gimmick", I do not regard it as a substitute for sound monetary and financial policies in this or any other country' (p. 244).

INTERNATIONAL LIQUIDITY (1961–2)

In my hypersensitivity regarding linguistic and semantic sloppiness I was disturbed by the promiscuous use of the term liquidity, domestic as well as international. The term liquidity had been used in connection with *assets* and in connection with individual *debtors*, including individual *banks*. The use was gradually extended to *groups* of individuals, firms, and banks, and finally to whole *countries*, *groups of countries*, *the whole world*. The chief proponent of the extension to an entire country was the Radcliffe Commission in Britain, which in 1958, in its *Report on the Working of the Monetary System*, held that the old concepts 'quantity of money' and 'amount of bank reserves' were too narrow and had better be replaced by the wider concept 'liquidity'. The chief proponent of the concept of international liquidity was the International Monetary Fund, in its staff study *International Reserves and Liquidity* (Washington, 1958). The main idea was that an expression was needed for the combination of official reserves and borrowing rights. In 1961–2 I wrote an article protesting the looseness with which the term could be used; the National Bank of Belgium published it under the title 'Liquidité, internationale et nationale', and I included it later in a collection of essays under the extended title 'The Fuzzy Concepts of Liquidity, International and Domestic'.[30]

Among my misgivings to the extension of the concept to groups of individuals, firms, and banks was the troublesome question 'whether debts among members of the group and payments for intergroup purchases are to be included or "netted out"' (p. 251). There can be no unequivocal answer, because the problems are different for intragroup and for external debt-paying capacities; at least two different concepts are involved here. 'In some cases a clear answer will be almost impossible because one "person's" money or near-money is another "person's" debt and it may not make much sense to ask for their combined liquidity.' (p. 252). For heterogeneous groups, or the country as a whole, 'aggregate liquidity' cannot be meaningful until the intent of the question is specified. 'The term "liquidity" is concise only at the expense of precision', but 'what we need is not a [better] term ... A term in search of a meaning is a rather useless thing; a meaning in search of a term can easily be accommodated by imaginative word-coiners, provided the meaning is clearly and unambiguously specified' (p. 253).

Analogous difficulties trouble the analyst of so-called international liquidity. To designate the assets as well as the liabilities of the reserve-currency countries as

> liquidity of the international monetary system contributes nothing to the problem – except a bit of confusion. It would be better if we admitted that the liquidities of banker-countries and depositor-countries, like the liquidities of bankers and depositors are not additive (p. 255).

My objections to the extension of the concept of liquidity to groups, countries, and the whole world have been overruled by the profession. The new meaning of the term became conventional – and

I had to yield. I do not think that I was wrong in my resistance, but perhaps I was too fussy. I have later used the term in its new meaning without further protest.

The last two sections of the article became, somewhat expanded, the first two sections of a new essay 'Further Reflections on the Demand for Foreign Reserves' in my 1964 volume of collected essays.[31] In the section on 'Reserves for Contingent Liabilities' I explained why 'no amount of foreign reserve may be adequate for a country that indefinitely continues a policy of maintaining effective demand in the face of an excess demand for foreign currency at fixed exchange rates' (p. 264).

I went on to discuss that

> the accumulation of monetary reserves . . . represents a formation of capital that remains unproductive (or almost so) in its present form and becomes productive only through its eventual use. . . . For a nation to hold 'unnecessarily' large foreign reserves is to forego productive domestic investment in order to be prepared for unlikely accidents (p. 266).

On the other hand, I realised that the decision to hold reserves beyond anticipated needs may be based on undesirable side-effects of the measures that could be instrumental in precipitating the use of reserves, namely, accelerated monetary expansion or appreciation (or upvaluation) of the currency (pp. 266–7).

I examined the question of the optimal size of the monetary reserve of the nation, first on the assumption that the reserve was held by official monetary authorities, then that reserves of foreign or international moneys were held only privately in a system of free floating. Whether it is 'as a rule socially beneficial to make reserve-holding a government function' depends on 'whether the social marginal cost of reserve-holding is lower than the private marginal cost, and whether the social marginal product . . . exceeds the private marginal product' (pp. 267–8). Later analysts of these questions have overlooked my tentative conclusions, which included considerations regarding (1) economies of risk-pooling through partial centralisation of foreign reserves (in banks sufficiently numerous to safeguard competition) and (2) external benefits of reduced fluctuations of exchange rates (especially greater job security for labour employed in the foreign-trade sector of the economy). If external economies are substantial, 'it might be argued that . . . inventories [of foreign contingency reserves] held by private business in trade and industry are apt to fall short of what would be socially optimal' (p. 271).

On the other hand, the concept of a private demand for foreign reserves implies the reserve holders' awareness of their opportunity costs: they forego alternative uses of their resources. But 'if central bankers or governing boards make the decisions about reserve holding, they are not themselves sacrificing anything nor are they even aware of the fact that they are imposing a sacrifice upon the nation' (p. 276).

Several authors discussing the demand or 'need' for monetary reserves have the notion of 'real' demand in their minds – real in the sense that nominal amounts are corrected for changes in commodity prices. In discussions of 'inadequate international liquidity' it is often overlooked that a more generous provision of international reserves [and borrowing rights] to national monetary authorities 'may induce credit policies leading to rising prices with the result that the real reserves end up no higher than they were before' (p. 275). If this is so, inadequate liquidity can only temporarily be made adequate, until prices catch up with the increase in liquidity expressed in terms of money.

A SURVEY OF REFORM PLANS (1962, 1964)

In 1961–2 I wrote for the International Finance Section 'Special Paper in International Economics, No. 3' (August 1962), a survey of plans for international monetary reform.[32] These special papers were intended to serve as teaching material for students. (It may be of interest to some that Special Papers No. 1 and No. 2 had been by Gottfried Haberler and Oskar Morgenstern, my friends and fellow students at Vienna in the early 1920s, both in the United States since the 1930s.) My survey of reform plans has probably become the most widely read of my publications in this area, chiefly in its revised edition, published by the International Finance Section in 1964 and also included in my collection of essays in the same year.[33]

I began the survey with a description of the system as it existed at the time, including an explanation of the operation of the International Monetary Fund. This was followed by a presentation of the charges against the existing system, in particular, 'difficulties with the balance of payments', 'inadequacy of international reserves', and 'danger of collapse'. Then came 'A Section of Plans'.

A main feature of the exposition was the use of T-accounts showing the sequence of changes in monetary reserves and demand deposits, domestic and foreign, private and official, that would be generated by the operation of the different plans. Documentation of sources – proposals as well as proponents – was exhaustive, accounting for 105 footnotes in the revised edition – an increase of 52 per cent over the first edition. The 'growth' of the literature between the two editions was extraordinary: after only one year, 37 new publications with new proposals or comments on proposals were calling for my attention.

In the 'Concluding Remarks' I explained my reticence regarding my support of any one of the plans examined. No plan can be judged to be the best irrespective of government policies in all areas. What can and should be done is to recognise inconsistencies and incompatibilities. Some plans are simply ruled out as long as people in charge or people of influence entertain strong views about certain economic and monetary objectives. I pointed this out in connection with monetary policies intended to maintain high rates of employment and growth and also fixed rates for foreign exchange (*International Payments, Debts, and Gold*, pp. 359–63). This theme had been present in a more primitive form in my first book, was most clearly stated in this survey of monetary plans, and was to be sounded in several variations in my later publications.

THE TRANSFER PROBLEM REVISITED (1963–4)

One of my earliest concerns as international monetary theorist had been the transfer problem. The two articles published in 1928 and 1930 addressed chiefly the problems of large payments of foreign debts and reparations. In the early 1960s, when Europeans and Americans began to be worried about the dollar glut and the continuing deficits in the balance of payments of the United States, I became convinced that this country was experiencing transfer difficulties. Commitments for foreign aid, military expenditures abroad, and private investments abroad added up to large financial transfers not matched by real transfers in the form of export surpluses. This interpretation of the balance-of-payments problem of the United States – continuing outflows of gold and increases in official short-term liabilities to foreign countries – occupied my thoughts and induced me to write two new papers for inclusion in the volume of collected essays which I had prepared for publication in 1964.

The first of these new papers appeared also in a German translation.[34] 'The Transfer Problem: Theme and Four Variations' stated the theme in the briefest form and then presented the four variations: (1) Britain, 1793–1816, during the Napoleonic wars, maintaining armies on the continent of Europe, giving loans and subsidies to allies, paying foreign diplomatic agents; (2) France, 1871–5, after the Franco-Prussian war, paying indemnities to Prussia; (3) Germany, 1924–32, after the First World War, paying reparations to the victorious nations; and (4) United States, 1950–63 [though continued for many more years], after the Second World War, giving foreign loans and grants, paying for military expenditures abroad, and making private foreign investments.

Comparisons of the absolute amounts (of current money) involved were meaningless, but 'the relative burden on the paying country' could be judged by ratios to relevant aggregates. I compared the foreign remittances with national-income estimates and with foreign-trade statistics. The former comparison may throw light on the budgetary problem of the paying country, not just in the sense of a fiscal or tax problem but in the wider sense of 'the problem of reducing the domestic intake out of a given national income'. The second comparison 'may help in sizing up the real transfer problem; the problem of increasing exports and/or reducing imports in order to have the trade balance adjusted to the remittances abroad' (pp. 374–5).

Before I embarked on an analysis of the transfer problem under conditions of economic growth, I engaged in the semantic analysis which I had found wanting in my article on 'Transfer and Price Effects' back in 1930. Now, in 1964, I

> distinguished, besides 'shortage of foreign exchange' and besides 'political difficulties', six types of economic loss; primary burden, terms-of-trade losses, losses through increases in the real value of the fixed obligations, transitional unemployment, transitional misallocations, and long-term unemployment. If these different types of economic loss are no longer scrambled together as 'transfer difficulties', analysts of the transfer problem will begin to understand one another. (p. 440)

In both cases, transfer under conditions of growth and transfer between stationary economies, the problem is to ascertain the 'warranted' rate of primary disbursements in the paying country; that is, that rate which, given the rate of primary disbursements abroad and given the countries' propensities to save and to import, is apt to create the desired increase in its balance of trade. (p. 441)

Of course, this warranted rate of increase or decrease in domestic disbursements would depend on price effects as well as income effects. Realising that the analysis of price effects was quite complex (unless one simplifies the argument by limiting the number of goods traded to two, or to two bundles of fixed composition), I had in 1943 analysed the transfer problem exclusively on the basis of income effects. This meant, in accordance with the conventional assumptions of multiplier analysis, that the (full or partial) solution of the transfer problem, that is, the adjustment of the trade balance to the financial transfer commitment, has to operate through changes in employment: in favourable cases, there could be increased employment in the recipient country, but in any case there would be reduced employment in the paying country. This conclusion applied to transfers between stationary economies. Now I saw that under conditions of economic growth in both the paying and receiving countries, changes in income and employment would still be the only equilibrating forces as long as one sticks to the assumptions of income-multiplier analysis; but it is now possible for employment to increase also in the paying country. If both countries have increasing amounts of real resources available, and if the receiving country expands its primary disbursement sufficiently to employ much or all of its increased capacity to produce, the paying country need not reduce its domestic disbursements, and therefore its employment, in order to achieve the required trade surplus.

I thought in 1964, and I still do, that this revisit to the transfer problem secured new insights. Unfortunately, the essay has failed to elicit any response from my professional colleagues. I suspect it was overlooked. In a volume containing some twenty pieces, most of them well known to the well-read members of the profession, a new essay tacked in between the old ones, can easily escape the readers' attention. Perhaps this notice will persuade some to look up the overlooked chapter.

THE MYSTERIOUS NUMBERS GAME (1964)

Another chapter in the same volume was also new but not overlooked, perhaps because it had an eye-catching title and was particularly suitable for teaching purposes. It was 'The Mysterious Numbers Game of Balance-of-Payments Statistics'.[35]

Since it dealt with statistical data, the chapter concerned itself only with the accounting balance of payments, but showed that its components can be arranged in many different ways.

> Where accounts are kept on a double-entry [book-keeping] system, so that the sum of all credits must equal the sum of all debits, the selection of categories of entries to make up the [credit or debit] *balance* determines, obviously, the categories of entries which make up the *offsets* to the balance . . . equal in amount . . . with the signs reversed. (p. 141)

What I call 'offsets' in my essay has later been generally called 'financing items', suggesting that the balance (surplus or deficit) of all items 'above the line' is financed by the items 'below the line'. Where the line is drawn, however, depends on the statistician's or accountant's understanding of the theories purported to interpret the data – and these theories as well as the understanding of the theories change over time.

I exhibited a set of twenty different reports of the balance of payments of the United States for the year 1951. These reports, published between 1952 and 1963, stated 17 different results for 1951. Exactly one half of them – dated between 1952 and 1957 – reported surpluses, the other ten – only one dated 1952, the other nine dated between 1959 and 1963 – reported deficits for 1951. The surpluses varied from $5029 million to $99 million; the deficits from $300 million to $995 million. The same basic data were used by all these reports, only their arrangement was changed. Most of the earlier reports recorded surpluses because this was in line with the theories of dollar shortage widely held at the time; later reports for the same year recorded deficits because, if the statisticians had continued to use the old arrangements of categories, they would have to record surpluses for later years when the dollar glut had become manifest and the theories of dollars shortage had been abandoned.

One lesson to be drawn from this exercise is that one must not believe that statistical data can tell their own story. We must not be taken in by admonitions such as 'let us look at the facts'. The so-called empirical facts, or records of observation, can neither suggest nor verify theories. Instead, they presuppose and contain large chunks of theory; and 'changes in the theoretical presuppositions or preconceptions may result in drastic changes of the observations, of the empirical data, of the supposedly stubborn facts [of history]' (p. 147).

Editor's note: Professor Machlup's contribution remained unfinished at the time of his death in 1983.

Notes

1. Where and when did I work? A few readers may be interested in the more personal aspects of my life. Since I was engaged in business and could not work in my office on matters not related to the business, I did my reading and writing at home between 6 and 8 o'clock in the morning and between 8 and 12 o'clock in the evening. I had trained myself to do with little sleep and my physical constitution rebelled only occasionally against this stern regime. (The rebellions took the form of stomach ulcers, which attacked me repeatedly from age 20 to the present – age 77.)
2. *Die Goldkernwährung* (H. Meyer, Halberstadt, 1925).
3. *Ibid.* Part 2, pp. 44–95.
4. Ricardo, David, *Proposals for an Economical and Secure Currency* (London, John Murray, 1816), p. 14. In Piero Sraffa (ed.), *The Works and Correspondence of David Ricardo*, vol. IV (Cambridge, Cambridge University Press, 1951), p. 59.
5. Spann, Othmar, *Die Haupttheorien der Volkswirtschaftslehre* (Leipzig, Quelle & Meyer, 5th edn, 1920), p. 24.
6. *Die neuen Währungen in Europa* [Finanz- und Volkswirtschaftliche Zeitfragen] (Stuttgart, Ferdinand Enke, 1927).
7. Schacht, Hjalmar, *Eigene oder geborgte Währung* (Leipzig, Quelle, 1927).
8. 'Währung und Auslandsverschuldung: Benerkungen zur Diskussion zwischen Schacht und seinen Kritikern' [Currency and Foreign Indebtedness: Comments on the Discussion between Schacht and his Critics], *Mitteilungen des Verbandes Österreichischer Banken und Bankiers*, vol. 10 (no. 7/8, 1928), pp. 194–208. A rather free translation, under the title 'Foreign Debts, Reparations, and the Transfer Problem', was published in my book *International Payments, Debts, and Gold* (New York, Scribners, 1964; London, Allen & Unwin, 1966; enlarged edition, New York, New York University Press, 1976), pp. 396–416.
9. Keynes, John Maynard, 'The German Transfer Problem', *Economic Journal*, vol. 39 (March 1929), p. 6.

10. Keynes, cited in the preceding footnote; Ohlin, Bertil, 'The Reparations Problem', *Economic Journal*, vol. 39 (June 1929), pp. 172–8; Haberler, Gottfried, 'Transfer und Preisbewegung', *Zeitschrift für Nationalokönomie*, vol. 1 (January 1930), pp. 547–54; Machlup, Fritz, 'Transfer und Preisbewegung', *Zeitschrift für Nationalökonomie*, vol. 1 (January 1930), pp. 555–60.
11. 'Die Theorie der Kapitalflucht', *Weltwirtschaftliches Archiv*. vol. 36 (October 1932), pp. 512–29.
12. 'La Crise Monétaire et Financière', Société des Nations, Hors Série 51, Genève, 2 June 1932.
13. 'Die Währungs- und Kreditkrise', *Schmollers Jahrbuch für Gesetzgebung, Verwaltung und Volkswirtschaft im Deutschen Reich*, vol. 57 (no. 3, 1933), pp. 49–64.
14. 'Règlementation des devises en Autriche', Société des Nations, F/Tres/8, Genève, The German original, 'Das Österreichische System der Devisenordnung', 5 June 1932.
15. 'The Theory of Foreign Exchange', Part I, *Economica*, New Series, vol. 6 (1939), pp. 375–97; Part II, *Economica*, New Series, vol. 7 (1940), pp. 23–49. Reproduced in Ellis, Howard S., and Metzler, Lloyd A. (eds), *Readings in the Theory of International Trade* (Philadeplphia, Blakiston, 1949; Homewood, Ill., Irwin), ch. 5, pp. 104–58; also in Machlup, Fritz, *International Payments, Debts, and Gold* (New York, Scribners, 1964; New York, New York University Press, 1976), ch. 1, pp. 7–50; also in Machlup, Fritz, *International Monetary Economics* (London, Allen & Unwin, 1966), ch. 1, pp. 7–50. The essay was published also in Spanish, German, and Japanese translations. (All page references in this section will be to the reproduction in my volume of collected essays.)
16. Chipman, John S., 'A Reconsideration of the "Elasticity Approach" to Balance-of-Payments Adjustment Problems', in Dreyer, Jacob S., (ed.), *Breadth and Depth in Economics: Fritz Machlup – The Man and His Ideas* (Lexington, Mass., Heath and Company, 1978), pp. 48–85.
17. Perhaps I may now, in 1980, add a commentary to this statement about 'erratic' changes in expectations. Economic analysis is least complicated if one can reasonably assume that all or most economic agents expect present prices (rates) to remain unchanged; it is still manageable if one can assume expectations that prices will continue to move in the same direction and at the same pace as they have over the previous period (or even more slowly), or that they will revert to some previous level; analysis becomes too messy and unmanageable if expectations differ so widely that the dispersion of expectations cannot be described and, moreover, if they change from day to day or hour to hour.
18. 'Eight Questions on Gold: A Review', *American Economic Review*. Proceedings, vol. 30 (February 1941), pp. 30–7. Reprinted in my book *International Payments, Debts and Gold* (New York, Scribners, 1964; 2nd edn, New York, New York University Press, 1976), ch. X, pp. 228–38; also in Machlup, Fritz, *International Monetary Economics* (London, Allen & Unwin, 1966); Japanese translation in 1973).
19. 'Period Analysis and Multiplier Theory', *Quarterly Journal of Econo-*

mics, vol. 54 (November 1939), pp. 21–2; reprinted in Haberler Gottfried (ed.), *Readings in Business Cycle Theory* (Philadelphia, Blakiston, 1944), ch. 10, pp. 203–34; translated into Spanish and German.

20. I had become economic editor of the Blakiston Company and developed for it a series of economic monographs, texts, and volumes of readings. After a take-over of the company most of its books were republished under other imprints.
21. 'Elasticity Pessimism in International Trade', *Economia Internazionale*, vol. 3 (February 1950), pp. 118–37. Reprinted in my book, *International Payments, Debts, and Gold*, pp. 51–68. Page references in the text will be to that volume. Translated into Japanese (1973).
22. Several writers confuse the Lerner formula with another formula by Alfred Marshall, which relates to reciprocal-offer curves. Those who speak of a 'Marshall–Lerner formula' have slipped up on their reading assignments.
23. 'Three Concepts of the Balance of Payments and the So-Called Dollar Shortage', *Economic Journal*, vol. 60 (March 1950), pp. 46–68. Reproduced in Allen, William R. and Allen, Clark Lee (eds), *Foreign Trade and Finance* (New York, Macmillan, 1959), ch. 5, pp. 97–123, and in Machlup, Fritz, *International Payments, Debts, and Gold* (1964, 1966, 1976), pp. 69–92. Page references in the text will be to the last-named volume. The article was translated into Japanese in two versions (1953 and 1973).
24. 'Dollar Shortage and Disparities in the Growth of Productivity', *Scottish Journal of Political Economy*, vol. 1 (October 1954), pp. 250–67. Reprinted in *International Payments, Debts, and Gold*, pp. 93–109. Page references in the text are to that volume. The article was translated into Japanese (1955 and 1973) and Portuguese (1955).
25. Alexander, Sidney S., 'Effects of a Devaluation on a Trade Balance', *International Monetary Fund Staff Papers*, vol. 2 (April 1952), pp. 263–78.
26. 'Relative Prices and Aggregate Spending in the Analysis of Devaluation', *American Economic Review*, vol. 45 (June 1955), pp. 255–78. Reprinted in *International Payments, Debts, and Gold*, ch. 8, pp. 171–94. Page references in the text are to this collection. The article was reprinted also in *Selected Economic Writings of Fritz Machlup*, edited by George Bitros (New York, New York University Press, 1976), ch. 14, pp. 255–78. Japanese translations of the article appeared in 1955 and 1973, an Italian translation in 1971.
27. 'The Terms-of-Trade Effects of Devaluation upon Real Income and the Balance of Payments', *Kyklos*, vol. 9 (no. 4, 1956), pp. 417–52). Reprinted in *International Payments, Debts, and Gold*, ch. 9, pp. 195–222. Page references in the text are to this collection. Japanese translation in 1973.
28. 'Equilibrium and Disequilibrium: Misplaced Concreteness and Disguised Politics', *Economic Journal*, vol. 68 (March 1958), pp. 1–24. Reproduced in *Essays in Economic Semantics* (Englewood Cliffs, New Jersey, 1963; New York, Norton, 1967; New York, New York Universi-

ty Press, 1975), pp. 43–72; and in *International Payments, Debts, and Gold* (1964, 1966, 1975), pp. 110–35. Page references in the text are to the last-mentioned volume. The article was translated into Spanish (1962 and 1974), French (1971), and Japanese (1973).

29. 'Comments on "The Balance of Payments" and a Proposal to Reduce the Price of Gold', *The Journal of Finance*, vol. 16 (May 1961), pp. 189–93. Reprinted partly as ch. VI, partly as ch. XI in *International Payments, Debts and Gold* (1964, 1966, 1975). The part on the Proposal is on pp. 239–44 of that volume. Page references in the text are to that chapter. The two chapters were translated into Japanese (1973).

30. 'Liquidité, internationale et nationale', *Bulletin d'Information et de Documentation, Banque Nationale de Belgique*, vol. 37 (February 1962). Slightly revised English version, 'The Fuzzy Concepts of Liquidity, International and Domestic', *International Payments, Debts, and Gold* (1964, 1966, 1975), ch. XII, pp. 245–59. Footnote references in the text are to that volume. The chapter was translated into Japanese (1973).

31. 'Further Reflections on the Demand for Foreign Reserves', in *International Payments, Debts, and Gold* (1964, 1966, 1975), pp. 260–76. Japanese translation in 1973.

32. *Plans for Reform of the International Monetary System* (Special Paper in International Economics, no. 3, Princeton, N.J., International Finance Section, Princeton University, August 1962). An abridged version was included in *Factors Affecting the United States Balance of Payments*, Subcommittee on International Exchange and Payments, Joint Economic Committee, Congress of the United States, 87th Congress, 2nd Session (Washington, 1962). Part 3, pp. 209–37. Translations appeared in German (1962), Italian (1962) and Japanese (1963).

33. Revised edition of the Princeton Special Paper, no. 3 (March 1964). Reprinted in the *International Payments, Debts, and Gold* (1964, 1966, 1975), ch. XIV, pp. 282–66. Russian translation (1966), Japanese (1973).

34. 'Das Transferproblem: Thema und vier Variationen', *Ordo*, vol. 14 (1963), pp. 139–67. The English version, 'The Transfer Problem: Theme and Four Variations', became ch. XV in *International Payments, Debts, and Gold* (1964, 1966, 1975), pp. 374–95. Page references in the text are to that book.

35. Chapter VII in *International Payments, Debts, and Gold* (1964, 1966, 1975), pp. 140–66. Japanese translation (1973).

3 Aerial Roots

Paul Streeten

I was born in 1917, still but barely into the Austro-Hungarian empire, although I was not aware of it at the time. But there were echoes of it in the interwar years and, having lived through these and then again much later through the declining British empire, not to say anything of the post-Watergate, post-Vietnam USA, I regard myself as something of an expert on imperial decay.

I was born Paul Hornig, son of Wilhelm and Berta Hornig. My father died when I was less than two. He had been a businessman, dealing in feathers, and from all reports a dilettante in many fields and a great entertainer, full of the wit that was common in Viennese café society. After the death of my father, we (my mother, my younger brother Walter and I) joined my mother's sister, who was married and had, in due course, two daughters. I grew up in this slightly extended family, with two mothers, for Annimaedel (the name all four children gave to my aunt Anna) really brought us up while my mother ran a little knitwear shop.

My childhood was a happy one. My mother and her three sisters were close to each other and, together with their husbands, attracted an amusing group of admirers. Willy Reich and Siegfried Bernfeld were advisers on my sexual education (though not every one of their pieces of advice was followed). Otto Neurath, the logical positivist, unified scientist, and inventor of isotypes, a kind of pictorial statistics, took an interest in us children. There were many psychoanalysts, such as Otto Fenichel, a translator of Shakespeare called Flatter, journalists and politicians, a novelist Brunngraber, a composer Karl Popper was a member of a group that played handball on Sundays in the Vienna Woods, though he was not regarded as one of the brightest. My uncle Paul Stem wrote a regular column headed 'People's Doctor' for the Social Democratic daily *Arbeiterzeitung*. Paul Lazarsfeld and Marie Jahoda, whom I met again later at the University of Sussex, did a study of unemployment, *Die Arbeitslosen von Marienthal*. I particularly remember a family friend called Poldi Bandler who constructed a whole toy world for us children, with a life-like imitation of the skyline of Manhattan. Whenever I cross the

Triborough bridge and set eyes on the Manhattan skyline I think of him.

One of my earliest economic memories is overhearing in about 1922 a grownup conversation during the Austrian hyper-inflation, in which one person said the Krone (the crown) was rising (*aufsteigen*). I imagined a grand, queenly woman ascending a mountain. A bachelor *Hausfreund* (especially devoted to my aunt Annimaedel) of those days was a lawyer named Walter Froehlick, who had some influence on my becoming an economist. He was a member of the circle of Austrian economists round Mises, Haberler, Hayek and Machlup. He was very liberal in the Manchester sense, although also liberal politically, for he defended under the Dollfuss and Schuschnigg regimes many political prisoners of the Left.

Walter Froehlich had a great admiration for theory construction and a certain contempt for empirical research. One of his favourite stories was that told of Mrs Einsteen's visit to the latest and largest observatory. 'What do you do with these telescopes?' she asked. 'Well, we look at the stars to find out whether the galaxies are receding and are trying to test the theory of the continuous creation of the universe against that of an initial big bang', they replied. 'Ah, I see', she said. 'It's the sort of thing that my husband does on the back of old envelopes.' Although a Catholic by religion, Walter Froehlich was of Jewish origin. He migrated to Marquette University in Milwaukee and we were friends until his death.

It was not difficult to acquire a social conscience in the Austria of the inter-war period. I remember having to write an essay as a child of about eight years old on the subject 'If any would not work neither should he eat' and making it the occasion of a harangue against the idle rich.

I was politically active from the age of ten: marching, carrying flags, singing, demonstrating. Until 1933, these activities were legal, and after 1933, they were carried on underground, with the continual threat of arrest and imprisonment. I carried messages, especially during the 1934 attack of Dollfuss on the workers, attended meetings, distributed illegal news sheets. The socialist youth movement filled most of my time and interest, and though I have revised many opinions of these days, the underlying spirit still colours my views. Austrian socialism or Austro-Marxism was a very special brand of radical socialism. Although we read Marx and Engels, as well as the Utopian socialists, Otto Bauer (the leader of the party) had given it a

Keynesian stamp before the *General Theory*, so that it combined a revolutionary streak about ultimate objectives with a strong democratic-reformist element about the path.

Both the Christian Social Party and the Social Democrats had their private armies: the *Heimwehr* and the *Schutzbund*. I believe that they contributed to the political instability of Austria, the burning of the *Justizpalast* in 1927 and the deterioration of political cohesion afterwards. When nearly half a century later, I served on the Royal Commission on Environmental Pollution and we investigated the fast breeder reactor, I, together with other members of the Commission, saw one of the greatest threats of the fast breeder reactor neither in accidents, nor sabotage, nor terrorist attacks but in the need to arm personnel for the protection of the power stations and in the danger that such private armies could lead to reduced civil liberties and greater political strife.

Another major influence in my youth was Max Adler, a scholar who attempted to combine Marx and Kant (and, incidentally, was another courtier of my aunt Annimaedel). He argued that not only space, time and causality are *a priori* categories, but also the reference to other rational consciousnesses, the social *a priori*. All thinking (and, of course, morality), both pure and practical reason, has an inevitable reference to other rational minds. Adler tried to purge Marxism of vulgar materialism. I found his approach and philosophy appealing.

He was also a Hegelian and argued that social progress is achieved by the oppressed class overthrowing the unjust order of exploitation and establishing a higher synthesis in which the 'contradictions' of thesis and antithesis of the old order are overcome. Alas, all subsequent experience of liberation movements has shown that the oppressed, when they gain power and influence, often adopt some of the worst features of their oppressors: consider the black liberation movement; the black middle class is full of Babbitts; and the women's liberation movement, which has sponsored women who swear and bang the table; not to speak of the Soviet Union's or the Khmer Rouge's betrayal of social ideals.

I attended the lectures of Max Adler, of Moritz Schlick the philosopher who was shot dead in the *aula* of Vienna University, of Erich Voegelin, of the psychologist couple the Buehlers, and others while I was still at school. The driving force was only partly scholarly interest, though I enjoyed reading philosophy, psychology and sociology, but revolutionary fervour. I hiked in the Vienna Woods with my troup, camped out, and met weekly in a 'Heim' for political discussions.

The youth movement of which I was such an active member had itself an interesting origin. Its roots go back to the time before the First World War, when people like Wynecken elevated youth to an end in itself, and affirmed a youthful lifestyle that was in revolt against urban, bourgeois culture: they wore sandals and open-necked shirts, rejected smoking, drinking, ballroom dancing (dancing round a campfire was all right) and other features of urban life, sat round campfires and opted for free love. This *Wandervogel* had no political content. But youth cannot be an end in itself. The war, and the fact that youth is a passing phase, altered all this after 1918. The heritage of some of the elements of the *Wandervogel* was taken over by youth movements which, however, became politically extreme, both of the right and of the left. Both the Hitler youth and the *Roten Falken* (the red falcons, as we were called) had inherited some of the ethos of the pre-war youth movement. I remember how this gave rise to some odd and soul-searching conflicts: should we help in organising a trade union meeting in which beer was served? (We were passionate teetotallers as well as anti-smokers.) Should we participate in a workers' meeting at which cigarettes were smoked? Long debates were devoted to such dilemmas.

I had two conversions or rather turning points: at the age of about 15, and at the age of 18. The first was from hiking and camping and athletics and group life towards intellectual and private interest, at that time psychology and sociology. It began with reading some articles by Alfred Adler, the founder of Individual Psychology, and it linked up with social psychology for it was concerned with the best way to bring up children: whether in a family or in a collective, and I welcomed the idea that communal education was best. I had offered a *Matura* thesis, an optional dissertation, on graduating from high school. The subject was Mass Psychology. I enjoyed tremendously reading for this paper and writing it. I had a very stimulating high-school teacher, Haeussler (he taught philosophy and German literature), and he encouraged me in my interests. He turned out to be a Nazi (although simultaneously a member of the fascist *Heimwehr* and the Socialists), and after the war took to drink, but he was a powerful influence in my youth. Count Leinsdorf, a figure in Robert Musil's *The Man Without Qualities*, remarked that all these people in the superstructure are so unreliable: the Austrian equivalent of the *trahison des clercs*.

The second turning point occurred one or two years before I left Austria, and prepared me for the English approach to politics. It was away from revolutionary action towards democratic reform, away from collectivism towards individualism and away from party doctrine towards the individual conscience. In particular, I began to distrust the Communist doctrine that the end justifies the means and saw that certain means must be rejected, however good the ultimate end. It was, at the purely personal level, a 'shifting involvement' like that analysed by Albert Hirschman (whom I got to know, admire and like later) in his book *Shifting Involvements: Private Interest and Public Action*, a shift from intense involvement with politics and public life to a period of preoccupation with private affairs. Rousseau said that the more time citizens spend thinking about public matters, and the less about their own private affairs, the better the society. I felt increasingly out of sympathy with this view, and agreed more with Oscar Wilde who said that socialism would take too many evenings. I began to resent the time spent on organisational matters. But I continued to participate in political discussion groups (Helene Bauer, Otto Bauer's wife, conducted one), and was the leader of one, although my turning point was reflected in the fact that we discussed not only political issues but also literature, psychology and sociology. At that time I got to know the psychologist August Aichhorn, whose book *Wayward Youth* made a deep impression on me. I remained a radical socialist intellectually, though I had become a conservative emotionally. It may not be easy to understand that this was quite a difficult step, for much of the philosophy of the underground youth movement was more in line with Bakunin's, Lenin's and Stalin's teachings than with social democracy. It was, however, made easier by the Popular Front, the common cause with all anti-fascist forces, that the Communists then advocated.

I had started to study law at the University of Vienna and had already passed the first *Staatspruefung*, with distinction in Canon Law, of all things. Law, in Austria, was the academic path to sociology and political economy, but the main determinant was the need to earn a living and I had assumed I would become a lawyer. I attended the lectures of Othmar Spann, an authoritarian political economist who emphasised the whole as preceding the parts. He presented the universe as a great, all-encompassing mind, of which the state, the nation and their institutions (the university, the church, the stock exchange) are more substantial and significant aspects than any mere individuals. He illustrated this vividly by an imaginary walk round the *Ringstrasse*, in which one passed from the Bourse to the *Votivkirche*, to the university, and the natural history and art museums. Although I never swallowed his political philosophy, I was intrigued and fascinated by the man. He fell out with the Nazis, I think spent some time in prison, and was more in line with the pre-Hitler Austro-fascism. In a quite different way I was also impressed by the teaching and writings of Hans Kelsen, a philosopher of law in the positivist tradition. His scepticism and relativism contrasted with Spann's absolutism and universalism. I greatly admired university professors, and a life devoted to intellectual pursuits, and the idea of ever becoming a professor seemed to me then beyond the wildest dreams.

In Vienna we had court singers or court musicians. They were not singers at the court of the Habsburgs, but musicians who played and sang in the courtyard of the block of flats in which we lived. The inhabitants would wrap a few coins into newspaper and throw the packet out of the window into the court. But often the money was given to the court musicians to make them go away and permit peace and quiet to be restored.

These court singers became for me paradigmatic figures that later made me sceptical of the national income as a measure of economic welfare. Here was a case of people being able to extract money for the removal of a self-created nuisance. They did not produce a good, but a 'bad', and received in payment an anti-bad. Was this a rare exception or was it typical of other payments normally counted as net benefits? Nuisances or 'bads' can be generated by our enemies, by nature, or by the economic system itself. Those generated by our enemies call for an army and weapons of defence. Some would not regard these as additions to our economic welfare. The 'bads' generated by nature call for the anti-bads of protection against cold and heat, against the weather, against starvation, all that is needed to keep the body going. Should we not deduct these also from our accounts, not perhaps as regrettable necessities, like defence, but as preconditions of net income? Finally, what about the anti-bads that remove the nuisances created through pollution or by advertising and the social pressures of emulation? If people buy deodorants because the fear has been created in them that they will be ostracised if they do not use them, is this not exactly parallel to the court singers, or, worse, to the kidnapper asking for ransom or the blackmailer asking for money (though he may not have created the occasion for the blackmail)? But then not all demands for the removal of created gaping voids that require resources can be regarded as anti-bads. Some of the finest, as well as some of the lowest desires have been created by 'artificial' stimulation. The desire for truth, goodness and beauty, just like the desire to have the organ grinder leave, has been created, in the first case by educators, in the second by the musician. The organ grinder may produce such appalling noises that we pay him to take away his organ, or may produce heavenly melodies for which we are happy to give up a fortune. It follows that we cannot do without value judgements in deciding which are goods and which are anti-bads, which items add to our welfare and which bring us just back to square one. It was this discovery that made me look on economics as a moral study, as well as a study shot through with controversial assumptions.

In the final phases of the Schuschnigg regime, the university had been instructed to provide catholic political indoctrination. We had to write essays on political philosophy along Austro-fascist lines. This provided some exercise in writing entirely against one's conviction, yet with a certain relish, rather like an advertising executive who has to praise a product he does not believe in. There was strong cognitive dissonance, but no tendency to remove it by adjusting beliefs.

Things changed radically when on Saturday 12 March 1938 the Nazis marched into Vienna. We happened to have moved from a flat in the 8th district to a house in the 13th, a month before the *Anschluss*. Had it not been for this move, I am sure I would have been arrested and sent to a concentration camp. I was on several lists and the combination of being a Jew and politically active on the left would have been enough. But though enquiries were made at our old flat, I was not given away. I believe there was an SS officer who was a friend of mine and who had deleted my name from the list of those to be arrested. I witnessed the hysterical city on the day of the *Anschluss*: I walked through the streets, and saw the armoured Nazi cars cheered by the crowds. The Viennese, reputed for their *Gemuetlichkeit*, revealed faces distorted by hate mixed with ecstasy, as they shouted hysterically 'Heil Hitler', 'Sieg Heil', 'Ein Volk, ein Reich, ein Fuehrer'. It was a deplorable and frightening sight!

Attempts to leave the country and the destination were entirely haphazard: China, Peru, USA, England, to whichever country a visa could be acquired soonest. Sometimes we stuck pins blindly into the world atlas to determine the country of migration. We happened to live across the road from a British consular officer, who helped secure a visa for me (the queues at the consulates were endless) and through some English friends I acquired the affidavits and initial homes in England. I was the first member of the family to leave.

The transition from the turbulence, hysteria, fear and ghastliness of Vienna to the peace, tranquillity, and sunshine of the Principal's Lodgings in a Cambridge College, adorned by a very beautiful daughter of the Principal, was an extraordinary experience. I arrived just before Mayweek, in the events of which I participated, speaking as yet little English and finding the culture entrancing. Instead of political songs there were hymns in the College chapel, and instead of political discussions about sexual relations, guided by Ernst Fischer's books on the crisis of youth, there were theological lectures on extra-marital sex. But though there were superficial similarities, the underlying unspoken assumptions could not have been more different. I was enchanted, but also astonished by the Cambridge college life, the beauty of the Backs, punting on the Cam, the way people dressed for dinner, sang madrigals in college cloisters, attended concerts, and the light-hearted, ignorant way they viewed the world.

The group of people who had taken care of me in England called themselves the Knighthood or the Blue Pilgrims. They had their home in a house called The Chantry in Sevenoaks, and each member went by a symbolic Knighthood name. The founder, Beatrice Hankey, had been called Help, others were called Oriel, Charity, Faith, Hope, Romance, etc. Once I attended a meeting at the Chantry and the programme on the blackboard went something like this: Morning: Charity on Peace in our time; Una on Friends in Blue; Afternoon: Foolishness on the Lawn. For a moment I thought that one of the pilgrims had the code name Foolishness.

I had received a telegram in Vienna just before I left saying 'Friend in blue will meet you in Dover'. And on my arrival, there was a kind lady in a blue dress escorting me from the boat to the train to Victoria station.

The Knighthood was a wonderful group, its members truly saintly, and they had found a worthy cause in helping Austrian refugees escape. Two sisters, Marjorie and Dorothy Streeten, who lived in Hartfield, Sussex, were especially hospitable and made their home also mine. It was a period when I was impressed by the practical Christianity of the group, particularly that of my first hosts the Gibsons in Cambridge and then of the Streetens, and thought that I had religious convictions. I had not been brought up in any religion, and had not been conscious of being a Jew until attacked in school. In fact, when still at nursery school I once came home asking my aunt and uncle: 'Am I a Jewish?' The youth movement was atheistic. But I enjoyed the oceanic feeling, and the practical morality of the Knighthood in particular appealed to me. They also did a lot of work for the unemployed; they were the charwomen of history: clearing up the messes others had made.

At this time I felt that my change of direction was in contrast with and divergence from a great friend of mine in those years, Bill Davies. He was the son of the Dean of Worcester Cathedral and of a very gentle woman who was a member of the Blue Pilgrims. Bill had been at Balliol and when I got to know him was a lecturer in philosophy at Aberdeen University. He lived in the Bothy, a bachelor don establishment in Old Aberdeen. Soon afterwards he won a Fellowship to All Souls. He invited me to stay with him at All Souls and that was my first introduction to Oxford. I met and enjoyed after dinner talks with A.L. Rowse, Radcliffe Brown, and other luminaries.

Bill, coming from the cathedral close, a family with independent wealth and the Edwardian life-style of the rich, had become a communist, though he disapproved of the Hitler–Stalin pact. At the outbreak of war he immediately volunteered for the navy and died heroically when the cruiser *Electra* was sunk in the Pacific. There was a raft but it was not large enough to hold all the victims. He was last seen swimming away from it.

I spent holidays with Bill, driving and camping. He had a delightful imagination, both analytical and poetical, lyric and epic, and was able to take flights of fancy from the most humdrum circumstances, from some cloud formations or the branches of a tree. He would paint a romantic picture of our beloved Oxford by moonlight, where the buildings looked like an enchanted fairyland structure, made of chocolate that you could break off and eat, while you floated in a dream through its streets. I introduced him to Hermann Hesse and Otto Neurath, he introduced me to Yeats. But the tension between our opposite paths between religion and radical politics, between public and private affairs, we never resolved.

The International Student Service looked for a university place for me and with characteristic generosity Aberdeen University (Aberdeen being proverbially maligned for its stinginess) was the first to offer me a place. Alec Cairncross was then secretary of the Scottish International Student Service and was instrumental in getting me placed. I arrived there in the late summer of 1938. My desire had been to read sociology, but Aberdeen had no sociology department, so I was diverted into Political Economy.

I was in Aberdeen from the autumn term 1938 until Whit Sunday 1940, but in Sussex both at the time of Munich and at the outbreak of the war. In the early morning of that sunny Whit Sunday two friendly policemen, who addressed me as Paul, asked me to pack a few things in my bag because there was a need for a temporary internment quite near Aberdeen. It turned out to be much longer, and was my farewell to Aberdeen. Before that memorable event foreigners had undergone a laborious inquisition that was to establish their degree of reliability. Tribunals had been set up, and the one before which I appeared was chaired by Professor Taylor, a future Principal of the University and then professor of law. People were classified under three categories. A, B, or C. C meant internment as a suspect character at once. B meant regular reporting to the police, but freedom otherwise. A meant clearance, and freedom without reporting. I was put into category A and told I would be not only free from all restrictions but allowed to join the war effort.

As soon as war broke out, I had volunteered for the air force, even though I did not have British nationality. I appeared before another tribunal, was interrogated, and eventually received ironically, and with characteristic British muddle, my calling-up notice in the internment camp. When German troops overran Belgium and Holland, and Fifth Columnists were rumoured to have appeared everywhere, the British authorities panicked and gave orders to intern all aliens of German and Austrian nationality, including those who had been completely cleared by the tribunals, but who lived in coastal areas. We were shunted from Banff outside Aberdeen to an unoccupied housing estate in Huyton near Liverpool, to seaside hotels in Douglas on the Isle of Man, and eventually to Canada. I remember one man, who already had become a lecturer at Aberdeen University, crying on the train from Banff to Liverpool. In the camp in Banff, which was run on a combination of friendliness and muddle, I was allowed to sit a University exam, supervised by the crying lecturer, on the strength of which I was awarded in 1944 an Ordinary MA.

My Aberdeen teacher in economics was Lindley Fraser, in many ways a brilliant man who received me very kindly. He had written a book, *Economic Thought and Language*, which is underrated by the profession, and which I was given as a class prize. It contains a careful, occasionally almost scholastic, dissection of the meaning of economic concepts, in some ways not unlike the taxonomy that Fritz Machlup practised later though it was inspired by Fraser's classical education at Oxford. It is a book full of illuminating insights.

The person who welcomed me warmly and from whom I learned much was the Principal (The Princ as we called him), Sir William Hamilton Fyfe. A fine classical scholar with a sense of wit and irony, he ran the University more like a school. He took me into his family, introduced me to Aristotle and Toynbee, and, though considerably older, become a true friend.

There was the dour, yet kindly philosopher Laird who taught me first the distinction and then the possibility of eliminating the distinction between right and good. After Fraser had left for London, he took over the Political Economy class and taught it from a purely philosophical point of view.

Perhaps the most flashy character of those days was Rex Knight, professor of psychology. He was a superb lecturer, an ingenious showman and attracted mass audiences. His wife Margaret, in a quieter vein, probably was the better scholar. I was then very interested in social psychology and presented a paper to a student society stimulated by Ernst Kris's and Edgar Zilsel's work on the mythology of the hero, on the psychology of biography, and how, in some lives, biographies do not reflect what people do, but people's lives reflect their biographies, their stereotypes, their images, the roles they are expected to play.

Internment was horrid: not so much for the discomfort, meagre and tasteless food rations, often disagreeable company, crowded conditions, boredom, and tedious work, though all these were there: but mainly for being out of action at a time when one wanted to be in the midst of things. Some authors have recently maintained that the internees were quite happy with their lot and regarded it as an enforced but welcome holiday. This is quite wrong. All of us hated and resented the enforced idleness. And it was humiliating to have been rejected by the Austrians as a Jew, and imprisoned by the English as an Austrian. But Harold Nicolson and Richard Crossman, after a few months, helped to reverse this stupid action.

On 3 July 1940, we were moved back to Liverpool and embarked on our voyage to Canada. This voyage on the *Ettrick* was one of the most horrible experiences in my life. We were herded together, behind barbed wire on the ship (so that escape would have been difficult if the ship had been torpedoed), and slept in three layers: hammocks, beneath which were tables, and under the tables. There was only one meagre meal a day. The sanitary conditions were appalling. Many suffered from sea sickness and dysentery and there was no medical help. Count Lingen, the grandson of the Kaiser, organised a gang of cleaners with mops and buckets that restored order to what had become sickening chaos.

In another part of the ship were German prisoners of war who were treated much better because they had Red Cross protection. The ship ahead of us, the *Arandora Star*, had been torpedoed, and more than six hundred interned refugees perished. (Another ship, the *Dunera*, went to Australia. Its passengers were both ill-treated and robbed.) Curiously, the least disagreeable feature of this voyage was the crammed space. It is then that I discovered that, while food, water and sanitation are basic needs, shelter and housing are not, but are an acquired taste.

On arrival in Quebec on 13 July, after having moved up the estuary of the St Lawrence, we were driven through the town to our first camp, with police sirens wailing from the Black Marias. We were told to strip naked and money, watches and other valuables were taken from us. We never saw them again. The camp was strongly guarded by layers of barbed wire and towers with armed sentries and searchlights. At night the huts, whose windows were surrounded by barbed wire, were locked. One poor elderly disturbed and confused refugee who wandered about after curfew was promptly shot.

Physical conditions in Canada, after a few days of utter confusion, were better than they had been in England. Food was plentiful, the huts were well heated, and we were provided with prison uniforms, including jackets with a large red spot on the back. The Canadians seemed very pleased that they could contribute to the war effort by at last having got hold of some real, particularly dangerous enemies, disguised as civilian fifth columnists, and were correspondingly nasty to us.

We started again a successful camp university. We slept in double decker beds and in the bed next to me was Klaus Fuchs, later famous for being revealed as a Soviet spy. Other fellow internees were the scientist (now Sir) Hermann Bondi (whom I had known well in Vienna) who tried to teach me mathematics and later became chief scientist at the Ministry of Defence, Tommy Gold the astronomer, now at Cornell – both originators, together with Fred Hoyle, of the steady-state theory of the universe – and a wonderful older, melancholy art historian named Johannes Wilde, who educated a small group of us in Venetian art, while we were sitting in the dusk on iron girders.

After about six months in various Canadian camps, the British Parliament began to realise that they were wasting assets in these camps, as well as committing an injustice (questions were asked in Parliament, including one about myself), and a humane Quaker prison commissioner, Alexander Paterson, was sent out to Canada to select people for return and release. It was the height of the blitz, and some preferred to stay in Canada. When I visit nowadays Toronto and look through the University faculty directory, I come across the names of many people who were with me in the camp. Those sent to Canada had been men below thirty years, (regarded as particularly dangerous) plus some 'suspect' older characters, such as a Commander of the International Brigade in the Spanish Civil War, a Colonel Kahle, and other non-Jewish political refugees. We returned on the small liner *Thysville*, but in a large convoy, during Christmas 1940, to a heavy air raid in Liverpool but far from being set free were interned once again in Huyton, near Liverpool, where we had been before being sent to the Isle of Man. It was a cold winter, no heat, little food, crowded conditions. But I listened to self-organised lectures on spying given by the First World War chief spy Captain von Rintelen. (He had written a book, *The Dark Invader*, and told us: 'never mind for which side you work the principles are the same'.)

After another two or three months I was released, on the condition that I joined the Pioneer Corps. I had set my heart on something more active and more interesting than digging trenches and painting sheets of corrugated iron, but I accepted happily the condition.

The Pioneer Corps was much better than internment, but it had some similarities. It was recruited from mentally defective NCOs and officers, criminals, conscientious objectors and 'enemy aliens': some of the best and worst human material. I was a private. The officers and NCOs were also often ex-criminals of low intelligence, compensated by cruelty. The work was tedious. But we had our evenings off, and though not free, were not behind barbed wire.

In the Pioneer Corps I came across Arthur Koestler, who had joined the same 251 Company. His ideas of the oscillations between *la vie tragique* and *la vie triviale* were illuminating of much of our experience, both in internment and, later, in action. These oscillations account for the army slang and the convention and formulae that attempt to assimilate the tragic to the trivial. For the trivial plane the experiences of the other are nonsense – overstrung nerves, hysteria. When we live on the tragic plane, the joys and sorrows of the other are shallow and frivolous. I admired Koestler for refusing the privilege of a private room and exemption from duties of manual labour in return for writing a complimentary history of 251 Pioneer Corps Company. But he was a bully: selfish, anti-social, always jumping meal queues.

But after two years, access to combatant units was granted to specific individuals, after a process of careful selection. I had at that time distinguished myself as a long-distance runner, and it was as a result of this that I was given the opportunity to be interviewed in London for a very hush-hush job. One day we were told on parade that we had to pick English names and cover stories in case we were taken prisoners by the Germans. Otherwise we would be treated as traitors and shot, being still of German/Austrian nationality. Without much thought I thus converted myself in a few seconds from Hornig to Streeten and assumed the cover story of my adopted family. The two 'maiden aunts' were very pleased by this disguise.

The interviews for admission to the Commando X-troop were conducted in a large London hotel converted into army barracks. That was the beginning of my service in No. 3 or X-Troop of Inter-Allied Commando (it had a Polish, Belgian, Dutch, Norwegian and French troop), which was called by the Marine officers to whom I was later attached 'Indian Army', whether for its initials (Inter-Allied) or for the swarthy appearance of some Jews, I still don't know.

We were trained in Aberdovey and sent on courses to Achnacarry in Scotland, the Isle of Wight, and other places. It was great fun, more like a super holiday camp with a lot of exercise. One of the happiest days in my life was when I was promoted to Lance Corporal. This seems to me to refute Fred Hirsch's theory of positional goods. Not all of us wish to be Generals or Field Marshalls. The much more numerous intermediate ranks are just as satisfying to most of us. Therefore, the number of cherished 'positional goods' is much greater than is allowed by Fred Hirsch, whose uncle, incidentally, served in my troop.

The camaraderie of our Commando troop was considerable. It was helped by the fact that we lived in private billets of our choice and took part in a wide range of exciting activities. We organised discussions with the villagers and held Town Meetings. It was the time of the Beveridge Report on Social Security. I remember participating in a debate in which we slayed Beveridge's five evil giants, ignorance, hunger, disease, unemployment and squalor, and my giant was squalor. My opponent was a Welsh novelist, Berta Ruck (Mrs Oliver Onions). The current scepticism about the welfare state takes me back to those days, when the notion had gained acceptance that every citizen should be guaranteed a minimum survival level of living. This was regarded as a spur to human effort, not a deterrent. The safety net was not condemned as a safety hammock, but convertible into a trampoline.

There were many fine men in the troop, some of them with characteristics quite different from those that one appreciates in civilian or academic life. The characteristics by which we judge people in extreme situations, not only in battle or in a long stretch of time of physical danger but also after a very tiring route march or on a difficult exercise, are in some ways more fundamental than those by which we judge people in ordinary life. If we were hanging onto a raft that can barely hold two, would he push me off, or help me onto it? If I were wounded, would he carry me to safety under fire? Or if, after a long march, there is little food, would he snatch the last morsels? But occasions rarely arise to test for these characteristics and we may, therefore, fail most of the time to evaluate people, including our friends, by these ultimate tests. I observed that people who in ordinary circumstances of daily life are quite inconspicuous can become heroes in a crisis. Perhaps the nearest occasions parallel to these in ordinary life are deaths, divorces, or scandals. (Again, Koestler's *vie tragique* and *vie triviale*, when we transform psychology into mythology.)

On 26 May 1943 I was detached from my troop and attached to 41 Royal Marine Commando and trained for the invasion in Sicily. My first impression of action was: what a shambles! We did not land on the beach that had been planned for, did not occupy the pillbox, and as it turned out somebody had even forgotten the wire cutters to cut the barbed wire.

My second impression was that even on the front line there are long periods without action, just waiting, though in the first week after landing we were ordered not to sleep. The order was not obeyed.

My third impression was the frequency with which orders to go into battle were repealed. On numerous occasions we were already in ships from which landing craft were to be launched or in formation in a harbour, only to find that the action for which we had been trained had been called off.

Sicily was in many ways exciting. The sun shone, the scent of spices was in the air, the fields were full of melons to which we helped ourselves freely, there were abandoned large barrels of wine, and the forsaken bays were lovely for swimming. I relieved the boredom of the periods of waiting by organising games and theatricals with the multitudes of grubby children, whose dramatic sense was delightful when they acted out roles of passion, romance, love and sacrifice in beautiful settings. We established good relations with the Sicilian population who genuinely appeared to welcome the invaders.

A few weeks after our first landing on 9 July on the Southeast coast of Sicily at Pacchino I was severely wounded. I regard that day as a clear watershed. On the evening before the landing behind the lines in Scaletta, South of Messina, near Taormina, I was still walking through the streets of Catania, in full possession of my limbs and fit and able, and never after was I to have the full power of the use of my left foot and my left arm: no more punting, rock climbing, skiing, running.

We landed behind the lines on the road and railway line from Catania to Messina along which the Germans were withdrawing, in order to prevent them evacuating too much of their weapons and too many of their men. We established a small bridgehead and were just about to enlarge it (I had by then been promoted to the dizzy rank of Sergeant), when an 88 mm gun shell hit the railway platform from which I was operating and knocked me out. There followed days of delirium and unconsciousness, alleviated by morphine. I presume that a surgical field unit evacuated me by sea to Catania. From there I was moved to Alexandria and to the Fifteenth Scottish General Hospital in Cairo. I was later told that I was not expected to survive. I was never on my feet in Egypt, but could see from my hospital bed on one side the pyramids and on the other the eucalyptus trees and the Nile. I was evacuated in a hospital ship, without convoy, at Christmas 1943 to Glasgow, then moved to Sussex. I still carry pieces of shrapnel in my neck, skull and arm as mementoes.

The hospital period spanned about a year, at the end of which I returned to Aberdeen to collect my MA degree. In hospital in

Hayward's Heath and then Pyrford I had given up the idea of resuming my studies and was looking for a job. I was offered a job on the *Financial Times* and was already looking forward to taking this up when discharged, when the possibility of a grant under the Further Education and Training Scheme turned up. I was accepted by Oxford and Balliol to read philosophy, politics and economics. I arrived on a cold winter day late in 1944, my left arm strapped high on a complicated contraption of steel and webbing that doctors thought might restore the nerves in the brachial plexus that had been damaged by shrapnel.

It was before the end of the war and Balliol consisted partly of undergraduates unfit for military service, partly of exempted chemists and other scientists, and partly of a sprinkling of much older discharged service men. This driblet increased to a flood after the end of the war, when quite senior ex-officers, accustomed to the dens of vice of Cairo and Kuala Lumpur, returned to undergraduate status, under the supervision of the proctors.

I had wonderul tutors, Maurice Allen and Thomas Balogh providing a balanced team in economics, with the exception of one philosophy lecturer at New College to whom I was farmed out, who had a sumptuous tea on a tray served for himself without offering me a crumb. He recommended only his own writings. Donald Mackinnon I liked enormously, particularly when he told me: 'You see, Paul, the idealists do not take reality seriously' or 'God is not the solution to the problem of this world, God is the problem posed by this world' or 'It is the un-get-throughsomeness of things that the theory does not do justice to'.

From Frank Burchardt I learned a lot of economics because he was always crystal clear: but from Tommy Balogh more because he was so confusing that I had to go back to my room and work it out myself. The best tutors are not the clearest. I enjoyed listening to Sir Hubert Henderson poking gentle fun at economic models and forecasts. Michał Kalecki was another inspiring lecturer. His limited knowledge and idiosyncratic use of English was an advantage, for he had to express himself in the simplest terms and presented quite complex models in the most lucid way. I don't know whether the confusions of Thomas Balogh or the simplicity and lucidity of Michal Kalecki taught me more. I do know that having done philosophy contributed to my understanding economic theory better, and having done politics made me understand applied economics better. No Oxford-trained man can confuse identities with equalitites, the way Cambridge did in the early days of the Keynesian savings-investment controversy. The third stroke added to the equality sign makes a crucial difference.

And then there were the other undergraduates (Donald McRae, Julius Gould, Ned Crosfield, Noel Gates, Ernest Gellner, Leonard Minkes, Martin Milligan) with whom I drank endless cups of cocoa round the fireplace, in which the few pieces of coal were rationed. The heat of our debates was in stark contrast to the cold of the rooms as the hours advanced.

The ceremony of handshaking, at which no hands are ever shaken, is traditional in Balliol. At the end of every term each undergraduate appears separately before the Master and the tutors in his subjects, and the tutors report to the Master about his performance, talking about him in the third person, as if he were absent. The Master then makes a few remarks. I remember on one occasion my tutor, Maurice Allen, saying: 'Master, he is dexterous in handling concepts, but does not always carefully work out each step in an argument.' The Master, A.D. Lindsay, turned to me and said: 'Go and work out each step!'

I stayed on at Balliol first as a lecturer, for one year, and then as a Fellow. A group of economists from the Institute of Statistics, Balogh, Worswick, Burchardt, Alan Flanders and myself, welcomed a group of German economists to Oxford, to instruct them in the progress economics had made during and after the war and some of us visited them in return in Germany at a conference in Oberhausen. These meetings produced my first published article in a German journal on the theory of the firm. The first article published in England was on the theory of profit and was accepted by Arthur Lewis for the *Manchester School*. Both these early efforts are critical of established theory.

When I had been awarded my Bachelor's degree in Oxford, I was thinking of a subject for a doctor's thesis. I then wanted to apply the theory of duopoly or oligopoly to the relations between countries. I had been impressed by R.F. Kahn's 'Notes on Ideal Output' and thought that the same ideas could be applied to the decisions of governments whether to devalue, or adopt alternative trade policies. Foreign exchange reserves had their parallel in spare productive capacity, and expectations of retaliation played exactly the same part. One could also apply it to tariff policy or export subsidies. Today, we apply game theory to the analysis of such situations. My supervisor, J.R. Hicks, discouraged me from embarking on a theoretical thesis and suggested tramp freights as a more suitable subject. The connection was that this was an example of imperfect competition in international trade. I was not very interested in tramp freights, was elected to a Fellowship by Balliol College, and dropped the idea of doing a doctor's degree. I think it was G.M. Meier who took up the tramp freights for his thesis.

Particularly memorable was the Oxford-Cambridge-London seminar, that took place in these three places in turn. The participants were students from the three universities who read and discussed papers. Harry Johnson and Jan de Villiers Graaf were regular and brilliant performers.

In 1955–6, I was invited by Johns Hopkins University to be a visiting fellow and took leave from Balliol. The Johns Hopkins University economics department was a firmament of superstars: Simon Kuznets, Fritz Machlup, Evsey Domar were there, as well as Edith Penrose, Clarence Long, Mark Perlman, Richard Muth and some very good graduate students. Among the visitors was Don Patinkin. We attended the brilliant seminar of Simon Kuznets, and I also learned much from Machlup's taxonomy. The chairman of the department was Heberton Evans, not a particularly distinguished economist, but one who had the ability to attract first-class people and to create a collegiate atmosphere. This is more difficult in the United States than it is in England or Europe. For American culture lacks the third place. The first place is the home, where men mow the lawn, wash dishes, play with their children and make love to their wives. They also give dinners or cocktail parties. The second place is the office, where they bend over their typewriters and word processors and research or teach. There are also seminars and workshops. But there is no place or occasion for casual get-togethers. Austria and France have coffee houses and cafés, England has pubs and Oxford has common rooms, where people can meet, talk, bring guests to meet their friends, or just put up their feet and read the papers. For me this third place is very important and I miss it in America. Yet, Johns Hopkins' economics department came nearest to producing this atmosphere of 'unstructured' meetings, where one could discuss or not discuss one's ideas with colleagues.

In Oxford, the conditions for the third place were ideal. Patrick Corbett and Marcus Dick, the philosophers, Colin Leys the political scientist, and we economists had continuing discussions and exchanges of drafts. It was interdisciplinary work at its best. Thomas Balogh's approach to economics and policy making was not very different from Otto Bauer's type of social democracy. After I had become a Fellow, we collaborated on several articles and enjoyed a continuing exchange of ideas. I found it relatively easy to put into the shape acceptable to the profession the brilliant intuitive insights Thomas generated. In particular we were critical of the advocacy of floating exchange rates as a method of combining independent national policies with integration into the world trading and financial system. I remember writing an article in the early 1950s on the subject. Harry Johnson showed it to Milton Friedman who wrote that it reminded him of a beautiful abstract picture which had no relation to reality. Yet, cannot much of Chicago economics be described precisely in these terms? We also criticized the neo-classical approach to education which attributes economic yield to educational inputs, equated to years of formal schooling.

My collaboration with Gunnar Myrdal was quite different. In about 1949 he had asked me to translate his *Political Element in the Development of Economic Theory* into English. I found his critical approach to economic concepts and system building and his analysis of the role of valuations correct and a long period of fruitful collaboration followed. Later I collected his methodological writings in a book *Value in Social Theory* and was stimulated to write my introduction on 'Programmes and Prognoses'. I still think that it contains a valid critique of welfare economics, but nobody took any notice. By the time I worked with him on *Asian Drama* (with Michael Lipton and Bill Barber) he had acquired a contempt for detailed argument and preferred to paint with a broad brush. He chided me gently for devoting so much space to a critique in my appendix on the capital-output ratio in Asian economic planning, by saying it was filigree. He described himself as a cheerful pessimist, by which he meant that while he thinks the chances for improvement and reform are small, this calls all the more for putting all our efforts into trying to bring them about. The philosophy fitted well into mine of the pedantic utopian.

Among younger collaborators I found Frances Stewart and Sanjaya Lall particularly congenial. They both combined fine analytical minds with a profound concern for human beings and a sense of what is important and realistic in economic analysis. They each had an individual style, expressed in their writings. My earlier collaboration with John Black on productivity growth and the balance of payments was in some ways the mirror image of that with Balogh. John Black was very good in formalising ideas and expressing them in diagrams.

I have always been better as a critic than as an apologist or propagator or advocate. (Was it Thomas Beecham who said, when he noticed an elephant shitting on the stage in the procession scene of Aida: 'Ah, I see, not only an artist but also a critic!') I was an early critic of the theory of the firm, of growthmanship, of welfare economics, of the Common Market, of simple-minded models, of balanced growth, of floating exchange rates, of the incremental capital-output ratio, etc. Perhaps this is why I never felt altogether comfortable when put in charge in the late 1970s of the Basic Needs work in the World Bank.

I have never been a 'man of action', at any rate not since my youthful conversions, though I enjoyed and learned a lot from my work in the Indian Planning Commission, the British Ministry of Overseas Development, the Commonwealth Development Corporation, the Royal Commission on Environmental Pollution, the Government of Malta, and the Policy Planning and Program Review Department of the World Bank. I have never lost much sleep over the fact that nobody followed my advice. But I am intrigued by the reasons for the gap between thinkers and doers, between academics and practitioners. It is more than a gap: it is often a real conflict. And the task of bridging it or resolving the conflict I have always regarded as an exciting challenge.

My first experience of practical work, College administration and a brief spell in India apart, occurred in 1964, when I was asked to join Barbara Castle, the first Minister of Overseas Development, in the newly elected Labour Government. Sir Andrew Cohen was her Permanent Secretary and Dudley Seers her Director General of Economic Planning. I was asked to be his Deputy. They were exciting times, because I did not yet know how narrow the scope is for changing the thick, syrupy flow of history.

Thomas Balogh, who had become the Prime Minister's economic adviser, thought that the regular civil servants conspired to frustrate the efforts of Labour reform. To me they do not seem so much conspirators (with one or two exceptions) as people longing to be filled with a sense of direction, but without such leadership following precedent and avoiding rows as the least risky course. They seemed preoccupied with what is negotiable, what others will accept, rather than with what is right. The first paper that crossed my desk was on concessionary interest rates on loans to underdeveloped countries. At that time, there was only the full Treasury rate or zero rate. No single argument in that long paper was concerned with the merits of the case, but all the arguments turned on such issues as whether domestic local authorities or nationalised industries would not also ask for the concessionary rate, once it was granted to low-income countries. As a result of this pre-occupation, I suspected, the British tended to lose out to the most tenacious, often reactionary, negotiators: to the French on international monetary reform, to the Norwegians on North Sea oil, etc.

My Oxford education and my civil service experience made me aware of the need to include political variables and political constraints in economic analysis. But my experience with my colleagues in the British civil service also made me see the importance of formulating clearly what is desirable, independent of any constraints, however Utopian it may seem in the light of what is acceptable, feasible, negotiable. I concluded that we need pedantic Utopians or Utopian Pedants, with a full command of details, but also a vision, informed phantasy. The reason for this is partly that excessive pre-occupation with the feasible is a recipe for defeat, but also partly my experience that events change, and what seems impossible at one time may suddenly turn out to be implementable, and if we are not ready with a carefully worked out plan, we shall miss an opportunity for reform.

I also discovered that the human race consisted of two types: molluscs and mammals. (And perhaps each of us is at different times more one or the other.) Molluscs are those of hard veneer, unyielding and tough, but when you push you get into a squishy mess. Mammals are soft and warm and yielding outside, but underneath lies a firm, strong backbone. I was astonished by the way men who had upheld firmly one point of view, completely shifted their ground when the system of rewards and penalties made this opportune for them. Good examples of mammals were our Commando officer James Monahan and Bill Davies.

I was struck by the parochialism of the Labour Party in power. In opposition, and in the election campaign, there were numerous declarations of solidarity to the international community. In some obvious ways the world seems to be much more 'one family' than it was over forty years ago. The jet plane, the telex, satellite TV, container ships, super tankers and super ore carriers have brought us together and television has destroyed old images. An advertisement for the Concorde airliner said: 'The world is about to be halved in size'; Marshall McLuhan tells us that 'the new electronic interdependence recreates the world in the image of a global village'. The numerous activities of the United Nations, the stupendous growth of the multinational business corporation, the attempts to weld continents into common markets, the flourishing global voluntary organisations have provided us with an institutional framework of international cooperation.

But this framework is unused or is used to inflict damage on others, in the name of the national interest. In many ways we have turned inwards, with an increasingly short-sighted view of the interest of our own nation and its citizens. The socialist parties of the industrial countries of the West were pioneers of international solidarity before the First World War, but this internationalism collapsed with the war. Now friendly references to international matters in national plans, publications, manifestoes, speeches and other declarations are considerably less common (as well as less convincing) than they were seventy years ago. The phrase 'workers of the world unite' would have no appeal, almost no meaning, to a modern factory worker. As Dudley Seers and I wrote in a joint article in 1972: 'Labour's record was discreditable, especially in contrast to the promises before the election (which some of us were naive enough to believe). Particularly damaging was the rejection of any attempt to lead public opinion to accept a more international, development-oriented strategy.'[1]

Early in my Ministry days, I discovered the law of the racket, according to which a good action, institution or procedure is soon highjacked by the wrong people and twisted in their favour. Voluntary Service Overseas (the British equivalent of the Peace Corps) was used to subsidise the teaching of English in the schools of the rich and thus reinforced privilege and wealth differentials. The low-priced book scheme, intended to make books available to Indian students at subsidised prices, was used by a publisher with political connections to dump his remaindered copies of out-of-date textbooks. It is also called the Le Chatelier Principle in mathematics, or, by the great Indian wordsmith Raj Krishna, in the Indian context, First-Round-Socialism. In subsequent rounds the rationing, import controls or licences reinforce monopolies and privilege.

Although I am now marked as a development economist, my interests have not always been in this field. A tutorial fellow has to teach the whole range of subjects, though the fact that we were two economists at Balliol permitted Thomas Balogh to teach applied economics and me to teach economic theory. My special areas were public finance, international trade, welfare economics and methodology.

Three influences converged to produce my interest in development in the early 1960s. First, there was my critique of the writings of Rosenstein Rodan and Nurkse on balanced growth, although this critique could be equally applied to the European Common Market. The essay on unbalanced growth appeared in fact in my volume on *Economic Integration*. Second, Gunnar Myrdal called upon me again to help him with his Twentieth Century Fund Study of Asia, which appeared eventually as *Asian Drama*. And, underlying these two tributaries, there was my already mentioned interest in the world community and my objection to the national state and nationalism as a form of heresy. But armchair thinking preceded field work, for my first visit to India was in 1963, after my contributions to *Asian Drama* had already been written. India was the first underdeveloped country in which I spent some time, if pre-war Austria is not counted as underdeveloped. Yet. Rosenstein Rodan and Chenery started their work on development by analysing the Italian South, and Rosenstein Rodan and Kurt Mandelbaum had written earlier about the development of Eastern Europe. So when today we welcome back development economics into the mainstream of economic analysis, which, however, has been enriched by the insights development studies had gained in the intervening thirty years, it is, in one sense, a homecoming to the concerns of the early pioneers.

Of course, without a thorough training in mathematics, one feels nowadays like a handloom weaver in the days after the invention of the power loom. But the thought is made bearable by the fact that most of the power loom weavers (with some notable exceptions) seem to be weaving the Emperor's clothes.

I have taken a special interest in and acquired a great affection for two countries; one very large with 700 million people, the other very small, with 300,000: India and Malta. The contrast between the two taught me much about the role of foreign trade, of technology, of special interest groups, etc. Prime Minister Mintoff of Malta only had to go down to the docks and address the dock workers in the language they understood, and they would reduce their wage demands. As Jagdish Bhagwati has said about Barbados, 'there was evidently no sensible distinction between partial and general equilibrium analysis'. Hence Malta's is the great economic success story of Europe. India, at first the darling of the development community, has later been much maligned. Some of the high-cost 'inefficient' import substituting industries most economists have condemned have now turned out to be successful exporters. Agriculture flourishes and there has not been a famine since independence. Against many predictions, and against many centrifugal forces, India has kept together as a single nation and has become a major industrial power. It is the world's largest democracy. The swings in the opinion about India's performance have been more violent than those of Indian policy, which has pursued a steady course.

In 1963, I accepted an invitation by P.C. Mahalanobis to work in the Indian Statistical Institute in New Delhi with Pitambar Pant on problems of Indian planning. Pitambar was a brilliant, charismatic figure, who used his double position as head of the Indian Statistical Institute in Delhi and of the Planning Division in the Indian Planning Commission to integrate the two, so that I became in fact a member of the Indian Administrative Service and worked on the tough 1963 Morarji Desai budget. Pitambar Pant had formulated the 'minimum needs' strategy, concerned with the rapid eradication of poverty (in spite of the mythology of recent writings that the pioneers of the 1950s had ignored poverty). But as he believed in the iron law of Pareto's income distribution, the way to attack poverty is by rapid growth of the whole economy. Our work in the early 1960s in India and in the late 1970s in the World Bank had identical aims, but differed only with respect to the means. The experience of my later work in India gave me a foretaste of my later work in the British Ministry of Overseas Development.

There is an Austrian expression: *Zivilcourage*. It is not quite translatable. 'Moral courage' would be claiming too much, and 'spiritual courage' even more. It is certainly not correlated with physical courage, for I have seen men of great physical courage lacking it completely. It means that you have the guts to say something contrary to the rest when opinions round a table have been uttered and everyone agreed on something that you believe is wrong. It is different from intellectual integrity, for saying nothing is consistent with integrity. I have always admired it, found it rare and valuable.

I have lived through two world wars (the first not wholly and not consciously), one *Anschluss*, three revolutions or putsches, and two emigrations. It may be as a result of these upheavals that I do not consider myself as having any roots, at least not roots in the ground: more aerial roots like antennae that reach out across the sky and that make me a citizen of a world community.

I regard the role of accident in my life as crucial. Few important events were planned or turned out as intended. The fact that I came to England, that I read economics rather than sociology or law, and became an economist, that I am an intellectual rather than an athlete, that I met the girl who was to become my wife in 1950 in Washington and now live in America are all accidents. Even my name and the fact that I am still alive after being shot to pieces. Yet, *ex post* all these accidents look like some kind of design.

Note

1. Seers, Dudley, and Streeten, Paul, 'Overseas Development Policies' in Beckerman, Wilfred (ed.), *The Labour Government's Economic Record 1964–1970*, (Duckworth, London, 1972).

4 An Emigrant from a Developing Country: Autobiographical Notes I

Nicholas Georgescu Roegen

When asked by Paul Schilpp to write his *Autobiographisches*, Albert Einstein, at sixty-seven, felt as if he were being asked to write his own obituary. One of the numerous things that differentiates me from Einstein is that even at eighty-two I do not feel that these biographical notes represent my auto-obituary. Those who have had as splintered a life as mine are likely to invert the old adage – *dum spiro, spero* – *dum spero, spiro*. Only by hoping and hoping could I live through four dictatorships as well as three wars all in my own backyard.

I have written these recollections only because they could serve as an instructive case study of life during the world's convulsions and upheavals that marked this century. The disconnected episodes threaded by my life are indeed relevant for such a purpose, even though I can describe them rather imprecisely, for I have never kept records of my daily happenings, never had a good memory for names, not even for faces (a failing that ruined many of my social ties).

I grew up and lived for many years in places and among a people that were not well-known outside their border at that time. History has changed all beyond recognition. Certainly, children in Romania no longer play, as I did, with antique coins gathered from almost any excavation in the town of my childhood. Having been a witness to that old world of seventy, sixty, or even forty years ago I considered that even some details of my past should have their place in this account.

I wish that I could but I cannot begin with the typical ingratiating preliminary by mentioning the notable feats of some ancestors. I never met my paternal grandparents who died before I was born; nor have I learned what exactly they used to do in life. My mother came from a humble family; her mother and three of her five siblings were illiterate. My maternal grandmother lived with her unmarried daughter in a small adobe house half of which was below the ground level, a traditional design which was both inexpensive and thermally efficient. It was still standing as a lone relic when I visited Bucharest twenty years ago.

Constanța, the town where I was born in 1906, had then only 25,000 inhabitants (now, more than 300,000). It was then an ethnic mosaic of Romanians, Greeks (some of whom may have descended directly from dwellers of the ancient Greek emporium, Tomis), Germans, Jews, Armenians, Turks, Tartars, and a few Bulgarians. Each nationality lived by its own precepts for felicity, but there never was even the smallest racial strife. I had classmates who wore the fez and turned towards the south during the morning prayer. Because the environment of my childhood was truly cosmopolitan, my ethos has remained so ever since.

My parents had a decent income, yet stringent in many ways. My Western friends are often flabbergasted on learning that I cannot ride a bicycle. But for my parents' income a bicycle meant a golden Cadillac. They could not buy me even shoes with laces which were one *leu* (then exactly 20 US cents) more expensive than those with buttons, although I yearned for the former. My mother, an amazing addict to work, taught needlework in a trade school for girls until the 1930s. My father was an army captain when I was born. A couple of years later, he happened to come upon a higher ranking officer slipping away with some meat from the soldiers' stock. During the ensuing altercation my father struck him. For striking a superior my father should have been court-martialled, but in view of the nastiness of the situation he only was pressed to retire, a typical face-saving procedure of bureaucracy. He had thus time to turn towards me to guide my development with immense love and patient understanding. Effortlessly I learned to write and read by the time I was four. My earliest occupation was to write the sequence of numbers from 1 to 99 on any piece of paper I could find (a sign of budding mathematical inclination, according to Lord Snow). My first mathematical discovery was how to write 'one hundred', 100, and beyond. My second mathematical discovery, about which I can still remember my father's happy smile, was the Eratosthenes sieve. I was eight when he died, and I have missed him not only as a father but also as a *man* that would prepare me for the plunge into the future harsh life.

In 1913, I became acquainted for the first time with war. Romanian armed forces had been sent into Bulgaria to put an end to a lingering episode of the Balkan war. No shots were fired, but the returning soldiers brought with them two threats. One was cholera, and plenty of it. That was why, as it was explained to me, we had to boil the water. The other, which was political, I realised it much later via my economic studies of Romania. Because of its relevance for the cunning of economic phenomena, it deserves a parenthesis here. Bulgaria had been an integral part of the Ottoman Empire whose religious precepts prevented the emergence of private landed property, implicitly, of landlords. The Romanian soldiers, mostly peasants, thus found out that landlords need not exist and after their return commented openly about it. An aristocratic but wise Parliament voted with quasi-unanimity to set the stage for a radical agrarian reform, an action, curiously, taken under no pressure whatsoever from Communism.

Nothing much happened during my first years of school. I only had less time to play around the Roman sarcophagi excavated from old Tomis. But I despaired of always having my hands stained with ink from the inkwell we had to carry to school. In my third grade there came a new teacher, Gheorghe Rădulescu, who was to influence my educational development in a profound way. He endeavoured to stimulate children of ten or eleven, like myself, by problems that normally require algebra. Just for a deserving record: 'Good morning hundred geese.' 'But we are not one hundred,' objected the gander. 'We would be one hundred if we were twice as many, one quarter more, and plus one goose.' Whatever inborn mathematical aptitude I had was not outstanding, but that early training developed my lasting love for mathematics.

At that time, a newly founded military *lycée* was in tremendous demand for its unique excellence. Admission was through exams. According to the general principle of that time for the allocation of public educational funds, only children of parents of modest means could enter the exam for scholarships, of which there were only twenty-three; the exam for thirty fee-paying places was held separately. Rădulescu insisted on preparing me to try for a scholarship, saying that if I won all he wanted was a demijohn of one of the famous wines of the region. For the exams I went with my mother to Bucharest. The competition for scholarships was frightful, more than 900 pupils. For the written tests, tables were arranged in a huge military *manège*. I learned that I got the twenty-third scholarship (the last) from the results that came out the very day Romania entered the war against the Central Powers (27 August 1916). On our return to Constanţa we saw the name of my teacher on one of the earliest lists of 'killed in action'. My child's soul began to be terrorised by the thought that perhaps, as in a mythical old Romania legend, his life had to be the price paid for my success.

Before long, under attacks from all sides, we had to leave Constanţa in the greatest hurry by the last train of refugees. We spent the next two years in Bucharest under German occupation, living first with my grandmother in her old house. After schools opened, my scholarly duties were overtaxed by my lining up from midnight to dawn for the bread rations, and by my earning a little money selling newspapers on the street, moving the rubble of interrupted constructions, tutoring even grown-ups. During whatever free time I had, I read a few well-known authors, but since I was limited to secondhand paperbacks, I hardly benefited from my choices. From books I also learned chess but could only replay old games by myself. My love for chess has never left me, although no significant talent for it has ever graced me.

I must not fail to mention an enduring trauma caused at that frail age by the sight of blood dripping from the moribund wounded piled up like sardines in horse carts that kept coming from the front to a hospital across the street. It was worse than if, as a grown-up, I had been on the front line.

With the cessation of hostilities late in 1918, the military *lycée* returned from the unoccupied zone to its old home. A newspaper notice advised the students who had remained in the occupied zone to join the school. From some discarded wood pieces with an old rusted handsaw I made a chest for my belongings. My mother and my younger brother rode with me to the railway station in a hired horse cart. There was none of the usual emotional quivering at the separation: we believed that two years as a refugee under German occupation had tempered me sufficiently for an unknown and disarrayed reality. That we were not immediately confuted, as it was natural to be, was only because I joined an education institution, well-supervised, disciplined, and, moreover, virtually isolated from the outside world.

The *Lycée* of the Monastery on the Hill was so called because it was situated on top of a hill, around a monastery church dating from 1499, of moderate but harmonious proportions and adorned by delicate, sober stone carvings. The buildings of the school, some of which were erected on the foundations of the old cells, consisted just of classrooms, a dormitory, a mess hall, a gymnasium, an infirmary, a couple of homes for teachers, a barrack for soldiers, a stable for the work horses, and a power plant. Briefly, a nearly self-sufficient settlement virtually isolated from the outside world. Most teachers lived in a nearby town and shuttled every day by a horse carriage. The students were not permitted to leave the school at all except for the summer vacation or for the shorter ones, at Christmas and Easter.

Everything, from meals, books, and clothing was provided free to the scholarshippers and, because of the inflation, practically to others, too. We wore a uniform and were submitted to a mock-military discipline. Each class was supervised by a distinguished officer, a few of whom later became university lecturers or professors. Between reveille at six and breakfast (black bread and tea) there was a half-hour of sustained trotting up and down the hill, save in case of blizzard. Except Sunday, five hours were devoted each morning to fundamental courses, with two hours of physical exercises in the afternoon (which together with *solfeggio* sessions formed my indescribable terror) and three hours of study after another tea. There was nothing else one could do but study even in the few non-programmed hours. And this is what I kept doing. Many teachers had a PhD and were eventually called to university chairs. I may mention Octav Onicescu because he is known especially in Italy for his work on probability.

My aptitude for mathematics was noticed and sustained by two teacher officers, alumni of the *Lycée*. When I was thirteen (in the eighth grade) they introduced me to *Gazeta Matematică*, a review that even during the World Wars never failed to appear on the fifteenth of every month ever since it was founded (and financed) by a handful of enlightened engineers in 1895. It was a periodical devoted to medium-level articles, short notes, and especially proposed problems and their solutions. It covered matters up to the level of the average bachelor's degree in the United States or of the European special *lycées*. One may imagine my elation when so early in life I saw my name in print under a solution, a proposed problem and a later note. *Gazeta* was a remarkable institution that fostered the mathematical interest of the youth also through stringent national competitions for some four to five prizes. It was not only because of luck that I got the second in 1922 and the first in 1923. My addiction to mathematics did not interfere with my other studies. Each year until graduation in 1923 I was ranked first in my class. The human capacity for pride is usually limitless, and my pride was certainly so when seeing my name carved on the marble of the honour list. Of course, I regret not having a photograph of that scholastic testimonial which has been blasted into dust by the present regime as it has done with many truly important memorials.

Although the heavy programme of my *lycée* covered far more than the normal curriculum for seven years – more mathematics and more Latin – I had to take separate exams for some of the next grade's courses. By the end of the 1923 summer, I had also passed the exam for the 'baccalauréat', a killing wringer, which was necessary (and sufficient) for the entrance to the university. After a sustained curriculum of thirty hours of solid classes per week and my additional efforts, my general knowledge was an operational toolbox. When in 1950 I told Harvie Branscomb, the Vanderbilt Chancellor, that as much as 75 per cent of my working knowledge came from my secondary education, he branded me as facetious.

But in a distant retrospect, the system of the *Lycée* of the Monastery on the Hill was a blessing but not an unadulterated one (a thought that probably will displease the still living alumni). To live, year after year, isolated from the ordinary society, following a programme on which one had no influence of any kind, sitting in class next to one and the same classmate, and sharing the same dormitory room with an almost invariable group was a most inadequate conception for preparing one to meet other people and develop fruitful relations according to the opportunities of each case. The vacations spent with the family did not help either. Given the situation, everyone endeavoured to wait hand and foot on the 'tourist'. I do not doubt that because of this long extrasocietal period of my life I did not master the vital art of developing auspicious social ties with new acquaintances, or even the manners of cultivating the ties I fortuitously made. That is a far from small defect. Of two scholars known to me, one a much better scientist, the other a far more amiable personality, an Ivy League university chose the latter because he sold himself quickly and to more people.

The issue of where I should go to the university came up tragically, not for me but for my mother. Friends of my parents when paying some attention to me as a child used to ask what I wanted to be in life. My invariable answer for as long as I can remember was: 'Mathematics teacher.' That had remained my life dream. So, I entered the mathematics department of Bucharest University. But my poor mother had dreamed to see me an engineer, a rich man without material worries, and cried bitterly over my foolish decision not to go to the Polytechnic School (where I was exceptionally invited to join without the entrance exam). But I could not renounce my own dream (so I thought then).

Public education, the overwhelming institution in Romania, was free and welfare-minded. This time, too, I was allowed to enter a competition for a modest first-year scholarship open to students from families of low means – which I won. The department of mathematics consisted then of six professors and two lecturers. From the competitions of *Gazeta Matematică* I knew four of them. The academic demeanour was like that usual on the continent at the time: the professor behind the desk, the students seated on their benches, ordinarily no dialogue. Together with a classmate I edited and lithographed the lectures on analytical mechanics of Professor Dimitrie Pompeiu (who was already world-famous for his contributions to the theory of functions), but he could not have cared less for our enthusiastic project. The only men who descended into the student's milieu were Professor Traian Lalescu and Albert Abason, a lecturer. They helped us form a student association for scientific activities.

The requirement for the 'licence' was four courses per year for three years. There were no graduate courses. After the licence anyone could submit a dissertation for a doctor's degree. The curriculum was specifically classical; for example, it included a full year of elliptic functions but not a single lecture on modern algebra or topology. There was little variation from year to year. An exception: while I was in my last year, Anton Davidoglu, who ordinarily taught mathematical analysis, offered at his pleasure a special seminar on the singularities of differential equations. What I learned from his masterly exposition helped me to arrive at the peculiar results of my 1936 paper 'The Pure Theory of Consumer's Behaviour'. Curiously, in 1926 I did not think that it could be of value to me. Ordinarily, only George Țițeica, a founder of the differential projective geometry (a highly interesting field now fallen into oblivion), used to vary the topic of his free course for the third year. One that I cannot forget because of the beauty Țițeica instilled into it was the isoperimetric problem in its most general conception. Țițeica's lecturing taught me an affix to what I had learned from my *lycée* teachers. His lectures went so smoothly, so clearly, so impeccably that many students left his classes with the illusion that they had understood absolutely all and need not study any more. How unhappy must have been that great teacher to see that too many students failed his courses. All perfection, so it seems, has its drawbacks.

At the university there was nothing that could be called a library; however the Carol I Foundation had a good, convenient, library to which we had free access. But the new books, which in the post-war years came out in waves, were available only from bookstores. To be able to buy some and also to supplement the meagre support from my mother I did some tutoring. In my last year I even accepted to teach in a *lycée* newly established in a small town for the special purpose of making secondary education accessible to peasant children. On that occasion, witnessing the peasant's staunch yearning for learning was an impressive revelation for me: rain or snow, pupils came on foot from villages miles away. In that year the university courses were often interrupted by student demonstrations, symptoms presaging worse things to come.

In June 1926, I graduated with the highest grade: *foarte bine*. And for the coming academic year, I got a position at my old *Lycée*, where I could prepare in seclusion for the next hurdle: the 'aggregation'. That term, without a correspondent in English, denoted a special exam to qualify as a secondary teacher. It consisted of a deeper test of the licence materials and of the ability to teach secondary classes. The committee was presided over by Samuel Sanielevici, a professor at the University of Iaşi where the exam took place. (As my mathematics teacher, ten years earlier during the German occupation, Sanielevivi boxed my ears although he seemed to like me very much. Curiously, the only other teacher to have done so was my fateful Rădulescu.) I again ranked first for men, and in the competition for women so did my future wife, Otilia Busuioc, who had been my classmate from the first university year. I chose the teacher position at the boys *lycée* of Constanţa and applied for a scholarship to study for a PhD in Paris.

On that occasion, in October 1927, I went to see Traian Lalescu, towards whom I rightly felt most attracted. Lalescu was a remarkable mathematician who along with Vito Volterra and Erik Ivar Fredholm broke new ground for the theory of integral equations. But he also was interested in the welfare of his country. Repeatedly he endeavoured to submit economic problems to scientific methods. Everybody knew of 'Lalescu's curve' for salary adjustment. Having felt very badly about the lack of statistics, with great pathos he succeeded in convincing me during that visit to study statistics further, not pure mathematics. 'Mr Roegen, when you come back from France, we will have to do some great work together,' he said.

In November I left for Paris and, as we planned, registered myself at the *Institut de Statistique*. After completing my course requirements (for which I ranked first) I returned home for the first time in 1929. Naturally, with a heart jumping with felicitous expectations, I went, immediately to see him, only to learn that he had died just a few days earlier. For a while, I was unable to turn away from the housekeeper who informed me of still another tragic loss in my life.

In the fall I was supposed to return to Paris to complete my dissertation. A snag came up that deserves mention because of its interesting sociopolitical object lesson of the kind Pareto's *Mind and Society* is full. The rule was that the scholarships for studies abroad be given from a special fund by a commission of university delegates on the basis of academic recommendations. Until 1928 the Liberal governments respected that rule, so my first two scholarships came automatically. But the new government of the National Peasantist Party (the party I joined years later with great zeal!) began distributing scholarships to their own favourites by administrative decision in disregard of the rule. The head of the office for the scholarship fund decided one day to indiscreetly inform me that the fund was almost exhausted. I went to plead my case to the Secretary General of the Treasury who, shamefully, told me that only the 'commission' distributes the scholarships. Troubled, my mother found that a former colleague of hers could obtain for me an audience with Mihail Manoilescu, the renowned advocate of industrial protectionism, then Minister of Industry. But Manoilescu barely looked at my credentials from the University of Paris and he, too, sent me to 'the Commission'. Time and again, my mother approached Al Lapedatu, an elementary school teacher from Constanţa, then a National Peasantist deputy in the parliament. A pure idealist, he could not believe my story but promised to try. Next day he handed me my application with the administrative resolution of that very Secretary General: 'It is approved.' The only time, I believe, when I got a scholarship by favouritism. The work for my degree was thus saved.

For many students life in Paris was not easy. There were no dormitories nor mess halls for students. We had to rent rooms in hotels (old apartment houses) with which the entire Latin Quarter was studded and ate in fixed-price restaurants, most of which sold books of meal coupons at a discount. With the unavoidable *pourboire* the simplest meal was from five to six francs, and the continental breakfast at the 'bistro', about two. Monthly rents (no bath) varied around 300. My stipend was 800 francs per month, which amounted to about $32 of that period. Since what remained after food and shelter was next to nothing, I had to rely on some money from home. Fortunately, there was, just like in Romania, absolutely no tuition fee. With holes in the soles and even the uppers of the shoes and with worn-out shirts, students in general were nevertheless happy, very happy to be able to learn and learn. That episode of my life often came vividly to my mind in connection with the situation of past decades when almost everywhere scholarships have been viewed just as salaries.

Contact between professors and students was, just as in Romania, at arm's length. On a couple of occasions I was able to speak with Professor Lucien March at the General Bureau of Statistics where he was a director. Alfred Barriol, a man who was the incarnation of good will, taught financial mathematics and also was a director of the PLM, the greatest railway company in France. He graciously lent me an old calculating machine to use in preparing my dissertation. The machine was two feet long and so heavy that I had to transport it by cab! However, I believe that even though all who studied in Paris would agree with the poet who said that

> Tout homme a deux patries,
> La sienne et puis Paris
> (Everyone has two fatherlands,
> one's own and then Paris),

all have also remained with a strong bitter aftertaste because of the way French students jeered at their foreign colleagues by calling us *métèques*, a deriding term meaning 'stranger' in ancient Greek.

In addition to my obligatory courses, I attended regularly two others. The first was an uninspiring course on finite difference equations offered by Henri Lebesgue at the *Collège de France*. The second was the epochal course of mathematical analysis taught at the *Sorbonne*, by Eduard Goursat, another great. Bent with age at seventy, Goursat entered the classroom after, as was the *Sorbonne* decorum, an *enchaîneur* wearing a neckpiece with the university seal announced '*Messieurs et Mesdames, Professeur Goursat*'. At this point we all stood up. Men like him deserved that and would deserve it even today. What Goursat, moving slowly and speaking very softly, wrote on the board, just as in Țițeica's case, never needed the sponge for correction.

Occasionally, I also attended some conferences bearing on the theory of probability offered by Maurice Fréchet at the *Institut Henri Poincaré*. Because Gaston Julia was a rising star in mathematical analysis I also went to one of his lectures. On that occasion, seeing the man who entered the classroom had a black globe as a head, I was shocked to the point of fainting. Julia had to wear such a total masque with just small holes for eyes and mouth because a shrapnel had exploded on his face during the First World War. He was what the French called a *gueule cassée*. Burning with patriotism, young French intellectuals, like him, fought on the first line of fire. Their momentous story was told by Julienne Félix in a luminous epigraph about her brother Robert, 'who, at the age of four, discovered the rule of casting out nines; and, at the age of seventeen, was a student at the *Ecole Normale Supérieure*; [and] who, at the age of nineteen, died for France'. Mathematics being taken as a case in point, after the old greats – say, Borel, Cartan, Darboux, Fréchet, Goursat, Hadamard, Lebesgue, Picard, Poincaré – departed, there was hardly anyone to replace them. I have kept wondering ever since whether the highest stratum of intelligentsia should not be exempt from going on the battlefront. The answer is difficult and no cost-benefit analysis could settle it.

My only other extracurricular contact was with Fortunat Strowski, an expert on Blaise Pascal who had a seminar on that philosopher. Şerban, the son of my former professor of astronomy, Nicolae Coculescu, introduced me to it. Şerban (Pius Servien, by pseudonym), was developing into a critical philosopher of probability and an initiator of statistical analysis of languages. He took me to the seminar because many participants, even Strowski, had trouble with Pascal's argument for the incommensurable lottery advantage of believing in God. Incredibly, even after several meetings I was unable to convince them that, if $e \to 0$, while $G \to \infty$, $e \times G$ may be finite, even infinite. Together with Şerban, they all demurred at an analytical definition of probability.

Because the novelty of the field kept my interest alive, I attended my required courses scrupulously. As one would expect, I never missed a single lecture of Emile Borel, even though his course did not add much to his available textbooks on probability. Borel, just like Lalescu, had multiple extracurricular activities and often came unprepared. Once he was stuck, unable to think of the next move for some embarrassing minutes that seemed like ages. When I spoke to suggest a way out, not only Borel but also everyone present at once fixed their eyes upon me as if spelling out 'Who are you to help Borel?'.

One of the most valuable experiences for me was the unusual *Cours de statistique*, recently introduced by Albert Aftalion. An outstanding economist among the French, Aftalion proved himself in that task a devoted and talented teacher as well. He had used statistical data in his studies of business cycles and of money. But after hearing of Karl Karsten, Warren M. Persons, and the so-called Harvard Economic Barometer (all mentioned often in his lectures), he became convinced of the need for a systematic method. To be sure, the title of his course stood as a curious nonsense on the graduate programme posters of the Faculty of Law to which he belonged. However, Aftalion, although without much mathematical training, must have taken great pains to prepare his lectures, for the task of teaching exponential trend to law students was Herculean. So, all his lectures were to a tee. And to judge from the fact that the University Presses of France published a lithograph of his course in 1928 and followed with several reprints, his programme kept attracting students. Aftalion endeavoured to make us see what is actually obtained by the use of a statistical formula rather than to know how to manipulate it. Witness his splendid metaphor I have always used in my classes: partial correlation serves to put out the sun, as it were, so that we can see the relevant stars. Admirable, penetrating thoughts such as these have disappeared from the French writings with the disappearance of the Aftalions, the Borels, or the Poincarés. When I was a visitor at Strasbourg University in 1977/78 it chagrined me to see that, as my colleagues told me, the fashion was to write *à la* Lacan (the psychoanalyst), that is, in a verbose, foggy style. For instance, J. Attali, the economic counsellor of M. Mitterrand, mixed even music with economics in his *Bruits* (1977). After a glowing review of it in *Le Matin*, I wrote the editor wondering how M. Mitterrand could know when his counsellor speaks of economics and not of music. Harry Johnson's blunt (and certainly too strong) verdict, that France has no genuine economists anymore, was not surprising.

I also paid a visit to François Divisia, another intellectual wounded on the battle front, who was lecturing at some of the special schools in Paris. His remarkable *Economique rationnelle* appeared the same year and in the same collection as Darmois' *Statistique mathématique*. In a friendly atmosphere, we talked about his dynamic index and about his solution for the industry whose average cost was constantly higher than the demand for its product (a point that especially struck me). But knowing then only little economics, I was unable to benefit much from that encounter. The third economist with whom I came in contact was Jacques Rueff, who taught the regular course on monetary phenomena, which he limited to statics. A second volume of his *Théorie des phénomènes monétaires* (1927) supposed to deal with dynamics never came out. Rueff already moved in highest society, he was Inspector General of Finance, one of the most powerful bureaucratic posts, and the right-hand of Charles Rist in the frequent international monetary arrangements (including Romania's). From his course it seemed clear that the science of economics was not his true calling, a point confirmed by his ending as the only economist to be elected to the prestigious *Académie Française* which could include only forty 'immortal' *littérateurs* and by the great success of his, a ballet-comedy, *La création du monde*.

The course I avidly absorbed was mathematical statistics, not only because of my great interest in it but also because of the immense delight it offered me as a mathematician. It was taught by Georges Darmois, who had succeeded Borel in that chair. Darmois was both a consummate mathematician and an inspired and devoted teacher who had a warm faint smile for all of us. His *Statistique mathématique* that just came out in 1928, reflected his exceptional comprehension of the particular nature of statistical analysis. Because of the extent of the problems covered as well as the elegant mathematical treatment, that treatise was by far the best at that time and, in my opinion as an old hand, a lasting paragon. Darmois's contributions to statistics pertain to many other branches, but his *Statistique* did not count little in his election as President of the International Institute of Statistics (1953–60).

The reader does not need to be told why I chose a topic of mathematical statistics for my dissertation: 'On the problem of finding out the cyclical components of a phenomenon.' As was the practice then, when I thought it to be good enough I deposited a copy of the manuscript with the secretary of the Faculty. Naturally, Darmois was nominated the chairman of my committee, which also included Alfred Barriol, M. Huber, Lucien March, and Jacques Rueff. My defence on 27 June 1930 was received with the highest qualification, *très bien*, but the committee liked my work so much that all members signed my diploma adding '*avec les félicitations du jury*'.

On 7 July, Borel communicated to the French Academy of

Sciences (C.R. pp. 15–17) a *résumé* of my periodogram method and the October 1930 issue of *Journal de la Société de Statistique de Paris* contained nothing besides my dissertation in full. My method permitted the discovery of all the numerical parameters of a time series of the form

$$y = Q(t) + \Sigma_i B_i \cos(a_i + \omega_i t) + e_i,$$

where $Q(t) = \Sigma_k A_k t^k \exp(b_k t)$, and e_i, an independent error. As I found out after I could read English, my method has some points of contact with that proposed by Arthur Schuster in 1898 which served as a basis for virtually all subsequent writers. But my approach still is superior, I believe, to all similar periodogram analyses because, after the replacement of the above formula by an equation of finite differences, it takes into account the random covariances resulting from that transformation. The fact that Professor Joseph Schumpeter used it in his 1939 *Business Cycles* and that an ampler presentation in English appeared in the *Proceedings of the International Statistical Conferences* (1947) and was reprinted in *Econometrica* (1948), ought to have arrested the attention also of those who were not acquainted with the French sources. But references often follow a devious link. It is because Herman Wold probably did not know my French sources that he did not mention my work in his 1938 dissertation, a less powerful method than mine. And, by inertia, he did not correct this omission even in his 1968 article in *JESS*, in this way influencing virtually all subsequent writers. So, I must content myself with Borel's and Darmois's recognition of more than fifty years ago, which is a long time indeed. As many have rightly exclaimed, the scholar's only award is that one's peers should know what one has done – good or, even, bad.

Having learned from Darmois some of the epochal contributions of Karl Pearson, I began longing for the possibility of studying with him. Luckily, I obtained a scholarship for that – about £15 per month, far more than for Paris because of London's higher cost of living. The trouble was that I did not know even what 'good bye' meant. Luck helped me. In Paris I had known a young Englishman, a master of French, Leonard Hurst. In late November 1930 the economic crisis was biting deeper and deeper, two Hurst youngsters were out of work, the small bedroom of Leonard's father, who had recently died, was vacant. So, the Hursts were willing to take me as a paying guest, seventeen shillings and a half (a little over $4) per week. That was very little, indeed. But the Hursts were a working class family, living in a realtor's small house on Leicester Road, the working class section of Putney which was separated by a common from the other, of the highest class. We subsisted usually on potatoes, cabbage and gravy, with bread and lard for breakfast. However, for more than one year, the Hursts surrounded me with great attention and warm consideration, things that cannot be bought. Priceless indeed was the patience of Mrs Hurst, a retired elementary teacher, who helped me learn the new language which for a long time kept sounding to me as an uninterrupted sequence of diphthongs without consonants. Once, in despair I thought of giving up and returning home.

After I could command a few basic words, I gathered all my courage and went to see Karl Pearson. He received me so naturally that I immediately felt as in heaven. The Galton Laboratory at the University College was a small institution set primarily on research; almost all visiting fellows had a doctoral degree. One could see Pearson almost any time, unannounced through a secretary. His office was long; between his desk and the door there was a couch and some chairs around a tea table. Every working day around three o'clock, tea and biscuits were served for Pearson and anybody who wanted to join him. News about one's own or other's work were then passed around. In addition to meeting Karl Pearson I soon had other surprising experiences for my Continental background. The first was the possibility of checking books out of the library. I must confess that I said then to myself 'this library would not last long'. Yet it has. I made another discovery when one morning a fellow standing at the foot of the stairs in the laboratory stopped me to ask where I was going. After I told him that I was going to Professor Pearson's class, he replied that for that very reason I must see the bursar. I did, only to find out that I had to pay tuition, in my case ten guineas or so per semester. I felt outraged – even in Romania one did not have to pay for going to school! Another surprise was that everybody at University College was very friendly. Before coming there I even asked myself what word they would use instead of '*métèque*'.

What is truly great you did not learn from Pearson's classes; you learned it from the immense number of his contributions to which he would inspiringly direct you. Pearson was a unique scholar, amazingly prolific in a vast range of interests. In addition to laying single-handed the proper foundation and forging the basic tools of statistical analysis as we know it today, he made important contributions to applied mathematics, the theory of elasticity, anthropology, sociology, eugenics, biometry, and, with a singular insight, to philosophy through his *Grammar of Science* (which, regrettably, is not properly appreciated by present tastes). To any topic that would be touched in a casual conversation, Pearson could add an enlightening observation. He was also a hard worker *sans pareil*: his writings number almost seven hundred. He was a stern, acidulous at times, defender of his positions. The man who appeared under this face in several bitter controversies – theoretical, with R.A. Fisher, and political, with many others (including J.M. Keynes, and A. Marshall – was nonetheless a most considerate and warm teacher. He invited me to spend a weekend at his country home in Surrey, and wrote with a quill (as he always did) a detailed travel schedule for me. It could not have passed through my mind as a possibility, but when I arrived he was on the station platform. Damning the fact that there *had* to be a wedding that very day to hire the only horsecab in the village, Pearson, at seventy-five, insisted on carrying my valise over a couple of miles to his home.

One of his greatest prides was his method of determining distributions of random variables – observed or theoretical – by moments. The idea had its roots in the Laplace transform of the characteristic function of the moments m_i. I already knew that from Darmois, from whom I also learned Pearson's method of using only the first four moments for constructing distributions of virtually universal application. As I see it in retrospect, Pearson's method is analogous to an arithmetic approximation, say, of π as 3.1416, *i.e.*, to retain only the most relevant moments, m_1, m_2, m_3, and m_4 from their infinite sequence. Pearson's stroke of genius consisted of the additional observation that every one of these moments represents an important structural characteristic of the frequency curve: the location, the dispersion, the asymmetry, and the kurtosis (one of the several terms coined by him). The seven types of distributions obtained by that method found splendid applications in the studies of sampling distributions by Student and R.A. Fisher. But Pearson expected that one may go much further than that, namely, to arrive at some general formula for the moments of sampling, moments which could lead to an analytical expression of the generating function for some particular cases at least. The problem of moments seemed to dominate the day. Several statisticians of note – e.g., V. Romanowsky, C.C. Craig and even R.A. Fisher – had already dealt with it. So, I decided to try my hand at it, too.

In the conference I had with him Pearson encouraged me and even seemed pleased that I would work on his *Lieblingsthema*. The result of my steady effort over a full year, during which I could hardly do anything else, was a long memoir that occupied forty-three pages of the May 1932 issue of *Biometrika*. But the long list of tedious, repelling formulae for the moments of sampling moments (six quarto pages of them!) did not seem to reflect any regularity; they could only dispense other students from sweating if they needed any. The only meaningful result was a proof of the fact that the semi-invariants of large samples from normal distributions are uncorrelated, and, further, that this property characterises the normal distribution. (This last theorem, for any sample size, was proved later by R.C. Geary, also by using moments.)

Science often advances by negative results, such as the impossibility of perpetual motion or of a speed greater than that of light. Perhaps, the long list of formulae in my memoir served as proof that Pearson's expectation was not realisable. Be this as it may, Pearson's method of moments, even that of four moments, has not prevailed but not because its role has been taken over by that of the Bayesian analysis. The real reason, I submit, is to be found in the sociology of the literati. The tone of R.A. Fisher in referring to Pearson's method, which undoubtedly was a valuable innovation of a man his senior by more than thirty years, who also had ploughed and sown where Fisher was then harvesting, certainly wounded Pearson deeply. The result was an unsavoury rift that marred the relationship of those two great minds. So, after he followed Pearson in the Galton chair in 1933, Fisher felt no inclination (as it might be natural) to propound or support any idea of his foe. Nor did the statisticians of the later generations, who were interested rather in maintaining good bridges with the new pontiff of *Biometrika*.

The shelving of Pearson's idea of four moments is most regrettable. To wit, Sir John Hicks in a paper summarised in *Econometrica* (April 1934) proposed to use it for determining the frequency distributions of investment risks. Stochastic dominance could also be applied with much greater precision if the involved distributions were determined by Pearson's method rather than relying only on the stochastic intervals established by the standard deviations. Particularly nowadays computers could be programmed to print out the proper frequency curve without waiting. But there are sufficient signs that statisticians now return to Pearson's conception of statistical analysis.

Pearson was a Machian who did not like to erect science on pure creations, such as those used by R.A. Fisher. Nothing, in my opinion, would constitute a better portrait of Pearson as the forceful writer he was and of his profound attachment to the method of moments than the first stressed sentence of his very last (and greatly enlightening) paper published in *Biometrika* of June 1936, a couple of months after his death: *'Wasting your time fitting curves by moments, eh?'*

Once, Pearson suggested that I pay a visit to the London School of Economics where Arthur Bowley was lecturing. But I had already studied the French translation of Bowley's textbook. Above all, I said to myself that I wanted at first to be a pure mathematician, instead I have become a statistician. I have nothing to do with economics and I do not wish to become an economist, never!

However, sometime in 1931, someone from the Rockefeller Foundation came to the laboratory to explain to me the programme they had then for post-doctoral fellowships and to test my interest in a fellowship in the United States; I suspected that no other but Pearson was behind that move. In my dissertation I applied my method to the series of rainfall in Paris because I was convinced that the economic cycles are not symmetrical like the trigonometric cosine (a conviction that was the source of a paper of mine to be mentioned later). Yet when shortly thereafter I received the application form, optimistically, I already saw myself working with Warren M. Persons at the Harvard University Economic Barometer on the application of my method to their three curves system. Perhaps some property of a Fourier series may save the day. After my return to Romania I received the favourable notification of the award of a Rockefeller Fellowship for the academic year 1933. Two reasons stood in the way of my leaving at that time: my mother was seriously ill and my first substantial project, *Metoda Statistică*, was not yet ready for the printer. The volume of over 500 pages, combining the viewpoints of Pearson and Darmois, appeared in 1933. It still could serve in the course aimed at explaining the significance of concepts rather than at manipulating formulae. On the side, I wrote a couple of didactical pieces and also a paper on a problem broached in a particular case by H. Poincaré. Over hurdles of differential and functional equations I proved that only for three distributions (one of which is the normal one) are the most probable and the probable values of a characteristic parameter equal (1932).

It may be well to explain now that, just as A. Burk became A. Bergson, my present legal name appeared first on *Metoda Statistică*. In all my previous papers and the dissertation my name was Nicholas St Georgescu, as it appeared in Schumpeter's *Business*

Cycles, and, strangely, was kept unchanged by R. Fels in his condensed version of that work. In the first edition of M.G. Kendall's *Advanced Theory of Statistics* I was even indexed as 'St Georgescu'.

By October 1934 I was ready for the voyage to 'the Moon', as it may have seemed at that time to anyone from Romania. The Rockefeller Foundation booked me on the *President Roosevelt*, a United States steamship of only 11,000 tons but apparently very sturdy. It trailed the Mauretania through a ferocious fall storm of the mid-Atlantic without any damage, whereas the *Mauretania* had a mast broken and several wounded. We docked two days late and, moreover, on a Saturday. Until Monday when the Foundation offices would open, I hesitated to walk farther than the corner of the hotel: New York stunned me not as much by the skyline from the ship as by its internal agitation. Stacy May, the director for the social sciences, was a kind, friendly person, highly competent for that job, who contributed in great measure to making my work and life during my stay totally enjoyable. The Rockefeller Foundation continued to be the splendidly oriented institution it has always been.

Cambridge seemed quite companionable in comparison to New York; no agglomeration of any kind then. After finding easily a room next to the Harvard Yard, I tried to locate the offices of the Harvard Economic Barometer and was quite intrigued to find that no one seemed to know anything about that organisation. Asking and searching, I finally found out that the organisation petered out soon after the 1929 Black Tuesday because just the week before it predicted that all was in perfect order. The organisation thus no longer existed when I counted on it in my application, but I had no way of knowing that. The whole thing, I feared, was vitiated *ab ovo*. Once more, I felt the earth sinking under my feet.

Thinking that something could nonetheless be saved by contacting the person who was teaching statistics, I obtained an appointment with Professor W. Leonard Crum, a highly respected statistician. I was stopped cold when he routinely just asked me: 'What can I do for you?' Ill-at-ease, I told him my reason for being there and hazarded to ask whether I could visit his research outfit. After the obviously discouraging answer, which I had expected, I left with my heart heavy with despair. (Later, I learned that Crum not only had written a neat paper on periodogram analysis for the *Handbook* of H.L. Rietz, but he also had been an important associate of W. Persons.) There was only one solution left, I thought, to ask Stacy May to send me back to Bucharest.

But after sleeping on it, it occurred to me to approach the professor in charge of business cycles theory. After all, it was Albert Aftalion, a specialist in that field, who had made me aware of the importance of periodogram analysis. At that point, praying more than hoping, I asked for an appointment with Professor Joseph A. Schumpeter, a rather strange and completely unknown name to me then. Like Traian Lalescu seven years earlier, but in a much subtler manner, Schumpeter trapped me in his own scientific bailiwick. Instead of simply asking what he could do for me, he wanted to know what I had done and what I wanted to do. On hearing about the topic of my dissertation, he immediately called E.M. Hoover, then his assistant, to see together how my method could be used for Schumpeter's planned *Business Cycles*. Learning that I had a degree in mathematics as well, without any ado Schumpeter also invited Wassily Leontief who at the time taught mathematical economics. You can remain here – I said then to myself – to see how your method would work on economic time series and, in addition, try to learn more than you knew from Divisia's *Economique*. Leontief's lectures were a model of clarity. We quickly became intimate friends, and so did later his wife, Estelle, and mine.

Schumpeter was a great teacher but only for those students who were sufficiently advanced to see the gist of his remarks, almost every one a valuable suggestion even for a doctoral dissertation. Naturally, I stayed out of his classes for some time to come. But Schumpeter had still other attractions for any would-be student of his. He was still single, living as a guest in Professor Frank Taussig's sumptuous house. Taussig even seemed to look after Schumpeter as after a younger brother. I once saw Taussig pulling Schumpeter's collar up as they were walking together in the Yard on a chilly day. Schumpeter was then the darling of all Harvard Houses where he was constantly invited for an enchanting afterdinner speech. Above all, he found time to preside over the weekly meetings of a circle of Rockefeller Fellows from Europe who happened to be there at the same time with myself. They were Oskar Lange, Fritz Machlup, Gerhard Tintner, and Nicholas Kaldor (who arrived one year later). The meetings concentrated on mathematical economics and lasted endless hours after dinner. Leontief, Ed Hoover, and Paul Sweezy (another Schumpeter assistant) also were among 'the regulars', nonetheless the foreign accent still dominated. Machlup usually attended only when the topic involved diagrammatical analysis in which he was a deft expert. Kaldor was a special figure in the group.

When he first learned about its main interest, he demurred joining it. 'I do not understand mathematics,' he said. He came nonetheless by curiosity once and continued as an active participant; he was so well trained in economics that often he was able to better by a verbal argument a mathematical point. Almost every mathematical paper published by the members of the group during that period had first gone through the severe wringer of our meetings. Schumpeter always came forward with a helpful, inspiring suggestion, although a favourite student of his once taxed him as a fake because, as he claimed, in Schumpeter's formulae on the black board some sign was always missing. The circle's star of mathematical economics was Lange. He was a very friendly colleague always ready to spice the conversations with little stories and much humour. There was a great deal of unassuming socialising among the fellows of the circle, including Schumpeter. Now and then, Schumpeter would offer a dinner, with a menu composed by him, in an upstairs room of the Harvard Club. Those memorable dinners lasted so late in the night that we were the last and had to lock up the Club.

At that time the fashion in the United States was that statistics serve mainly business needs. The most advanced level was represented by Edmond Day's textbook. Crum's course followed an elementary text he had co-authored. So, there was no reason to approach him again. I attended just a few of Taussig's classes because my economics was not yet up to their level and also because each session consisted of continuous dialogues between Taussig and the students about the previous assignments, a rather typical teaching style in the USA. It made me recall my gaffe in Borel's class. I found two other professors of great help. Edward V. Huntington, the author of *Continuum* (1917), one of the earliest monographs on order types, was a man born to be a kind and efficient teacher. He taught a related course from which I learned for the first time things I used twenty years later in some papers on the nature of pure uncertainty. E.B. Wilson, the devoted pupil of J. Willard Gibbs, then connected with the Harvard School of Public Health, crossed over to the Department of Economics where he lectured on mathematical economics as a sort of preparatory acclimatisation for the graduate students of that time. He was familiar with Pareto since his substantial review of the *Manuel* in 1912. In the *Quarterly Journal of Economics* his papers were intercalated with mine and often he passed the chalk to me for the class lecture.

Sometime in May 1935, Stacy May sent me a flat travelling stipend urging me to visit other universities so that I should not go back to Romania 'without knowing America'. Although not happy with the idea of leaving my Harvard nest, I drove across the Continent as far as the small community of Palo Alto; Stanford did not yet exist as a town. On the way I stopped first in Chicago, where I had the good fortune to meet Henry Schultz; he died together with all his family a few years later in a car accident. Schultz was a very pleasant as well as interesting host with whom I explored his renowned notion of statistical demand and his recent incursions into Paretian theory. In Bloomington, Indiana, where I stopped to see C.C. Craig, who had written on moments, I also met Harold T. Davis, who was to become a great mentor of dynamic economic systems. Davis had a niche at the turn of the staircase in his home where he kept a copy of Newton's *Principia* behind a continuously burning candle. It characterised the spirit of that prolific writer who advanced knowledge in several directions.

No one could have thought of bypassing Colorado Springs, the seat of the Cowles Commission. Alfred Cowles, III, a former stockbroker who had escaped unscathed by the 1929 crisis but became seriously ill, established that institution so that he could be busy but without any worry. It was a highly attractive visit, which combined Cowles's almost daily entertaining with exciting meetings at the Commission. The prominent members were Charles F. Roos and Victor von Szeliski. The Commission's project was to find a mathematical formula for predicting the stock exchange market. A few papers on that topic appeared in the first volumes of *Econometrica*. Our discussions easily reached a heated level for I was strongly opposed, as I have always been, to describing historical, that is, unique processes by a mathematical, necessarily ahistorical formula.

The person I wanted to see in California were Holbrook Working, a statistician mentioned by Aftalion, and Griffith C. Evans. Evans, a mathematician famous for his signal contributions to a domain developed by H. Poincaré, D. Hilbert, and V. Volterra and now almost deserted, had also written a highly appreciated monograph in which he considered the equilibrium of a market that depends also on the price change. At that season, Working was on vacation. Evans was giving a summer course to a small class of students with little, hybrid knowledge, which once he turned into a seminar for my work on Pareto, probably with little effect. In the ultimate analysis what we got out of California was just a touristic interest and gasoline at seven cents a gallon.

On the trail back, I stopped first in Princeton where I met a Romanian scholar, David Mitrany, who had been the editor of the *Manchester Guardian* and was a specialist in agrarian problems. Being invited to join the Institute of Advanced Study, he was able to arrange for me to see Albert Einstein. Naturally, I did not feel much enthusiasm for that since I did not see what I could say to Einstein. Just to say something on meeting him, I mentioned that in my model of stochastic choice I used a hyperbolic quadratic form similar to that of his ds^2. Visibly unimpressed, he passed on to ask me whether I played any musical instrument. Probably disappointed by my negative answer and out of kindness towards a strange youngster, at the end of the visit he said that mathematical economics must be a right endeavour. I missed a great opportunity: to ask his opinion about the entropy law. But at that time I did not know, what I learned thirty years later, that he was a great defender of it.

I next stopped in New York and New Haven. In New York I saw Harold Hotelling, whose name was already on the lips of every statistician and mathematical economist. Not having kept notes, I cannot remember what precisely I talked about with that great, yet modest and gracious, scholar. But circumstances being as they were then I could not have thought of asking his possible afterthoughts about the paper he had written on natural resources in 1931. I thus missed another unique opportunity.

In New Haven, I called on Irving Fisher, already retired. A convinced vegetarian because that regime had saved him from tuberculosis in his youth, he invited us to a Sunday dinner when everyone had turkey except him. He then conducted me through a basement full of shelves with numberless reprints of which he liberally gave me many more on diet and his ideas about 100 per cent stable money than on economics. But some helped me to become aware of his solid economic contributions. Like many *emeriti* nowadays, Fisher must have been unhappy with his younger colleagues, for when I told him that I had not yet come in contact with any Yale economist, he shot back, 'Don't worry, there is none'.

My stay in the United States allowed me to know also the multiple faces, good or bad, of that great, soul-searching and soul-stirring nation. To begin with, my wife (who having been ill could not travel together with me) landed in New York on the day before the Thanksgiving of 1934. I had reserved a room at the Iroquois Hotel, recommended to me as clean and moderately priced. After the Thanksgiving dinner my convalescent wife felt sick and I asked the room service to bring us two teas and two rums (an old wives' recipe). But the switchboard girl harshly admonished me: 'We do *not* serve liquor in this establishment!' We had to make do with tea only, but I kept wondering thereafter how I could have known that the Iroquois was dry. Next day as my eyes fell on two brass plaques on each side of the entrance, one with 'Iroquois', the other with 'Restricted', I thought that I solved my puzzle. It was only an illusion, for when I told my story as a joke on tourists, my Harvard friends assured me that 'Restricted' meant 'Only Caucasians'. My surprise turned into a shock when next year I saw the main street of Brookline (a suburb of Boston) dressed up with huge placards full of Nazi slogans. And I was bewildered when a professor's wife confidentially told us that anyone with Jewish ties stood a poor chance of promotion at Harvard. According to some, Henry Schultz in retaliation had turned down the invitation to occupy a special, heavily endowed chair recently created at Harvard. But apart from the shocking discrimination against the blacks and isolation of the orientals, in my journey across the whole country I found no other symptom of racial hostility. America had to be then, as always, a melting pot.

At the time, motels did not exist even as a name. Rarely there were 'cabins'. Most of the time we stopped in homes with a sign 'overnight guests'. At 75 cents on the average, including at times a farmer breakfast, we were received friendly, our accent notwithstanding. On some occasions, the host adjusted my carburetor or even washed my car. They would also make tea for my wife when she happened to be sick.

By and large, the United States enchanted me sufficiently to tell my flabbergasted Romanian friends how marvellous it would be if Romania could by the impossible become the forty-ninth state. I also was happy to serve as president of the Romanian Society for Friendship with the USA. I was often taxed as a traitor, neither then nor now an unusual type of reaction almost everywhere.

During my stay of one year and a half at Harvard I published in quick succession four papers. It was from Schumpeter's remarks that I began to admire Pareto's work on mathematical economics to which I later added with enthusiasm his overpowering sociological edifice. From the outset I realised that Pareto's mathematical skill wavered from highs to lows. In his 1896 *Cours*, for example, he was up on Irving Fisher who in a review of the work wrongly censured him for a point concerning the integrability of total differential forms. On the other hand, in his *Encyclopédie* article (1911) Pareto claimed to derive the indifference varieties from the simple, common assumption that the quantities demanded depend on the price constellation and the quantities initially possessed. The claim involved an undetected mathematical slip which I exposed in my first paper on economics (*Quarterly Journal of Economics*, 1935), in which I also touched upon the integrability issue as well as on that of time in choice. In the next paper (*Review of Economic Studies*, 1935) I attacked a new problem, the pricing of limitational factors, in connection with which I endeavoured to define 'limitational' more broadly than Ragnar Frisch, the originator of the term, had done. Kaldor (*Review of Economic Studies*, 1937), as if bent on confirming my above-mentioned opinion about his talent, pointed out that I had overlooked one limitational type. As there were no copies of *Review of Economic Studies* in Romania, I learned about Kaldor's point only after my return to the United States in 1948, when it helped me arrive at a general analysis of limitationality in opposition to the kin concept of limitativeness I introduced then.[1]

I wrote the third paper (*Quarterly Journal of Economics*, May 1936) at the invitation of Taussig, the editor, to serve as an honest broker on a controversy between A.C. Pigou and Milton Friedman concerning Pigou's recipe for measuring the elasticity of demand. In his criticism, Friedman adopted a strict interpretation of mathematical constant, while Pigou's argument considered a *nearly* constant elasticity of demand. What I wrote was a lecture about the absurdity of qualifying a dimensional entity as small or as large and also showed how the assumption of a very large number of demanded commodities may lead, depending on the type of utility function, to either a zero or a finite value for the income elasticity. The verdict was against Friedman. As we all know, if you disagree with him however little, Milton Friedman would clobber you: 'You are *totally* wrong!' So I felt immensely gratified when Milton introduced me before a lecture at the University of Chicago as the only economist who had proved him wrong. Of course, my lecture, on Brazilian monetary inflation, 'was *totally* wrong'.

The leading article in the August 1936 issue of the *Quarterly Journal of Economics* was my fourth essay 'The Pure Theory of Consumer's Behavior'. It was a solid essay not because of its size (forty-eight pages) but because it covered several entirely new aspects of that subject. I began by formulating a special postulate (later known as the continuity postulate) and showed it to be indispensable for the existence of indifference varieties. So, I regret to have to disappoint those who have kept attributing my postulate instead to Herman Wold. True, in his 1943/44 articles he did formulate a similar postulate but failed to cite my article although it had been advertised by Paul Samuelson in two 1938 articles on 'revealed preference'. In my article I also related the consumer choice to indifference directions subject to a few transparent axioms which entail the peculiar property that a non-preference direction, if prolonged, retains that quality. Topologically, it means that the indifference planar elements form a convex structure relative to the origin of coordinates. In one section I deal with another novel problem, the stochastic binary choice (between two alternatives). The way I approached it led to a stochastic distribution of some particular varieties at every point of the commodity space. One surprising result was that stochastic indifference is not transitive, a point which formed the object of numberless lucubrations until very recently. The model also cast light on Taussig's famous description of actual demand as a penumbra. Probably because its mathematics is hard going, subsequent writers have preferred a scheme based on a stochastic distribution of the ordinary indifference varieties. However, my exposition was not faultless. An error, which remained undetected until 1958, was exposed in my contribution to Ragnar Frisch's *Festschrift* (*AE*, ch. 5). On that occasion, I established a few relevant theorems and an unexpected result: assuming that A is the most frequently chosen in the binary alternatives (A, B) and (A, C), A may nonetheless be the least frequent choice in the multiple one (A, B, C).

I consider the 1936 essay as one of my salient contributions to economic theory and, to judge by Paul Samuelson's repeated praises of it, a pathbreaking development of the theory of choice. The piece of evidence is the clarification of the integrability puzzle which originated with the lesson Vito Volterra wanted to teach in his critical review of Pareto's *Manuale*, namely, that although a total differential equation is *always* integrable for two variables, this is not true for more than two. Hence the paradox, which tormented Pareto thereafter: why the indifference varieties can always be derived from market data for a world of two commodities but not necessarily for one of more than two. Volterra has never made a more infelicitous intervention and no other mathematician seems to have duplicated Volterra's example of the disorienting muddle one can create in a field by taking account only of mathematics. Volterra did not see that integrability is not the economic issue, the economic issue is whether the market data entail a transitive order of *binary* choice, the cornerstone of Pareto's theory. Volterra confused a mathematical concept – the integral varieties of a total differential equation – with an economic one – the indifference varieties. This is what I have denounced in several places and, in an accentuated way, in the conclusion of that paper. To prove my point I showed that the integrals of $Xdx + Ydy = 0$ may also represent a family of spirals around a focus, in which case no ordering can be established even in a purely formal way. Furthermore, to forestall the objection that my argument was relevant only for a two-dimensional case, I pointed out that the intersections of the three-dimensional indifference elements, $Xdx + Ydy + Zdz = 0$, with a budget plane form a two-dimensional structure in no way different from that of the two-dimensional $Xdx + Ydy = 0$, and demonstrated that non-integrability of the former would correspond to spirals, and integrability to closed curves.

Schumpeter realised that, because of what I had published before coming to Harvard and the four articles worked out during my short stay there, at the age of thirty I was a promising scholar. Due primarily to his judgement, Harvard wanted to keep me on. Schumpeter also wanted to write an economic analysis in collaboration with me. But incredible as it must seem, I declined – not the only time when I fouled up my scholarly career, but the worst such case. Schumpeter, together with the others at Harvard seemed to hope nonetheless that after looking at conditions in Romania I would return and arrangements for that possibility were made. The day before our sailing, sometime in late May, Schumpeter came to New York and took us to dinner at the Waldorf Astoria (still in splendour then) to convince me to accept his outstretched hand. Only after many years was I able to comprehend how hurt he must have been by the refusal of an inconsiderate youngster. Yet he later wrote me several times urging me to change my mind. Perhaps, it is for the better that those letters, testimonials of my maleficence, have been destroyed together with all my old files by the Communist regime. Our cabin on the SS *Washington* was covered with so many flower bouquets that at first I thought it was for another couple, a honeymooning one. My Harvard friends wanted to say 'Bon voyage and come back'.

That happened more than fifty years ago and I cannot recall, not even imagine why I made that inconceivable gross blunder. The Georgescu Roegen of that time appears to me now as another individual, another mind. One reason that interfered with my vision was that all my education had been supported by the public funds of Romania and that even my Rockefeller Fellowship counted on a spot earmarked for Romania, just as the other Fellows were for each country. I ought therefore to serve in the capacity expected of me. Yet I cannot believe it was just the call of the wild.

On the way back to Bucharest I stopped for a while in England via Paris. Hitler had remilitarised the Rhineland just a couple of months earlier; France could not react alone and Great Britain was not willing to indispose the Führer. Under the government of Léon Blum, in Paris almost every packet of cigarettes or of matches contained a small label with *'pour qui et pourquoi*, a slogan painted even on the sidewalks. All that gave me goose pimples.

At the London School of Economics, I just caught the tail of a series of seminars held by F.A. von Hayek. My knowledge of monetary matters was quite slim then, but after listening to Hayek's splendid and methodical exposition I became aware of one infirmity of my mind, that of not being able to feel at home in monetary theory. After earnest efforts all I could gather from the revered literature are the endless controversies not only between the Keynesians and the monetarists, but also between the members of one and the same fraternity. Monetary theory has no leading analytical thread. Bankers and financiers are generally successful only because they ignore the economists. The monetary domain appears to me as a 'phantasmagoria', to use Irving Fisher's characterisation of the economic world with the difference that I do not believe that it can be clarified by the torch of mathematics. Max Planck, as we know, found even economics too entangled for his mathematical propensity.

Understandably, I have written only one paper on monetary matters, 'Structural Inflation-Lock and Balanced Growth'.[2] In my personal experience with the galloping inflation in Romania and with the troubles caused by the slowing down of inflation in Brazil after the fall of the João Goulart government I found inspiration for that paper. Its moral, in which I have never ceased to believe, was that in most cases inflation is a perverse way to govern: it switches real income from some people to others surreptitiously and without divulging the pickpocketing. Because the essence of his theory can be explained by one of the simplest economic diagrams with the 45° line, Keynes immediately became the darling of economists. But he became even a dearer darling of politicians who could thus fulfill their demagogic promises by government spending without any tax increases, now a catholic policy. To me, Keynes and especially the

Keynesians seem to have believed that because a diabetic feels better with shots of insulin, everyone else would also feel better if given such shots. This fable pinpoints Keynes's definite impact on economic epistemology: all that counts in economics are the aggregates, structure is irrelevant.

At the London School of Economics I was looking forward to meeting R.G.D. Allen, whom I admired for his remarkable paper on utility theory. But he seemed rather cool. Perhaps, in a somewhat un-British way, he resented the exposure of a mathematical slip of his in the Appendix of my 1936 paper.

During short stops in Oxford and Cambridge, I met Jacob Marschak, in whom I was to find great support later, and the Hickses, kind, approachable and interesting as they have always been. Sir John thought that the issue of non-integrability was a will-o'-the wisp, as he put it later in his *Value and Capital*. I was unable to move him an iota, for the existence of a utility function was a matter of pure faith for him.

It was a great surprise for me to find Vienna as enchanting as ever despite her retrogressions from the First World War and the shock she suffered through the 1929 crisis. Young statisticians, economists, and philosophers would meet informally in small groups to settle the universe anew. Tintner was already back from the United States at the Institute for Business Cycle Research. The Institute, headed by Oskar Morgenstern, followed a similar conception to that of Ernst Wagemann, the founder of *Konjunkturforschung*. One member of the Institute was an exiled Romanian mathematician, Abraham Wald. He worked out a few vignettes of mathematical economics, but later was the inventor of sequential analysis. The whole atmosphere contrasted with the gun powder I could already smell.

Notes

1. *Analytical Economics: Issues and Problems*, chs 7 and 10 (Cambridge Mass., Harvard University Press, 1966).
2. *Energy and Economic Myths: Institutional and Analytical Economic Essays*, ch. 7 (Oxford, Pergamon Press, 1976).

5 Confessions of an Incurable Romantic

Irma Adelman

Writing my intellectual autobiography is an assignment which I have long postponed, primarily out of fear. Such a retrospective self-appraisal would inevitably make me stand naked in front of myself, influence the rest of my career and impart a sense of, hopefully premature, semi-closure. A gentle reminder by the editors has now made me grit my teeth, lay my trepidations aside, and commence.

I was born in Cernowitz, Romania, in March, 1930. Amusingly enough, Joseph Schumpeter had played an unwitting role in my parents' marriage. My mother was a law student at the University of Cernowitz while Schumpeter was teaching there. She was being courted by my father, a businessman ten years her senior. She decided to reject his suit, took her qualifying exam in economics from Schumpeter, and returned to her home town. A few months later, she was informed that Schumpeter had lost her examination paper, and that she would have to take the exam again. She returned to Cernowitz, was met by my father who, in his sorrow at being rejected by her, had shaved his head and lost about fifteen pounds. Her heart went out to him and she reversed her decision.

FORMATIVE INFLUENCES

The formative influences on my life and values were my parents, my early education, and the trauma of the Second World War. My mother, a very attractive, intelligent, and vivacious woman, never got to practice law. My father claimed that her working would ruin his credit rating and the quota of Jewish lawyers imposed by the Romanian government in the 1930s meant that by choosing to practice she would take bread out of the mouth of a Jewish male *pater familias*. So she concentrated her boundless energy and ambition on me, a single child. She was determined (poor woman) that I would be as attractive as possible given my original, rather unpropitious, endowments and that I would have the career that circumstances had conspired to rob her of. Her efforts imbued me with a view of the perfectibility of individuals and society that have dominated my teaching and research.

My father was a socialist businessman, a not unusual paradox among East European Jewish businessmen at the time. He had been studying at the University of Kiev, in the Ukraine, when the Russian Revolution broke out, and was a Zionist Menshevic, a socialist reformer. When the Bolsheviks won, he fled to Romania. He had been scheduled to be shot, but the officer in charge of the firing squad turned out to be a friend of my uncle's and enabled him to escape. From my father I gained my commitment to social reform, my compassion for the poor, and my sense of outrage at social conditions that generate mass poverty and mass deprivation.

Despite being Jewish, my early education in Romania was at a French Catholic nun's school, Notre Dame de Sion. The Jews are said to own 'guilt' and the Catholics to have a lifetime lease on it. My early education therefore left me with a mammoth sense of primordial guilt, that was later reinforced by the guilt of the survivor of the Holocaust. The expiation of this guilt through the only mechanism it can be expiated – service to humanity – has been a primary driving force in my life.

The Second World War left an indelible mark, even though I escaped comparatively unscathed. My father had had the foresight to leave Romania in 1939 for Palestine, so that the entire nuclear family survived intact. The main impact of the war on me was the wrenching break in personal attachments involved in becoming a refugee, and the experience of mass religious hatred. I remember my father telling me when I was six that I might be reviled for being Jewish, but that I should be proud of this fact. Since I knew not what being Jewish was, and had been taught by the nuns that pride is sin, this talk left me totally bewildered. The war imbued me with a sense of rootlessness, a suspicion of mass ideologies, a sense of the impermanence of any state, a lack of attachment to possessions, and a sense of personal worthlessness. It also induced a sense of belonging nowhere and everywhere, that is the mark of the cosmopolitan, and a feeling of 'There but for the grace of God go I' towards the less fortunate, akin to Rawl's initial state of ignorance. On the positive side, I learned that the only thing one can rely on is one's human capital – one's knowledge, skills, and character – because all else can be taken away at the bellow of a demagogue. My later fascination with stochastic shocks, with non-linear dynamics, and socio-political view of economic development also have their roots in my Second World War experience.

There was never any doubt in my mind that I had to become an intellectual. It was my only comparative advantage (I was an uncoordinated, roly-poly and cross-eyed youngster), and my parents and world view had predisposed me to see in education my only potential for achieving a moderately stable and socially productive life. After finishing high school in Palestine and fighting in the Israeli war of independence, I enrolled in 1949 as an undergraduate at the University of California at Berkeley. I chose business administration with a minor in public administration not because of my interest in these subjects – had I let myself pursue my own inclinations I would have studied French and German literature and art history – but rather because of my perception of the primary needs of the nascent State of Israel, the furthering of whose interests I was dedicated to. But this was not to be! Shortly after coming to Berkeley, I met my husband, an American PhD candidate in physics, fell in love, married, and stayed. In making the decision to marry and stay, I felt very guilty at putting my personal happiness ahead of my duty to Israel. I felt I was betraying Israel by not returning there.

I sailed through undergraduate school, shifted to economics in graduate school, and obtained my PhD six years later after having entered as an undergraduate. My graduate education was sadly lacking. At the time, Berkeley was very weak in economic theory and in mathematical training. Robert Dorfman was the only ray of light in the graduate programme and I shudder to think what I would have become had I not been able to benefit from his tutelage. I supplemented the graduate programme in economics by taking courses in statistics, mathematics, and in agricultural economics, where, together with Arnold Zellner, Zvi Griliches and Yair Mundlak, I learned my econometrics from George Kuznets. I also benefited greatly from the influence of my husband, Frank Adelman, who taught me a view of scientific method involving a continual iterative interaction between theory and experimental or statistical 'stylised facts' that is natural to applied physicists but still not to economists.

RESEARCH

From the perspective of a historian of doctrine, the research process appears planned *a priori*; from the perspective of the author, it appears as a series of unplanned choices that are guided by personal interest and a sense of the importance of the issues, and are made in response to opportunities, both external and self-generated. Although both perspectives are correct, I shall adopt the latter in this narrative.

My early research was eclectic, but there were a few common threads, arising from my values and early experiences: concern with dynamics, both cyclical and long run; concern with stochastic processes; and concern with aggregation procedures. 'The Dynamic Properties of the Klein-Goldberger Model', 'Business Cycles, Endogenous or Stochastic?', 'A Stochastic Analysis of the Size Distribution of Firms', my first book, and my work on hedonic index numbers (1961) were all facets of these concerns. There were also some methodological predilections, which have stayed with me throughout my entire career, and which reflect my scientific predispositions: a view of the world as an interdependent system; a view of the world as real and of scientific research as holding up a, hopefully nondistorting, mirror to it; and an inner compulsion to contribute to the elucidation of real world issues that affect the welfare of a large proportion of the world's population.

The Klein-Goldberger paper arose when my husband, a physicist, one day expressed a desire to try programming a simple problem and asked whether there was anything in economics that might be suitable. I suggested the Klein-Goldberger model. This was in 1955, before the days of Fortran; all programming was in machine language. I remember spreading out a large sheet of paper on the floor, with a map of the computer memory, and keeping track of the location of individual variables after every operation. Nevertheless, when we ran the problem there was only one error in the code! After we finished the computer runs, my husband taught me a valuable lesson. He said: 'Now it's up to you to milk the results.' The writing of the paper was excruciating: we composed it jointly and fought over every word in every sentence, finishing only one or two paragraphs per night. This paper, which confirmed the Frisch hypothesis of random origin of business cycles, has been identified as one of the best twenty articles in *Econometrica*, and achieved the status of a 'classic' in business cycles and in simulation of economic systems.

My first book, *Theories of Economic Growth and Development* (Stanford University Press, 1961), was originally written as the development theory section of an undergraduate text on economic development jointly with I. Mears and A. Pepelassis. The publisher, McGraw-Hill, objected that my section was at a more advanced level than the rest of the book and insisted that it be taken out. I then revised it, making the text more lucid, but, when it came to seeking a publisher, I became racked with doubt. It seemed to me that the book contained little that was original, and that when I was describing the interactions of socio-cultural and institutional features of societies with their economic development I did not know what I was talking about. So, for a few months after finishing the revision, I held the manuscript. But this troubled me. Paul Baran, then my colleague at Stanford, noticed that I was upset and asked me why. When I blurted out my concerns, he said: 'It's all very simple, Irma. Let the market decide! Send the book to a few publishers, and see whether they take it.' Amusing advice from the then only Marxist economist teaching at an American university . . .

This book, with its associated doubts, set the stage for one of my consistent lines of research: how the economic growth of nations is affected by and, in turn, affects economic and political institutions, and sociocultural structures and values; and how institutions and economic structures and choices affect the diffusion of benefits from economic and institutional change. I felt the need to understand these processes better and to base my understanding on empirically generated hypotheses and stylised facts. This is the line of research with which Professor Cynthia Taft Morris became associated.

I first met Cynthia Taft Morris in Washington DC, in the summer of 1962, when we were both Research Associates at the Brookings Institutions. We both had just moved to Washington, following, like the Biblical Ruth, our husbands' careers, and were both a little disoriented by the need to build new professional bases for ourselves. Our work together that summer was the beginning of a lifetime friendship and association. After the summer, Cynthia Morris combined teaching at American University with part-time work at the Agency for International Development (AID), in the research division headed by Hollis Chenery. And I started teaching at Johns Hopkins University, in Baltimore, and was brought by Hollis Chenery into his research division with a vague mandate to roam through the AID files and find something researchable. I found the AID country reports – monographs generated by AID offices in the field as annual reports on their respective countries. This was before the days of general data banks; indeed, even before the days of published comparable figures on per capita GNP! The reports were variable in quality and reliability, but had undergone some vetting before being sent to Washington, and, at least in principle, were uniform in coverage. They were treasure-troves of up to date information concerning political and sociocultural country situations together with quantitative and descriptive information on industry, agriculture, investment and international trade. Naturally, the information had to be cross-checked, especially for political bias and lack of comparative experience with other developing countries, but nevertheless offered an invaluable starting point. I became very excited about the potential of these country reports for generating information usable in research on interactions of economic social and political facets of economic development. Also, in reading psychological literature, I had come across the use of factor analysis. This technique seemed to offer an ideal statistical vehicle for exploratory research on interactions about which there were no validated theories. I asked Cynthia Morris whether she would be interested in collaborating with me on this project. And so, *Society, Politics, and Economic Development – A Quantitative Approach* (Johns Hopkins University Press, 1967) was born.

A word about our professional collaboration may be in order: Cynthia Morris had had polio as a teenager and has been on crutches ever since. As a result, her mobility has been limited. She therefore informed me early in our collaboration that she did not wish to be involved in presenting papers at conferences, professional meetings, etc.; that task would be up to me. Unfortunately, her less visible role has led the profession to underestimate her contributions to our joint work.

In 1965, when the major work on *Society, Politics, and Economic Development* was done, it occurred to us that it would be interesting to see how applicable the hypotheses generated by this research on contemporary development were to the historical development process during the period of the Industrial Revolution. This research was especially appealing to Cynthia Morris, whose training was as an economic historian with a strong institutional bent. She then started working on gathering comparable information on twenty-three countries for the period 1850–1914. In 1972, I met Herman Wold, at a talk on the methodology of partial least squares and, more generally, on soft modelling that he gave at the World Bank. I got very excited by his philosophy and approach, rare among mainstream statisticians, to which I resonated. Ever since finishing *Society, Politics, and Economic Development*, I had been looking for distribution-free methods of melding partial prior specification with sample information. (While my philosophy was Bayesian, there were two reasons I could not go the strict Bayesian route: I did not want to specify a specific prior distribution, especially with the type of discrete, ranked data that characterised my work on interactions between social, political, and institutional features of societies and their development patterns. I also wanted to deal with interdependent systems, and this is still difficult with present Bayesian techniques.) Herman Wold's approach seemed to be the answer. I started working with him in the early stages of the development of the partial least squares approach, and through him became aware of the work of Svante Wold, on disjoint principal components models. It is this latter approach that Cynthia Morris and I used in our historical work. Little did we know, when we started this research in 1965, that it would be twenty-three years before our historical work could culminate in a book describing what role institutional and political forces had played in inducing the very diverse economic responses of individual countries to the challenges and opportunities offered by the early Industrial Revolution in Great Britain! Our book, *Comparative Patterns of Economic Development, 1850–1914* (Johns Hopkins University Press) appeared only in 1988. In this book, I finally persuaded Cynthia Morris to put her name as first author, both as a means of reflecting our relative contributions to this work and a means of partially rectifying the general misconceptions about her contributions to our past joint research.

Of course, during the twenty-three years that it took to complete this book, there were several detours on the way. The most important was our joint and my separate work on income distribution in developing countries. In 1969, the Agency for International Development came under fire from the US Congress for not paying enough attention to the spread of benefits from its projects. (It would appear that international junkets by Senators and Congressmen have some uses!) Cynthia and I were asked to undertake a study of the breadth of participation, both economically and politically, by developing countries' populations in the development process. The result was *Economic Growth and Social Equity in Developing Countries* (Stanford University Press, 1973). While generally taken as having confirmed Kuznets' U-hypothesis, our results confirmed a reverse J-hypothesis. We found that the share of income accruing to the poor first declines rapidly, then less rapidly, and then, depending on the policy choices made, either levels off (the reverse J) or starts increasing (the U). Politically, as the indigenous middle class and urbanisation increase, and as education and communication improve, the influence on policy of non-elite groups starts extending to the middle class and to workers in the modern sector. But we found that the greater political participation of these groups does not redound to the benefit of the poor. Indeed, the middle class benefits at the expense of both the poor and the rich.

We were deeply shocked by our findings. Up to then we had believed in the benign view of economic development offered by modernisation-scholars and the trickle-down hypothesis imbuing mainstream writings on economic development. Were it not for the function-free statistical technique we adopted for our study, and were it not for our inductive empirical approach, we would have adopted an *a priori* specification confirming the modernisation-cum-trickle-down theories. We would then have ascribed the poor statistical fit to poor data and small sample size. It is also fortunate that we undertook an arduous effort to obtain direct information on income distribution, despite the virtual lack of published studies. Of over 200 books and more than 1,000 articles on individual countries published in the previous ten years, we found income distribution information in only one – Samuel Barber's study of South Africa – for 1948! We found a list, prepared by the United Nations Statistical Office, of income distribution studies in developing countries that had been carried out but had not been published, and then proceeded to use the leverage of AID field offices to obtain the studies themselves. We were also fortunate to find the comparative study by Christian Morrisson, written as his PhD dissertation, with income distribution estimates for Sub-Saharan African countries. This data, though of lesser reliability than the data for the more developed countries, played a critical role in generating the initial decline of the income share of the poorest. We submitted our report to AID and then did not publish the results for two years since we feared that our findings would be used as an argument to curtail resources for foreign-assistance rather than direct resources to more poverty-oriented projects and programmes. We felt free to publish our findings only after we were convinced they would do no harm: by 1973 the decline in foreign-assistance was already underway and new evidence concerning increasing urban unemployment despite rapid growth was making it clear that all was not well with the development process.

Our findings in this book led to the second major strand in my work: that dealing with income distribution and poverty, both descriptively and from a policy viewpoint. Two articles, 'On the State of Development Economics' and 'Development Economics – A Reassessment of Goals', summarise the effect my shock had on my research. In the former I argued that the fundamental failure of development economics had its roots in several methodological deficiencies: the failure to take a sufficiently broad systems approach; the failure to monitor results adequately; the pervasive search for panaceas and for simplicity and simple guidance rules; and insufficient humility and insufficient professionalism in our approach to development. In the latter article, I argued that the goals of development should become the creation of the social and material conditions for the realisation of human potential by all. This goal should replace the goal of self-sustained growth; rather, growth should be viewed as an instrument for the achievement of poverty reduction – a goal to which I referred as 'depauperisation'. Mark Blaug (1985) calls this paper my most readable and controversial article.

I joined the World Bank in 1971 and started a research programme aimed at seeing whether an approach to economic development policy exists that would spread more of the benefits of development to the poor. This was genuinely an open question, since the history of the early phases of the Industrial Revolution in developed countries had also exhibited a decrease in the share of income accruing to the poor. It seemed to me that finding such an approach would require generating a computer-laboratory in which experiments with policies and programmes could be carried out and evaluated. This laboratory should represent how economic actors interact in an actual economy, portray the governmentally set rules for markets and behaviour, incorporate all the instruments for intervention and all the variables that are important in mediating the impact of the economy, of governments, and of the rest of the world on the poor. Having seen how the simple (simplistic?) *a priori* models that identified single-cause development prime-movers or bottlenecks had led the development-policy formulating community into advocating a seriously flawed development process, I rejected the methodology of specifying a two- or three-sector model with one or two classes of actors, solving it for its comparative statics implications, and then basing policy recommendations on these findings. Rather, I argued for building a complex but realistic computer-model and then simplifying it *a posteriori,* on the basis of sensitivity experiments. This returned me to the methodology of digital simulation, introduced into economics by my first major published article, on the Klein-Goldberger model. I asked Sherman Robinson, who was then an Assistant Professor at Princeton, to join me in this research. (I had first met Sherman Robinson when, as a PhD candidate at Harvard, he asked me for the *Society, Politics, and Economic Development* data for use in his dissertation. When he finished, he sent me a copy of his dissertation, and I was impressed by it.)

We first thought that the appropriate model structure for our research on income distribution would be offered by a Johansen model. But it then became clear that, since our purpose was to model structural change and large-programme interventions, a model like Johansen's, that is expressed in linear rates of growth, might miss effects that are of the same order of magnitude as the impacts of the experiments themselves. Sherman Robinson suggested that we change our formulation to solving for the levels of the endogenous variables rather than, as in the Johansen model, for their rates of change. And so, the first large-scale computable general equilibrium model (CGE) was born. The model was quite large (it contained over 3,000 endogenous variables); mixed neo-classical and structuralist features; incorporated non-homogeneities in investment and government behaviour; had an endogenous demand for money; two loanable funds markets (one official and one unorganised); two policy regimes (a tight-money regime with fixed money supply and rationing, and a loose-money regime with fixed interest rates); and some elements of industrial organisation within sectors (four firm or farm sizes, with different behaviour rules and different credit and foreign exchange access by large firms). The model was applied to South Korea, a country for which we both had a feeling. The initial reactions to our model specification were sceptical. Our critics contended that we would never be able to solve the model, and that, even if we were able to solve it, we would not be able to understand what was going on in the model. We proved them wrong, however, on both counts. Our book, *Income Distribution Policy in Developing Countries: The Case of Korea* (Stanford University Press), finished in 1975, appeared in 1978. In it, we were able to identify the important policy variables, explain how the model worked, and gain a feeling for the relative importance of different policy interventions. (The first general presentation of the model was in 1973, at a World Congress of the Econometric Society, in Toronto. There we met with John Whalley, then a graduate student writing his dissertation with Herbert Scarf, and he asked us many questions about solution-techniques, and about the feasibility of solving other than toy models. The first written reports on the model were in 1973 and the first publication, giving our rather pessimistic policy conclusions based on our comparative statics experiments, was in 1975, as part of my paper calling for a shift in emphasis away from economic growth and towards poverty alleviation as the major goal of development policy.)

In the policy experiments we performed with our CGE model we found that policy interventions aimed at increasing the equality of the size distribution of income were very difficult. Of the roughly 3,000 endogenous variables in the model only two, rural–urban migration and the agricultural terms of trade, had a perceptible impact. The size distribution of income was exceedingly stable, even large-scale programmes produced effects that altered only the second decimal of the Gini coefficient. Most interventions altered the incidence of poverty (i.e. the functional distribution of income), especially between the rural and urban poor and near poor, without changing the relative magnitude of poverty (i.e. the size distribution of income). In the absence of changes in the distribution of assets or institutions affecting the access of the poor to factor and commodity markets, only changes in development strategy, equivalent to large packages of mutually coordinated programmes, could alter the relative magnitude of poverty by engendering the right kind of economic growth. Absolute poverty was easier to reduce than relative poverty. This conclusion was confirmed by our dynamic experiments and is consistent with the conclusions from models for different countries, with different closure rules, and different structural specifications (Adelman and Robinson, 1988).

After the book was finished, Sherman Robinson joined the World Bank and shifted to work on industrialisation and trade with generic CGE models. He simplified the specification of the Korea-CGE model, based on the intuition gained from our sensitivity and policy experiments; improved the solution algorithm; improved the trade specification; and based the model-calibration explicitly, rather than only implicitly, on the Social Accounting Matrix (SAM) accounting framework. His work did a great deal to disseminate the use of CGE models among academic researchers and in the policy-planning community. Amusingly enough, however, with the currently renewed interest in the impact of IMF-inspired structural adjustment programmes on the poor in debt-ridden developing countries, many of the monetary, macroeconomic, industrial-organisation, and credit-allocation mechanisms that he ripped out of the Korea-CGE model, in an effort to arrive at a simpler generic model, are being reintroduced into CGEs of the 1980s, one by one.

I continued my work on income distribution policy and, becoming increasingly discouraged about the potential for policy impact on development assistance and on development policy after the two oil shocks, increasingly turned to non-policy work on institutions in development and economic history.

In 1977, I was invited to hold the Cleveringa chair at Leyden. This was a chair established by the Queen of the Netherlands to commemorate the resistance of Leyden University, led by Cleveringa, a law Professor, to the Nazi order to fire all Jewish Professors. The chair was to deal with some issue affecting human rights, be staffed by a social scientist on a one-year basis, and rotate between a Dutch and a foreign professor. I was the fourth holder of the chair, the second economist after Tinbergen. In my inaugural address, 'Redistribution Before Growth – A Strategy for Developing Countries' (1978) I advocated asset redistribution before, rather than after, improvements in the asset's productivity: land reforms before improvements in agricultural productivity and mass primary education before a major push on industrialisation. Asset redistribution before improvements in productivity would enable growth-promoting measures to go hand in hand with equity-improving measures, thereby greatly enhancing the potential for improving the lot of the poor through economic development. The profession has accepted the call for increased emphasis on primary education while ignoring the call for land reform as unrealistic. In 'Beyond Export-Led Growth' (1984) I advocated a temporary shift during the low-growth-in-world-income-and-trade period of the 1980s towards agricultural development in an open trade regime as a mechanism for accelerating domestic industrialisation and increasing equity (the ADLI strategy). I used the generic CGE model of Korea developed by Sherman Robinson to demonstrate the superiority of this strategy in a low-growth world environment over export-led growth.

At the same time, Cynthia Morris and I intensified our work on economic history. After finishing the historical book in 1988, we felt that we had enough insight into the complex interactions that determined the diversity of country responses to the industrial revolution in Great Britain to be able to specify a simultaneous equation, partial least squares model of nineteenth-century economic development using Herman Wold's statistical methodology (Adelman, Lohmoller and Morris, 1988). We are now working on a monograph comparing historical and contemporary development patterns.

POLICY WORK

My policy work started early in my career, and I have always felt that it offered both the motivation and new insights for my research. My first involvement with policy started by accident. In 1963, AID in Washington received an urgent request from its Vietnam office for a statistician who would design a rural income-expenditure survey in the Delta. I did not quite understand why this was so urgent, but was eager to travel so I volunteered. When I came to Saigon, I was struck by two things: the Vietnamese population did not seem to be committed to the war and the security situation was much worse than depicted by either military or diplomatic communications from Saigon. I reasoned that with incorrect information, correct decisions could not be made in Washington, and, with the arrogance of youth, started on a one-woman fact-finding mission. My starting point was why the Vietnamese population was not committed to the war. I soon realised that an important part of the answer was that, with existing tenurial conditions, the rural population had a large positive incentive to keep a low level of military activity going: due to the war, most of the landlords had left the rural areas, and rents had not been collected for as much as three years. At existing rents, pacification would mean an indebtedness of about 1.5 years' output! This led me to argue for a United States supported land reform of the land-to-the-tiller variety as a higher probability alternative than the military approach to ending the war. Buying all the land of the Delta at market prices from the landlords would have cost only about half the annual military budget! Upon returning from Saigon, I spent much of my effort for about three months peddling this view to the policy establishment. I gained a hearing, but, alas, the military approach prevailed. Many years later I met the director of the Saigon AID mission again and asked him why the consumption-expenditure survey had been such a high-priority item. His answer: 'The country may be burning, but Washington still wants to know: what's GNP?' – a sad, but accurate comment on bureaucracies.

My work in development planning started early, has given me some insight into methods of policy-formulation and a great deal of personal and professional satisfaction. In the 1950s and 1960s, work in economic development was by and large non-technical except in one area – that of development planning. This area, which started with Tinbergen's formulation of planning and his hierarchic view of state-economy interactions, offered scope for the use of all techniques of econometrics and operations research. The technical part of my soul could therefore find satisfaction in this branch of work. That period also offered scope for the influential foreign adviser. Both coincided in my work on South Korea's Second Five-Year Plan, summarised in *Practical Approaches to Development Planning – Korea's Second Five-Year Plan* (1969).

My involvement in Korea started fortuitously. I was sitting in the office of a friend at AID in the summer of 1964, and he was complaining that his boss (Hollis Chenery) wanted him to go to South Korea, whereas he wanted to go to Turkey. I said: 'I'll go!' I went under AID auspices in early 1965, wrote a critical report on the institutional setup for planning in Korea, and returned home expecting never to return. To my great surprise, my recommendations were implemented, and I was called back to assist with the work on the plan. We wound up using all the econometric and operations research techniques then known to formulate investment, credit and foreign exchange allocation for the next five-year plan. The plan, initiated in 1967, involved a shift towards export-led growth, after a 50 per cent devaluation to realign exchange rates, substantial reductions in tariffs and in the scope of protection to reduce distortions, and a doubling of interest rates to reduce inflation and increase savings. The shift towards export-led growth was a natural recommendation for an economy with highly developed human resources (a level of education three times the average for an economy of its per capita income); a very small internal market (per capita income in 1965 was about $70); and a very poor natural resource base (hence high import coefficients). I was not sensitive at the time to income distribution issues, but the plan worked out very well for poverty as well, tripling the incomes of the poor in ten years, because of the very egalitarian distribution of assets. Korea had had two major land reforms in the early 1950s, and had universal primary education. In 1972, I received a Presidential decoration from President Park, the Order of the Bronze Tower, for my work on the Second Five-Year Plan. The citation reads:

With deep interest in the wellbeing of the Korean people. Mrs. Irma Adelman, the professor at Northwestern University, has devoted her efforts with superb competence to the economic development of the Republic of Korea and thereby greatly contributed towards attaining the goals of economic self-sufficiency pursued by the Government of the Republic of Korea. Her valuable donation and service has gained for her the appreciation and admiration of the Korean people.

But when, in 1973, President Park turned from benevolent dictator to oppressive despot, torturing and jailing the opposition, I felt I had to resign from any advisory role in South Korea, after checking with my previous Korean co-workers that my resignation would not place them in jeopardy.

My final direct involvement with policy came in 1971, when I joined the World Bank. A paper summarising the findings of my work with Cynthia Morris on income distribution and development was circulating as a working paper at the Bank. McNamara's speech writer, who was looking for material on this subject, came across the paper and used it as background for McNamara's Chile speech. This was the speech that signalled a change in Bank policy towards emphasis on poverty alleviation in lending to developing countries.

With my change of emphasis in development policy towards income distribution and poverty, I lost all popularity with planning agencies in developing countries themselves. For a while, I was popular with international agencies with a poverty orientation: the ILO and the World Bank, in particular. But as their interest shifted towards debt and trade problems, this policy involvement stopped as well. Whatever policy influence I now have is indirect: through my academic research and policy writings.

CAREER ISSUES

So far, I have not touched on how the particular issues affecting professional women – discrimination; handling the multiple demands of home, child and career; and managing two careers – impinged on my life and career. I hit discrimination against women for the first time when I got my PhD in 1955. I was totally unprepared for this. I was a foreigner to the United States, and I had not realised that, like democracy in ancient Greece, the Horatio Alger myth characterised the United States as an open, mobile society did not apply to American women. In the 1950s, discrimination against women in US academia was incredible. I had graduated from a top institution, at the top of my class, in a period of high demand for college teachers. Nevertheless, when it came to entering the job market, no one would waste a recommendation on a low-probability hire. At the time, openings were not advertised, and were publicised only through a network of personal contacts. When I applied for a teaching position at San Francisco State, the chairman suggested that I might look for a position in a local private high school! In the end, Berkeley hired me on a one-year appointment as a Teaching Associate – a position routinely given to third-year graduate students who have passed their field examinations. Then came six years, all on one-year, non-tenure-ladder appointments, at Berkeley, Mills College (a local private elite womens' college, where I became aware of the many phenomena described in Betty Friedan's *Feminine Mystique*), and Stanford. By then I had published my first book, the Klein-Goldberger article, two other articles on business cycles, my articles on sampling and hedonic index numbers, and one on the use of Markov chains to predict the long-run size distribution of firms. The quantity and quality of my publications would have been sufficient to earn me a solid promotion to tenure in any first rate institution, had I been male. And still, I had no leg on the tenure ladder . . .

The hardest thing during this period was to keep from getting bitter. I thank my lucky stars that I had the maturity to realise that, if I were to allow the process to make me bitter, the world would have won its fight against me, regardless of the ultimate professional outcome. I forbade myself the making of invidious comparisons with males, and ordered myself to consider myself as part of a Cairnes-type non-competing group. And yet, had the process continued much longer, I would not have been able to hold out against being corroded by bitterness. Still, I was fortunate: I was employed continuously, at first-rate institutions, and worked with excellent colleagues, with whom I interacted on a par. My work relationships with my colleagues and students were easier than those of males: women are used to interacting as equals with more senior males, my Assistant Professor colleagues did not consider me a threat, and the educator-maternal role with students came easily.

Then, I got a break: my husband became bored with his position at the Livermore Laboratory, and obtained a more challenging position in Washington, DC. I used the Hungarian Connection (from Tibor Scitovsky, at Berkeley, to George Jaszy, at Johns Hopkins) to indicate my availability, and was offered a regular Associate Professorship at Hopkins, at the princely salary of $10,000 a year, a 60 per cent increase on my previous salary at Stanford. We moved, I met Cynthia Morris, became exposed to policy through Hollis Chenery at AID, and could use my tenured status to engage in longer-term, riskier, research which culminated in the Adelman–Morris publications. Still, salary discrimination continued. When I complained to my chairman at Hopkins about the lack of a raise for three years despite high productivity, I was told to solicit alternative offers, as indication of my opportunity cost. Within a week, I obtained two offers, one from Maryland at 60 per cent higher salary, and one from Northwestern, at 80 per cent higher salary. The Northwestern position looked especially attractive, because there was an active interdisciplinary group in economic development, and because several of my would-be colleagues, George Dalton, Karl de Scweinitz, and Jonathan Hughes, shared my broad-ranging institutional interests. My husband found a satisfactory position in Chicago, and, in 1966, we moved.

I was very happy at Northwestern. I liked the department, my colleagues, the size of the school, the quality of the students, the attitude of the administration, and, last but not least, the computer centre. I continued my collaboration with Cynthia Morris, and would have happily stayed at Northwestern except for my husband's work situation. His position at a research laboratory in Chicago proved to be unrewarding – so, again, we had to move. We spent a very happy year in 1971 at the Center for Advanced Studies in Behavioral Sciences, in Palo Alto. Influenced by Vietnam, my husband tried during this year to switch from defence physics to work on urban social science problems. We worked on a model of urban politics, which incorporated many novel features, but was only published in book chapters and conference proceedings. We hoped that, at the end of the year, we would be able to find joint teaching positions. But our timing was wrong: 1972 was the beginning of the academic recession, and departments were even more than usually concerned with credentialling. I tried to get us hired as a package-deal, and almost succeeded at Cornell. But, in the end, my husband's end of the deal fell through.

After the year at the Center, we moved to Washington once again. I took a job at the World Bank, my husband continued his work on the urban book, and we continued the search for joint positions. For one year, I was the major breadwinner in the family. I then learned how heavy the psychological burden of being the major breadwinner actually is. I would wake up in the middle of the night in a cold sweat, wondering what would happen to the family if I were to suffer an incapacitating accident, or be fired. I now know that what I was trying to do was wrong, even had it succeeded: my husband should have got a job on his own merits rather than as part of a package deal. I felt inadequate for being unable to give him what he wanted (a professorial position in the social sciences) and he resented my efforts and support, though asking for them. When I gave up, he found a position in his old career within a week! I did not know whether to laugh or cry.

At the end of the year at the World Bank, I took a professorial position at Maryland. Maryland was a commuter campus, and this meant that both students and faculty only came there for a purpose, retreating to home or office in Washington in between. I missed the college atmosphere typical of non-urban campuses, such as Berkeley, Stanford, or Northwestern. My husband and I were both working too hard and had no energy left to build a social life. We started drifting apart, interacting only on the level of practical problems or when going to an event at the Kennedy Center. Finally, the inevitable happened: we separated and, in 1980, divorced.

When we separated, I became a free agent, and when Berkeley's Department of Agriculture and Resource Economics enquired about my potential interest, I jumped at the opportunity. My work on poverty had made me realise the importance of agricultural development, and I was painfully aware how little I knew about agriculture, and how much more difficult agricultural development was than industrialisation. I hoped that through exposure to my colleagues' work I might learn about agricultural economics, agricultural technology, and about the physical bases of agriculture. I have not been disappointed. Since joining the Department in 1979, I have learned a great deal about these issues, but I still have a great deal more to learn. Indeed, I expect agriculture–industry interactions and patterns of agricultural development to be a focus of my research in the coming years.

Thus, my response to the twin problems of discrimination against women and two careers, was high geographic mobility. I once counted that we had owned more houses than cars! We moved whenever a Pareto-optimal move was possible, and alternated in initiating moves.

My female students occasionally ask me: 'When is a good time to have a child, if I want to also have a career?' My answer is: 'Either in graduate school or once tenure is assured.' (As a result, I wind up with a fair number of pregnant dissertation advisees...). I myself had chosen a different timing, which did not make my early career any easier. Our son was born in 1958, when I had a very precarious hold on an academic career. The most difficult parts about melding childrearing with career were the tremendous physical stamina it required, the constant guilt at not being a full-time mother, and the constant anxiety that something might happen to him while I was at work. At the time, day-care facilities were very few and of dubious quality, so, for the first ten years of his life, I had a live-in help. After that, I had day-help, at first five days a week, then two, then one. He was an easy child, intelligent, energetic, charming, and with a great sense of humour. Our relationship has remained close, though there have been a few rocky patches in the last ten years.

Like all autobiographies, my story is, fortunately, still unfinished. However, I do not anticipate many new departures; just a deepening of old lines of research and a continuation of my present, satisfying, personal and professional lifestyle.

But then, who knows?

Bibliography

Adelman, Irma, 'A Stochastic Analysis of the Size Distribution of Firms', *Journal of the American Statistical Association*, pp. 893–904, 1959.

Adelman, Irma and Adelman, Frank L., *The Dynamic Properties of the Klein-Goldberger Model*, pp. 596–625, 1959.

Adelman, Irma, 'Business Cycles – Endogenous or Stochastic?', *Economic Journal*, pp. 783–96, 1960.

Adelman, Irma and Griliches, Zvi, 'On an Index of Quality Change', *Journal of the American Statistical Association*, pp. 535–48, 1961.

Adelman, Irma, *Theories of Economic Growth and Development* (Stanford University Press, Palo Alto, 1964).

Adelman, Irma and Morris, Cynthia Taft, *Society, Politics, and Economic Development: A Quantitative Approach* (Johns Hopkins University Press, Baltimore, 1967).

Adelman, Irma, *Practical Approaches to Development Planning: Korea's Development: A Quantitative Approach* (Johns Hopkins University Press, Baltimore, 1969).

Adelman, Irma and Morris, Cynthia Taft, *Economic Growth and Social*

Equity in Developing Countries (Stanford University Press, Palo Alto, 1973).

Adelman, Irma and Robinson, Sherman, 'A Non-Linear, Dynamic, Microeconomic Model of Korea: Factors Affecting the Distribution of Income in the Short Run', *Discussion Paper 36, Research Program in Economic Development* (Princeton University, 1973).

Adelman, Irma and D'Andrea Tyson, Laura, 'A Regional Microeconomic Model of Jugoslavia: Factors Affecting the Distribution of Income in the Short Run', *Development Research Center* (World Bank, 1973, mimeographed).

Adelman, Irma, 'On the State of Development Economics', *Journal of Development Economics*, pp. 3–5, 1974.

Adelman, Irma, 'Development Economics – A Reassessment of Goals', *American Economic Review*, pp. 302–9, 1975).

Adelman, Irma and Robinson, Sherman, *Income Distribution Policy in Developing Countries: The Case of Korea* (Stanford University Press, Palo Alto, 1978).

Adelman, Irma, *Redistribution Before Growth – A Strategy for Developing Countries* (Martinus Nijhof, The Hague, 1978).

Adelman, Irma, 'Beyond Export-Led Growth', *World Development*, vol. 12, pp. 937–49, 1984.

Adelman, Irma, *A Poverty Focussed Approach to Development Policy*, pp. 49–65 (Transactions Books, New Brunswick and Oxford, 1986).

Adelman, Irma, Lohmoller, Jan-Bernd and Morris, Cynthia Taft, 'A Latent Variable Regression Model of Nineteenth Century Economic Development', *Giannini Foundation Working Paper No. 439* (University of California, Berkeley, 1988).

Adelman, Irma and Robinson, Sherman, 'Macroeconomic Adjustment and Income Distribution: Alternative Models Applied to two Economies', *Journal of Development Economics* (forthcoming, 1988).

Blaug, Mark, *Great Economists since Keynes: An Introduction to the Lives and Works of One Hundred Modern Economists* (Wheatsheaf Books, 1985).

Morris, Cynthia Taft and Adelman, Irma, *Comparative Patterns of Economic Development, 1850–1914* (Johns Hopkins University Press, Baltimore, 1988).

6 The Life of an Economist
Charles P. Kindleberger

RECRUITMENT

It is virtually a theorem that economists start out intellectual life specialising in some other subject and switch about age 20. Sir John Hicks began in mathematics, John Williams in English, Max Millikan in physics, Robert Solow in sociology, etc. The one counter-example known to me is Paul Samuelson who wanted to be an economist for as long as he can remember, but he is *sui generis*. The reason, I believe, is that young people grow up in a fairly homogeneous environment, and become aware of the fascination of complex social interrelations only on reaching a certain maturity.

Too much attention is given in the United States from too early an age on choice of career, if this view that some careers can be judged only as one comes of age be correct. Another element in the equation is one's relations with one's father. Later at MIT when guiding students, I several times had promising young men decide to leave economics for law. In two cases, it had turned out that their fathers were lawyers. At college, during a period when men rebel against fathers, they had been moved by a charismatic teacher and, following him as father substitute, had been seduced into economics. When the rebellion stage had passed, a basic affinity for the law reasserted itself and economics was abandoned. The same problem existed at MIT on a wider scale in science, where bright young people, enticed by a specific Pied Piper in secondary school, had come to a university specialising in science and technology when they ultimately wanted different careers. In the 1950s, before undergraduate concentrations in humanities and social sciences proliferated, the economics department had a bimodal selection of undergraduate majors, an early cohort of weak students who failed to be admitted into popular departments, such as electrical engineering, whom for the most part we failed and expelled, and a second delayed group that came into economics in the third year or even the first term of the fourth year, having finally decided that mathematics, science, or engineering was not their basic bent. Many of these went on to graduate school –

elsewhere, for we resisted the temptation to keep them on as graduate students – and had successful careers.

One should not make too much of adolescent rebellion, despite Mark Twain's statement that it was remarkable how much his father had increased in intelligence and judgement between the time Mark Twain was 15 and when he became 21. A small set of economists follow their father's footsteps. Historically, the most distinguished are perhaps John Stuart Mill and John Maurice Clark. Among contemporaries Sir Alec Cairncross, Walter Heller, Lord Kaldor, Sir Donald MacDougall, Walter Salant, and Paul Samuelson have sons or daughters in economics. George Stigler once suggested that professorships in economics be made hereditary, but I do not know whether he had a candidate for his successor.

I had a lawyer father, and there was perhaps a certain amount of resistance to following that career, which he would have chosen for me. In college, my start was in classics – Latin and Greek – but I switched at the end of the second year into economics, ostensibly because of a pedantic and disagreeable teacher in Horace. Certainly I was not moved by the excitement of my first courses in economics which were badly taught by graduate students little older than me (the mature members of the department were not great teachers either). In retrospect, the cause, in a world sliding into depression, was the innate appeal of economics gradually dawning on a young man outgrowing adolescent enthusiasms.

The 1930s attracted people into economics because they wanted to understand why the system was breaking down. Curiosity is a more effective stimulus to work in economics than the desire to make a particular kind of living, or than the wish to do good in the world. The profession attracts brains counter-cyclically, although it may now turn out that stagflation will prove to be as powerful a magnet as depression in the 1930s which brought in Samuelson, Friedman, Meade, and similar giants.

In the preface of *The World in Depression, 1929–1939*, I have commented on the chances that permitted me to work on ships in the summers of 1929 and 1930, and led to the Graduate School of International Studies at Geneva, Switzerland, under Sir Alfred Zimmern, in the Summer of 1931. These experiences pointed the choice to international economics.

FORMATION

Depression makes economic education attractive, but it does not help finance it. My family was hard hit, and I was unable to win one of the few fellowships available in economics at that time. By luck, I was offered financing at Columbia by the alumni of a social fraternity that was in danger of collapse and needed a few more bodies to establish a critical mass. They offered to pay my way to law school, but had no objection when I chose economics. The opportunity in the fall of 1933 came after I had worked for a year as an office boy in a marine-insurance brokerage firm.

Columbia graduate education in economics at that time suffered from several drawbacks. First was the sizeable number of master's candidates relative to the PhD programme, who filled classes but were for the most part not serious economists. Secondly, many faculty had part time jobs elsewhere in the city, typically at the National Bureau of Economic Research downtown, which made contact between students and faculty difficult. Thirdly, the faculty – notably Mitchell, Clark, Angell, H. Parker Willis, and the like – had not been led by the 1929 crash and depression to rethink lectures developed in the 1920s. An instructor in international trade on one occasion, reading from notes, said 'Take the price of wheat at $2.00', which produced a murmur from the class which knew that the price was nearer fifty cents, and that the notes were 10 years old.

I would argue, however, that graduate education is produced far more by one's fellow students than by the faculty. At Columbia we lacked the numbers of outstanding students that Harvard had in those years, but benefited enormously from one-year transfers from Chicago of Milton Friedman and Allen Wallis, from Rockefeller fellows from Europe – Fritz Machlup, Michael Heilperin, E.A. Radice, E.F. Schumacher. The biggest stimulus for me was the transfer to Columbia from Cambridge, England, in 1935, of H.H. Villard who had attended the Keynes' seminar. This was before the *General Theory* had actually appeared, but Villard was an evangelist, and the Columbia students felt an excitement akin to Keats' 'On First Looking into Chapman's Homer', as he communicated the new approach to what we now call 'macroeconomics'. In 1936, Villard and I organised an informal seminar that met in the apartment of Arthur R. and Evelyn Burns. That proved as stimulating as any organised instruction. It also helped me get a job at the Federal Reserve Bank of New York, when W. Randolph Burgess attended one evening and

I arranged through him an interview at the Bank.

These paragraphs are unduly severe on the Columbia faculty. In the School of Business, H.P. Willis arranged for many of the students in his seminar to publish their papers in a symposium entitled *The Economics of Inflation*. I choose not to look back now at that misguided effort. B. Haggott Beckhart encouraged me as a first-year graduate student to submit a term paper on competitive exchange depreciation for publication. James Angell and I never completely agreed whether equilibrium in the balance of payments meant no net gold movements, as he thought, or no net movement of gold and short-term capital, as I insisted, but he commented faithfully in long single-spaced letters on each chapter as I submitted it to him in 1936 and 1937, after leaving the university, and I have tried to follow his example. And Vladimir Gregorovitch Simkovitch was a never-ending source of stories. Eli Shapiro recounts hearing him say to Michael Florinsky, who had mentioned teaching: 'Mihail, let me tell you about teaching (pronounced teachink): take one cup of ideas, mix (meex) with a bucket of water, give students one drop an hour.'

REAL WORLD

The 1930s were not a good time to get an academic job. Aaron Gordon said later that in 1934 the Harvard Department of Economics had requests for only one teacher. It went to E.M. Hoover who had waited longest. The next year there was again one job, and it went to Gordon (today our top students have four or five offers each). I do not recall that I contemplated applying for an academic job. I wanted to understand the foreign-exchange market. The Federal Reserve Bank of New York job did not open up right away, and I spent the summer of 1936 in the US Treasury Department under Harry Dexter White, working with Frank Coe on purchasing-power-parity calculations for the French franc which was devalued in the fall. After three months, on 1 October 1936, I switched to the New York bank, working half-time in the Foreign Research Department on British problems and half-time in the Foreign Department in a small section on foreign exchange with Emile Despres.

As it happened, I did not get into academic life for twelve years, largely because of the war and post-war recovery. For one who ends up teaching, that is too long, but a year or better, two, is highly desirable. Too long is likely to make it impossible to perform effectively as a scholar. An agricultural economist who spent forty years in research in the Bureau of Agricultural Economics and on retirement received a grant to distill his experience into a book found it impossible. Having written two-page policy memoranda for forty years, that is what he knew how to do; unfortunately 200 two-page memoranda do not make a 400-page book. An economist going directly into government who wants to hedge against the possibility that he will later prefer academic life should publish a couple of articles before settling into government. That is more difficult today in the highly competitive scholarly world than it was in the 1930s. In addition, Columbia University before the Second World War, still retained the German requirement that a doctoral candidate must submit seventy-five printed copies of his dissertation, which it then used to exchange with other universities and build its library. I had no money for this purpose, but luckily my new wife did. The cost was $2000 for 600 copies. Columbia University Press wanted to publish only 400 copies to be sold at $3.00 retail, of which we would get back half. After subtracting seventy-five copies for Columbia and 25 for personal distribution, 300 copies at $1.50 each would yield $450 for a net loss of close to $1400. With difficulty I persuaded the Press to print 600 at my expense, writing the loss on investment down to $1250. When these were exhausted, the Press asked me to finance a new printing, an opportunity which was declined.

The Federal Reserve Bank of New York was a splendid place to work in the 1930s, partly because of Allan Sproul, later president, and John H. Williams, the economist-vice-president who commuted from Harvard, and partly because I worked with Emile Despres who became one of my closest friends. Allan Sproul belonged in a Pantheon of great men I worked under – in most cases far under. It includes General George C. Marshall, General Omar N. Bradley, and William L. Clayton. My contacts with the last three were on the whole remote; Mr Sproul wrote me a letter some five years before his death in 1978, and we kept up a correspondence. John Williams was the originator of the key-currency concept, which I have traced back to 1932, when he served with E.E. Day as a US representative to the Preparatory Commission for the World Economic Conference of 1933. It is a concept which originally did not seem very striking, but one that has had tremendous survival value, coming back to mind time and again.

Emile Despres had one of the finest minds I have known, subtle, sophisticated, penetrating. He has not left the mark in economics that he should have done, because he was a perfectionist, one who was unable to submit formal papers for publication until he had worked on them still more. The profession contains many economists with his disability. It is an enormous waste of resources. The opposite combination of an easy flow of words but little to say is also encountered. When Despres was teaching at Williams College, which then had no graduate programme, it was said that the best graduate education in the United States was obtained by getting a job as an assistant professor there, near him.

In February of 1939, before the German invasion of Czechoslovakia, I accepted a job on the economic staff of the Bank for International Settlements. This proved a mistake, as outbreak of war cancelled the monthly meetings and much of the work of the Bank. It was interesting to see Per Jacobsson close at hand in that environment, although I did not find myself in sympathy with his economic views. When Paris fell in June, 1940, Despres who had transferred to the research staff of the Federal Reserve Board in Washington arranged a job for me there, in the international section.

The economic staff of the Federal Reserve System is often regarded as a reservoir of talent, available for deployment, since the operating functions of the System do not require all that research. In the summer of 1940, the Board was turned to provide manning for the American side of the Joint Economic Committee of Canada and the United States. Alvin Hansen on leave from Harvard to the Board was made chairman; I became secretary. The Canadian chairman was William Mackintosh of Queens University, and the secretary Alexander Skelton of the Bank of Canada. Among the other American members were Harry Dexter White, Jacob Viner, E. Dana Durand. It was interesting, and working full time on Canadian problems for two years, I acquired a great deal of information, with, however, a high rate of obsolence. Moreover, the assignment contained the seeds of its own destruction. As soon as the Committee had introduced American and Canadian groups working on common problems, as in price control, lend-lease, production priorities, and the like, to each other, the Committee was asked to withdraw. In the spring of 1942, it turned to post-war problems of Canadian-American relations. These lacked immediacy, given the state of war. Accordingly when Emile Despres invited me to move again to OSS in the summer of 1942, I did.

William J. Donovan had been a distinguished general in the First World War, a New York lawyer, and a man with the seminal idea that the armed forces in the United States would leave a lot of things undone. To fill the gaps, he built an Office of Strategic Services (OSS) that later developed into the Central Intelligence Agency. A major division was the Research and Analysis Branch (R and A), which had a Board of Analysts, including as economists, Emile Despres and Edward S. Mason. In the economics division were sections to work on intelligence on enemy production, manpower, agriculture, and estimate war materiel.

In addition to economists, Research and Analysis branch had geographers, political scientists, and especially historians. There was a methodological struggle between historians and economists. When it came to estimating Russian wheat production, for example, Russian historians claimed that the economists could hardly make a contribution if they did not know how to read Russian, which would give them access to crop reports and the like. The economists, on the other hand, claimed that with data on acreage, historical yields and weather they were in better position statistically to estimate output, and the wisps of evidence from the daily press were diversionary rather than helpful. Over the years I have become more sympathetic with the historians' position as I read econometric studies strong on technique and weak on background. OSS had some brilliant successes using both techniques combined. Walter Levy could determine when to bomb given plants for hydrogenation of oil by reading German railroad-rate schedules obtained through Switzerland. When feedstock coal began to move in volume, German railroads lowered the rate, and railroad rates of course had to be published. Donald Wheeler's manpower section collected obituaries of soldiers from local newspapers of German towns adjacent to Switzerland and with census data blew up the sample into an estimate of German casualties on the Eastern Front.

In due course it was revealed that the American Air Forces were ill prepared to bomb enemy targets, having at best some vague Douhet-Seversky notions of bringing the enemy economy to its knees by battering it back to the Stone Age. When these notions seemed inadequate for operations, the Air Forces in Europe and in Washington sought help from OSS. R and A set up an Enemy Objectives Unit in the Economic Warfare Division of the US Embassy in London. Chandler Morse, Walt W. Rostow, and William A. Salant were the first OSS economists to man it in the fall of 1942. In February, 1943, I changed places with Morse. EOU had an initial problem in winning the confidence of the American air forces who had started out using

British intelligence with its long headstart. It was done by finding a British mistake. EOU was not privy to Ultra, the source of intelligence using decoded German radio traffic. Air Ministry intelligence came to depend upon it too much. Using aerial photographic interpretation (see Constance Babington-Smith, 1957), Polish intelligence which came to Britain in enormous volume, prisoner-of-war interrogations and every possible source, we concluded that the Folke Wolf plant at Bremen had moved to Marienberg, Poland. The Air Ministry claimed it had not, wrongly as it proved. From that time on, the Air Force was willing to listen to its most unmilitary economists.

War is a relatively simple economic problem. The objective function has only one argument – winning – instead of difficult trade-offs among growth, stability, income distribution, etc. in peace-time, and one constraint, to keep the domestic civilian economy moving. Full mobilisation is an equilibrium in which one can not increase the military effort by transferring one person from home front to fighting services – an ideal that Britain approached but Germany never did, although the British failed to achieve optimum allocation among air, navy, and ground forces. EOU economists articulated a theory of bombing which rested on the premise of invading Europe – Air Chief Marshal Harris thought the war could be won by bombing alone, a Douhet-Seversky position, with hammer but no anvil. Our theory of bombing combined intuitively – the theories had not been developed yet – input-output on one hand, and capital theory on the other. Intuitive input-output theory said that in a complex interdependent economy, to take out one row of inputs – such as ball-bearings or oil – would bring the whole economy to a halt. Capital theory held that it all had to be done within a time constraint, since given enough time, labour could be substituted for any missing input. These theories have doubtless been formalised and extended in such organisations as RAND since those primitive days. We thought of 'depth' – the time today's output was behind its ultimate use on the fighting front – and the 'cushion', or availability of inventories, civilian supplies, and the like, that could be diverted to protect military uses. Such targets as steel or electricity were rejected on grounds of both depth and cushion. We were initially ignorant of the time it takes to build an effective striking force and of tactical problems of deep penetrations into Germany, problems handled in any event by the air forces, but which affect target selection.

In due course, the problem was posed as how best to use strategic air forces to ensure success of the invasion of Europe. EOU found itself in a controversy on this issue, a debate between various analysts who advocated bombing railroad centres or marshalling yards, and our own view of driving military trains bringing reinforcements and material back from the landing site by cutting a ring of railroad bridges of a certain size. Railroad centres in our view had a cushion of civilian traffic close to 85 per cent. Interdicting all railroad traffic by destroying bridges (which took three weeks to repair as opposed to four hours for bombed track) was required. The debate still goes on. In his autobiography, *From Apes to Warlords*, Lord (Solly) Zuckerman defends attack on railroad centres, and dismisses the economists as a priori, unscientific and amateur. The controversy is pursued in *Encounter* for November 1978, and June 1979.

I was privileged in May and June 1944, to assist with tactical bombing operations during the invasion on the intelligence side, and in July to join G-2 staff of 12th Army Group commanded by General Bradley, in due course aided by Robert V. Roosa.

Having been overseas from February 1943, to June 1945, with one brief respite, I was anxious after V-E day to go home. Despres again came to the rescue. Many OSS staff had transferred into the Department of State to work on post-war problems such as German reparations. Despres himself was scheduled to go with Undersecretary Clayton to the Potsdam meeting concerning the occupation, and needed a backstop. I made it back to Washington by 12 June and after a week's leave was busy in the Department of State. That fall I tried to switch out of occupation issues and worked briefly on the British loan. German problems remained exigent, however, and soon I was back in the Division of German and Austrian Economic Affairs with Rostow, William Salant, Harold J. Barnett, and others of OSS days. This continued until June, 1947, when the Secretary of State, G.C. Marshall, broached a European-wide recovery plan. I moved into that work in the Department.

Just as we had intuitively reached the essence of input-output theory and capital theory in EOU, so in the Department of State we intuited the theory of second-best. A number of firms in Allied countries wanted to acquire German firms for one and another reason; theatres to show films, a sewing-machine plant to replace a direct investment that had fallen to the Russians, a monopoly such as 4711, and the like. Our division insisted that there should be a moratorium on direct investment in Germany until after monetary reform. This, of course, is the theory of the second-best. When markets don't work, don't use them. Revisionist historians assume that the United States as a capitalist nation was anxious to buy up German industry cheap. In actuality it was easy to persuade our betters of the wisdom of the policy. Secretary Byrnes came from South Carolina, General Clay from Georgia, Undersecretary of State Clayton from Texas. We had only the word, 'carpet-bagger', reminding them of the army of locusts that had descended on the South after the Civil War, to have them understand the merits of waiting.

On the Marshall plan, most economists served as advocates rather than objective analysts. I happened to be located at the cross-roads of a series of country and commodity committees. It was revealing how each country expert wanted more, not less, aid for the country he was analysing, and each commodity expert thought Europe needed more of his product. In retrospect, what is disturbing is the fact that we argued that Europe had a balance-of-payments deficit that had to be made up, whereas in the intermediate run, of course, as Machlup later pointed out, foreign aid determined the deficit, rather than the deficit foreign aid.

Worse, we argued as if we could forecast the needs of seventeen countries in twenty-six commodities for four and a quarter years as if it were a partial-equilibrium problem and any saving in any commodity would change the overall aid bill. In fact we were so fearful of revealing the limits of our knowledge to the Congress that no one dared change the original calculation of $5.2 billion for the first year and a quarter. The result was that when a change was required in any of the twenty-six commodities, another change was made in a residual figure. The joke among the statistical staff was that computers in the basement of the Pentagon building which we used were unable to produce any other answer than $5.2 billion for the next several months.

Those where years of hard work, with one-week vacation in 1945, none in 1946, or 1947. In 1948, I had an operation, lost weight, and decided to quit government for an academic job. Some part of the decisions was the belief that President Truman would be defeated for the presidency in the fall of 1948. That proved wrong. None the less I looked around for an academic job. An invitation to give a seminar at Princeton turned out badly. Professors Lutz, Graham, and Viner took strong exception to my defence of the Marshall plan, holding rather the belief that appropriate budget balancing and exchange depreciation by European countries could have restored equilibrium. The same seminar at Yale had the bad luck to find Viner on hand in

New Haven, invited to the seminar, and no more receptive. Finally, Richard Bissell, who had been the chief staff member on the Harriman economic report analysing the Marshall plan's economic impact on the United States, told me of an opening at MIT. I applied, visited the campus, was not asked to give a seminar, which may have been fortunate, and got the job.

ACADEMIC LIFE

Many people find it anomalous that MIT should have an economics department at all, much less a good one. Its existence is only partly accident. Francis A. Walker, a distinguished economist of the nineteenth century, had been president of MIT. Davis R. Dewey, brother of John Dewey, was for forty years secretary-treasurer (and one year president) of the American Economic Association, which he ran from his MIT office. It was thought that most engineering students went into business, and that they should know something of industrial relations. Many state certifying agencies in engineering required some exposure to economics. At one time the department of economics was half devoted to labour economics, the other half to everything else. Then it was able to recruit Paul Samuelson. His availability rested first on the resolve of a tiny minority of Harvard faculty not to hire him, because he made them uncomfortable, and second, his interest in staying in Cambridge. With his appointment, a positive feedback process set in, and economics at MIT grew by itself.

MIT turned out to be a superb place to spend the following thirty years. Its micro-sociology was highly effective. The economics department was housed on two floors in the same building with the Sloan School of Management and the Faculty Club. There was easy and informal intercourse within the department, at lunch where members without engagements filled up the same round table each day, and with economists in the Sloan School, some of whom had joint appointments with economics. The faculty was relaxed, tolerant, supportive, as opposed to some departments in other universities, which are divided and antagonistic. Many of us take on the coloration of our environment. If one goes to a third-rate place where few people do research, one is unlikely to do research. At MIT everyone worked hard, stayed on the campus in the office, accessible to colleagues and students.

There is a possibility I made a mistake in the 1950s, by not seeking to repair omissions in theory, mathematics, and later econometrics that were produced by weak training in the 1930s, and twelve years away from the academy. It is true that the journals were not full during the war years, but I had not been keeping up – as few in government service do – before and after the war. One colleague reassured me, however, saying that it was a mistake to convert a literary economist into a second-rate mathematical one. Moreover, I began to be pushed into economic history by the chance of agreeing to give a year's course on the 'Economy of Europe' at Columbia in New York, one day a week, a rare assignment in the United States, though ordinary in France and Italy. I had no trouble preparing material for the second term; that came out of State Department experience. For the first term I needed a running start, and worked up a little history. One by-product was the 1951 *Journal of Political Economy* article on how differently various countries in Europe responded to the fall in the price of wheat in the 1880s. From then on economic history took more and more time.

Thirty years at MIT have produced books rather than articles. What is irritating, however, is a reputation based on a moderately successful textbook, written to help educate a large family, rather than on original work. Textbooks are syntheses of work of others.

MIT has been a splendid place to teach not alone because of the tolerance and support of one's colleagues. The students are of very high quality. Graduate admission is highly competitive, with perhaps 300 to 400 applications each year for openings that the department intends to hold down to twenty-five, but which seem inescapably to inch up to nearer thirty-five. Micro-sociology appears to decree that the optimum size of a scholarly department is on the order of 100 graduate students and twenty-five to thirty faculty. Increasing economies to scale obtain below these levels; diseconomies above. There is always a temptation to yield to pressure and to grow a little. But beyond a certain size, students do not know each other, faculty has less frequent informal contact.

I am puzzled by the outcome of my teaching. MIT graduates in international economics include Jagdish Bhawati, William Branson, Carlos Diaz Alejandro, Miltiades Chacholiades, Ronald Findlay, Ronald Jones, Stephen Hymer, Stephen Magee, Robert Mundell, Egon Sohmen, Jaroslav Vanek. It is hubris perhaps to claim Bhagwati and Mundell for MIT since they both studied widely elsewhere, Bhagwati at Cambridge, Oxford, and Chicago under Harry Johnson;

Mundell at Washington, London under James Meade, Chicago under Harry Johnson. This sort of peripatetic education, seeking out great men to work under is surely the best possible. MIT has had its share of whom one of the more original was Staffan Burenstam Linder. The distinction of MIT graduates in international economics reflects the fact that students educate each other rather than learn from faculty. If faculty can communicate enthusiasm for the subject which incites the students to work on their own and with each other, little more can be contributed. But I have a very pungent recollection of the remark of an MIT graduate, not my student, saying to me after a party, and somewhat in his cups, that MIT had done so well in international economics because my old-fashioned approach confused the students who were forced to work the subject out independently for themselves.

In the course of thirty-two years, my wife and I have had three sabbaticals abroad: in Geneva, Oxford and Paris, Kiel and Rome. Each carried research deeper into European economic history and further from the pure theory of trade. International money represented a compromise and a continuing interest. Preoccupation with history led further from pure theory in a seminar at Harvard that lasted two years and produced a book, *In Search of France*, written with two political scientists, two sociologists, and an historian. Interdisciplinary research, I concluded from that exercise, is hard work, productive, but should be undertaken later rather than sooner, after one has spent years within one's own discipline. Departmental divisions strongly discourage such research. It is erroneously thought by many that the best explanation is the one that manages to stay within a given discipline, and indeed within a given technique. I once asked a visiting European scholar how he liked teaching at . . . Not much, he said. All the students reason like Professor . . . At Chicago, he went on, everyone is a Becker, looking for economic explanations of all sorts of phenomena that are normally thought to lie outside the purview of that subject. And as for the MIT 'fryer', referring to chickens available in American supermarkets that are exactly alike in size, weight, taste, they are superb at taking a model, manipulating it mathematically, then testing it with econometrics, but they are all identical.

Literary economic history, or historical economics as I sometimes call it, is not the fashion of the ongoing MIT, but it is a splendid way to occupy one's retirement.

References

Basington-Smith, C., *AirSpy* (New York, Harper & Row, 1957).
Zuckerman, S. (Lord), *From Apes to Warlords* (New York, Harper & Row, 1978).

7 Reflections on the Drive to Technological Maturity

W.W. Rostow

INTRODUCTION

Having accepted the invitation of the editors of the *BNL Quarterly Review* to reflect on the evolution of my 'intellectual developments, theoretical debates, and so on', I was, for a time, puzzled as to how to proceed. The unlikely catalyst proved to be a single sentence written by two respected old friends:[1] 'Rostow's book, published in 1960, generalised to all human history and to all the future a model based on the experience of eighteenth- and nineteenth-century Britain, partially repeated by the United States.' So far as the intellectual basis for *The Stages of Economic Growth*, its structure and pretensions to universality are concerned, they are quite wrong; and I shall shortly indicate why. But I have not responded to much more extreme and colourful misstatements of my views. As I said in the introduction to the volume of the International Economic Association reporting the 1960 Konstanz conference on the take-off:[2] 'As for the take-off, it will have to look after itself... Like all intellectual constructs it will survive only if it meets the hard pragmatic test of usefulness to others – if it illuminates problems that deeply concern them. No market is – or should be – more ruthlessly competitive than the market place for ideas.'

I have replied temperately to critics on a few occasions for sake of the record or because editors or publishers insisted.[3] But I do not, in fact, believe such defences much matter. The market for ideas is, indeed, oligopolistic; but over a reasonable period of time I don't think attack or defence (the equivalent of advertising) much affects the elasticity of the demand curve facing a given author.

Thus, the offending sentence generated by my friends on the Charles River triggered this piece not because it stirred me to gladiatorial combat but because it recalled that in my current research and writing one little discussed stage is proving highly relevant to a key phenomenon in the world economy.[4] The neglected stage is the drive to technological maturity.[5] The key phenomenon is the rapidly emerging capacity of the more advanced developing countries to absorb sophisticated industrial technologies and, with the special advantage of lower wage rates, to compete successfully in a widening array of manufactures with the older industrial states of Western Europe, North America, and, increasingly, Japan as well. They are collectively beginning to repeat the process whereby, say, Germany and the United States closed the gap separating them from Britain as of 1815; and Japan closed the gap separating it from Western Europe and the United States as of 1955.

In this perspective, the drive to technological maturity has thus moved on to centre stage, to a degree replacing with the passage of time and progress the much-discussed take-off. This has happened for two underlying reasons: because most of the population of the developing regions now lives in countries experiencing the drive to technological maturity; and because it is in this stage that technological absorptive capacity accelerates and the efficient use of the most modern technology spreads from a few sectors across the whole terrain of industrial and agricultural output and the services. At its close, an economy must normally rely for growth on the flow of new technologies emerging from the global investment sector we call R & D.

I shall begin by briefly recalling the origins and character of *The Stages* analysis, with special attention to drive to technological maturity; and then suggest briefly the relevance of this stage to three major problems on the world scene: development assistance policy; managing the competition between older and newer industrial societies; and phasing out the Cold War.

HOW *THE STAGES* CAME ABOUT

I am sceptical that anyone – including the creator – can provide a full and accurate account of how he hit upon a given idea. It's generally a messy, only half rational business. But I am reasonably confident that the following sequence was the framework from which my notion of the stages of economic growth emerged.

The story begins with a kind of informal black market economic theory seminar in 1933–4, when I was a sophomore, majoring in

British history, at Yale. The seminar was conducted on Thursday nights by a talented graduate student, Richard M. Bissell Jr., fresh from a year at LSE. (As I recall, this meant we read Wicksteed as well as Marshall.) I was one of Bissell's four students. He was one of the most gifted expositors I have ever known, presenting to us the bone structure of both micro- and macro-theory, a good deal of it in mathematical terms.

Before the year was out, I decided, aged 17, to devote my professional life to combining history with economic theory in two senses: using economic theory systematically both to illuminate economic history and to explore the complex interactions of the economy with the non-economic sectors of society. And this is what I have tried to do ever since.

I set to work immediately on the British economy and British society of the nineteenth century. By the time I had completed my doctoral thesis (formally 1940, in fact 1939) I had concluded that neither British growth nor fluctuations could be explained without introducing the large forces at work in the world economy, including the interaction of British growth with growth in other countries. When I came, after the Second World War, to publish my first book, I stated the proposition as follows:[6]

> Much of Britain's investment was foreign investment, related to development on distant continents, in which Britain participated, but which British initiative did not wholly determine. And the course of events at home, in other respects as well, derived in part from forces generated abroad. The fluctuations and trends in Britain were shared, with variations, by most other areas in the world. It is likely that the optimum unit for the study of economic history is not the nation, but the whole inter-related trading area.

While teaching at Cambridge, England, 1949–50, and preparing to settle down as an economic historian in the United States, I began to work out a way to make good that vision; that is, to capture the interplay between the forces of national development and those generated in the world outside. Two conclusions emerged: the task required the study of certain pervasive international phenomena (e.g., cycles, prices of major commodities which enter in international trade on a large scale, the impact of wars); and, equally, it required a method for analysing the stories of national growth. It was in contemplating the latter requirement that I decided I had to formulate my own theory of economic growth – a process carried forward by a memorable discussion with D.H. Robertson.[7]

I had also concluded by that time that conventional economic theory suffered from four weaknesses which rendered it grossly inadequate as a framework for studying and teaching the history of the world economy as it had evolved since the mid-eighteenth century. First, it could not accommodate within its structure the process by which major new production functions were generated and diffused. It provided no credible linkage between science, invention, and the production process. And there is no way a serious economic historian can accept the evasions which seem to have satisfied a good many theorists; for example, to render innovation exogenous or embody it in gross investment; or to treat it as an incremental consequence of widening the market or learning by doing; or to bury it in the 'residual', or the marginal capital-output ratio, or 'intermediate production'. Secondly, mainstream theory provided no credible explanation for trend periods, longer than conventional business cycles, in the prices of basic commodities relative to manufactures. Thirdly, it provided no credible linkage of conventional business cycles to the process of growth. For a historian it is palpable that cycles are simply the form growth historically assumed. The separation of cycle and trend, of the Marshallian short from the long period, is an act of intellectual violence that cuts out the heart of the problem of both cycles and growth. But it will be recalled that 1950 was a time when mainstream business cycle theorists were ringing the changes on the interaction of the multiplier and the accelerator, thereby effectively separating growth from cycles, relegating innovation to exogenous investment.[8] Fourthly, contemporary economic theory provided no mechanism for introducing non-economic factors into the analysis of economic growth when it was quite clear that economic growth – notably in its early phases but, in fact, throughout – could not be understood except in terms of the dynamics of whole societies.

Thus, as I began teaching the history of the modern world economy at MIT in September 1950, I worked simultaneously on *The Process of Economic Growth*, which, among other things, tried to remedy these weaknesses. That study has remained the theoretical framework for my work in historical and contemporary economic analysis down to *The World Economy: History and Prospect* and beyond.

The first modest, unnoticed appearance of the take-off was in *The*

Process, first published in 1952.[9] The take-off arose as an inescapable discontinuity from my own research and the papers of my seminar students, as together we turned around in our hands the stories not simply of Britain and the United States, but also of Belgium and France, Germany and Japan, Sweden, Russia, and Italy, Argentina, Brazil, Mexico, Turkey, Canada, Australia, and others. The discontinuity was inescapable because I began with the proposition that modern economic growth resulted from the generation and efficient absorption of increasingly sophisticated technologies. And if one studies the introduction into the economy of new technologies, one must disaggregate down to the level of the sectors (sometimes even to particular factories) where the new technologies are introduced. The discontinuity induced in those sectors – and related sectors – by the absorption of new technologies is then obvious; and it is quite possible to trace out in rough approximation at least the consequences for the aggregate performance of the economy induced by these multiple linkages.

Parenthetically, I would note that modern economic theory has focused on either the firm or the national economy; and it has not successfully linked micro- to macro-analysis. That is, in part, because it had no place in its formal structure for the analysis of sectors. Alfred Marshall wrestled with, but never solved, the problem with his representative firm and other devices. As an examination of any contemporary mainstream economic textbook reveals, modern economists generally ignore the problem. Behind this evasion is, explicitly or implicitly, the assumption of a Walrasian equilibrium in which, with technology and other Marshallian long-period factors fixed, labour and capital yield equal marginal returns in all uses. Indeed, with such assumptions, why bother with sectors?

Dynamic growth analysis, embracing the generation and absorption of new technologies, requires the sectors because it is in the sectors that the dynamism initially occurs, altering the marginal rates of return in substantial segments of the economy and, therefore, patterns of investment, the allocation of labour, and other structural and institutional characteristics of the economy. That is why serious economic history is full of sectoral analysis for which there is no counterpart in mainstream economic theory where, via micro- and macro-theory, we blithely take our students from 'one side of the moon – [to] the other without knowing what route or journey connects them'.[10]

In any case, my seminar students and I went about our business in the early 1950s by trying to link technological, sectoral, and aggregate analysis as we examined growth patterns, case by case. If any one country in this initial array of case studies was of particular importance, it was neither Britain nor the United States. It was Japan. Here was a nation rooted in a wholly non-western culture whose movement through the pre-conditions and take-off could be analysed within precisely the same framework – by answering the same matrix of questions – as the nations of the West. After Japan, the major Latin American countries and Turkey which entered take-off in the 1930s were most illuminating.

By 1955, having conducted projects and written books on Russia, China, and US policy towards Asia while teaching economic history,[11] and having worked over the concept for five years in my seminar and applied it – and seen it applied by my students to many countries – I was ready to write an article on 'The Take-off into Self-Sustained Growth'.[12]

THE DRIVE TO TECHNOLOGICAL MATURITY EMERGES

Up to this point I did not attempt to distinguish any stages beyond take-off and the arrival of self-sustained growth. This, for example, is the formulation in the 1956 *Economic Journal* article:[13]

> The sequence of economic development is taken to consist of three periods: a long period (up to a century or, conceivably, more) when the preconditions for take-off are established; the take-off itself, defined within two or three decades; and a long period when growth becomes normal and relatively automatic. These three divisions would, of course, not exclude the possibility of growth giving way to secular stagnation or decline in the long term.

But as I worked forward with my seminar students, two further definable stages emerged within the general rubric of self-sustained growth; the drive to technological maturity and high mass consumption. The former was defined as follows in *The Stages* (1960):[14]

> After take-off there follows a long interval of sustained if fluctuating progress, as the now regularly growing economy drives to extend modern technology over the whole front of its economic activity. Some 10–20% of the national income is steadily invested,

permitting output regularly to outstrip the increase in population. The make-up of the economy changes unceasingly as technique improves, new industries accelerate, older industries level off. The economy finds its place in the international economy: goods formerly imported are produced at home; new import requirements develop, and new export commodities to match them. The society makes such terms as it will with the requirements of modern efficient production, balancing off the new against the older values and institutions, or revising the latter in such ways as to support rather than to retard the growth process.

Some sixty years after take-off begins (say, forty years after the end of take-off) what may be called maturity is generally attained.

The essentially non-economic process behind this stage, permitting it to happen, is the build-up within the society of scientists and engineers, workers and entrepreneurs, foremen and managers, capable of absorbing – and motivated to absorb – the backlog of relevant, hitherto unapplied technologies. This implies not only an extension of education at every level and the emergence of a wide range of modernised institutions, but also a succession of generations each born into and taking for granted a technologically more sophisticated world. The upshot is the progressive diffusion, beyond the relatively few leading sectors of take-off (quite often confined to one or a few regions), of modern attitudes and motivations as well as modern technologies. The emphasis on the process by which the expanding backlog of technologies comes to be absorbed should be contrasted with the virtually universal assumption of mainstream economics that all profitable inventions are incorporated into the capital stock as innovations and, therefore, no technological backlog exists. Moreover, since neo-classical economics assumes that net value product is equated at the margin in all uses, it is quite unnecessary to consider the allocation of investment resources as opposed to the aggregate proportion of GNP invested and the over-all marginal capital-output ratio.

In the three academic years beginning in September 1955, as I elaborated and refined the processes beyong take-off, I directed a project and wrote a rather long book focused on the interplay of American domestic life and foreign policy.[15] It included a substantial introductory historical section covering that interplay from the beginning of the American republic to 1940. As I noted in the preface to *The United States in the World Arena*, it was my wife who suggested that I use the emerging, refined version of the stages of economic growth to help frame the analysis. (The other two concepts used for that purpose were the national style and the national interest.) *The Arena* went off to the publisher in August 1958; and we left for a sabbatical year in Cambridge, England.

It was initially my intention to use the year to begin writing a two-volume book on the stages of economic growth, embracing the full historical and contemporary evidence then available bearing on the concept; but I agreed to a request of the Cambridge economics faculty that I deliver eight lectures to undergraduates in the Michaelmas term of 1958 on 'The Process of Industrialisation' and packed what I had to say about the stages into those lectures. Since I wrote them during each week in a small office in the tower above the Marshall Library, for delivery on Friday mornings, they were rather fresh – a fact, I think, appreciated by students, who are shrewd in these matters.

After an interval in public service (1961–9), I returned to academic life, resumed in Austin my seminar on the history of the world economy, refining along the way my theory of economic growth and its various components, including the stages.

So far as the drive to technological maturity is concerned, those refinements can be tersely summarised as follows:

- The identification of the political and social problems which typically characterise the drive to technological maturity (and other stages).[16]
- The demonstration, from post-1945 experience, that the drive to technological maturity, typically requiring about forty years beyond take-off in the pre-Second World War era, could be transitted more briskly under appropriate conditions.[17]
- Confirmation from improved historical and cross-sectional statistical data that a sharp rise in the proportion of GNP invested occurred during take-off and a further rise in the drive to technological maturity after which the investment rate tended to level off.[18]
- Evidence from improved historical and cross-sectional statistical data that the drive to technological maturity was typically the stage characterised by the maximum rate of growth.[19]

DEFINING STAGES: GNP *PER CAPITA* VERSUS TECHNOLOGICAL VIRTUOSITY

Before turning to the contemporary relevance of the drive to technological maturity, it may be useful to compare briefly how stages of economic growth have come to be defined by the World Bank, by Kuznets and his followers, and by me.

The World Bank uses as its overriding criterion GNP *per capita* in constant US dollars.[20] It then arrays nations as 'low income', 'lower middle income', 'upper middle income', 'industrial market economies'. Aware that this criterion involves some important anomalies, the Bank provides some corrective calculations and categories. For example:

1. Calculations are presented indicating how GNP *per capita* would vary if purchasing power parity rather than exchange rates were used in making the conversion from local currencies into US dollars.
2. For unexplained reasons China and India are lumped together in a separate category as well as arrayed with other 'low income economies'. In my view, the separation is legitimate because these two most populous nations in the world combine vast low income rural sectors with some of the most technologically sophisticated industrial sectors in the developing world.
3. Oil exporters and importers are averaged separately as well as among 'middle-income economies'. This is presumably because the World Bank is conscious that, depending on the oil price, an oil export or import position can distort the implied linkage between GNP *per capita* and stage of development. 'High income oil exporters' are also separated out to distinguish them from poorer developing countries which export oil (e.g. Nigeria, Indonesia).
4. 'East European Non Market Economies' are separately presented because of dollar conversion and more general data difficulties.

Kuznets, in his apparently head-on, across-the-board clash with my concept of take-off at Konstanz, argued rather modestly in the end that the data were simply not sufficient as of 1960 to validate the assumed course of the investment rate and that the concept of entrance into the 'early phase of modern growth' was a better designation than 'take-off'.[21]

But an important difference did exist between us. It lay in his insistence on measuring the critical transition primarily in terms of a sustained rise in income *per capita* and a shift of labour out of agriculture *versus* my insistence that such aggregate movements reflected a deeper process which required explicit analysis; i.e., the absorption of new technologies in particular sectors which, along with their multiple linkages, accounted for the structural changes Kuznets used to identify modern economic growth.[22] Here is Kuznets' summary statement of his criteria.[23]

> Let us begin by agreeing that modern economic growth displays certain observable and measurable characteristics, which in combination are distinctive to it, i.e., were not evident in earlier economic epochs... What these characterics are is a matter for discussion; but I believe that agreement could easily be reached on some of them, e.g., those relating to rates of growth of national product, total and *per capita*, and to structural shifts that commonly accompany them. Let us assume for purposes of illustration that identification of such growth requires a minimum rise in *per capita* income sustained over a period of at least two or three decades, a minimum shift away from agriculture, and any other identifiable indispensable components of modern economic growth that we may specify.

Later Kuznets used the single criterion of accelerated urbanisation to date 'the beginning of modern growth' emerging with dates virtually identical with my dates for the beginning of take off.[24]

Kuznets himself did not define stages beyond the beginning of modern growth; but Ohkawa and Rosovsky, in an evidently Kuznetsian spirit, arrayed three phases of modern growth in Japan in a fashion easily reconciled with my stages, the dating being, for all intents and purposes, identical.[25]

The primary criterion for defining my stages of growth, up to the stage of high mass consumption (which is a joint product of the level of consumption *per capita* and the income elasticity of demand), is the degree to which an economy has or has not absorbed efficiently the pool of then existing technology relevant to its natural resource base and the sectoral structure of its economy.

OHKAWA–ROSOVSKY	WWR STAGES OF GROWTH
A. The First Modern Phase of Modern Economic Growth, 1868–1905	
I. Transition, 1868–85	Pre-conditions for take-off (late period)
II. Initial Modern Economic Growth, 1886–1905	Take-off
B. The Second Phase of Modern Economic Growth, 1906–52	Drive to technological maturity (choice of military option; postwar recovery; completion technological maturity on civil basis)
III. Differential Structure: Creation, 1906–30	
IV. Differential Structure: Economic and Political Consequences, 1931–52	
C. The Third Phase of Modern Economic Growth, 1953–present	High mass-consumption

Thus, the difference between Kuznets' approach to growth measurement and mine is simple enough. Kuznets and I wholly agreed that the systematic application of science and technology to specific sectors was the basis for the sustained rise in real income *per capita* and structural change that distinguished modern growth from all previous history. By his own description, 'frustrated' by the difficulties of measuring formally the generation and sectoral diffusion of technology, he settled for GNP *per capita* and structural change, notably under the highly aggregated headings of primary, secondary, and service sectors.[26]

Although Chenery has refined these categories somewhat and, especially, characterised growth patterns according to the development strategy pursued, he has generally dealt with technological absorption on a highly aggregated structural basis.

Using statistical and other data, I have preferred to deal with the evolution of national economies by disaggregating down to the sectors in which the major technologies are actually introduced and then linking sectoral to aggregate national income analysis and structural change. In effect, Part Five of my *World Economy: History and Prospect*, covering the history of twenty countries, containing about two-thirds of the world's population, generating perhaps 80 per cent of global product, is a sustained exercise in that method. This disaggregated approach, coming to rest on the rapidly changing pool of existing technologies, is, I believe, highly relevant to the three contemporary issues to which we now turn.

IMPLICATIONS FOR INTERNATIONAL DEVELOPMENT POLICY

The first of these issues is development policy. It arises because, as noted earlier, most of the population of the developing regions lives in countries experiencing the drive to technological maturity. By the method of identification I applied in *The World Economy*, this group includes China and India; the major countries of Latin America, a considerable group of countries in the Pacific Basin (e.g., Taiwan and South Korea); Turkey and, potentially, some other countries of the Middle East now caught up in the tragic pathology of the region.

This is a quite different state of affairs than in the 1950s when a good deal of development thought and policy was generated and, to a degree, institutionalised. Then most of the developing world (including China and India) was struggling to get into take-off, moving through, or completing that phase. Under heavy pressure from relatively falling export prices for basic commodities after 1951, some of the Latin American countries were also experiencing rapid deceleration in their leading sectors of take-off. They were, it turned out, in a rather painful transition to the more diversified and sophisticated technologies and sectors of the drive to technology maturity, a fact which became apparent in the 1960s. Turkey was in a similar transition.

In his engaging Presidential Address delivered at the meeting of the American Economic Association in December 1983, W. Arthur Lewis cited the following 'list of new models invented by development economists of the 1950s and 1960s':[27]

Two-gap model	dependency
unbalanced growth	indicative planning
vent for surplus	appropriate technology

Dutch disease	big push
dual economy	growth pole
disguised unemployment	rising savings ratio
structural inflation	low-level equilibrium trap

Almost all of these concepts arose from analyses of countries struggling to move from what I would call the pre-conditions for take-off into the take-off or to make the transition from take-off into the drive to technological maturity. After that transition, one hoped, they could rely increasingly on private international capital markets, rather than official aid, to supplement capital formation from domestic sources. And to a significant degree that has happened.

The developing world can now be roughly split between countries in or beyond take-off and those often hard cases which have not yet entered take-off; and this fact is, indeed, reflected in the increasing reliance of the former group on private rather than official capital imports.[28]

The shift of the more advanced developing nations to private capital markets has not, of course, ended the need for formulating international development policies towards them. Immediate problems posed for such nations by excessive debts, slow OECD growth, high OECD unemployment, and the consequent rise of protectionism are all on the agenda and by no means resolved. Before the debt burden is somehow lifted and rapid growth resumed in the more advanced developing nations (with important advantages to the OECD countries) large additional official as well as private aid transfers will be required; although higher OECD growth rates and lower interest rates combined with liberal trading arrangements would do just as well in most cases.

We shall return to OECD relations with developing countries in the drive to technological maturity in dealing with the second issue of policy identified in this paper. Before doing so, I would note one problem of domestic development policy which has risen autonomously in more advanced developing countries in every region; i.e., the need to shift the balance in the economy from the state to the private sector, from planning to market.

The existence of excessively large public sectors resulted from the convergence of technical economic and political forces and certain strongly held attitudes in the developing countries of the 1950s.

On the economic side, there was the pattern, set for some in the 1930s by the inability to earn or borrow, at tolerable rates, sufficient foreign exchange to avoid highly protectionist import substitution policies. These led directly to insufficient competition in domestic markets, idle industrial capacity, damping the entrepreneurial quality of both the private and public sectors. Foreign exchange rationing was also a policy that required large powerful bureaucracies to decide what should be imported. In many countries that process was the heart of what passed for 'planning'. On the political side there was the fear of explosions in the volatile cities and a decision, in effect, to exploit the farmer on behalf of the urban population. This had, of course, the effect of reducing incentives in the agricultural sector and slowing the rate of increase of agricultural production, forcing increased grain imports at the expense of manufactured good imports required for industrial development.

With respect to attitudes, the 1950s were times when, on balance, capitalism was an unpopular word, socialism a popular word among the educated elite in the developing regions. Capitalism was associated with colonial or quasi-colonial status, representing an intrusive external power. There was also considerable sentimental appeal in socialism during the 1950s: some of the European social democratic governments were doing quite well; Mao's Great Leap forward and Chinese Communist policy in general generated a considerable appeal among those who did not investigate it too deeply; and even Khrushchev's boast that the USSR would soon outstrip the US in total output had a certain credibility in the late 1950s. To all this one can add that many of the emerging political leaders were intellectuals or soldiers, both types inherently suspicious of the market process and inclined, for different reasons, to have excessive faith in the powers of government administration.

Obviously, the answer now is not and should not be a compulsive Friedmanesque reliance on the market process. But the time has come to examine afresh and sceptically the accumulated economic functions of government, and to strike new balances between the public and private sectors – balances which would exploit the potentialities of private enterprise and competitive markets a good deal more than they are exploited at present.

The drive to technological maturity is peculiarly relevant to the public-private sector balance because public authorities have proved everywhere clumsy and inefficient in trying to manage the production of the increasingly diversified manufactures which characterise the drive to technological maturity; and, much more than was the case a generation ago, the private entrepreneurs now exist in the developing world capable of producing diversified industrial products competitively for world markets.

Although this complex and rather sophisticated set of problems confronts a good many countries in the drive to technological maturity, others have still not moved into take-off. Indeed, some of these, notably in Africa, have regressed in terms of real income *per capita* in recent years.

Their plight was made vivid by a question put to me by an African agricultural technician attending an international centre in India where I spoke in 1983. He said in effect: 'Many African countries became independent twenty years ago but have not entered take-off. What's wrong with your theory?' When laughter had subsided I discussed the wide range of mainly non-economic forces which have historically determined the length of the period I call the preconditions for take-off; short for Japan (thirty-two years from Commodore Perry's arrival, only seventeen from the Meiji Restoration); long for China (110 years from the Opium Wars), even longer for Mexico (120 years from independence). Evidently no uniform time period could be defined for developing the pre-conditions for take-off. I concluded that, basically, the people of each country, suffused with their respective cultural, social, and political heritages, would determine if, when, and how their entrance into sustained growth would begin; each case would be different; but the advanced countries – especially their development economists – owed the lagging aspirants more thought and attention than they had been thus far given plus a good deal of patience. The African heritage, including arbitrary boundaries derived from colonial history, was likely to make the interval between independence and take-off rather long but, I would guess, less than for China or Mexico.

By definition, the problems the Africans confront are extremely difficult. If not, they would have long since been solved given the aspirations of the people, the efforts of many dedicated men and women on the spot, and almost forty years of sustained international political and social science attention to development.

These laggard cases, of course, transcend Africa. At one end of old Hispaniola is the Dominican Republic whose political and economic progress since 1965 far exceeds the visions of the greatest optimists, of whom there were few; at the other end, Haiti. There are the two Yemens, Burma, and Bangladesh. And, intellectually as challenging as any, the Pacific Islands, some of which are even denied tourism by their geography.

A part of the challenge posed by these hard cases is that our profession cannot usefully come to grips with them unless we economists are willing to make cultural, social, and political factors – as well as history – a living part of our analyses. We paid a price in our studies of and prescriptions for more advanced developing countries when we set these factors aside, as we have often done. But still we could find areas of usefulness. This is much less likely to be the case in analyses of the pre-conditions for take-off.[29]

But my point here is that the emergence of a large part of the developing world into the drive to technological maturity has dramatised the wide range of countries we have traditionally included in the rubric 'developing'. *The World Development Report, 1986* records among countries called 'developing' a GNP *per capita* range from $110 (1984) *per annum* (Ethiopia) for $7260 (Singapore). (This range of 1 to 66 compares to a range of less than 1 to 4 among 'industrial market economies'.) The average for 'low income' developing countries is $260; for 'upper middle income', $1950. Clearly, in dealing with a spectrum of this sweep a uniform 'development economics' does not suffice. Shiva Naipaul wrote: 'To blandly subsume, say, Ethiopia, India, and Brazil under the one banner of Third Worldhood is as absurd and as denigrating as the old assertion that all Chinese look alike. People only look alike when you can't be bothered to look at them too closely.'[30]

So far as development aid policy is concerned, the major conclusion is that, while each country, like each student or doctor's patient is unique, we need, broadly, two types of policy: one addressed to pre-take-off countries, the other to countries in the drive to technological maturity, a subject to which we now turn.

BROAD IMPLICATIONS OF THE CONTEMPORARY DRIVE TO TECHNOLOGICAL MATURITY FOR OECD RELATIONS WITH DEVELOPING REGIONS

My second proposition is that the developing countries now in the drive to technological maturity are destined to be at once a major source of trade and growth for the OECD world and a major challenge to its primacy. This is because they can be expected to experience their maximum growth rates; and these are almost certain to be higher than those in OECD. These countries are also moving quickly into a position where they will be able to absorb the technologies of the Fourth Industrial Revolution (microelectronics, genetic engineering, etc.). This is, in one sense, repetition of an old story. Britain, for example, experienced a mixture of economic opportunities and strains as the United States, Belgium, Germany, France, and Italy acquired the technologies of the Second Industrial Revolution (railroads, steel, etc.). The Atlantic world as a whole confronted a similar adjustment when Japan and Russia acquired those of the Third (electricity, internal combustion, chemicals, etc.). Now the whole of the industrial North confronts in the decades ahead a parallel challenge as the more advanced countries of Latin America (led by Brazil), of the Pacific Basin (including China), plus India, having pretty well caught up with the first three industrial revolutions, acquire the fourth.

This proposition requires a bit of elaboration. First, then, growth rates. Table 7.1 and Figure 7.1 exhibit the behaviour of growth rates *per capita* in relation to real income levels (and roughly equivalent stages of growth) for the period 1960–70. Historical sequences of growth rates exhibit similar patterns of rise and subsidence with the growth rate surge of 1950–72 something of an explicable exception in the OECD world.[31]

The reason for the peak growth rates during the drive to technological maturity is, as suggested earlier, that the progressive expansion in the size and quality of the cadres of entrepreneurs, engineers,

Table 7.1 Income levels and growth rates, 1960–70

	Population 1967 (millions)	GNP per capita 1967 US $	Average Annual Growth Rate 1960–70	Approximate Stage of Growth
		$	%	
United States	199	3,670	3–2	High mass consumption
Group 1 ($1,750–$3,670)	307	3,120	3–3	
Group 2 ($1,000–$1,750)	238	1,490	3–5	
Group 3 ($700–$1,000)	444	930	6–5	Drive to technological maturity
Group 4 ($400–$700)	161	550	4–4	
Group 5 ($200–$400)	299	270	2–9	
Group 6 ($100–$200)	376	130	2–6	Take-off pre-conditions
Group 7 ($50–$100)	1,580	90	1–7	
World	3,391	610	3–2	

Source: Thornkil Kristensen, *Development in Rich and Poor countries* (New York, 1974), pp. 156–9. Stages added by W.W.R.

Figure 7.1 Income levels, annual growth rates, and approximate stage of growth, 1960–70

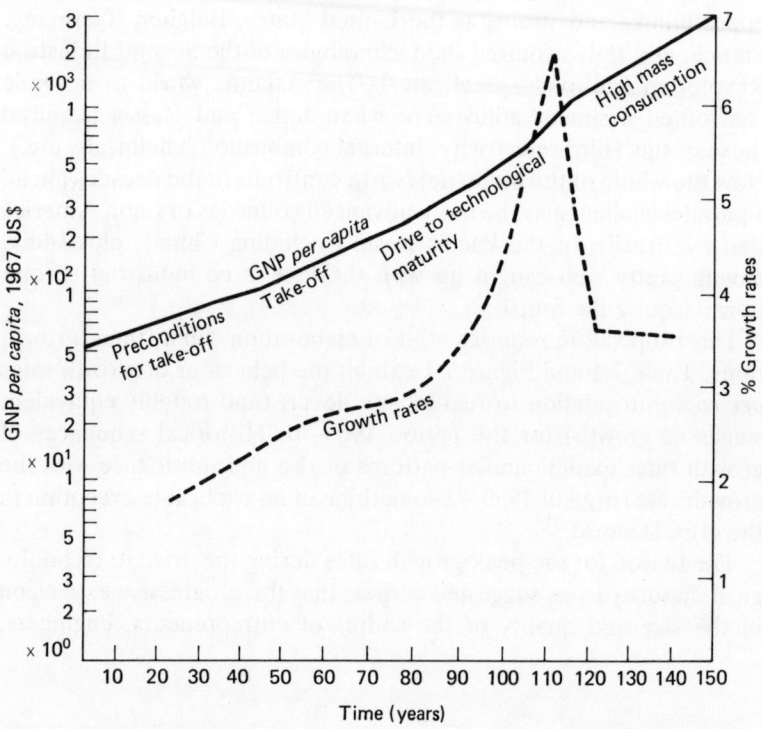

Source: same as for Table 7.1.

Note: The US price level (GNP deflator) increased by approximately 3 times between 1967 and the third quarter of 1986.

foremen, skilled workers, etc. increases the society's capacity to absorb rapidly the backlog of unapplied technologies. That accelerated absorption elevates growth rates in the affected sectors and those linked to them. The investment rate rises not because the savings rate rises with the rise in average income *per capita*, as the generalised Keynesian consumption function suggests, but because profits rise in the new, more sophisticated, fast-moving leading sectors; and a high proportion of profits are ploughed back by ebullient entrepreneurs. Thus, as I have argued since the 1956 Take-off article, rising investment rates are substantially a result of accelerated growth *via* the absorption of new technologies in key sectors, rather than its initiating cause.[32]

The question then arises: Are the more advanced developing countries likely to be able to absorb and apply efficiently the technologies of the Fourth Industrial Revolution? These technologies have four distinctive characteristics: they are closely linked to areas of basic science also undergoing revolutionary change; they are galvanising the old basic industries as well as agriculture, forestry, animal husbandry, and the whole range of services; they are immediately relevant to developing countries to a degree depending on their stage of growth; and they are each so diversified that no single country is likely to dominate them as, for example, Britain dominated the early stage of cotton textiles and the United States the early stage of the mass produced automobile.

Meanwhile, the developing regions have been mounting a human revolution of their own. Overall, the proportion of the population aged 20–24 enrolled in higher education in what the World Bank calls 'lower middle income' countries rose from 3 to 10 per cent between 1960 and 1982; for 'upper middle income' countries the increase was from 4 to 14 per cent. The increase in India, with low income *per capita* but a vital educational system, was from 3 to 9 per cent. For Brazil, fated to be a major actor in this drama, the increase from 1965 to 1982 was from 2 to 12 per cent. To understand the meaning of these figures it should be recalled that in 1960 the proportion for the UK was 9 per cent, for Japan 10 per cent.

There has been, moreover, a radical shift towards science and engineering. In India, for example, the pool of scientists and engineers has increased from about 190 000 in 1960 to 2.4 million in 1984 – a critical mass only exceeded in the United States and the Soviet Union. In Mexico, for example, the annual average increase in Mexican graduates in natural science was about 3 per cent, in engineering 5 per cent, in the period 1957 to 1973. From 1973 to 1981 the comparable figures were 14 per cent to 24 per cent, respectively – an astonishing almost five-fold acceleration.

Even discounting for problems of educational quality, the potential absorptive capacity for the new technologies in the more advanced developing countries is high. Their central problem – like that of most advanced industrial countries – is how to make effective the increasingly abundant scientific and engineering skills they already command. This requires, in turn, an ability to generate and maintain effective, flexible, interactive partnerships among scientists, engineers, entrepreneurs, and the working force.

I would guess that, despite current vicissitudes, the developing countries of the Pacific Basin (including China), India, and those containing most of the population of Latin America will absorb the new technologies and move rapidly forward over the next several generations. Much the same would happen, I believe, if the Middle East could find its way from its chronic, tragic bloodletting to a twentieth-century version of the Treaty of Westphalia.

Thus, if my view of what lies ahead is broadly correct, and the late-comers continue to gain ground, the world economy and policy face an adjustment familiar in character but unprecedented in scale. The advanced industrial countries (including the USSR and Eastern Europe) now constitute about 1.1 billion people, or, say, 24 per cent of the world's population. At least 2.6 billion people, or about 56 per cent, live in countries which will, I would guess, acquire technological virtuosity within the next half century. Moreover, population, in the decades ahead, will increase more rapidly in the latter than the former group. We are talking about a great historical transformation.

The phenomenon of poor countries catching up with the rich goes back, in fact, at least three centuries from, say, the rise of Britain relative to the initially more advanced Netherlands and France. But the dynamics of the process has attracted less attention than it deserves.

David Hume was, at once, the first analysis of what has been called the rich country–poor country problem and the most eloquent advocate of reconciliation rather than confrontation.[33]

> It ought ... to be considered, that, by the encrease of the industry among the neighbouring nations, the consumption of every particular species of commodity is also encreased; and though foreign manufactures interfere with them in the market, the demand for their product may still continue, or even encrease. And should it diminish, ought the consequence to be esteemed so fatal? If the spirit of industry be preserved, it may easily be diverted from one branch to another; and the manufacturers of wool, for instance, be employed in linen, silk, iron, or any other commodities, for which there appears to be a demand. We need not apprehend, that all the objects of industry will be exhausted, or that our manufacturers, while they remain on an equal footing with those of our neighbours, will be in danger of wanting employment. The emulation among rival nations serves rather to keep industry alive in all of

them.... I shall therefore venture to acknowledge, that, not only as a man, but as a British subject, I pray for the flourishing commerce of Germany, Spain, Italy and even France itself. I am at least certain, that Great Britain, and all those nations, would flourish more, did their sovereigns and ministers adopt such enlarged and benevolent sentiments towards each other...

Nor needs any state entertain apprehensions, that their neighbours will improve to such a degree in every art and manufacture, as to have no demand for them. Nature, by giving a diversity of geniuses, climates, and soils, to different nations, has secured their mutual intercourse and commerce, as long as they all remain industrious and civilized.

Hume's elaboration of his argument came to rest on two propositions for the short and medium run:

1. the composition of trade would change, but the rich country should benefit in an open trading system from the two-way expansion of trade with the up-and-coming poor country; but
2. to cope with the inevitably increased competition in certain sectors, the rich country would have to adjust its output and use of resources, exploiting its advantages in 'the mechanic arts', transport facilities, banking institutions, etc.

In the long run, Hume granted that economic leadership might prove transient; but he regarded that proposition as part of a philosophy of history rather than a guide to current policy.

Adam Smith's position on the rich country-poor country problem was close to Hume's but not identical.

1. A rich country had a number of inherent advantages over a poor country which ought to permit it to retain its lead, barring failure to conduct correct policies.
2. Despite higher real wage rates, these advantages included lower unit labour costs, resulting from the greater division of labour, in turn made possible by the abundance and cheapness of capital. They included also a more elaborate and efficient transport system, reducing the relative prices of basic commodities.
3. Therefore, a rich country could afford to move towards free trade where it would enjoy the advantages of a large and productive commerce with its partners in the world economy, even with its potential military adversaries.

The flavour of Smith's views is well captured in the following passages:[34]

> The more opulent therefore the society, labour will always be so much dearer and work so much cheaper, and if some opulent countries have lost several of their manufacturers and some branches of their commerce by having been undersold in foreign markets by the traders and artisans of poorer countries, who were contented with less profit and smaller wages, this will rarely be found to have been merely the effect of the opulence of one country and the poverty of the other. Some other cause, we may be assured, must have concurred. The rich country must have been guilty of some error in its police [policy].
>
> A nation that would enrich itself by foreign trade, is certainly most likely to do so when its neighbours are all rich, industrious, and commercial nations. A great nation surrounded on all sides by wandering savages and poor barbarians might, no doubt, acquire riches by the cultivation of its own lands, and by its own interior commerce, but not by foreign trade.

With Britain's primal take-off of the 1780s and its post-1815 widened lead in the new technologies, the rich country-poor country debate shifted to the legitimacy of tariff protection for infant industries in a country lagging technologically behind the front runner. The seriousness of the issue was heightened by the perception of Alexander Hamilton in 1791 that more than money was at stake:[35] 'Not only the wealth but the independence and security of a country appear to be materially connected with the prosperity of manufactures.' By and large, Hamilton's formula, with its security as well as welfare strand, was to be the fundamental rationale for industrialisation in relatively underdeveloped countries over the subsequent two centuries. It was first accepted in countries of the Atlantic world conscious by 1815 of the widened technological gap with Britain. Thus the American and Continental tariffs of the post-Napoleonic period.

Britain was the only nation to move into take-off in the first graduating class in the last quarter of the eighteenth century. The next graduating class of, say, the second quarter of the nineteenth century included the United States, Belgium, France, and Germany. It was the movement of this second class to the drive to technological maturity – the stage beyond take-off – that revived the rich country–poor country anxiety in Britain. In the last quarter of the nineteenth century, post-Civil War America drove its railroads to the Pacific, rounded them out with feeder lines, and pushed population to the limits of the frontier; Bismark consolidated his empire, which exploited fully its potentialities in the age of coal and steel, surpassing British steel production in the 1880s. Britain became conscious that its time of lonely primacy was passing and that late-comers did indeed command the potentiality of catching up with early-comers. Alfred Marshall was one of the most thoughtful commentators on the process. He reflected not only on the long run industrial prospects of the United States, Germany, and France but also of the British dominions and Japan, Russia and China (with 'great futures'), and India.[36]

In the more than two centuries since Hume generated a lively discussion among his contemporaries of the rich country–poor country problem, two important empirical studies bearing directly on the economic issues it poses were conducted: *Industrialization and Foreign Trade*, mainly the work of Folke Hilgerdt, and Eugene Staley's *World Economic Development*.[37] They were products of the League of Nations and the International Labour Office, respectively, as their secretariats looked to the future with considerable prescience during the Second World War. Hilgerdt's study constitutes, in effect, a systematic analytic test of Hume's propositions, based on statistical data covering the years 1870–1938.

Its three major findings were:[38]

first, that until about 1930 the growth of manufacturing, far from rendering countries independent of foreign manufactured goods, stimulated the import of such goods;

secondly, that again up to about 1930, those countries in which manufacturing developed most rapidly as a rule increased their imports of manufactured goods more than did other countries; and

thirdly, that after the breakdown of multilateral trade early in the 'thirties', this relationship between the growth of industry and of trade in manufactured goods was severed.

But Hilgerdt's story was distorted by the pathology of the inter-war years as well as by the autarchic economic policies of the Soviet Union. Nevertheless, the process of mutual adjustment envisaged by Hume went on and is well captured in Hilgerdt's conclusion on the

186 Reflections on the Drive to Technological Maturity

Figure 7.2 Four graduating classes into take-off: stages of economic growth, twenty countries

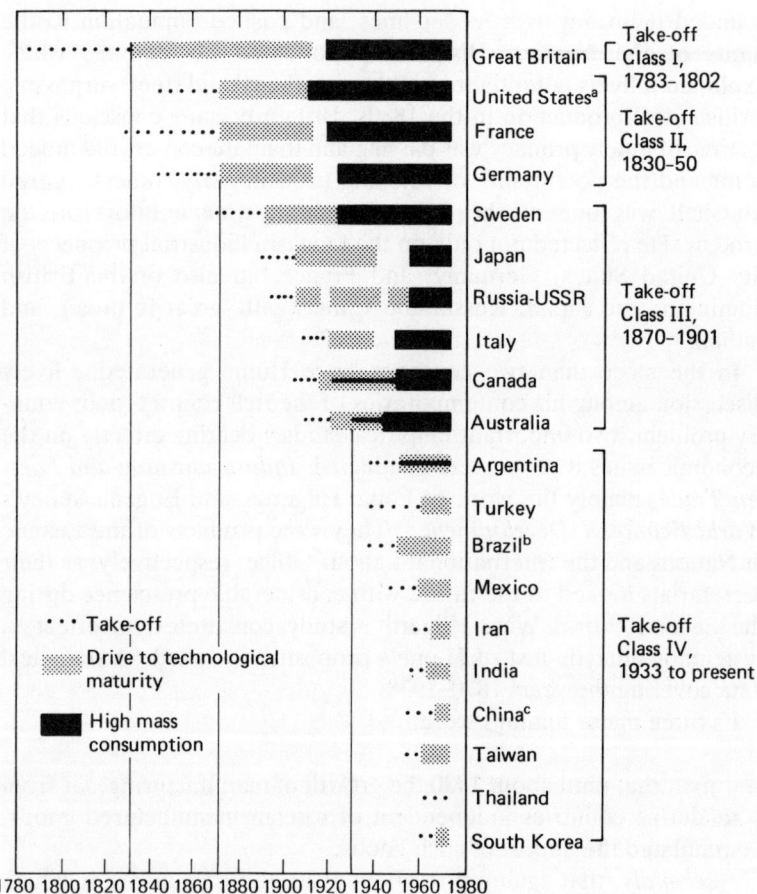

Notes: [a] New England regional take-off, 1815–50.
[b] São Paulo regional take-off, 1900–20.
[c] Manchuria regional take-off, 1930–41.

Source: See *The World Economy: History and Prospect* (Austin: University of Texas Press, 1978), p. 51 and Part Five.

changing composition of manufactures as 'poor countries' industrialise, and on the related problem of 'adaptation' in 'rich countries'.[39]

While normally the import from older industrial countries is thus not likely to decline as a result of industrial growth elsewhere, these imports are likely to change in character, for the countries in which industry develops will diversify their demand for consumption goods and increase their demand for manufactured capital goods. Different supplying countries will thus be differently affected; and even those able to raise their sales may experience some difficulty in affecting the necessary adaptation. Under normal conditions, however, time for adaptation is likely to be afforded, for in the majority of countries, particularly those with a dense population, there are strong forces resisting the industrial development which is accordingly, as a rule, relatively slow.

The resistance to industrial development appears to have diminished sharply in the second half of the twentieth century.

Staley's substantial monograph is, in fact, a policy manual on the rich country–poor country problem. His objective was to define policies which would yield the greatest mutual benefit to advanced industrial and developing countries. With a barrage of statistical data he drove home the first of Hume's *dicta*; i.e., growth in less advanced countries enlarges exports from more advanced countries to adjust to the expanded competitive exports of the rising, less advanced countries.

The take-offs of the major Latin American countries and Turkey, beginning in the 1930s, inaugurate the fourth graduating class. They were joined in the 1950s and 1960s by India and China as well as by the extraordinarily dynamic smaller countries along the western rim of the Pacific. Although strongly affected by the rise and subsidence of the relative price of oil, their role in the world trade for the period from the early 1960s to the early 1980s broadly validates the three basic Hilgerdt propositions:

1. The period down to 1981 was marked by an extraordinary expansion in manufactured exports from developing countries;
2. This surge was accompanied by continued high (but lesser) rates of increase in exports of manufacturers to developing countries;
3. There was an evident sensitivity of exports from developing countries to the rate of growth of advanced industrial countries; but the shift towards manufactured exports altered the relationship.

This diversification away from primary products does not mean that foreign demand no longer matters. Developing countries depend on developed-country markets for their manufactured exports; short-run fluctuations in the demand for their exports due to fluctuations in growth in industrial countries can still be important. But the diversification of exports toward manufactures has changed the medium- and long-run competitive position of developing-country exports in developed-country markets ... Developing-country exports increased twice as fast in relation to developed-country income in the 1970s; for each 1 percent change in real income in developed countries, the volume of developing-country exports increased by only 0.9 percent in the 1960s, but by 1.7 percent in the 1970s.[40]

As we all know, things have not gone as well in the 1980s. Both the rich and poor have slowed down to their mutual disadvantage, under the weight of chronic high unemployment in the Atlantic community and severe debt problems in important parts of the developing regions. Protectionist pressures have palpably strengthened. The world economy, taken as a whole, does not appear particularly industrious or civilised.

HOW TO ORGANISE AN INDUSTRIOUS AND CIVILISED WORLD ECONOMY

Jean Monnet used to say that nations should not come together to negotiate but to stare at a common problem. When they have explored the problem together a solution will emerge. When the solution is translated into action, legitimate areas for negotiation will naturally appear at the margin.

Right now we are dealing, after a fashion, with some of the most acute short-run problems in the world economy. We are, for example, buying time by rolling over the international debts of important developing countries; and we have co-operated to bring the dollar down closer to purchasing power parity. But we are still far from long-run solutions to these problems, and others are being swept under the rug. International gatherings of Common Market and OECD leaders – let alone the United Nations – are still mainly dialogues of the deaf. In good part, that is because we are without a clear agreed vision of our great common problem. Lacking a common vision working politicians concentrate on the short-run idiosyncratic problems of their own economies and their possible impact on the next election. Such parochial considerations never wholly disappear. But solutions to national problems would come easier if consensus were reached that the great long run common task is to work together to assure that the inevitable transition in the contours of the world economy takes place without either a neo-mercantilist fragmentation or war, both of which are clearly possible. When we stare at the hard, inescapable facts long enough, the solution likely to emerge – if we have the will to seize it – is to set about organising together an industrious and civilised world economy which will exploit the large constructive opportunities open to us and fend off the dangers. One of the straightforward, immediate common interests that should render this vision potentially attractive even to the least visionary politicians is the significant degree to which prosperity in developing countries still depends on momentum in the advanced industrial countries and the fact that high momentum in the countries moving well through the drive to technological maturity should render exports to those countries a substantial leading sector in the next OECD boom.

Briefly, the larger task of Humeian reconciliation has three dimensions. First, within the advanced industrial countries there must be an acceptance of the fact that the great era of expansion of the welfare state (from, say, the 1870s to the 1970s) is over. Historians are likely to judge a limit was reached in the mid-1970s when the great surge, which had brought welfare outlays in the major OECD countries from 14 per cent of GNP to 24 per cent, peaked out. Politics addressed to the division of a pie assumed to be automatically expanding must give way in significant degree to concerted national efforts to assure the pie will continue to expand.[41]

Secondly, if we are to find solid ground between hegemony and chaos, something new and difficult but not impossible will be required. Western Europe, Japan, and the United States will have to generate the collective leadership no one can now provide on his own. They will have to work with each other and the developing regions to exploit the possibilities and make the peaceful adjustments cooperation could render realistic and mutually profitable.[42]

Thirdly, the intensified cooperation required between the more and less advanced nations requires some institutional innovation. Although I can not argue the case fully here, I am inclined to believe that the process of adjustment is likely to be pursued most effectively through greatly strengthened regional organisations containing societies at different stages of modernisation. The United Nations, as a whole, is too big for serious business and lends itself to sterile and over-simplified political polarisation. Regional organisations are smaller, closer to the day-to-day pragmatic problems which must be solved and, potentially, their operation can be softened and the risk of confrontation reduced by a sense of a neighbourhood.

Specifically, strengthened enterprises should be encouraged in the Pacific Basin, the Western Hemisphere, and Euro-Africa. In happier times, a Middle East regional organisation might be envisaged and one for South Asia, the basis for which already exists. In the Pacific Basin, the Asian Development Bank might be the organising centre; in Latin America, the Inter-American Development Bank and the OAS; in Africa, the African Development Bank and OAU. The World Bank and IMF would engage actively in each region. The advanced industrial countries might work with all these groupings although their relative roles would evidently vary with their historic and current interests.

There would be no lack of items for serious regional agendas: urgent debt, trade, and balance-of-payment problems; cooperative exploration of possible applications of new technologies; cooperation to deal with acute environmental problems; and cooperation in assisting the pre-take-off hard cases in which more advanced developing countries of the region should play a major role.

IMPLICATIONS FOR THE COLD WAR[43]

Historically, completion of the drive to technological maturity has proven to be a dangerous age. We have seen in this century two efforts by Germany, one by Japan, and one by Russia to seek hegemony in their regions when they, as late-comers, finally caught up technologically with early-comers, and were led to challenge the primacy they had earlier established. As its imperialist stirrings round about the turn of the twentieth century suggest, the United States was by no means exempt from this temptation to assert itself in the global arena of power and did not wholly resist that temptation.

Evidently in a nuclear age, both the pursuit of hegemony by a new major power and the defence of their interests by resistant older powers must be conducted with restraint if a cataclysm for the human race is to be avoided. Thus, the Cold War has proceeded now for four dreary decades in three rough cycles marked by successive phases of vigorous but still cautious Soviet efforts to exploit perceived laxness or weakness in the non-communist world and belated and rather restrained efforts to retrieve their positions by the United States and others who shared its interest in preventing Soviet hegemony in Europe, Asia, or elsewhere. We are now in the third relatively quiet interval in the Cold War, the other two being 1953–5 and 1969–72. The question is: can we convert this interval into a progressive liquidation of the Cold War or will we behave in such a way as to induce a fourth downswing? Is a soft landing possible? The answer relates in part to a fairly steady trend which operated quietly as these noisy, dangerous, and often bloody cyclical phases proceeded; i.e., the diffusion of effective power away from both the United States and the Soviet Union. This resulted not only from higher postwar growth rates in Western Europe and Japan than in the United States – and their catching up in technological virtuosity – but also from the dynamism of the developing countries that moved successfully into technological maturity. The combined total of US and USSR GNP may have declined from about 44 per cent to 33 per cent of the global product between 1950 and 1980.

First, Soviet difficulty in absorbing effectively the new technologies and, more broadly, reversing the protracted decline in the productivity of its economy poses searching political and institutional problems which may divert its energies to domestic concerns unless the non-communist world provides temptations to adventure too attractive to resist, too easy to exploit.

Secondly, the dynamism of the countries caught up in the drive to technological maturity is likely to strengthen a perception already widespread in Moscow; namely, that the power of nationalism, the diffusion to the developing regions of increasingly sophisticated technologies, and the diminished attraction of communist development dogma and methods make it increasingly clear that the emerging world community is not going to be dominated by the Soviet Union or by any other single power.

Thirdly, if the non-communist world can mount a reasonable approximation of the three-dimensional policy required to fulfil Hume's injunction to be 'industrious and civilised', a rather good foundation exists for initiating evenhanded, serious negotiations with Moscow to bring the Cold War peacefully to an end.

The narrower conclusion to be drawn is for development economists. In retrospect, the pioneers of development economics of the 1950s focused sharply (and understandably) on how to make the transition into Simon Kuznets' Modern Economic Growth, Arthur Lewis' Industrial Revolution, Paul Rosenstein-Rodan's Big Push, my Take-off. Our common task two generations later is to understand better and prescribe more wisely for two cases: where the preconditions for take-off have proved particularly difficult and for the drive to technological maturity.

Notes

1. Neustadt, Richard E., and May, Ernest R., *Thinking in Time: The Uses of History for Decision-Makers* (New York, The Free Press, 1986), p. 207.
2. Rostow, W.W., (ed.), *The Economics of Take-off into Sustained Growth* (London, Macmillan, 1963), p. xiii.
3. For those who may be interested, my responses to critics are to be found (beyond the Konstanz volume) in *The Stages of Economic Growth* (Cambridge, Cambridge: at the University Press, 1971) (2nd edn), Appendix B; *The World Economy: History and Prospect* (Austin, University of Texas Press, 1978), pp. 778–9 (note 2); 'Development: The Political Economy of the Marshallian Long Period' in Meier, Gerald M., and Seers Dudley, (eds) *Pioneers in Development* (New York, Oxford University Press, 1984), pp. 232–7 and 247–9; and my review of Maddison, Angus, *Phases of Capitalist Development*, in *The Journal of Economic History*, December 1985, vol. 45, no. 4, pp. 1027–8.
4. I say 'little discussed' because a recent study substantially focused on 'semi-industrial' countries is much concerned with what I would call the drive to technological maturity. The study is: Chenery, Hollis, Syrquin Moise, and Robinson, Scott, *Industrialization and Economic Growth* (New York, Oxford University Press, for the World Bank, 1986). Balassa, Bela, *The Newly Industrializing Countries in the World Economy* (New York: Pergamon Press, 1981) is also focused on specific countries beyond take-off. These valuable studies, however, are primarily concerned with the relative success of export-oriented (if not export-led) growth patterns. Chenery and his colleagues have more to say about the progressive absorption of sophisticated technologies than Balassa; but their method for dealing with the degree of technological absorption in the course of the whole growth tension is highly aggregated; i.e., via the relative scale of 'intermediate' industrial production in the structure of GNP.
5. Characteristics of the drive to technological maturity are defined and illustrated in *The Stages of Economic Growth*, ch. 5. See also *Politics and the Stages of Growth* (Cambridge, Cambridge University Press, 1971), ch. 4.
6. *Essays on the British Economy of the Nineteenth Century* (Oxford, Clarendon Press, 1948), pp. 12–13.

7. For reference to my discussion with D.H. Robertson, see *The Process of Economic Growth* (Oxford, Clarendon Press, 1953, 1960), pp. 5–7.
8. For my reaction at the time to mainstream cyclical analysis of the period, see 'Some Notes on Mr. Hicks and History', *American Economic Review*, vol. XLI, no. 3, June 1951, pp. 312–24.
9. *The Process of Economic Growth* (Oxford, Clarendon Press, 1953), pp. 17, 71, 103–8.
10. Keynes, J.M., *General Theory* (London, Macmillan, 1936) p. 292.
11. These enterprises yielded *The Dynamics of Soviet Society* (New York, W.W. Norton, 1953, 1967); *The Prospects for Communist China* (New York, Technology Press, MIT, John Wiley, 1954); and *An American Policy in Asia* (New York, Technology Press, MIT, John Wiley, 1955).
12. *Economic Journal*, vol. 66, February 1956, pp. 25–48.
13. *Ibid.*, p. 27.
14. *Stages of Economic Growth*, p. 9.
15. *The United States in the World Arena* (New York, Harper & Row, 1960).
16. *Politics and the Stages of Growth*, pp. 98–183 and 196–218.
17. See, for example, the extraordinary rates of technology absorption and growth of Taiwan and South Korea in chs. 45 and 47 of my *World Economy: History and Prospect*.
18. See, *ibid.*, pp. 55–9, and my *Why the Poor Get Richer and the Rich Slow Down* (Austin, University of Texas Press, 1980), pp. 275–88.
19. *Why the Poor*, etc., ch. 6 as a whole.
20. See Table 1 and relevant notes in the 1980 edition of World Bank's *World Development Reports*.
21. Rostow, W.W. (ed.), *The Economics of Take-off Into Sustained Growth*, p. 43. In his 1971 *Economic Growth of Nations: Total Output and Production Structure* (Cambridge, Mass, The Belknap Press of the Harvard University Press), pp. 61–9, Kuznets quietly capitulated to the Rosenstein Rodan-Arthur Lewis-Rostow view. He concluded that the net domestic capital formation proportion rose 'from about 5 or 6 per cent at the beginning of the modern growth process' to a 'characteristic' 15 per cent as a peak terminal value (pp. 64–5).
22. Here is how I compared Kuznets' full criteria for modern growth *versus* my criteria for take-off in *The World Economy: History and Prospect* (p. 778 n. 2):

> 'Kuznets' full criteria for modern growth are: the application of modern scientific thought and technology to industry; a sustained and rapid increase in real product per capita, usually associated with high rates of population growth; a shift of the working force out of agriculture to industry and services; significant contacts with the outside world. My view of what lies at the heart of take-off and the beginning of modern growth is the effective absorption of a limited range of modern technologies, yielding a high rate of expansion and significant scale in an identified leading sector complex, with evidence of spreading effects, bringing about in the usual case an acceleration of increase in GNP per capita, a rise in the investment rate, and an acceleration of the pace of urbanisa-

tion. I regard accelerated urbanisation as evidence of the 'lateral spreading effects' of leading sectors'.
23. *Economics of Take-off*, p. 42.
24. *World Economy: History and Prospect*, pp. 778–9, where sources are indicated and minor discrepancies between Kuznets' dates and mine discussed.
25. Ohkawa, Kazushi, and Rosovsky, Henry, 'A Century of Japanese Economic Growth', in W.W. Lockwood (ed.), *The State and Economic Entreprise in Japan* (Princeton, Princeton University Press, 1965), pp. 52–3. The comparison of the two sets of stages is presented and discussed in my *Politics and the Stages of Growth*, pp. 378–9.
26. For discussions of Kuznets' dilemma and his acknowledgment of it, see, for example, my review of his *Economic Growth of Nations: Total Output and Production Structure* (Cambridge, Mass., The Belknap Press of Harvard University Press, 1971), in *Political Science Quarterly*, vol. LXXXVI, no. 4, December 1971, pp. 654–7. Kuznets' discussion of the problem is on pp. 314–43.
27. Lewis, W. Arthur, 'The State of Development Theory', *American Economic Review*, vol. 74, Number 1, March 1984, p. 3.
28. For a full discussion of the changing structure of the international capital accounts of developing countries, see, especially, *World Development Report, 1985* (New York, Oxford Press for the World Bank, 1985). Virtually the full text is devoted to the evolution of foreign borrowing, repayment, rollovers, etc.
29. The reader of Part Five of my *World Economy*, providing short economic histories of twenty countries plus stages of growth identifications, will note the disproportionate amount of space allocated to the pre-conditions period and the inevitably large part played by non-economic factors in the argument.
30. Naipaul, Shiva, *An Unfinished Journey* (London, Hamish Hamilton, 1986), pp. 34–5.
31. For a full discussion, see my *Why the Poor Get Richer and the Rich Slow Down*, ch. 6, 'Growth Rates at Different Levels of Income and Stage of Growth'. The accumulation during the depressed inter-war years and the Second World War of unapplied technologies makes the acceleration of growth rates for post-1945 Western Europe and Japan somewhat less of an exception than at first appears.
32. For further discussion, see *ibid.*, especially pp. 275–88. Also, *Pioneers in Development*, pp. 232–7 and 247–9.
33. *David Hume Writings in Economics*, Rotwein, Eugene (ed. and intro.) (Madison, University of Wisconsin Press, 1955), pp. 79–82. For an account of Hume's and other views, see, especially, Hont, Istvan, 'The "rich country-poor country" debate in Scottish classical political economy', ch. 11 in Hont, Istvan, and Ignatieff, Michael (eds), *Wealth and Virtue: The Shaping of Political Economy in the Scottish Enlightenment* (Cambridge, Cambridge University Press, 1983).
34. The quotations are to be found, respectively, in Istvan Hont, *op. cit.*, p. 300 (where original sources are provided), and Smith, Adam, *The*

Wealth of Nations, edited by Edwin Cannan (New York, Random House, 1937), p. 462.
35. Hamilton, Alexander, 'Report on Manufactures' (1791), in *Alexander Hamilton's Papers on Public Credit Commerce and Finance*, McKee, Samuel (ed.) (New York, Columbia University Press, 1934), pp. 227.
36. Marshall, Alfred, *Industry and Trade (London, Macmillan, 1919, reprint, New York, Augustus M. Kelley, 1970, Reprints of Economic Classics)*, chs III–V, especially pp. 95–106, 157–62.
37. League of Nations, *Industrialization and Foreign Trade* (New York, distributed in the US by International Documents Service, Columbia University Press, 1945), with a Preface by A. Loveday, Director of Economic, Financial and Transit Department, dated July, 1945. The full reference for Staley's study, commissioned by the ILO, is: *World Economic Development* (Montreal: International Labour Office, 1944).
38. *Op. cit.*, p. 5. This summary passage is from Loveday's Preface.
39. *Ibid.*, p. 117.
40. *World Development Report, 1984* (New York, Oxford University Press for the World Bank, 1984), p. 43.
41. This argument is elaborated, for example, in my article published in *The Washington Post*, December 28, 1986.
42. This argument is elaborated in 'Is There Need for Economic Leadership?: Japanese or American?' *American Economic Association Papers and Proceedings*, vol. 75, no. 2, May 1985.
43. The following argument is elaborated in 'On Ending The Cold War', *Foreign Affairs*, vol. 65, no. 4, Spring 1987, pp. 831–51.

8 The Radical Reflections of an Applied Economist
Henry Phelps Brown

In my lifetime I have seen economics become a profession. When I began my university studies in the 1920s, the tradition remained that political economy was a field of literary and philosophical discourse which any serious-minded and cultivated person could enter. But a rapid change was in progress. Already before the First World War the amount of statistical information was growing rapidly, under American stimulus. During the war the Government became involved in economic affairs as never before, and as economic troubles deepened after the war it accepted a new responsibility for the direction of policy. These changes created a widespread sense of the need to achieve a greater understanding of economic affairs, and to train more people to handle the materials of economic administration: so the British universities generally came to provide distinct courses in economics, supported, if not by separate departments, at least by a staff of specialised teachers. The Second World War carried the interpenetration of government and business farther. The increased attention to planning in the years that followed, with the relative expansion of that sort of function in the private as well as the public sectors, brought new openings for economists. They were able to show their usefulness in posts for which their training specially suited them. The former relations of remoteness and sometimes contempt between the practical businessman and the economist were superseded by acceptance of the economist as a necessary member of the staff.

By the later 1950s economics had thus become distinguished and established as a profession, both academically and occupationally. Meanwhile its academic status had been enhanced by its having developed a distinct body of theory and of statistical or econometric methods. Theory was being advanced to levels of great logical rigour and complexity, mainly by the application of mathematics. The graduate schools were giving an intensive training in the newly developed methods of handling quantitative data.

It might appear that these two developments, the occupational and the academic or theoretical, were linked. To some extent they obviously were. Most evidently this was so in the training of the new profession: the equipment which gave that profession its special usefulness was derived in great part from the assembling of quantitative economic information and the development of sophisticated methods of analysing it which had raised the professional status of academic economics in recent years. But as I look back what strikes me is the extent of divergence. The conspicuous achievements of economic theorists in the last half century have been made in a rarified atmosphere: the starting point of their inquiries may have been an issue of contemporary importance, but they have abstracted only such elements as would fit into a cohesive system, and they have been more attracted by the intellectual difficulty of problems than by any application to practice. The outcome has been work of great intellectual distinction but – here appears the divergence – it has not contributed to the qualities by which during the same years the economist has gained acceptance as a staff officer and adviser.

What are those qualities? The economist who is employed in that capacity commands a body of specialised information, and is equipped to analyse, assess and present it: in particular, he is trained in statistical methods. More than this, in matters of policy he brings to bear an approach, under the title of 'the allocation of resources', which though it may seem commonplace to him, often makes a fresh contribution to the decision-making of others, through the reduction of choices to marginal variations, and the calculation of opportunity costs. If he is to be valued as an adviser he must also have the ability to see situations in the round, have empathy for human nature, and be able to enter into the outlook of the people of the country as that has been moulded by their history. But what do these assets of the economist by occupation owe to what are generally regarded as the advances made by economic theory in recent years? There seems almost to be a negative relation. One economist who had held the highest responsibilities as an adviser told me that when an able young man who had taken honours in economics at the university joined his staff, he had to begin by unlearning his advanced theory. Another adviser whose responsibilities had been no less high told me that an entrant whose graduate work had been wholly in economic history would be as eligible as one who had been drilled in economic theory and econometrics: both could learn much of their work only after entry to the service, and the economic historian would have the advantage of not being prone, as the others were, to process data in detachment from their context. But in any case, one has only to compare the content of paper after paper in the learned economic journals with the problems that confront the administrator or adviser: not even remotely can he be guided, stimulated or informed by their profound, rigorous but remote reasoning.

Again, recent years have seen the extension of business consultancy as a distinct form of professional service. Some of those who prove their worth by providing this service are economists by training; many are not. A training in economics is not found to be an outstandingly useful preparation for a consultant's work, still less an indispensable qualification. Yet an outsider coming fresh to the academic field might expect the science of economics in the universities to bear the same close relation to business consultancy as physiology and pathology bear to consultancy in medicine.

This divergence between the economics of the dons and the administrators concerns me greatly. It is the issue I most want to raise as I look back now over the years of my own acquaintance, such as it has been, with both sides of the divide.

But I may well be told that my concern is uncalled for. The distinction between the pure and applied departments is common to many branches of study. It is common also to find within the ambit of the same science both the advanced theorist, the exploratory and problem-solving mind on the frontiers of knowledge, and the practitioner who makes useful application of a more limited body of principles. Nor is this, the argument goes on, to admit any distinction between what is and what is not inherently capable of practical application: on the contrary, the most abstract and hypothetical trains of reasoning may lead to discoveries of practical significance. The function of economic theory, in any case, is not to provide an explanation of this or that particular set of observations, but to construct a paradigm, a complex of interrelationships, which we carry in our minds and which enables us to cast the data presented in a particular inquiry into an intelligible order. To assess the justification of advanced economic theory by simply asking what use it is to someone immediately concerned with the problem of the competitiveness of British exports, or the shortage of skilled manual workers, is simply a vulgar error.

The need for theory is not in question: theory is tantamount to explanation, and to give up careful theorising would only leave the field clear for theorising of a wild and hasty kind. But there is still a good deal of economic theorising going on that cannot avail itself of this justification. This is because of the special handicap under which the economist labours, in his inability to test his theories, especially by controlled experiment. Ideally, the need to account for certain observed occurrences should suggest a theory, and this theory, or inferences drawn from it, should then be brought back again to the test of fact: but this test can seldom be made by the economist, because the theory necessarily isolates the operation of a small number of factors, whereas the data record the effect of a great many. This drastic limitation should, as Marshall said, confine the economist to 'short chains and single connecting links' of analysis and deduction, inserted at appropriate points in his empirical studies, but in practice he tends to feel that it sets him free for composing problems and building models. Since – it is no fault of his – he cannot be always working under the check of empirical relevance, he comes upon no boundary line to divide the theory that is applicable to actual situations from that which is outwardly the same, being made up of similar components, but has become artificial. Before long he is making models in which the components do indeed bear the names of entrepreneurs or holders of money balances, trade unionists or investors, but these are such stereotypes that the patterns they form and problems they pose seem, like chess problems, to owe their interest to their intellectual difficulty, and not to any identity between the pieces on the board and the flesh and blood of those they nominally represent: nor to any help their solution will give in the world's work.

But there is another way in which the basic limitation of the economist is likely to make him more of a theorist, and this holds for those who are most anxious to be of practical use. I speak now not of the refinements of theory, but of the theory of contemporary policy. A pressing problem arises, and the economist is asked to advise: can he say only that he must be given time and resources to conduct a detailed investigation? Ricardo showed how a method lay ready to hand that might yield speedier insights. Its results, moreover, would have both generality and certainty. This method is to abstract the essential and dominant propensities of the agents concerned, and to assemble these elements in a model whose workings can be traced, if not simply in the mind's eye, then by a process of deduction from premises, very possibly with the aid of mathematics. The conclusion will have general applicability, if it has been derived from basic elements of widespread occurrence. Contrast this with the limited scope, the 'ad hoc-ery' as we call it now, of the recommendations that emerge from the study in depth of any one problem. The conclusion of the Ricardian method will also, unless the premises are wrongly selected or an error can be demonstrated in the reasoning, have certainty. Contrast this with the uncertainty and the tentative proposals which are all that is commonly attained at the last by those who have tried to take so much more into account. With a clearly thought out theory, the economist can at least approach all the tangle of contemporary problems with an assured orientation. Without it, he is floundering in empiricism, moved now this way and now that by anecdotal evidence.

Or so it has seemed; but my doubts have grown with the years. These doubts are not about the insights that models of the economic system can afford, but about the components and the comprehensiveness of these models: are the models made up of the factors and processes that enter substantially into the actual course of economic affairs, and do they therefore take account of the reactions which measures of policy will meet with in practice? In particular, do they distinguish the variety of factors that affect the different components of the aggregates assembled under any one such heading as investment, real income, or unemployment? The Keynesian system showed how variations in effective demand could arise so as to change aggregate employment, and how within this system a high level of employment could be maintained by the use of appropriate fiscal and monetary operators. This was always subject to the constraints of the balance of payments and of cost push by trade unionists; but when in outstanding and blessed contrast to so much that had gone before, for twenty years and more after the Second World War the Western economies generally maintained a high and stable level of employment, many of us believed that the Keynesian theory had shown how to prevent the recurrence of large-scale unemployment. Only with the creeping rise of unemployment in the later 1960s was our attention brought back to the structural factors affecting employment in particular industries and regions within any one country, and to the effects on employment of a changing share of the international market; the complexities of investment decisions; and the uncertain, sometimes halting rhythm of technical advance. Western Governments are faced in common with the necessity for contracting the capacity of their steel industries: is it only for fear of cost push that they do not proceed in common to sustain effective demand?

Or consider the countries of low income, and what the economic theory of development has done for them. That the two-sector models that were formerly so plentiful had little impact on the paddy fields I think highly probable. But I wonder also whether the theory of economic development has served to shape the strategy of policy effectively as it might have done if it had dealt with the obstacles and opportunities that present themselves as salient to those charged with practical responsibilities in the field; or if it could help to explain why a given country has developed more effectively than a neighbour of similar natural endowments.

Again, we have seen the application of economic theory to the struggle against inflation in the western economies. Monetarism passes lightly over the processes by which prices, costs and incomes are fixed and changed in detail by the volition and consent of individual and collective human agents, and the inertia of those people's expectations. If the present increased reliance upon monetary constraints produces so sharp a reaction among businessmen and trade unionists that governments draw back, we may be told that the economic policy was correct, but the short-sighted or politically motivated resistance of the public did not give it a chance.

Economic theorists seized on the Phillips curve as a demonstration of the determination of the movement of the general level of wages by the market forces of supply and demand; they were taken aback when the number of unemployed – their index of the excess of supply over demand – and the rate of rise of wages doubled side by side. They would have avoided their misinterpretation if they had remembered what Marshall said long ago about the propensity of Ricardo and his followers to suppose 'that the world was made up of city men'. This propensity, he said,

> caused them to speak of labour as a commodity without staying to throw themselves into the point of view of the workman; and without dwelling upon the allowances to be made for his human passions, his instincts and habits, his sympathies and antipathies, his class jealousies and class adhesiveness, his want of knowledge and of the opportunities for free and vigorous action. They therefore attributed to the forces of supply and demand a much more mechanical and regular action than is to be found in real life; and they laid down laws with regard to profits and wages that did not really hold even for England in their own time.[1]

In sum, I doubt whether the economist by building models whose components are believed to be general propensities of economic agents, can come close enough to the actual economic component of human affairs for the working of his model to be a guide to policy. We do not know how far the assumptions out of which the model is built represent accurately so much as it covers; and we do not know how much it leaves out.

But here, it may be said, econometrics comes to our aid: it can draw out relations from the data, and check hypotheses by testing inferences from them against the facts. The great value of the range of statistical studies now included within econometrics is not in question, but in the particular use proposed for it here econometrics operates under severe constraints. Because economic time series are affected by common causes, like sticks floating together down a stream, regressions between them must have interpretations placed upon them from without – the theory must be imported into the statistics and not drawn out from them. The Phillips curve was a notable example of this. In cross-section analysis the difficulties remain of determining the direction of causality, and knowing whether a variable appears in its own right or as a proxy for a latent factor. It seems to me therefore (so far as a layman is entitled to an opinion) that the wide and vigorous extension of econometrics has been a mixed blessing. It has brought great benefits by its concentration of interest on quantitative evidence and methods of making the fullest use of it. But the availability of the computer, and the fascination of getting numerical answers out of it to the most complicated questions, have led economists too often to be cavalier in reducing their problem to a computable form, and naive in interpreting their findings.

But by now many of my colleagues will have had too much from me. They will have seen me not only turning away from advanced theory, but calling in question the use of theory at any level in order to draw measures of policy directly out from it for practical application. For good measure I have even thrown in some thoughts about the limitations and temptations of econometrics. My colleagues will feel that these judgements are at best highly subjective. 'This surely is a peevish fellow', they will say. 'He objects to other people doing things after their own style, because it's not the style that suits himself. He presumes to erect his personal preferences into general laws. He does not realise that in the methodology of economics, all debates in the end are only about tastes, and manifestos come down to little more than advice on "how to be more like me".'

There is force in this, as an observation of what does tend to happen. Because methods are hard to assess by their results, they are likely to gain their acceptance instead by the intellectual satisfaction they give to those who use them, and of course this varies with each user's own talents and temperament. It seems the most efficient arrangement, moreover, that each person should work in the way that comes most naturally to him. It must also be observed that, given the diversity of talents, the highest prestige attaches inherently to the intellectual power of the masterly theorist. The rest of us recognise his gifts as outstanding. It may be that there are gifts of handling complex detail and forming sound practical judgements, that are actually no less rare, but because their application is hedged around by the circumstances of particular cases they do not stand out like the ability to prove a new theorem. The more abstract the material, the more evident is the intellectual power of those who master it. For this among other reasons the economic theorist moves among his fellows with a certain majesty.

And more than this: those of us who prefer to see each problem in its circumstantial setting may have to be warned that instead of priding ourselves on our fidelity to the facts we should examine ourselves for mental laziness. We like information for its own sake, we are naturally readers of the press, we like to envisage what has been going on in lively colours and in the round. We are responsive to the play of personality, aware of the variety of human nature as it is moulded in different societies and periods, and we are constantly reminded of how the actual course of events differs from the determinate composition of forces in a mechanical model. Our inquiries convey the feeling which the war correspondent gains when he reaches the front line, that he is looking directly into the springs of action. Yet any intelligible account of transactions, any reasoned history, implies a theory: any user of our studies is bound to be concerned with the firmness and representativeness of the evidence, and the rigour and generality of the reasoning. It is here that the impulse towards realism may be defective. When we recreate a scene before our eyes, we are not abstracting, we are not reasoning: we may be missing connections and constraints, we may make statements that analysis would show to be downright fallacies. But for the type of mind that likes to see things as they are, that sort of hard thinking may be uncongenial; and the realist's criticism of the unreality of theory may only provide a rationalisation of his own reluctance to make the mental effort that theory would require of him.

There is force in these remonstrances that I hear my colleagues making. In particular I agree with them on the temptations of empiricism, and the need for the application of a framework of analysis, with the consequent value to be set upon a rigorous training in theory – even though, as will appear shortly, I do not think that this training should be carried to such advanced levels as it commonly is carried today. But I cannot agree that when we have pointed out how different methods appeal to different temperaments we have said the last word about their relative usefulness. Perhaps that would be so if we were concerned with the nature of economics: economics is what economists do? But it certainly is not so if we raise the question that, I realise now, has underlain the disquiet of these reflections of mine – the question, namely, of what is the object of the economist.

This is a different question from that of the scope and method of economics. It is also a more embarrassing question. If the object of the economist is simply to study economics as that subject now stands, then he is free to occupy himself within a wide range of intellectual tasks, and suit his personal inclination in both his choice of subject and the way he works. But suppose we ask what is the use of all this, and consider whether the foremost object of the economist should not be to gain an understanding of the economic aspect of human affairs so as to be able to contribute to their healthier development? That seems a very natural and widely acceptable object; but if we really believe in it, we are calling in question the validity of much contemporary work. The difficulty lies not in the abstraction of economic processes from their social setting, but in the return from that abstraction to policy applied to human affairs. The mental process that the economist performs has no counterpart in daily life: advice based on the separation of economic from other influences on human behaviour is liable to be stultified by what it has abstracted from. I have heard an eminent economist say that he could only recommend the policy that was economically advisable: whether it was socially acceptable was for others to say. But this seems to me as if a medical specialist were to recommend a drug as the best treatment for neuritis, but add that whether the patient's stomach would revolt against it was for a dietitian to advise. Economic 'aspects' may be detached analytically; 'the economy' may be separated conceptually from society, but the behaviour of 'economic agents' is affected by influences from which the theorist abstracts. Effective policy recommendations must take account of those influences.

This is to rediscover the obvious: it is to say that what actually happens in the economy occurs as a process of history. It depends upon human attitudes and expectations, cultural inheritance, waves of feeling, the power of personalities, the impact of particular events, sometimes on sheer chance. Any one problem on which the economist is called to advise is part of the ongoing affairs of a society. He needs an understanding in which the quantitative relations established within the framework of economic analysis are combined with empathy and imaginative insight.

If we ask what training is appropriate for the entrant whose object is to be an economist of this kind, our findings are disturbing. For it does not appear that training in the great intellectual advances that have been made in economic theory in recent years are helpful to this end. The insights yielded by economic analysis are essential but they are those of quite elementary analysis. My contention is that the economist who is best equipped to understand the working of the economy around him and to advise on policy needs in point of analysis the equipment that is needed by the economic historian, and no more. I take this to be the analysis of demand and supply, distribution, international trade, and money, as these are developed in a text for undergraduates. It stops short even of what is expected nowadays of the most able undergraduates in their final examination. I doubt whether more concepts or relationships than are contained here will in practice be drawn upon even by those who can handle them with facility, in work upon particular problems at the highest level of responsibility. The entrant would also receive thoroughgoing training in statistical methods. For the rest, his course would include much economic, social and political history: this is essential. The course would also provide for the study in detail of some contemporary societies and their recent changes.

This marks a conception of the professional economist different from that which prevails today in our universities. But I believe it agrees with the habit of thought and the working equipment actually used (whatever their academic training) by those economists who have gained experience in posts of responsibility as advisers on issues of practical policy. A divergence between what the academics like to teach and the training that practical men wish they would give is an old story, and economics would not be the first faculty to hear it. But the professionalisation of economics is still recent. The economics of the chair has less grounds for self-confidence than it might have relied upon some years ago. Our metal may not yet have set in the mould. We may be moved to some reassessment and reformation. Our conception of the professional economist may yet become that of the economist who is equipped to understand mankind – as Marshall said, mankind and not economic man – to understand mankind in the ordinary business of life.

Note

1. Marshall, Alfred, *Principles of Economics* (1890), Appendix B, Section 6.

9 On the Career of a Microeconomist

William J. Baumol

For as long as I can remember – certainly by my early teens – my desire to be an economist was never in doubt. In retrospect I can see that this was no accident. Both my parents were self-educated immigrants, but educated they were, as few undergraduates are today. Literature, older or current, language, politics and economics were constantly discussed in our house in a most fascinating manner, and I was expected from childhood to participate fully in the discussions. My father with his lower class background (his parents had run a tavern in a small town in Poland) was driven by passionate concern for humanity, and emotion ruled his talk. My mother, by contrast, coming from a line of Jewish Lithuanian intellectuals, epitomised logic and careful reasoning in pursuit of the same objectives. Both parents, particularly my father, were avid Marxists. The combination was irresistible. I was infected by their interests and their concerns. My reading provided a sampling of Marx's logical convolutions which, combined with tales of the adventure of the buccaneers of nineteenth-century business – Morgan, Vanderbilt, Gould, Rockefeller and others – sealed my fascination with the subject. Well before I entered college I had begun to read economic history, the works of the classical economists and the writings of Thorstein Veblen.

UNDERGRADUATE EDUCATION (1939–42)

I entered CCNY (the College of the City of New York) in 1939 as the great depression was drawing to an end and the threat of war hung over us. CCNY, then, was an extraordinary institution. There was no tuition charge and the students commuted from home every day by subway. The ambitious children of impecunious immigrants flocked to it as their ticket from poverty or grinding labour. Never did so many future Nobel Prize-winners congregate in one place. Passionate activity, discussion and debate flourished everywhere. The dining room was surrounded by alcoves each had been claimed by a permanent discussion group – there was the Trotskyist alcove, the Socialist alcove and one of every other variety. (There was even an alcove at which future comedians or rather, comic social commentators, some of them to become famous later, practiced their craft without let up.)

A number of economists of note emerged from there, Kenneth Arrow, Julius Margolis and Jules Joskow among them. But while CCNY at that time had many gifted teachers, the department of economics had very few. It was clear to us students that many of them were thoroughly behind the times, and could not teach us about the work of Keynes, Chamberlin and Joan Robinson which were then at the frontier. Besides, many of them just could not communicate very well. There seemed to us to be little choice, and so we organised our own classes, each specialising in a different field, devouring as much of the relevant literature as we could and then lecturing on it to the others. I was assigned the microeconomics, and suspect that I learned more economics there than ever before or since. This experience has always engendered uncertainty in my views on teaching. Can it be that, at least for some students, what is considered to be 'bad' teaching is really teaching in its most effective form, because it forces students to think and learn for themselves? I have long advocated some controlled experiments in which parallel classes are held, some taught in the conventional way by teachers of good reputation while in the others students are asked to fend for themselves, guided only by past examinations, perhaps by a reading list, and with no access to the faculty. It is my conjecture that the first group will perform better on the examination at the end of the semester, but that in an examination five or ten years later the self-taught group will far outdistance the other.

THE DEPARTMENT OF AGRICULTURE AND MILITARY SERVICE (1942–6)

Graduating in 1942, I spent a few months in Washington working (though it may seem odd) in the Department of Agriculture. The shadow of the receding depression led graduating students to accept with delight virtually any reasonable job offer, and I was considered very daring by the others in my class when I held out for – and received – a salary of $2000 a year. Happily the job was not undesirable. It was a sort of think tank for the Department, and many of the group, some of whom I still see, were exceedingly bright and creative persons. The head of the Department was Frederick Waugh, a bright and fatherly figure who then and later made a number of significant contributions to the economic literature. It was under his guidance and that of my young colleagues that I first learned how microtheory can be applied to concrete issues.

Just before leaving for Washington I had been married. We were both very young, but the US had just entered the war and many others were doing the same. I have had many occasions to congratulate myself on the wisdom (or luck) that guided that decision. We have ever since worked (and enjoyed life) together in many areas, most directly in our work on the economics of the performing arts. But I am getting ahead of the story.

My years in the US Army are pertinent only for the correspondence course in linear algebra I took, and, while stationed in Rouen, the mathematics books I was able to buy and devour. There, incidentally I made lifelong friends with a French family whose fabulous cellar, including samples of every great vintage of the century, introduced me to the delights of wine which I still collect. Just after the war in Europe had ended some German prisoners gave me my first lessons in wood sculpture which I now teach at Princeton University. (Before entering the army I had studied drawing and painting at the Art Student's League in New York City and my second main field of study at CCNY had been visual art – painting and lithography, particularly.)

After returning from the war there was another brief stint at the Department of Agriculture. But this time the task was very different: the allocation of the US grain resources among the countries of a hungry world. Two prime lessons emerged from this experience – the high costs of the negotiation process and the complexities of the calculations of fairness. The first lesson flowed from the fact that all of the senior and more experienced members of the division were almost fully employed in diplomatic negotiations involving international agencies and other governments. As a result, the actual decisions were, to our astonishment, left to another young man of equal inexperience and myself!

It was not a task to make for an easy conscience. The refrain we heard from virtually every country was the same; we are hungry. If we had one shipload to go either to country A or to country B, what were we to do if the evidence showed that we had already sent enough to A this month to provide each of its inhabitants more calories than before the war, but that B, whose per capita grain receipts were higher than A's, was nevertheless well below its pre-war consumption level? We did not, of course, enjoy the luxury of indecision that is available to pure research.

THE LONDON SCHOOL OF ECONOMICS (1946–9)

I had assumed that on my return to civilian life I would begin my postgraduate studies. My application to the London School of Economics was rejected, and I wrote again asking when it would be possible to apply for the following year. As later came out, compassion was still part of the admission process, and it was decided to accept me as a student for the masters degree only. As explained to me later, at LSE they had never heard of CCNY and, in any event, my undergraduate record was hardly outstanding. But CCNY soon made up for its handicap. The training in fierce debating – quarter neither asked nor given – soon got me (in my view, undeserved) attention in LSE's justly famous seminars. To my amazement, within weeks I had not only been transferred to the PhD programme, but was also offered a part-time teaching post which became full-time the following year. Lord Robbins afterwards told me that he went back to the records to see where they had made their mistake in rejecting me, and decided that, on the record, they had been right, after all.

LSE was an extraordinarily stimulating place to be. Besides Lionel Robbins I got to know Friedrich Hayek, Arthur Lewis, Nicholas Kaldor and, later, James Meade, among the economists, and Karl Popper and Harold Laski outside the department. Among the students there were Frank Hahn, undergraduate Ralph Turvey and an Australian, David Finch (now at the World Bank) who (in 1948!) was writing a thesis on the theory of stagflation. The weekly Robbins seminar and the stimulation in the common rooms where one met for avid and fruitful conversation were experiences I have never duplicated. The erudition and broad knowledge of Robbins and Laski revealed what humanistic learning can be. Popper, who had not yet reacquired any professional logician colleagues, was prepared to report his latest derivations frequently to a new assistant lecturer who had taken a course or two in formal logic at CCNY. Hahn, Turvey and other young people were sources of a continuing flow of new and fruitful ideas. Meade and Hayek were also full of ideas which they constantly tried out on the delighted newcomers.

Because few English faculty members had anything like a PhD and did not take the degree seriously, it was possible for me to write my dissertation at the same time that I held a full-time faculty position. I had already planned my dissertation during my military service, and Lionel Robbins agreed to be its supervisor. He never begrudged me time or advice, which was always very helpful. The thesis, later published as *Welfare Economics and the Theory of the State*, took off from the Marshall–Pigou theory of externalities, then a neglected subject widely considered to be of minor importance. It sought to generalise the idea to as diverse a set of subjects as the behaviour of competitors, the difficulty of cartel formation and the theory of inflation (all of which we were already characterising as a prisoners' dilemma problem in the new fangled theory of games).[1] More than that, I hoped to derive from the logic of externalities the rationale for all government intervention in the workings of the economy – notions later echoed in works of Buchanan and Tulloch and the writings of Mancur Olsen. In the hotbed of discussion that constituted LSE the dissertation's ideas were very much a group product. We had made an effort to revive the famous Cambridge, LSE, Oxford seminar of the 1930s, and these subjects were discussed at the joint sessions, bringing in ideas from outside the LSE. Jan de v. Graaff played a leading part, he and I spending large amounts of time discussing one another's work on welfare economics.

In the course of that seminar's travels, incidentally, I also met Dennis Robertson, Joan Robinson, R.F. Kahn, J.R. Hicks, Lionel McKenzie and others whose names already were or were about to become legendary.

At LSE I gave two courses. Lionel Robbins invited me to lecture on economic dynamics, and my lecture notes for that course formed the basis for what was to be my first book, *Economic Dynamics*, which still survives. But in return for that plum I had to give a set of lectures on the American economy, a subject on which, most regrettably, I was dismally ignorant and which, I am sure, were an embarrassment to everyone, even if most educational to me. Much of the dynamics course, like so much else, followed Paul Samuelson's pathbreaking explorations which I merely translated into forms more accessible to students. People have sometimes been kind enough to suggest that my writing on the subject is rather clear. I have responded that I tried to write the book so clearly that even I could understand it – and that was, in all seriousness, the truth of the matter.

In both my lectures and the dissertation there were substantial sections on the relevant *dogmengeschichte* on which Lionel Robbins was enormously helpful. The graphic translation of the dynamics of the Ricardian model seemed to me an obvious interpretation of a system universally understood within the profession and generally agreed upon. I was amazed to find it singled out for special commendation in John Williams's presidential address to the American Economic Association the year after publication, and to see it cited by writers on the history of thought many times thereafter. Since then it has become clearer that the substance of Ricardian economics is far from being agreed upon, as my former student Samuel Hollander has found in his debates with the neo-Keynesians of Cambridge and Italy and even with George Stigler and Paul Samuelson.

Our happy three years in London were drawing to an end. We had used the opportunity to travel about Europe a good deal. British exchange controls in that period of post-war austerity prevented us from using either my small earnings or my wife's comparable income, both in sterling, for the purpose. Fortunately, I also received support from the US Government in US currency, as an army veteran, and that permitted our first visit to Italy, which we have loved ever since. Of course, young graduate students did not expect many comforts while travelling or in their domestic arrangements so a small income served very adequately. There were severe shortages and strict rationing still continued. In London the foreign students and their spouses shared any packages received from abroad with their English friends. Often we would all pick up our six-week ration of one egg and one slice of bacon at the same time and get together to celebrate the feast. Heating was a great problem with tightly rationed coal of poor quality burnt in an open fireplace the main source of warmth in the home. One winter our water pipes froze for three months and produced a great indoor flood when they thawed and burst in the beautiful spring of 1947.

The dissertation was completed on schedule, and I had the most delightful oral examination on record over whiskey and sodas at the Reform Club with my examiners, Marcus Flemming and Lionel Robbins who still considered my pursuit of the PhD an American aberration. Professor Robbins knew we were determined to return to the United States, but he nevertheless made me a very generous offer at the LSE if I were prepared to remain. After I had refused with thanks most deeply felt, he recommended me with his characteristic kindness to Friedrich Lutz who was then visiting LSE from Princeton. Within weeks I had received and accepted an offer of an assistant professorship for the following academic year, and have remained at Princeton ever since.

Lifelong friends were acquired at the LSE – Lord and Lady Robbins and their children, Sir Arthur and Gladys Lewis to whom we had the pleasure of extending their first dinner invitation after they were married, Anne Bohm who brought sanity and order to the postgraduate programme, Frank and Dorothy Hahn, and others as well. We have since made still more close friends in London where our visits (or theirs to the US) have assumed the nature of reunions. In particular, Lord Robbins in his role as Chairman of the Royal Opera at Covent Garden and as Director of the National Gallery has over the years provided us with access to London's cultural activities such as few are privileged to enjoy.

PRINCETON UNIVERSITY (1949–)

At Princeton we were immediately welcomed into the community and the department. Richard Lester was chairman, and he quickly made us feel at home. Lionel Robbins had also written ahead about us to Jacob and Frances Viner with whom we remained on closest terms for the rest of their lives. I did not know Viner's terrifying reputation (which was belied completely by his natural but often deliberately concealed kindness). Consequently, I was foolish enough to disagree with him avidly and energetically whenever it seemed appropriate to the astonishment of many of our colleagues. Viner, who was obviously unused to such a response, was delighted. We spent many hours each week locked in debate. From time to time I needed information on economic history or on the history of ideas and was always very pleased when in response to literally any such question he would talk without interruption for at least an hour providing an amazing stream of illuminating material from his bottomless stock of knowledge. He would also regularly, but apparently casually, make some unsupported theoretical statement which I was sure was quite incorrect and which he would then challenge me to disprove. Each time, after a considerable struggle on my part, the mathematics showed unambiguously that he was right.

Years later a friend of his in another city recounted how Viner told him of a young friend on the faculty for whom he had set himself the task of presenting a new, paradoxical proposition in economic theory every week. What an education that was.

The following year Lester Chandler joined the Department, and from him I learned what little I understand about money and banking. Later we wrote a textbook together which, though it was unsuccessful, was an introduction to the pleasures of collaboration.

On arriving at Princeton we met two advanced graduate students, Martin Shubik and Harvey Leibenstein, with whom we have remained close friends. Within a year or two the department attracted an extraordinary group of undergraduate students including Richard Quandt, Otto Eckstein and Gary Becker with whom I wrote an article on Patinkin's dichotomy analysis and the pertinent materials in classical and neo-classical economics. We felt, and I still do, that Patinkin's discussions of the invalidity of the dichotomy between the real and monetary sectors of the economy, and of the problems caused by the assumption that supply and demand functions are homogeneous in prices alone, were brilliant pieces of work and constituted an extremely illuminating contribution. But at the same time some of the classical and neoclassical authors he accused of the resulting errors were, in my view, quite innocent of the charges. It should be added that the dispute was conducted just as such disputes should be, and that Professor Patinkin and I have become good friends and see one another both in Israel and the United States.

CONSULTING ACTIVITIES

In about 1953 Paul Lazarsfeld, the great sociologist then at Columbia University, asked me to work with him on one of his research projects. I quickly accepted the invitation, anxious to get to know more about his path-breaking work, and, of course, because of the additional income which greatly relieved the assistant professor's traditional poverty. A key premise in much of Lazarsfeld's analysis was that while human behaviour is stochastic, the relevant probabilities of the different options in tomorrow's behaviour depend on the state of affairs today. Thus the probability that some individual will vote socialist in the next election will depend on whether he voted as a socialist or a Christian democrat in the preceding election. This immediately leads to the employment of the theory of Markov chains which yields exactly that sort of relationship. It also translates itself at once into a simultaneous system of stochastic difference equations whose coefficients are the relevant probabilities. It was this translation which had attracted Lazarsfeld to my writings, and the work I did for him was subsequently used in a substantial expansion of *Economic Dynamics* in its second edition. Later I also joined Lazarsfeld in two seminars, each lasting several weeks, one held in Switzerland and the other in the beautiful mountains north of Turin. There our families got to know one another.

Just after my work on the Lazarsfeld project came to an end I spent the spring and summer as a visiting professor at Berkeley. We travelled from Princeton to Berkeley by car with our two small children, making the country seem even more enormous than it is. At Berkeley we met many delightful people, notably Aaron Gordon, Robert Dorfman, (and for the second time) Harvey Leibenstein and their wives. I also met Joe S. Bain from whose work the theory of contestable markets would later derive so much, and Howard Ellis who was then approaching retirement.

Soon after our return to Princeton, where I had been promoted to full professor, I was introduced to another remarkable person, Wroe Alderson, who was then serving on an advisory committee to the Princeton economics department. Alderson was Quaker and a devoted advocate of their social goals such as the promotion of peace and elimination of poverty. He was senior partner of Alderson and Sessions, a management consulting firm in Philadelphia. After one evening together at a meeting he invited me to come to his office to see whether a consulting arrangement would suit us both. That arrangement lasted for nearly a decade. I would travel to Philadelphia about once a week and work on one or more of the many projects on which the busy company was engaged. In those years I got some sense of the way big business in the US is conducted. I worked with large firms and small, among them major firms in chemicals, steel, food products and a variety of other lines. I studied their policies on pricing, advertising, product line, location and all of the other areas of interest to economic analysis. The work made use of demand theory, mathematical programming, inventory theory and many of the other tools of formal economic analysis. It was a very valuable experience, teaching me how theoretical instruments can be applied flexibly to the complex and messy problems of reality, and, above all, suggesting how firms actually behave in reality. It also led me to revise many of my theoretical ideas, and two of my books originated from my work at the consulting firm. *Economic Theory and Operations Analysis* (1961) started off as a compendium of the analytical tools that had proved useful in application to business activities, with illustrations derived from experience with firms. In its later editions the book has gradually evolved more into exposition of economic theory with particular emphasis on very recent developments. The relationship between business experience and theory was still more direct in the case of *Business Behavior, Value and Growth* and its sales-maximisation model. Several years of association with members of the managements of large firms finally forced me to recognise that there was a systematic difference between the way matters were viewed by them and by the standard economic models. Of the recommendations made to our clients, my impression was that about 60 per cent were accepted and adopted. It became clear, eventually, that those which were rejected were not chosen fortuitously, but, rather, constituted a fairly predictable pattern. It ultimately dawned on me that virtually any proposal that promised to increase profits but did so by sacrificing sales volume was almost certain to be spurned. I began to modify my recommendations accordingly and, as I remember it, the acceptance rate rose substantially.

The natural reaction of a microtheorist to such experiences was a re-examination of the standard profit-maximisation models which we had all been taught to employ. I found out, eventually, that other economists had, on the basis of interviews and other forms of observation, also reached the conclusion that in practice firms pursue objectives more diverse and complex than just maximisation of profits. But in one important respect the consulting experience had taken me beyond that observation alone, for it had shown that other goals such as maximisation of sales or growth of assets each had their own implications for business decisions and to each of these there seemed to correspond optimal values of the firm's decision variables. In other words, abandonment of the profit-maximisation premise did not leave one with no choice but chaos and indecision. Rather, it called for decisions which are different but equally determinate, and which can be analysed using all of the traditional tools and methods – marginal analysis, mathematical programming, etc.

Some months of working on the formal analysis provided the model of sales maximisation (later supplemented by a model of growth maximisation) which constituted the basis of the little book

Business Behavior, Value and Growth (1959). If this model does constitute a contribution I believe it consists not in the observation that management may have objectives other than profit, but in the demonstration that other objectives are perfectly consistent with fruitful theoretical analysis, as was later demonstrated so effectively by writers such as Oliver Williamson and Robin Marris.

Let me emphasise that I never maintained and do not believe that all firms (or even all oligopoly firms) seek to maximise sales, or that they all share any other common and simple objective. I merely asserted and still believe that many firms have some objectives other than profit alone, and that for some which I encountered sales maximisation is a reasonable approximation to their somewhat more complicated goals. Those goals are, in any event, rarely formulated expressly (except for purposes of public relations), they may change from time to time, and they are at most pursued only in a rough and ready manner. Moreover, I believe that in aggregative studies of industry behaviour the differences between the predictions of profit and sales maximisation are apt to be minor and unimportant. But for analysis of the behaviour of individual firms I believe the distinction is vital, as the reactions of business clients to our recommendations made under the two premises suggests strongly.

Partisans of the profit maximisation approach have suggested that the behavior patterns called for by the two models may be difficult to distinguish, and they have questioned the evidence presented in *Business Behavior, Value and Growth* which, admittedly, is all anecdotal. They have pointed out, rather cogently, that long-run profit maximisation may require resistance to elimination of unprofitable sales in the short run. I certainly cannot prove the contrary. I can only suggest that the change in the nature of our recommendations constituted what amounts to a (very poorly) controlled experiment of a sort rarely possible for economists. Moreover, the resulting observations were generally supported by careful discussion with businesspersons with whom I had established rather close relationships and who had little reason to slant their answers.

After the sale of Alderson Associates when Wroe Alderson retired my consulting work continued through the firms Mathematica, and Consultants in Industry Economics (CIE), which I helped to found. This work has usually proved fruitful and stimulating to me in more general research. Microeconomists are peculiarly fortunate in this respect, for while academic consultants drawn from other disciplines generally contribute by application of the learning they have acquired through research and teaching, for them benefits rarely seem to flow in the other direction.

THE PERFORMING ARTS

Sheer misunderstanding led to my involvement in the economics of the performing arts. In about 1960, the Twentieth Century Fund and John D. Rockefeller III had decided that the time was auspicious for a systematic study of that subject. On enquiry they were told of an economist at Princeton who was knowledgeable about the arts as well as economics. The person who had steered them to me had, of course, confused my activities in painting and sculpture with knowledge of the finances and organisation of opera, theatres, orchestras and dance companies. My father had instilled in me a great love of the performing arts, but little knowledge of the economic side of these activities accompanied my wife's and my frequent attendance.

I agreed to a meeting on the subject, having first discussed the matter with a young colleague, William G. Bowen, with whom I had worked earlier (and who has since become President of Princeton University). Talking with the potential sponsors of the study I emphasised my ignorance of the subject and then, on the basis of my consulting experience, proceeded to indicate how I believed it should be analysed dispassionately, as though one were dealing with the economics of the most banale of commodities rather than one which commands widespread expressions of adulation (if hardly universal attendance).

As it happened, Bowen and I were then both heavily committed to other projects. When it turned out that the potential sponsors had, for better or worse, decided that we were the right persons to conduct the study, we found ourselves resisting what was to prove one of the most exciting projects we had ever undertaken – so poor can foresight be!

The research turned out to be a major undertaking. It lasted somewhat more than three years, acquired and analysed data from several hundred organisations, distributed questionnaires to about 150,000 audience members at more than a hundred performances in dozens of cities. A small army of students and other investigators was trained and sent out to collect the materials using questionnaires which had been painstakingly designed and pre-tested. All of this was planned meticulously by Bowen and the work was organised and supervised by my wife, with whom all my subsequent work on the economics of the arts has been carried out in full partnership.

The overall design of the study and the planning of the empirical work is all to be credited to my co-author. His skill in dealing with messy data made it possible to determine many fundamental attributes of the activities in question. For example, he was able to show systematically that the composition of audiences in terms of education, income, age and sex varied only minusculely from one art form to another or one city to another. Audiences in London were, essentially, no different from those in Houston, Texas – all highly educated, and well-to-do relative to the population as a whole. Generally no more than 2 or 3 per cent of the audience was made up of blue collar workers; opera with 7 per cent of the audience derived from this economic group, constituting the only exception. Many fascinating observations peripheral to our central topic also emerged from Bowen's calculations. For example, he was able to show that the proportion of women among the performance in an orchestra at that time was almost perfectly inversely correlated with the income of the orchestra – a very tangible index of sex discrimination!

In the early 1960s collection of economic data on the performing arts in the US was no routine matter. It often took my wife to back offices, basements and lofts, where figures sometimes had to be pieced together from scraps of paper that constituted the only records that some group had kept. Since that time much more such information has been collected and some of it published on a regular basis. Indeed, we were asked to design and, for several years, collect some of the figures that now appear regularly in the official US government publications.

My own part in the study involved a role in the determination of the overall objectives and the general research design. I also wrote most of the final manuscript. However, my one contribution I consider to be significant is the cost disease model, which has since been used to help explain the behaviour of the cost of education, the budgetary problems of cities, etc. The basic point is that the *live* performing arts (in contradistinction to those employing the mass media such as film and television) are extraordinarily unadaptable to productivity-increasing technical change. A Boccherini string quartet written in the eighteenth century which takes half an hour to perform, required two-person hours of performance time then and requires exactly the same amount of time today. Meanwhile, in much of the remainder of the economy productivity has been increasing virtually without interruption in a manner that compounds and accumulates. If wages in the arts do not rise far more slowly than those in the remainder of the economy (and the evidence indicates that they do not) this means that cost per performance in the arts must rise steadily at a rate faster than costs in the remainder of the economy, roughly reflecting the difference in the productivity growth that characterises the two sectors. Over the years this can add up to an enormous differential. I estimate roughly that a typical manufactured good which cost about the same as attendance at a performance in 1800 now costs only about one twentieth as much! This means also that the funds supplied to the arts by government or private philanthropy must generally increase year in, year out, at a rate exceeding the economy's rate of inflation if artistic activity is not to be forced to retrench. Constancy of *real* contributions is simply not enough for the purpose. This, then, is what has since come to be called the cost disease of the arts (I am delighted that it is also sometimes called 'Baumol's disease'). If the hypothesis is correct (and there is a good deal of evidence consistent with it)[2] it helps to explain many economic phenomena outside the arts, such as the shift of the labour forces in a number of countries out of manufacturing and toward the services, the increasing use of disposable products to avoid repair, the rising relative cost of medical care and education, etc.

Because such incidents are sometimes considered noteworthy it may be worth reporting that the cost disease model entered my consciousness quite suddenly and unexpectedly, though it had no doubt lurked in my subconscious for some time before. One night I awoke from a deep sleep at about 3 a.m. with the entire model clearly in my mind. I left the bedroom, went to the next room, jotted down a few notes, and immediately went back to sleep. The next morning I was able to write the idea up systematically. Later I will recount another such incident which occurred about fifteen years afterwards.

Our study of the arts was sponsored by a private foundation, the Twentieth Century Fund, which generously paid the considerable costs of this project. Moreover, the Fund was careful to avoid interference of any sort with the nature of the research or the contents of the resulting book. Indeed, it withstood pressure from a representative of some of the larger performing organisations to suppress or weaken some of the materials showing the high incomes of the members of the audience, a piece of information which, it was feared, would make it more difficult to obtain financial support from the government and other sources. Happily, these fears proved to be unjustified.

As a matter of fact, it is now widely believed that the opposite occurred – that because of the accident of timing (or, perhaps it was no accident but a matter of good judgement of its sponsors) the book is now said to have played a role in launching substantial government support in the United States. It appeared at the same time as another report sponsored by the Rockefeller Brothers Fund (*The Performing Arts: Problems and Prospects*, 1965), in which Bowen and I had a peripheral part. The Rockefeller report was prepared by a committee composed to a considerable extent of businessmen whose strong statement of approval of funding for the arts contributed political respectability to the attempt to induce the United States to embark upon the sort of public sponsorship so traditional in Europe. The simultaneous appearance of our own book, which for the first time provided systematic data and some degree of analysis on the subject, apparently contributed ammunition to the campaign for public support of the arts.

The book was launched with a burst of publicity orchestrated by the Twentieth Century Fund. There were front page stories in the *New York Times* and the *Washington Post*. Newspapers throughout the world carried substantial reports. We were most amused by the story in Pravda which reported that two respectable economists from Princeton University had just published a book showing how capitalism destroys the arts!

PRINCETON AND NEW YORK UNIVERSITIES

The economics department at Princeton was an extraordinarily harmonious group, indeed. I believe virtually all of my colleagues had a deep affection for one another. We were sorry when Friedrich Lutz returned to Europe a few years after we arrived. In addition to members such as Viner, Oskar Morgenstern, Richard Lester, and Lester Chandler, the Department was fortunate to acquire W. Arthur Lewis and Fritz Machlup, both of whom were to become close friends. The Lewises had their home a few doors from ours, and our children grew up together. His lovely and charming wife also proved to be my most talented sculpture student, and has had several successful exhibitions of her own. Sir Arthur's general wisdom, his analytic intuition and his meticulous historical scholarship have always constituted standards difficult for the rest of us to emulate. Fritz Machlup, whose unexpected death earlier this year has left a major gap in our lives, was an incredible generator of ideas and research undertakings which he pursued with amazing determination and energy. At age 77 he undertook a research programme which was projected to yield a work in ten volumes. Three years later he had completed the first three of those books, and work on the others was well on its way.

He and Oskar Morgenstern reached retirement age virtually simultaneously. On attaining their emeritus status at Princeton they were immediately offered and accepted full-term appointments at New York University, where each of them continued to teach with energy and devotion for the remainder of his life.

At just about the time Machlup and Morgenstern left for NYU I had begun to think about my position. By then I had been at Princeton for nearly a quarter of a century. Our children had grown and left home. It seemed high time to make some change in our arrangements. Yet leaving Princeton altogether was virtually unthinkable. Half our lives had been spent there and it contained most of our close friends, both outside the department and within it.

The solution to our dilemma was an invitation to NYU, first, to come as a visitor for a year. Aside from visiting appointments at the Stockholm School of Economics and Berkeley this was our first protracted period away from Princeton since 1949, and it was a return to the city of our childhood. The department in New York proved most hospitable and a pleasant place in which to work. The students were far more heterogeneous than those at Princeton, both in ethnic background and in quality of their earlier training. The best of them were of outstanding quality, and they constituted a fascinating and enthusiastic group.

Consequently, when the next year I was offered a permanent appointment on a half-time basis, and received the consent of Princeton to the arrangement, I agreed readily. As it turned out, it was the beginning of what, in my own view, seems my most creative period.

It actually began with the completion of an exclusively Princeton enterprise; two volumes on environmental economics written jointly with my (then) Princeton colleague, Wallace Oates. One volume was almost entirely devoted to theory while the second sought to assemble the available empirical materials, adding some evidence acquired by ourselves.

Among the results provided by the theoretical volume two will be cited as illustrations. The first deals with the victims of externalities. It has, of course, been known, at least since the work of Pigou, that (with some restrictions) optimal expenditure on reduction of pollution emissions (or other detrimental externalities) requires a charge or tax upon the polluter equal to the marginal social damage of his emissions. This 'polluter pays' arrangement forces the polluter to bear the full social cost of his emissions, and therefore, to undertake any preventative measure whose (incremental) cost is less than the value of the damage thereby avoided. But what about the victims? It would seem that simple justice calls for some sort of compensation to those whose health or even whose cost of living is affected by pollution. Indeed, this intuitive judgement is readily confirmed formally with the aid of the mathematical theory of fairness provided in the work of Duncan Foley, David Schmeidler, Serge-Christophe Kolm and others. Yet it is proved in our theoretical volume that, unless it can be provided in a way whose incentive effects are zero (i.e. as a 'lump sum' payment), *any* compensation to the victims of externalities, however small, is incompatible with Pareto optimality in resource allocation in the economy. There is a simple theoretical explanation of this result. In the presence of detrimental externalities there is a Pareto optimal level of use of resources *by the victims* to protect themselves from their effects. For example, it may be appropriate to insulate or air condition homes and workplaces, or it may be desirable to move them away from the source of pollution thereby, perhaps, increasing transportation costs in the future. But if compensation is based on the amount of damage suffered by the victims, such compensation payments will induce them to spend less on self-protection against that damage. In effect, such compensation payments reduce the marginal net yield of outlays on self-protection. Here we then have a clear example of a conflict (or, rather, a trade-off) between Pareto optimality and fairness.

A second illustrative result of our theoretical analysis relates to the choice between a tax upon the generator of externalities and a subsidy to induce him to reduce his emissions. Common sense suggests that at appropriate tax and subsidy rates the effects of the two will be the same – the donkey can be moved either with the carrot or the stick. But while this conclusion (which had often been repeated in the environmental literature) has an element of truth, it turns out that subsidies have a second consequence which is more than likely to offset its pollution decreasing effect. It is true that in the short run either the tax or the subsidy will induce polluting firms to emit less. However, at least in the case of perfect competition, in the long run, the tax on emissions may *not* reduce the emissions of any one polluting *firm*, yet it will reduce the emissions of the *industry* by encouraging the exit of polluters. On the other hand, *the subsidy is likely to increase the industry's emissions* by encouraging the entry of polluters. These results are certainly true when there is a fixed proportion between output and quantity of emission. A fixed Pigouvian tax, t, per unit of emissions then contributes to the firm's total cost the amount tky, where y is output and k is the emissions-output ratio. The resulting addition to average cost is tky/y = tk = constant. Therefore, the Pigouvian tax simply causes a uniform upward shift in the firm's average cost curve, and so does not affect the location of its minimum point, i.e. its profit maximising output or emissions level. Yet we do know from a standard supply-demand diagram that with curves of the usual shape a tax must shift the supply curve upward and therefore must reduce industry output and, hence, its emissions, and the opposite must be true under a subsidy.

The investigation of the empirical data also produced a number of what, to us at least, were surprises. We had thought that the explosion in the world's population and in industrial activity would show that there was fairly universal growth in the rate of environmental damage, but the results were far more mixed. In some cases such as lead in the atmosphere and the generation of solid wastes our conjecture did indeed turn out to be true or, at least, to be supported by the evidence. But post-war emissions control efforts had substantial beneficial effects on air and water quality with, e.g. enormous decreases in the sulphur and particulate content of the atmosphere in major cities of the US and the United Kingdom. In other cases, e.g. the concentration of pollutants in Lake Superior in the United States and the oxygen content of the rivers surrounding Manhattan, matters had been improving long before that. In several cases such as the depletion of oxygen in the Baltic and the concentration of mercury in tuna it transpired that there was good reason to suspect that the causes were natural (e.g. a secular decline in rainfall in the sources of water for the Baltic). We were most surprised to find (after an extensive search that took us to the conservators' quarters at the Louvre, the Metropolitan Museum in New York and St Paul's

Cathedral in London) that there seems to be no conclusive evidence supporting the view that the deterioration of ancient sculpture and of stone buildings is accelerating or that it is attributable to increasing emissions of pollutants. We found many newspaper stories claiming categorically that this was so, but careful review of the scientific evidence simply forced us to accept the verdict 'not proven'.

Perhaps partly in consequence of this work I was elected to the presidency of the recently formed Association of Environmental and Resource Economists (AERE), an organisation which has since grown and expanded its activities.

THE THEORY OF CONTESTABLE MARKETS

Soon after the two books on the environment[3] made their appearance, I found myself embarked almost accidentally on what I consider to be the most fruitful piece of research in which I have ever participated. The word 'participated' is used advisedly, since the results stemmed from the work of at least a half dozen persons beside myself – my co-authors, John Panzar, then of Bell Laboratories and Robert Willig of Princeton University, Elizabeth Bailey, formerly Vice-Chairman of the Civil Aeronautics Board and now at Carnegie Mellon University, Dietrich Fischer, Thijs ten Raa, then at New York University, and Gerald Faulhaber at Bell Laboratories. Obviously there were three centres of activity: NYU, Princeton and Bell Laboratories.

My systematic work on the subject began with a project I had undertaken under the sponsorship of the Division of Information Science and Technology of the National Science Foundation in which an incidental part of the task was to provide a non-technical document discussing the rationale for and principles for the determination of the proper amount of government financial support for the dissemination of scientific and technical information in general and of scientific journals in particular. Assuming that a large part of the argument would rest on the sorts of market failure associated with public goods and scale economies, I set about what I expected to be the tedious task of redescribing a set of elementary and straightforward principles. The public goods portion of the discussion turned out just as expected – exactly as it is so well described in the literature. However, the theory of scale economies and the associated phenomenon of natural monopoly seemed to resist simple explanation. Each time I attempted a description of the logic of some obvious proposition it seemed to acquire complexity and turned out not to be quite correct. For example, in the case of a publisher who provided a half dozen journals rather than only one, scale economies did not seem to account for the firm's multiproduct character. Why was the enterprise a multiproduct firm, and what would society lose by breaking up the publishing firm into six separate publishers of single journals? It was considerations such as this which later led Panzar and Willig to formulate their concept of economies of scope – the savings which a firm may (or may not) enjoy from simultaneous provision of a multiplicity of products – and which had previously led me to formulate the more technical concept of trans-ray convexity,[4] a formal criterion of continuous complementarity in the production of different goods as output proportions change. At the same time it became clear that natural monopoly which is defined to mean that production of the industry's vector of outputs is cheaper when carried out by a single firm rather than by any multiplicity of firms, is not quite the same thing as scale economies. Indeed, it was proved eventually that scale economies throughout the relevant region of output space are neither necessary nor sufficient for natural monopoly.

Meanwhile, Gerald Faulhaber, who had been sent by Bell Laboratories to carry out his graduate work at Princeton, had quite independently, starting off from some earlier work of mine, begun research on the theory of natural monopoly. He found implications which had escaped me completely at the time the original work had been prepared. When Faulhaber showed me some of his work and asked me to supervise his PhD dissertation, I was astonished at the degree of overlap with my own work at NYU. Indeed, using a single-product game theoretic approach, his work was at that point in many ways ahead of mine.

The developments were sufficiently seductive to attract the attention of others, notably Panzar and Willig at Bell Laboratories, Dietrich Fischer at NYU, and Elizabeth Bailey who then held positions both at Bell Laboratories and NYU and who quickly took on the task of liaison in addition to the valuable contributions she directly provided herself.

Faulhaber had already proved for the single-product case that the concept underlying and, indeed, appropriately defining natural monopoly is a mathematical relationship called subadditivity of total cost. Specifically (for the multiproduct case) let y^I represent the vector of outputs of the industry and let y^i be any vector of outputs assigned to a hypothetical firm, i, in any partition of the industry's outputs, so that $\Sigma y^i = y^I$. If C(y) is the total cost function of a firm in the industry, then that cost function is strictly subadditive if $C(y^I) < \Sigma C(y^i)$ for each and every set of y^i summing to y^I. In other words, the cost function is subadditive at industry output vector y^I if it is cheaper for y^I to be produced by a monopoly than by any larger number of firms.

Faulhaber had also proved in the single product case, first, that economies of scale are sufficient to guarantee that the firm's average costs will decrease, second, that decreasing average costs are sufficient to guarantee subadditivity, and, third, that the converse is untrue – that subadditivity is no guarantee of decreasing average cost. In other words, in the single-product case he had shown that an industry could be a natural monopoly even if it did not exhibit scale economies and its average costs were not declining.

Soon Panzar and Willig produced several sets of necessary conditions for subadditivity in the multiproduct case, and I provided a set of conditions sufficient for multiproduct natural monopoly, conditions which have since been used rather widely in empirical studies of cost functions and their implications for the structure of an industry.

Panzar and Willig, working together, proposed a concept which Dr Bailey and I had also put forth on the same day – the concept of sustainability of prices. A vector of prices charged by a multiproduct monopolist is said to be *sustainable against entry* if a) it provides revenue to the monopoly at least sufficient to permit it to cover its costs, and b) there exists no other vector of outputs which an entrant can sell at those prices and which will permit the entrant to operate without loss. In other words, sustainable prices permit the incumbent to prevent entry without recourse to retaliatory measures or strategic responses. This concept was formulated as a first step toward transformation of the natural monopoly concept from one which was normative (when is natural monopoly the most efficient industry structure?) to something that was more or less behavioural (when will natural monopoly be immune from entry?).

Faulhaber was able to prove that where both economies and diseconomies of scale are present (at different ranges of outputs), even if a firm is a natural monopoly, no sustainable prices may exist for it. He did this with the aid of a remarkable numerical counterexample. Consider three communities for which electricity generating facilities of given capacity are to be built. Suppose any one of the communities' needs can be met at a cost of $12 million, that any two of them can be served simultaneously for $19 million while all three of them can be served by a single plant for $30 million. Costs here are clearly subadditive since provision of the output by three separate plants costs $3 \times \$12$ million = $36 million, while two-plant production costs $12 + \$19$ million = 31 million. Both other options are, therefore, more costly than the $30 million outlay required for single-firm production. Yet, here, a single generating firm can find no prices which are sustainable. For if it were, for example, to propose to charge each community $10 million in order just to cover its $30 million cost, an entrant could offer to supply only two of the three communities at a cost of say $9.7 million each, thus more than covering the $19 million cost of the plant required for the purpose. Faulhaber's example thus showed that in some cases freedom of entry can prevent cost minimisation. But the bulk of our analysis was later to argue strongly for ease of entry.

A little later I provided a complementary theorem which rested on a result first derived by Frank Ramsey in 1927. As we know, where average costs are declining (and in a variety of related multiproduct cases), a firm which prices its products at their marginal costs must suffer losses. The question to which Ramsey addressed himself is if marginal cost prices are therefore precluded, what deviations of prices from marginal costs are required for the second-best allocation of resources, that is, for Pareto optimality under the constraint that supplying firms just cover their total costs? Ramsey was able to derive a formula for these second-best prices which was ignored by much of the economic literature for several decades but had by the 1970s received a great deal of attention. I was then able to prove (though the result took me completely by surprise) that a monopolist who decided to adopt Pareto optimal Ramsey prices would (under a set of rather reasonable assumptions) find those prices to be sustainable. In other words, such a commendable pricing decision would reward the monopolist by granting him immunity from entry.

I had arrived at this result in rather curious circumstances. My wife and I were attending a fund raising performance at one of New York's experimental theatres, and we were waiting in line to get in surrounded by persons in bizarre dress and make-up when, according to my wife, my face took on a rather distracted look. I told her that a theorem which hardly seemed plausible to me had come to me from nowhere, along with what seemed to me to be its entire proof.

Indeed, it transpired that the rigorous proof that emerged eventually did follow the outline that came to me suddenly in that theatre lobby, but it took weeks of hard labour by (a sceptical) Willig, Bailey (and myself) before it could be put into satisfactory form.

At about this time a small group of US economists was sent by the National Science Foundation to attend a conference in Leningrad, and Willig and I were among them. We sat up all night in the airplane discussing how our analysis of natural monopoly could be extended to other market forms and constitute the basis for a theory of the determination of industry structure. The vision had been mine, but Willig was to contribute the key step to its realisation. First, on our return, Fischer and I produced a paper showing how one can calculate the cost minimising structure of an industry, thereby determining whether it is or is not, say, a natural monopoly. For example, if it transpires that the industry's output vector can be produced most cheaply by say, four firms, one can say it is a 'natural oligopoly', and we showed under what circumstances this will be true. Similarly, we showed under what cost conditions the industry will be 'naturally perfectly competitive', etc.

Then Willig formulated the concept of what we were to call a perfectly contestable market – a market in which an entrant has access to all production techniques available to incumbents, in which the entrant is not prohibited from wooing the incumbent's customers, and in which entry decisions can be reversed without cost – that is, a market from which entrants can withdraw without loss of any of their investments. An example of an approximation to such a market is an airline route. If company A opens up for business on the route from New York to Los Angeles and business proves disappointing, he can simply withdraw and move them to another more promising route.

Where exit and entry are so easy and exit so costless incumbents are completely vulnerable to the threat posed by *potential* entry. It is possible to prove that, as a consequence, in a perfectly contestable market (a) no firm can earn any monopoly profit in the long run, (b) industry structure must always be efficient, i.e. the industry will tend to be composed of exactly the number of firms that can produce its output at minimum cost and (c) if two or more firms supply a given product to a market, in the long run the price of that product must equal its marginal cost.

Markets may be perfectly contestable even if they are characterised by scale economies in production and even if they contain only a small number of firms (even only a single firm). The theory thus generalises considerably the concept of perfect competition, showing how ease of entry and exit and the accompanying threat by potential entrants can elicit good performance even in industries with small numbers of firms.

It must be emphasised that our purpose was not apologetics. We do not believe that most industries are perfectly contestable or even nearly so. We do believe, however, that some industries with small numbers of firms *are* highly contestable, and that in those cases government interference with the market mechanism is difficult to justify. In other cases the contestability of the market can be increased by public policy and in those cases this will sometimes prove to be the most effective means to serve the public interest.

It should be added also that we are well aware of the heavy debt contestability analysis owes to earlier writing, and have tried to suggest some of its sources in our publications. But as Viner taught me long ago, one can never hope to achieve completeness in such an undertaking.

In my presidential address to the American Economic Association in December of 1981 I sought to provide a general introduction to the theory of contestable markets. This was followed several months later by the publication of our book with its lengthy analysis of multiproduct firms and industries and its examination of the market forces that determine the structure of an industry – whether it will emerge as an oligopoly, a monopoly or something else. As is to be expected, the analysis has generated controversy, raising legitimate questions many of which are still far from being settled. It has also led to a variety of research undertakings by others, both empirical and theoretical, and that has, of course, been most gratifying.

TOWARD FURTHER WORK

Happily, the area in which I work has experienced relatively rapid growth in the past few decades, and so my stock of teaching capital has undergone considerable obsolescence. Many of my former students and their contemporaries are now better equipped than I to teach the various courses in mathematical economics, virtually all of which I had inaugurated some thirty years earlier.

I flatter myself that this is not quite true in my research. In the two years since the appearance of the contestability book I have embarked on several other projects. I am working on applications of Duncan Foley's fairness concept to analyse the equitability of different rationing procedures, of peak-off peak pricing and of Pigouvian taxes on externalities. I am working on the theory of productivity growth and the feedback relationship between such growth and expenditures on research and development by private industry. I am also considering a study of the theory of nationalised industry – of the circumstances under which operation of a firm by the public sector may be superior in terms of the general welfare to operation by private enterprise, regulated or unregulated by government. Here it should be noted that analyses such as the theory of public goods are less pertinent than may at first appear to be the case since a public good can be produced by private firms if it is *financed* by government. If nationalised firms lack the incentives for efficiency provided by the market mechanism to private firms why, then, should government enterprise ever be preferred over private? I am working on a model which will, with a bit of luck, provide some answers and, perhaps, some additional insights.

In short, as yet there is no conclusion to my story – all I can offer is a status report on a continuing stream of research . . .

Notes

1. I am not certain the term 'prisoner's dilemma' had yet been invented; indeed, I seem to remember it was proposed by Professor A. Tucker at Princeton several years later. But the ideas of game theory had reached London and in discussions externalities were already being translated there into game theoretic terms.
2. The noteworthy exception seems always to have been a period of rapid inflation. Data for the period after the US Civil War, after the First World War and the inflation of the 1970s indicate that in such periods growth in cost per performance has not stayed ahead of the general price level. Presumably groups are not able to raise money quickly enough, and are therefore forced to retrench by reducing rehearsal time, simplifying costumes and scenery, etc. If this explanation is correct, it follows that the cost disease is not really in remission in such periods, but that its normal consequences are suppressed and emerge in a different form – that of reduction of standards and cutting of corners.
3. Baumol, William J. and Wallace, Oates, *The Theory of Environmental Policy*, Englewood Cliffs, N.J., Prentice Hall, 1975 and Oates, Baumol and Blackman, S.A., *Economics and the Quality of Life*, Englewood Cliffs, N.J., Prentice Hall, 1979.
4. For a formal definition see Baumol, W. Panzar and Willig, *Contestable Markets and the Theory of Industry Structure*, San Diego, Ca: Harcourt Brace Jovanovich, 1982, pp. 79–81.

Reference

The Rockefeller Report, *The Performing Arts: Problems and Prospects* (McGraw-Hill, New York, 1965).

10 A Fascination With Economics
Karl Brunner

The study of economics in the context of an institutionalised vacuum of knowledge is a peculiar experience. You reach in all directions with no sense of discrimination. Good fortune may intervene on occasion and guide you to the inheritance left us by great thinkers. But such exposure is disturbing. It stirred an awareness that my doctoral dissertation, marking the ritual exercise assuring entry into the academic confrerie with the blessing of the University of Zürich, be immediately committed to oblivion. Still, I was more than ever fascinated by the spectacle of man and his problems in society. I also judged, with better intuition than reason, that economics could offer me the best avenue to satisfy my curiosity. But the intellectual wasteland characterising the social sciences at Swiss Universities compelled a crucial decision between adaptation or departure. The offer of a grant by the Rockefeller Foundation determined the outcome. Four months at Harvard University and one and a half years as a visitor at the (then) Cowles Commission for Research in Economics (University of Chicago) introduced me to the American scene.

This experience produced utter confusion and urgent questions. The environment enjoyed at the Commission was in many ways admirable valued in human terms and measured by the skilled intelligence and technical expertise. But all this impressive exhibition of human ingenuity remained blurred and out of focus. What did all these layers of adroit analytics involve, what was their point and what did really matter? Was it the superior skill in using a mathematical theorem within a context of 'economic' vocabulary? Was it the 'technical complexity' and 'sophistication' of an argument, or was it the felicitous re-articulation of views bearing on economic policy within the dominant post-war consensus, or an 'innovative variation' of a well defined game fixed by some paradigmatic formulation? A master of the German post-war university scene advised me at the time to be guided by 'astounding and new ideas'.

My encounter with Milton Friedman opened indeed 'new and astounding' vistas. He violated the prevalent pattern of suggestively vague criteria addressed to the selection and evaluation of professional work. Most distressing was moreover the encounter with a group of economists systematically applying economic analysis (i.e. price theory) to social problems of our world. The resulting confusions yielded a fertile ground for the right environment, and UCLA at the beginning of the 1950s was for me the right place. The permanent discussion with a subtle mind (Armen A. Alchian), the impact of a lucid philosopher of science (Reichenbach), and the good fortune of questioning and determined students (Allan H. Meltzer, Tibor Fabian, later on Jerry Jordan and others) dispersed the intellectual fogs and gradually structured my thinking about economics and its role in our endeavour to understand the world.

This background influencing the evolution of my thoughts, addressed to the role and use of economics, guided my attention to three distinct major groups of problems. One covers the range of monetary analysis and policy and a second involves the nature of our cognitive endeavours expressed by our pursuits. The last strand of my persistent interests developed over time from my occupation with the previous two problems. There evolved a gradual understanding that economic analysis offers a systematic approach to the whole range of socio-political reality. These three distinct strands, however separated they may be on purely logical grounds, emerged in the actual practice of my thinking with a connected pattern. I wish to invite the reader to trace with me some of these aspects and interrelations.

ISSUES IN MONETARY ANALYSIS AND MONETARY POLICY

The Development of a 'Money Supply' Analysis

Monetary problems already attracted my interest as a student. But I became, as many others, absorbed with the 'Keynesian Revolution' and the study of Keynes' work. My old interest re-emerged however during the early years at UCLA and the detachment from the Keynesian orthodoxy was under way. This detachment was guided by many uneasy questions bearing on the profession's dismissal of the classical programme for monetary analysis. It was also encouraged by many discussions with Allan H. Meltzer during his doctoral work bearing on the 'money supply process'. So began a long and productive association which crucially influenced my work and ideas over many years.

My interest focusses during the 1950s most particularly on the total separation between 'policy' and monetary analysis. This separation was best revealed by the occurrence of two unrelated and independent languages used for the discussion of policy and the formulation of analysis. This analysis offered little help for a systematic approach to important aspects covered by policy discussions. And the latter frequently proceeded with arguments and formulation unrelated to any economic analysis. This feature still lingers at many Central Banks. Our professional literature contained around the middle of the 1950s suggestive approaches attempting to trace the behaviour of money stock or earning assets of banks' in response to actions undertaken by the monetary authorities. These approaches were indeed rather 'mechanical' in the sense that the behaviour patterns used in the arguments showed no exposure to economic analysis. But this failure was not an inherent property of what became known as the 'multiplier approach' to the analysis of the money stock. It occurred to me that a suitable exploitation of inherited attempts could articulate the problem within the context of an economic analysis recognising the operation of relative costs and yields on the crucial behaviour patterns. The result was an analysis of the 'money supply process' describing the joint behaviour of money stock, earning assets and interest rates resulting from the interaction between banks, the public and the monetary authorities. The behaviour of the money stock was made understandable by this approach as an outcome determined by interacting asset markets operating in response to Central Bank behaviour.

The formulation was deliberately chosen in order to 'navigate' the analysis between the empty exercises represented by (what I called once) a 'Forest of Jacobians' and the standard econometric approach relying on large models. The 'multiplier approach' lacks the 'neat elegance' much appreciated by our profession but does offer a procedure with useful advantages for anybody concerned with the real problems confronting us. It suggested a natural way to impose order constraints assuring a range of definite propositions about the results of the asset market interaction. It offered moreover a framework effectively geared to subsume important institutional aspects of the monetary system. The role of a shifting inter-bank deposit structure, or the consequences of changing reserve arrangements or of waning membership in the Federal Reserve System could be systematically evaluated in the context of this analytic framework. It offered also an opportunity to examine the dominant patterns shaping the behaviour of the money stock and to appraise the many assertions usually encountered in this respect. Thus emerged an assessment of the relative importance of the public's, the bank's and the authorities' behaviour in the evolution of the money stock over shorter and longer horizons. It yielded in particular a clarification of the conditions generating a 'reverse causation' in the relation between money and income. The occurrence of this phenomenon depends on very specific institutional arrangements. It requires either a massive interest elasticity of the banks' reserve and borrowing behaviour or a pronounced interest sensitivity in the supply of the monetary base. The latter condition is probably more important. But such patterns are not a natural property of monetary processes. They are the product of a Central Bank's institutional policy. Variations of these arrangements over time modify the relative contribution of 'reverse causation' to the observed association between money and income.

The analysis clarified moreover the meaning of loan ceilings occasionally imposed by important countries. It showed that this instrument hardly affected money stock and total earning assets. It created a captive market for government securities and lowered the relative cost of public borrowing and raised the cost of private borrowing. It presented a typical example of wealth redistribution proceeding under the rhetorical cover of an anti-inflationary device. And lastly, the monetary control procedure developed by the Swiss National Bank or experimentally applied by Professor Robert Rasche on behalf of the Shadow Open Market Committee emerged basically from this equilibrium analysis couched in terms of a 'multiplier approach'.[1]

The Study of Federal Reserve Policy-making

This research on the money supply process prepared the ground for a detailed examination of Federal Reserve policymaking jointly undertaken with Allan H. Meltzer. This work initiated a growing attention to the political economy of political institutions. We examined in particular the nature of the ruling conception guiding policies over the past decades. We also investigated the strategy associated with the ruling conception and the interpretations of events and actions made in this context. It became very clear that the Federal Reserve's policymakers shared with all other men the characteristic of a 'theorising animal'. Their view of the world was controlled by a theory associated in the 1920s with their major figures. Federal Reserve actions and interpretations during the Great Depression were rationally conceived in terms of this theory. The problem centred on the adequacy of this theory developed without any connections with and exposure to systematic economic analysis. This theory, centred on the notion that banks are 'inherently reluctant to borrow' (irrespective of costs and yields), gradually changed into the free reserve doctrine of the early post-war period. This tradition eventually faded away in the late 1960s and was replaced with the idea that the money stock is determined by a volatile money demand in the context of a more or less explicit IS-LM framework.

Several major results of our investigation were impressed on my mind. The history of monetary policymaking in the USA revealed to me, confirmed by many observations over the subsequent years, that only very special circumstances will produce a substantial change in conception and procedure well entrenched in the bureaucracy manipulating a political institution. It also revealed that policymaking is indeed rational. It involves however a rationality relative to the long-run interests and survival of a political institution not necessarily linked with systematic attention to the social welfare of the nation. A careful study of the minutes summarising the meetings of the relevant policy committee indicated moreover the tragic and persistent misinterpretation of monetary actions and monetary events all through the Great Depression. This judgement does not depend on hindsight. It can be justified by the knowledge available at the time. Lastly, the persistent misinterpretation of monetary evolutions, also visible in the public record, was ultimately expressed by the *negative* association between the Federal Reserve's actions and rhetoric description. This 'Orwellian inversion' (i.e. expansionary becomes contractionary and vice versa) of language affects the media's reporting and permeates the financial world to this day.[2]

The Major Issues in the 'Monetarist' Controversy

The discussion gradually evolving over the 1950s proceeded however with a broader focus beyond the issues considered so far. The monetarist 'counter-revolution' addressed some central tenets of the Keynesian position. The array of issues governing the discussions can be organised under four major groups. These problems refer to the nature of the transmission mechanism, the impulse patterns driving the economic process, the internal stability of the system and the relation between allocative processes and aggregative behaviour. The controversies proceeding under the various headings involved substantially more than erudite scholarly games. They reflected ultimately important aspects of the world bearing on the rationale of specific policies or of general approaches to policymaking.

The Transmission Mechanism The Keynesian tradition subsumed two interpretations of the transmission mechanism associated with two alternative interpretations of the famous IS/LM apparatus. One version guided the econometric approach to macro-analysis and most of the textbook discussion. It emphasises the substitution between money and financial assets represented by 'bonds' and excludes substitution between money and real assets. Monetary impulses are conveyed under the circumstances by the play of interest rates on financial assets. The interest sensitivity of money demand and of major expenditure categories in the national income accounts determines therefore the impact of monetary policy. This interpretation explains investigations bearing on the efficacy of restrictive monetary policy organised by the US Department of Commerce in 1967 which concentrated on the response of business firms' capital budgeting to the observed increase in interest rates. It also explains the rationale developed by the Council of Economic Advisors for an activist use of fiscal policy supplemented with an accommodative stance of monetary policy. This particular version of the Keynesian transmission mechanism directed to the operation of borrowing costs associated with specific expenditure categories. The framework guiding policymakers' interpretation produced the conclusion that monetary impulses reach the economy via a narrow segment of total national expenditures most exposed to the impact of borrowing costs. This sector became identified with construction activity. The burden of monetary policy would be imposed under the circumstances on an industry with high 'social and political priorities'. This 'social cost' of monetary policy could be avoided by confining monetary policy to an accommodation of prevailing trends guided by an interest rate set in accordance with the 'needs of the housing sector'. Activist management of aggregate demand was assigned on the other hand to fiscal policy.

Other policy issues reinforced attention to the nature of the transmission mechanism. This range of questions, motivated by policy problems, encouraged the systematic re-examination of this particular Keynesian strand. This re-examination was guided by an analysis of the social function of money as an asset emerging from the interaction between individuals in a social group. The self-interested search of interrelated individuals yields a pattern of asset uses minimising information and transaction costs in a world where information and transactions require the investment of valuable resources. But money as a transaction-dominating asset substitutes in all directions, and most particularly over the whole array of assets. The text-book version of the Keynesian story centred on interest rates and borrowing costs could not subsume the monetary evolutions of countries without an organised capital market. Observations from a wide array of countries suggest that money substitutes beyond financial assets with real assets. This broad sweep of substitution relations radically changes the nature of the mechanism transmitting monetary impulses to the economy. This change lowers the significance of Keynesian 'interest rates' as conveyors of monetary impulses and dismisses the role of relative borrowing costs. Some of the empirical studies designed to explore the efficacy of restrictive (or expansionary) policy appear thus to be misconceived or irrelevant. The monetary policy of accommodation loses moreover its justification.

A broader view was already contained in an alternative version of the IS-LM apparatus developed by Lloyd Metzler. In order to subsume an analysis acknowledging the full substitutability of money over all assets into a framework admitting only two assets all non-money items were lumped into a single asset juxtaposed to money. The 'interest rate' refers in this case beyond rates on financial assets also to returns on real assets. But the procedure severely constrains the relevant range of application available for the analysis. It could only be used for episodes exhibiting comparatively negligible variation in relative yields between financial and real assets. This limitation excludes most of the cyclic fluctuations unfolding in contexts of modest inflation. These fluctuations usually produce shifts in relative yields affecting the interaction between asset markets and the real sector. A useful analysis would thus explicitly represent the important strands of the money substitution process. This motivated the analysis of a three-asset model of interacting asset and output markets jointly developed with Allan H. Meltzer by the late 1960s.

This revision of the transmission process affected most particularly the crucial conditions ensuring the occurrence of monetary effects in the real economy. Keynesian analysis typically yielded statements emphasising the role of the interest elasticity of money demand. Samuelson and others actually characterised the difference between a Keynesian and a non-Keynesian view in terms of the relative magnitude of this interest elasticity. This characterisation reflected a persistent misconception maintained over the years by the Keynesian establishment. This misconception assumed that everybody shared the basic assumptions yielding the specific economic content of the IS-LM approach. It reflected thus a pervasive failure to recognise the nature of the issue. Our analysis implies in contrast to the accustomed Keynesian view the comparative irrelevance of the absolute value of the interest elasticity of money demand. The essential (i.e. necessary and sufficient) condition assuring the transmission of monetary impulses involves an order relation, irrespective of absolute magnitudes, between interest elasticities on the credit-market and on the money market. The extension of the transmission mechanism affected furthermore standard interpretations offered by our Central Bank bearing on the observed variability of monetary growth. This variability was usually interpreted to express corresponding disturbances in money demand. The extended analysis determines however that *all* disturbances from *all* over the economic system are converted into corresponding gyrations of monetary growth whenever policy is geared to accommodate interest rates. This difference in interpretation affects again the evaluation of monetary policy.[3]

The Internal Stability of the Economic System The 'internal stability' of the system opposed a dominant Keynesian position that the private sector is inherently unstable. This issue was again associated with important policy problems and determines very different views of policymaking. It modifies in particular the role assigned to the public sector. The Keynesian tradition views the government as the stabiliser of a flawed system. Under the alternative view the government's actions contribute, in conjunction with other shocks affecting supply and demand conditions, to maintain the system in motion. The system's internal stability operates to absorb these shocks and assures that the system converges forever to its normal position. Persistent deviations from this position, as in the 1930s, do not result from an inherent instability. They are produced by a long and massive series of negative shocks lowering aggregate demand beyond the system's shorter-run absorption capacity impaired by the information load imposed by the long series of shocks. Such a series is moreover (and usually) the creation of government. This conclusion contributed to the proposal that government policy would best serve the economy with a stable framework of reliably predictable actions.

The view of an unstable or meta-stable process contrasting with the classical notion of a system absorbing all shocks in a perpetual convergence around its normal position seems difficult to reconcile with pervasive patterns of monetary experience. These aspects attracted my attention in the late 1950s when I pondered in many discussions with Allan H. Meltzer and Armen Alchian the large differences in the level of monetary growth observed at peaks or troughs of cyclic fluctuations over time within a country or across time between countries. It dawned on us that neither the level of monetary growth nor of the money stock could be expected to affect significantly the real variables. The inherent stability of the system projects the persistent patterns bearing on these magnitudes into the price-level or the inflation rate. We settled at the time, as Milton Friedman did, on the idea that real effects are produced by monetary accelerations not yet absorbed into the prevailing price structure. It followed that a general recognition of persistent accelerations would shift the real effects to higher level time derivatives of the time path followed by the money stock. The role assigned to a non-passive and economically relevant aggregate supply interacting with aggregate demand determines ultimately the stabilising property of the private sector process. This interaction assures that monetary impulses cannot raise output permanently beyond its normal level. The property of an internally stable process precludes this result by eventually translating such impulses into price effects. The evolution of these ideas was spread over many years and became eventually fixed in our analysis by the end of the 1960s.[4]

The Impulse Problem The impulse problem dominated initially to some extent the public debate. Keynesians usually advance a thoroughly eclectic position with respect to 'cyclic' fluctuations in real variables. This eclectic position has recently been extended to explanations of inflation. The vision bearing on this issue is closely connected with the alleged flaws of the price mechanism associated with the denial of the system's internal stability.

The monetary analysis emerging during the 1950s attributed to monetary impulses a dominant role in the process generating business cycles and most particularly in the inflation process. The second strand bearing on inflation fully acknowledges the operation of real shocks modifying an economy's underlying condition. These shocks may significantly affect the price-level and over time our economic welfare. Their contribution to the persistent inflation remains however at the most quite modest. The first strand involving the fluctuations around the normal level, is much less robust and more sensitively influenced by specific conditions. The contribution of monetary accelerations (and decelerations) to economic fluctuations changes over time with the comparative mixture of monetary and real shocks. This mixture explains, at least in part, the variability of the lags acknowledged in the literature. This operation of monetary impulse in a context of shifting and unpredictable mixtures of shocks reinforced the notion of a non-activist approach to monetary policymaking.[5]

The Relation Between Allocation Processes and Aggregative Behaviour The last issue, centred on the relation between allocative processes and aggregative evolutions of the economy, may appear to be somewhat remote from policy issues. The rationale of large-scale model construction, pursued by the translation of a Keynesian tradition into an econometric language, was based on the idea that allocative processes determine the economy's aggregative behaviour. The monetary analysis evolving since the 1950s does not deny all possible spillovers from allocative processes into aggregative patterns. It contends however that this spillover is comparatively small and remains confined to the shorter-run noises in the aggregate data. This position reflects an assumption that aggregative evolutions and the detail of allocative processes are approximately separated to an extent increasing with the lapse of time.

The alternative conjectures about the processes governing an economy's aggregative evolution may be formulated in terms of a probability distribution covering the relevant dimensions of an economy. Monetary analysis asserts that the force shaping the *position* of this distribution are approximately independent from the forces controlling the location of individual elements *under* the distribution. The Keynesian tradition motivating an approach to large (and larger) econometric models asserts in contrast that the forces shaping the location under a distribution also determine its position. This difference affects in particular alternative proposals to control inflation. The first conjecture requires suitable monetary policy actions whereas the second usually leads to sequential proposals of incomes policy. The second conjecture influences furthermore the views bearing on the impulse patterns. It tends to encourage a diffuse eclecticism in this matter. Economic fluctuations are dominantly attributed to shifting combinations of allocative disturbances widely ranging over the private sector. The government possesses under the circumstances the only opportunity to smooth the aggregative fluctuations generated by the array of allocative processes.[6]

Government Deficits and 'Crowding Out'

The structure of this analysis evolving over the 1960s and early 1970s influences our approach to a systematic evaluation of permanent deficits in the government's budget. This issue moved in the middle of last decade beyond the pages of learned journals and was submitted to the public attention by the Shadow Open Market Committee.

The analysis anchored on the interaction between a credit-market and a money market implies that persistent and large increases in government debt induce portfolio adjustments. The resulting pressures on relative yields eventually lower the stock of real capital in the private sector. Government thus 'crowds out' real capital and lowers normal output. This conclusion is strongly contested on two grounds however. One strand invokes the public's rational expectations of tax increases matching the increased obligation to pay interest on new debt. The other strand emphasises that new tax liabilities change the agents' risk pattern. They restore with suitable hedging their preferred risk position revealed in a prior state. They purchase under the circumstances the new debt issued in accordance with their expected tax liability. The first strand removes the wealth effect and the second strand exorcises any substitution effect of deficits financed by issues of debt. With both effects removed the financial choice between taxes and debt is immaterial. 'Crowding out' does not result from a *financial* decision but from a *real* phenomenon expressed by the relative size of the government's absorption of real resources and the characteristics of the government sector's production process. Further reflection about this matter suggests that the difference between the alternative conjectures developed within the monetary analysis do not bear significantly on the longer-run outcome under appropriate assumptions about the public sector's production process. They influence mostly the views about the shorter-run impact on the economy. But the relative magnitudes of the effect on aggregate demand involved in this controversy seem to be of second order of significance.[7]

The Contribution of the 'Rational Expectations Analysis'

'Rational expectations' entered our scene during the last decade and substantially affected the nature of our discussions. Originally introduced by Jack Muth twenty years ago it lay dormant for many years until Robert Lucas effectively resurrected this idea. Its central theme advances a systematic extension of economic analysis to information problems. Men are not passive engineering particles. They grope and cope with their natural and social environment. They will thus exploit whatever information they may acquire. This theme was moreover developed in the context of new analytic formulation which extended the opportunities for useful explications of intuitive ideas. Such explication is hardly ever a trivial endeavour and the history of science demonstrates its creative dimension. This dimension became again visible with the appearance of the rational expectations analysis. It opened aspects to our attention beyond the direct explication of initially available ideas. This point may be exemplified for our purposes with the analytic explication obtained for the idea mentioned above that money stock and monetary growth exert no real effects. Rational expectations analysis provides an explicit form for the intuitive notion that we need to consider monetary acceleration for this purpose. It generalised the idea and directed our attention to unpredictable or surprising movements in the money stock not discounted into the current prices or prevailing price movements. It also provides a more powerful formulation addressed to an examination of the conditions controlling the absorption of monetary (or fiscal) impulses by price movements with little deviation of output from its normal level. Prior analysis could produce similar results in a somewhat 'mechanical fashion' by suitable adjustments in the elasticity of price expectations with respect to the current level.

The rational expectations analysis sharpened our awareness of the information problem. An intuitive sense of this awareness was brought to our work from many discussions with Armen Alchian during the early 1960s. These discussions led us to the nature of the information problem explaining the emergence of a wide range of social institutions, including money, middlemen, specialists of various kinds, etc. We understood that rationally behaving agents' exposure to incomplete information could explain the conjunction of 'long-run' neutrality of nominal impulses and their 'short-run' non-neutrality. The emergence of a rational expectations analysis made us aware that monetary analysis need attend more explicitly to the specification of the relevant information structure confronting agents. Two distinct patterns of incomplete information have been used in recent years. The pioneering work initiated by Lucas, Sargent and Barro relied on Phelps' 'island story'. It argues basically that local information is cheaply available whereas global information is costly. Global information beyond an agent's location accrues thus with a lag. Agents face under the circumstances an inference problem defined by insufficient information to separate local and global effects in observed local price movements. They do not know whether changes in specific prices represent relative or aggregative price changes. Their behaviour would moreover substantially differ with the interpretations of the observations. The structure of incomplete information determines ultimately the optimal inference made. Even this best inference deviates however from the true but unknown state. This wedge, produced by the specific form of incomplete information, assures the (transitory) real effect of monetary impulses. An alternative structuring of the problem emphasises incomplete information about the composition of contemporaneously known allocative and aggregative shocks. Agents face continuous changes in relevant conditions, but they do not know to which extent these conditions are 'permanent' or 'transitory'. Their behaviour over a wide range of activities depends on the other hand sensitively on their inferences made in this respect. Their best inferences will generally deviate from the true composition of the shocks. This deviation defines in this case the potential leverage of monetary impulses on real variables.

The second approach to the structuring of incomplete information offers in my judgement substantial advantages. The second type of inference problem affects the behaviour of agents much more pervasively than the first one. This would be confirmed by observations showing vastly larger investments to cope with a more reliable interpretations of contemporaneously known shocks than with the problem of lagging global information. Beyond these immediate factual issues loom important empirical problems exemplified by the credibility of Central Bank policy or the lamented unresponsiveness of prices to current conditions. These issues can be usefully subsumed under the second but cannot be explicated with the first inference problem. The range of relevant empirical problems requiring our attention thus suggests that the pattern of incomplete information be advantageously explicated according to the second version really initiated many years ago by Milton Friedman.[8]

The Monetarist Policy Rule

One subject, usually dominating the attention of wider circles, has been omitted so far. The 'monetarist rule' of a constant monetary growth is frequently assigned centre place in many of our disputes. It addresses indeed an important problem. This should not obscure however the central cognitive issues surveyed above. The monetarist rule derives from two distinct justifications. One strand is based on the 'internal stability' of the system supplemented with the dominance of monetary impulses. These conditions would indeed be sufficient to justify a 'monetarist rule'. But this argument lacks substantial force, and depends too much on seriously contested conditions. There is an alternative and in my judgement much more pervasively relevant argument in support of a constant monetary growth. The argument evolves from an examination of the case made on behalf of activist regimes or 'discretionary policies'. A close scrutiny of these arguments reveals without exception two crucial conditions invoked to establish the efficiency of activist policymaking expressed in one form or another. The first condition assures the policymakers' perfect information about the detailed structure of the economic process. The second condition rests on a particular implication of the sociological model of man expressed by the 'goodwill theory' or the 'public interest' theory of government. Both conditions are blatantly falsified by massive evidence. Our vision of the structure governing the economic process suffers under a diffuse uncertainty, whatever the policymakers', their staff's and academic advisors' subjective feeling may be. This diffuse uncertainty is exemplified by the array of econometric models producing very different answers to the quest for an optimal policy. An activist regime may thus 'luck in' and actually stabilise the economy, or 'luck out' and substantially destabilise the economy. An analysis of this problem shows moreover that the risks are asymmetrically tilted towards potential destabilisation. It follows that in the context of diffuse uncertainty a neutral strategy of constant monetary growth is optimal.

This conclusion is re-inforced by the rejection of the second strand more or less implicitly adduced in support of an activist regime. A political economy analysis of political institutions determines the basic ambiguity of such institutions. The information problem confronting citizens imposes very high costs on effective monitoring of a political agency. Such monitoring costs create opportunities for trade-offs enjoyed by the personnel operating political agencies. Private and self-interested behaviour replaces to some extent attention to the 'public interest'. These trade-offs are moreover reinforced by the diffuse uncertainty about the economy's basic structure and the resulting vagueness of the public interest. This environment fosters 'discretionary policies' exhibiting shifting patterns of unpredictable activism imposing serious information problems on economic agents. The subtle temptations of office shaped by inadequate monitoring opportunities resulting from the pervasive information problem need be removed by a constitutional or legislated constraint. Thus emerges the case for a neutral strategy operated as a policy of constant monetary growth. Diffuse uncertainty about the economy's structure and the political economy of political institutions constitute the crucial conditions of the justification. This argument needs however to be supplemented by an analysis addressed to the choice of benchmark level of monetary growth, and also to the important institutional and implementation aspects of such a policy.[9]

BEYOND MONETARY PROBLEMS

The search for a sense in our intellectual activities sharpened an awareness beyond the range of monetary phemonena. The struggle about purpose and content compelled my efforts to acquire a better comprehension of the logical aspects of our endeavours. It increasingly occurred to me that our behaviour and procedures expressed most particularly by prevailing language patterns frequently obstruct whatever degree of provisional and partial resolution could possibly be achieved. The nature of this obstruction deserved in my judgement some exploration.

The cognitive enquiry beyond 'money' involved however also the vision about content and range of economics. The inherited division of the social sciences appeared increasingly without logical or empirical justification. The broad sweep of Adam Smith's vision had been narrowed and confined to 'economic issues'. But economic analysis offers in my judgement the only usable analytic core in the social sciences. Political science and sociology define an important range of problems but provide no developed analytic framework to cope with these issues. The fashionable appeal to sociology over an expanding range of problems cultivated by many professionals seemed to sacrifice a potentially useful framework with a substantial empirical foundation for essentially *ad hoc* verbalisms and programmatic classifications or promises.

The Rules of the Game and the Idea Market

The market for ideas and intellectual products may be examined as any other market. We may investigate the patterns shaping the supply of intellectual products or affecting the demand. We may question the conditions controlling the survival of ideas on this market. We may particularly probe the dominant rules of the game which contribute to determine the supply and survival of ideas competing for our attention. A close examination of many argument patterns widely used in textbooks or used in papers published in leading professional journals influenced eventually my conjecture that our prevailing rules of the game contain important strands obfuscating the nature, significance or irrelevance of our intellecual activities and their products.

We hear on occasion that the social sciences address a subject matter inherently more difficult than the natural sciences. It would appear that the gods controlling social processes play an essentially hostile and non-cooperative game with the economics profession, whereas the gods controlling 'natural' processes play a cooperative game with the scientists. There is however an alternative conjecture emphasising the rules of the game dominating our activities. It is argued in particular that the rules of the game actually influencing our intellectual conduct contribute somewhat hesitantly to the relevant sorting between competing ideas. We should note however that the truth of this conjecture would not remove the other conjecture bearing on an inherent difference between natural and social processes. The truth of the second conjecture could simply aggravate the problem already recognised by the first conjecture. The immanent difficulties posed for the comprehension of social processes could thus re-inforce the obstructive effect of questionable rules of the game. A selection of some of our patterns cultivated in our learned endeavours drawn from a large sample may exemplify my concern.

The pervasive occurrence in many variations of the 'modality fallacy' offers some instructive information. We may encounter for instance a long series of possibility statements bearing on monetary policy. Somehow, by the end of the series of statements rather miraculously a categorical statement denying (or asserting) any relevant impact of monetary policy emerges. Alternatively, we find that monetary policy 'does not necessarily' modify the money stock (or anything) and is therefore potentially impotent. Both types of statements are inherently ambiguous and require careful scrutiny. A strictly logical interpretation of possibility statements simply conveys the information that the sentence subjected to the possibility modifier involves an empirical (i.e. non-logical) assertion. Similarly, the denial of necessity on a strictly logical interpretation means that the connections asserted are empirical and not of a logical nature. This meaning of the argument pattern is however quite innocuous and offers no grounds for the conclusions asserted.

The context of these argument patterns suggests however an alternative interpretation. The modality 'it is possible that something' is meant to convey that the 'something' should be considered to occur with a probability exceeding one half. The denial of necessity appears furthermore to reflect on many occasions the existence of alternative conjecture asserting the operation of different patterns. Statements are categorically judged in this manner simply on the grounds that an unsupported (stochastic) hypothesis can be invented or formulated. The argument pattern so widely encountered offers either no adequate grounds for the categorical statement advanced or no reason for the rejection of a particular conjecture addressed. The reader is lulled by the impressionistic effect of the linguistic evolution into a judgement lacking any relevant logical justification. This procedure is particularly rampant in critical objections addressed to a hypothesis (or theory) on the grounds that another hypothesis can be conceived (is possible). The substitution of impressionistic responses to a logical analysis of propositions subsumed by an analysis can be recognised moreover in many comparative judgements bearing on competing structures. The criteria seem occasionally affected by purely formal aspects with little attention to the empirical content obtained.

The role attributed to 'assumptions of a hypothesis' (or theory) offered for many years the most pervasive example of the ambiguous operation of the prevailing rules governing the idea market. A standard argument regulated the cognitive status of a hypothesis on the basis of the 'realism of its assumptions'. Milton Friedman's intuition understood very early the logical fallacy in this argument. In the absence of an explicit logical analysis of this issue the discussion initiated by Friedman's famous essay concentrated on intuitive and basically analogistic examples used by Friedman. The profession, represented by the published responses, refused to examine the logical merits of the problem and interpreted the needed clarification essentially as an ideological exercise. But an explicit logical analysis of the structure of hypotheses and their confirmation procedures establishes unambiguously that Friedman's intuition was right, whatever the relevance and effect of his argument may be. The standard argument pattern is logically untenable. Other patterns of our linguistic habits could be adduced to buttress my case but I wish to introduce just one additional example of great importance which has troubled me for many years. Econometrics emerged with a promise of ultimately assuring the victory of the cognitive adventure constituted by science. But this promise, still potentially inherent in the instrument shaped by econometric theory, has been converted into a travesty by the effort directed at large-scale model construction. The cognitive effort has been replaced by a numerological exercise on a level with astrology. Most of the models violate the essential requirements imposed on an empirical hypothesis, i.e. their empirical content remains on many occasions a mystery. Their actual use is a rigmarole of technical *ad hoc-ery* frequently conflicting with some of the explicitly advanced stochastic hypotheses used to infer a quantitative structure from the data. They are moreover logically impossible to test in their present form. They also contributed to an unfortunate confusion between forecasting exercises on the one hand and logically acceptable test procedures on the other hand. At this stage large-scale model construction should be understood not so much as a relevant cognitive effort but as rational wealth-maximising behaviour. The use of such models among political institutions directs moreover our attention to the peculiar socio-political incentive structures of political agencies. But this leads us to the last major strand of my intellectual experience.[10]

The Renaissance of Adam Smith's Vision

Our examination of Federal Reserve Policymaking in 1963/64 alerted me to the importance of institutional problems. It occurred to me at the time that our profession had unnecessarily and without adequate grounds sacrificed Adam Smith's broad vision of economics. Any cognitive efforts coping with monetary policy or inflation increasingly directs our attention moreover to consideration of socio-political aspects. But political science or sociology offered no analytic help in these matters. Many problems listed under these headings seemed on the contrary well designed for a systematic exploration with the aid of 'economic' analysis. I gradually accepted as a working hypothesis that economic analysis constitutes the basic apparatus potentially unifying the social sciences. The traditional partitions would at best survive, if at all, as specialisations of interest over subclasses of social phenomena.

The social sciences offer however beyond economic analysis a highly influential but also very undeveloped and ultimately very questionable alternative approach to social processes. The nature of this issue is best recognised by an examination of the intellectual background motivating radically different approaches to society. This background produces most particularly divergent evaluations of political institutions or of the operation of political agencies. It seems customary to reduce differences in views about socio-political arrangements to a purely 'ideological' dimension. The media and many professionals argue as if all views bearing on political institutions are condemned to a range beyond assessable cognition. This pervasive attitude is in my judgement fundamentally wrong and intellectually pernicious. The different evaluations of the operation of political structures reflect ultimately, so I began to recognise, two radically distinct perceptions of man. One perception was introduced to the social sciences by the Scottish moral philosophers of the eighteenth century. Man occurs in this view as a resourcefully coping, groping, and evaluating agent persistently bent on improving his lot according to his own best lights. This basic pattern of behaviour proceeds irrespective of any specific institutions. Such arrangements only modify the particular forms of man's self-interested expressions. An influential sociological tradition produced on the other side an entirely different perception. In this view man is totally shaped by exogenous social forces or entities. He is in the words of my colleague Michael Jensen a vacuous, aimless and passively reactive man. He plays a role determined by his position in society. He reveals no basic patterns invariantly operating over the whole spectrum of institutions. According to this perception man's self-interested pursuits are limited to the range of private property or the market place but wane in the context of political institutions.

The alternative perceptions present essentially two very different empirical assertions about man's conduct in society. They determine the different views and evaluations pertaining to social arrangement and most particularly to the role of political institutions. These differences can thus be recognised as the product of underlying perceptions which are in principle analysable and assessable. The easy reduction of all disputes about socio-political aspects to an 'ideological' dimension thus fails to recognise a cognitive problem of fundamental importance.[11]

The perception of man formalised by economic analysis appears to be substantially confirmed by a vast array of historical evidence. An application of suitably adjusted economic analysis to the operation of political institutions thus promises useful insights and answers to important socio-political issues. We obtain in this way, for instance, a better appreciation of the ambivalence of 'stabilisation policies'. We begin to understand why 'stabilisation policies' are at best randomly stabilising and mostly designed for purposes of wealth redistribution. We also recognise more clearly the dangers associated with any kind of policy-activism. The problem addressed in the context of monetary policy actually characterises the full range of government activities. Activist policy-making pursued by agencies imposing massive monitoring costs on the citizens usually produces the swamp of 'discretionary policies' with unreliable shifts, or stop and go. This erratic performance re-inforces however the adjustment burden imposed by natural shocks and destabilises the economy over time and in the average.

Lastly, the failure to recognise the alternative perception of man contributes to a widening influence of more or less indirect or subtle forms of essentially sociological explanations of inflation. Interpretations of price movements as 'self-generated, self-propelled and self-sustained autonomous processes' rely basically on a sociological role-playing pattern and cannot be reconciled with a 'resourcefully evaluating maximising man'. The fundamental issue influences at this stage our approach to the inflation problem. It affects in particular our judgement how to cope with it most effectively. Whatever the detail of the sociological approach may be, it will always favour, for reasons inherent in its basic perception, a complex set of political institutions controlling prices or wages. Once we recognise more fully the underlying nature of these differences we may discard easy ideological accusations and seriously consider the cognitive issues at stake. The rising importance of socio-political problems and institutional issues raises in my judgement the significance of economic analysis. The range of problems posed by our social evolution may encourage a new appreciation of Adam Smith's broad vision guiding our intellectual discipline. My own appreciation slowly evolving along the intellectual road, was shaped by many discussions with many colleagues in the profession. It was decisively influenced however by my colleagues and friends in Rochester (foremost William Meckling) and by my long-time friend Allan H. Meltzer. A younger and international group of friends has contributed its share in recent years. And I naturally hope that fate grants me future opportunities to continue to learn from them.

Notes

1. The reader may find a list of the major papers bearing on the issues discussed in the paper jointly authored with Meltzer, Allan H., 'Time Deposits in the Brunner–Meltzer Model of Asset Markets', *Journal of Monetary Economics*, January 1981. My paper on 'A Diagrammatic Exposition of the Money Supply Process' published in the *Schweizerische Zeitschrift für Volkswirtschaft und Statistik*, 1973, summarises the essential features of the accumulated analysis.
2. A detailed argument bearing on these issues may be found in 'Some General Features of the Federal Reserves Approach to Policy', February 1964, 'The Discrepancy Between Federal Reserve Policy and Federal Reserve Statements', February 1964, 'The Federal Reserve's Attachment to the Free Reserve Concept: A Staff Analysis', May 1964, 'An Alternative Approach to the Monetary Mechanism', August 1964, *Subcommittee on Domestic Finance. Committee on Banking and Currency. House of Representatives*. 88th Congress, Second Session, 1964. (with Allan H. Meltzer).
3. Some material pertaining to this section may be found in my paper on 'The Monetarist Revolution in Monetary Theory' in *Weltwirtschaftliches Archiv*, 1970. My 'Survey of Selected Issues in Monetary Theory' published by the *Schweizerische Zeitschrift für Volkswirtschaft und Statistik* 1971 also contains some relevant material. Lastly, the paper and comments jointly authored with Allan H. Meltzer and published in the volume on *Monetarism*, edited by Jerome Stein, Amsterdam 1976, may also be usefully consulted.
4. Relevant material on this point is contained in my paper on 'The Monetarist Revolution in Monetary Theory' and 'Inflation, Money and the Role of Fiscal Arrangements', in *The New Inflation and Monetary Policy* (London, Macmillan, 1976).
5. Note here also my paper on 'The Monetarist Revolution in Monetary Theory'.
6. Note here also my paper on 'The Monetarist Revolution in Monetary Theory'.
7. Aspects of crowding out appear in the paper published in the volume on *Monetarism* (note 3) and also in the second paper mentioned under note 4.

8. This section refers to current work jointly undertaken with Alex Cukierman and Allan H. Meltzer. A first piece was published in the *Journal of Monetary Economics*, October 1980.
9. The reader may find an extensive argument in my paper 'Controlling Monetary Aggregates' published in 1981 by the Federal Reserve Bank of Boston. A summary statement appeared in the Lloyd's Bank *Monthly Review* in the winter 1980/81.
10. The following papers provide additional information on these issues: 'Assumption and the Cognitive Quality of Theories', *Synthese*, 1969, 'The Importance of Rules in the Competitive Market for Ideas', *Schweizerische Zeitschrift für Volkswirtschaft und Statistik*, 1962; 'Econometric Practice Between Numerology and Empirical Science', *Journal of Economic Literature*, 1973; 'Some Reflections on the State of Econometric Practice', *Vielfalt der Wirtschaftspolitik*, Zurich, 1969.
11. The crucial ideas were developed in a paper jointly authored with William Meckling on 'The Perception of Man and the Conception of Government', *Journal of Money, Credit and Banking*, vol. 9, no. 1, Part 1, February 1977.

11 Economics as a Public Good

Herbert Giersch

PRELIMINARY REFLECTIONS

At least two conditions, in the author's mind, must be met to justify writing an autobiographic essay. The first one is age. With some tolerance, this criterion can be taken to be satisfied at 65. Secondly, there has to be a message worth getting across. After some reflection, the author managed to put into words what he intuitively felt through most of his life: economics is a public good with a potential demand far from saturation. Those willing to augment its supply can expect to earn a good living, and still maintain their self-respect.

Writing about oneself as an economist justifies using some economic jargon. Those who share the author's preference for micro- over macroeconomics and for open over closed economy models will not mind if he addresses the question of how he happened to find his place in the division of labour – interpersonal, intraprofessional, perhaps international – given his peculiar factor endowment and education and the good and bad luck of history in the last half century. It is, of course, the theory of international trade that should guide us to find an answer to this question, the more so if you consider that this theory – as August Lösch remarked – is most suitable for explaining the interpersonal division of labour, not so much the division of labour among entities called countries or economies. However, pure theory is so different from real life that trying to apply it in this particular case turned out to be rather disappointing. Nevertheless, abstract theory helps to raise good questions and it can be used as a guide in selecting facts and recollections.

An economist's 'déformation professionnelle' drives him to find (objective) explanations for the observations he made and remembered, the decisions he took and the experiences he gained. Strictly speaking, such a scientific approach to autobiography requires adopting the position of an impartial outside observer. Although this may not be wholly impossible, it has the drawback of producing a deterministic bias. Looking backward in this perspective, the author tends to see himself as a kind of pricetaker who always responded to given circumstances and changes: developing some talents and neglecting others – almost mechanically; adjusting his product mix to perceived changes in the structure of demand – quite opportunistically; exploiting some market *niche* – like a trader. This is surprisingly akin to what Latsis calls 'situational determinism'.[1]

Adopting this approach has, of course, the great advantage of providing for modesty in presentation. Moreover, it is in line with much of recent psychological teaching: aren't we the product of our environment, the slaves of that giant monster called society which then naturally has to bear responsibility for our failures as well as for any achievements? Many economists tend to fall into the deterministic trap by praising the invisible hand: suppliers are seen as selling what their customers are prepared to buy and make a profit to the extent that the demand curve happens to be sufficiently far on the right. If something goes wrong, they will be said to suffer from a deterioration of their terms of trade or from a deficiency of effective demand. Surely, there are enough macroeconomists around to support such determinism. It implies that the system cannot move ahead or expand without an external driving force – a goddess of history, a government development plan, a budget deficit. This, however, is a view of the world which the author does not share. As some readers may know, he considers himself a Schumpeterian and finds it necessary to stress the importance of suppliers' activities along the following lines: competition is monopolistic rather than atomistic; opportunities are given but can also be opened up by innovations, product innovations as well as process innovations; tastes are usually taken as given but are often waiting to be discovered and, if already there, to be cultivated up to high levels of sophistication; potential supply certainly needs complementary demand, but supply can create its own demand through aggressive selling and through the multiplier effects of those autonomous investments that arise from new knowledge and the competitive exploitation of long-run opportunities for growth and structural change. The invisible hand, to be sure, is a forceful coordinator but what it coordinates in a developing world is – apart from passive adjustment decisions in declining industries and firms – a crowd of ambitious plans pursued in active, if not aggressive, competition.

This point has been raised here to indicate the author's personalistic view of economic life in the market system in general, a view which is in contrast to mechanical interpretations that tend to support ideas of central planning and control, fine tuning and industrial policies. The reader will obtain some information about when and where this view developed. But there is also the touchy question of what in his personal life the author has to attribute to circumstances and what to his own endeavours and decisions. The answer is a rhetorical question: who can pretend to have found a solution to the imputation problem when so much complementarity is involved as in this case?

INITIAL CONDITIONS AND EARLY EXPERIENCES

Born and brought up in a small textile town in Lower Silesia (then a province of Prussia) I got an early taste of the 'social question' from both Grimm's fairytales and the historical folklore of those places that had seen the 1844 uprising of the weaver proletariat. The family background was lower middle class: peasants, petty traders in livestock and agricultural products, craftsmen. The way of thinking was bourgeois, entrepreneurial, sometimes criticised as mercantile or even Jewish, notably by neighbours and relatives rooted in the Prussian tradition. Civil servants in the family were envied for their leisure time and – particularly during the Great Depression – for their income security. Such envious views were also held by my father who was too busy to have enough time for me before 1929, but failed to earn enough income to pay for my education afterwards.

Having had to qualify for a scholarship during my gymnasium years I cannot claim to be one of those who made their way despite a poor performance at school. An idiosyncratic feeling that I owed a great debt to others developed in this period – to be quickly reversed after 1939. Two teachers deserve credit for having sensed my taste for languages and philosophy. On the quest for understanding why the economic conditions of the family had so dramatically deteriorated in the early 1930s and why the queues at the local unemployment office had become so long, I looked for facts, of course without having a theory, and gained reputation as a little expert in contemporary history. Newspapers (at home) made even more fascinating reading than detective stories (under the desk in the classroom).

But the news became more and more puzzling. Brüning was a statesman with a PhD in economics, like Stresemann before him, but he had no inspiring message, while Hitler was shouting and his Nazi followers were marching on the streets as if unemployment and poverty could be overrun by brute force. Was there no academic discipline to supply an answer, no profession of experts to speak up in public? Apart from unemployment, people were concerned about inflation, which apparently had wiped out my grandparents' savings a decade before. But if inflation had been the consequence of war, as was sometimes argued, how could it be a danger at a time when almost every politician talked about disarmament? Public opinion, it seemed to me, was profoundly disoriented. I remember hearing people saying that the country needed a strong man for action, no matter what kind of action he would initiate. In retrospect, there are good reasons to believe that world history would have taken a less disastrous course had good economics been forcefully supplied as a public good. Even as a youngster one could sense the vacuum.

The last three years in school were economically less distressful. This improvement encouraged a pious believer in the virtues of unselfishness and community spirit to become a rebellious young man who was proud of being called a sceptic. Nietzsche's writings, perhaps a bit misunderstood, nourished protest against the collectivist idealism propagated and shamelessly exploited by the Nazis. And a first love romance made me glorify the individual's role in the family. We would, of course, do better than our parents; and I would develop my intellectual muscles to avoid my father's mistakes, earning envy rather than the pity which some people had impolitely extended to me in our poorest years. Instead of a priest or teacher, I now wanted to become a columnist or lawyer to shock and challenge conventional wisdom. My increasingly individualistic beliefs were strongly confirmed when in April 1939 I was drafted into the compulsory German labour service ('Reichsarbeitsdienst') where collectivism and coercion served as substitutes for intelligence and motivation. The trade balance with these people was adjusted on the export side; in their own words; 'Giersch works slowly.'

University life was tantamount to liberation. At Breslau in 1940, law proved to be attractive to begin with, thanks to a young professor's praise for a beginner's unconventional argument for an esoteric case. Economics, inspected during the second term, turned out to be dull, except for Günter Schmölders' eloquent lectures on economic policy. Business administration, considered for pecuniary reasons, lifted the student's self-confidence to an unhealthy extent. The final choice came about by circumstances: Kiel University, which offered itself as an intellectual resort after I had been drafted into the Navy in 1941, did not offer a degree in business administration but, thanks to the Kiel Institute, first-class courses in economics, notably from Walther Hoffmann and August Lösch. I exploited this opportunity for two terms owing to a special agreement that allowed me to render military service on the premises of the very Institute for which I was to assume responsibility twenty-seven years after my Diploma Examination in 1942.

When the journey with the Navy, at the end of the war on a submarine boat, ended in a prisoner of war camp in England the half-baked economist became a self-appointed lecturer. He taught what a spontaneous social process could be seen to bring about even in limited freedom: bilateral exchange, a market for goods and services including cultural activities, money as a creature of the market, specialisation for a better living and self-esteem. In the best English liberal tradition, Colonel Vickers, the Commander of the camp, took it on his own to open up trade with the outside world: labour services were exported against food to raise the standard of living beyond the initial subsistence level. Watching this experiment before the background of past experiences in the German labour service while reading Adam Smith's *Wealth of Nations*, one of the few books of the camp library, was to become crucial for my view of the world.

One person noticed it at the time: the British Intelligence Officer (Mr Rossitter alias Philipp Rosenthal, the Chinaware manufacturer) who, after a lengthy interview on political and philosophical questions, decided in favour of my early release in October 1946. The cigarettes that served as a store of value on my passage to Northern Germany turned out to be vital for my parents who as refugees had to live on the 1000 or so daily calories the official rationing system could provide. After two months of search unemployment, mainly spent in full trains and railway station waiting rooms, I was hired by Walther Hoffmann to serve as his assistant at Münster University.

BETWEEN THEORY AND PRACTICE

Luck was on my side as Hoffmann was fully occupied in reconstructing the university beyond economics; he gave me full freedom to organise his seminars on Barone and Walras, on Viner and Hicks, and on Lange's and Lerner's economic theory of socialism. At last, I understood the allocation problem. Müller-Armack's seminars on the 'Social Market Economy', a term that was to become the trademark of West Germany's economic miracle, proved disappointing for lack of rigour, but they acquainted me with the importance of private property and the limitations of redistribution.

The dissertation on the question of how West Germany could arrange for the compensation of property losses caused by bombing and evacuation had been conceived already in the prisoner of war camp; it was submitted to and accepted by Hoffmann and Müller-Armack in late 1947.[2] The basic idea was that any redistribution to correct past war hazards could best take the form of a once-for-all change in the property distribution rather than that of a protracted interference with the process of income formation, exemplifying the principle 'redistribute now, grow later'. Contrary to the author's ambitious expectations it made no impact whatsoever on the vivid public policy debate. A private discussion of the issues with Friederike Koppelmann was more rewarding: it first led to a partnership in preparing for the oral PhD examination and later to a most happy marriage for hitherto more than three and a half decades.

The German currency reform of 1948, together with Erhard's courageous decision of lifting most price controls, came close to a controlled experiment of liberalisation. It demonstrated that sound advice – given by leading members of the economics profession – could have a high social productivity. The profession which had failed to prevent the Great Depression now showed itself to be capable of living up to my childhood's nebulous expectations. My career decision appeared justified.

Having read Keynes' *General Theory* with Herbert Timm in another prisoner-of-war camp against the background of Schacht's full employment policy after 1933, I was disappointed to hear Joan Robinson expound a vulgar Keynesianism in a guest lecture at Münster University. It was like Hamlet without the Prince of Denmark: a theory and a policy of full employment without wages. Macroeconomics was further discounted by reading of American stagnationists who visited Germany to recommend expansionist policies, erroneously assuming that we had Keynesian unemployment rather than the classical variety arising from the influx of refugees and the physical destruction of the capital stock. The relevant price was also conspicuously absent when Tinbergen lectured about the dollar shortage without mentioning the exchange rate. My training had surely not been the very best, but none of my teachers had ignored relative prices.

In these circumstances, Wassily Leontief who lectured at Harvard University's Salzburg Seminar to my surprise turned out to be an equilibrium economist. At least he was fully aware of the importance of substitution processes not captured by input-output analysis. The whole class was excellent as some names may indicate: Odd Aukrust, Gerard Debreu, L.M. Koyck, Göran Ohlin, Bob and Barbara Solow. An equally fascinating experience was the subsequent academic year (1948/49) as a British Council Fellow at the London School of Economics where I was most impressed by Lionel Robbins, Friedrich A. Hayek and James Meade among the full professors and by William Baumol, Graeme Dorrance, Terence Hutchison, Alan Peacock, and Ralph Turvey among the younger staff members. William Hutt and L.M. Lachmann as visitors enriched the Austrian flavour of the place, and so did Gottfried Haberler and Friedrich Lutz when they passed the LSE on their summer trip from the US to the European continent. How lucky to meet all these great men so shortly after the war.

Due to my interest in international economics, I found myself in Meade's seminar which offered a synthesis of macro- and microeconomics, Keynesian and classical thinking, positive and normative theory, planning and the price mechanism. The master showed how rigorous reasoning can go along with human kindness and fairness, embodied in a scholar whom I admired and still admire as the prototype of an Englishman gentleman. A paper written in the spirit of August Lösch on the locational consequences of a customs union[3] was my modest contribution to what still appears to me the best seminar I ever attended. The choice between Hayek and Laski – the political antipodes at the School – was easy for a young economist of my experience and persuasion, but I failed to grasp Hayek's economics, notably his theory of capital and growth, and the relevance of the hotly debated 'Ricardo effect'. Among the giants then teaching at the LSE I only missed Popper but nobody told me about him and his work. When a group of leading German economists visited the Oxford Institute of Statistics in March 1949 I was invited to act as an occasional interpreter during the conference. What struck me most was a remarkable international difference in the level of sophistication showing how much human capital Germany had lost under the Nazi rule.

Back home in Münster where Friedrike had temporarily replaced me as Hoffmann's assistant we married to start a race in which she would get our first child while I would complete the habilitation thesis on growth and employment that I had begun in London after having discovered Harrod's and Domar's seminal papers. She lost; but my product, although pleasing to the faculty, was much inferior in practice. While our son Volker was to become an applied economist pushing development in a structurally backward region, my study failed to reach the publication stage. Having moved to Paris to work for the OEEC (Organisation for European Economic Cooperation) I was struck by the contrast between the economics required in the real world and the empirically empty formal structures I had endlessly turned around in the tradition of what Leontief called 'implicit theorising'. Incidentally, it was on Leontief's recommendation that the Paris job was offered to me.

The group of economists in the OEEC, led by Cairncross and subsequently by Reddaway, included Juist Faaland, Koht Norbye, Jack Parkinson and Maurice Fg. Scott, all analytically well trained and much more versed in the art of interpreting current facts and figures than most economists I had met (except Hoffmann and Leontief). When the German balance of payments went into deficit after the outbreak of the Korean war my nationality made me the first choice for serving a working group of Erich Roll's Economic Committee charged with finding out the deeper reasons and possible cures. As many of the delegates were non-economists, most of the theory they used or were prepared to accept was home made (or 'do it yourself economics' as David Henderson recently called it), with no use for relative prices, exchange rates, elasticities, and other terms essential for understanding how markets work. Fortunately, Cairncross together with Per Jacobsson had previously been on a mission to Germany and established the authoritative conclusion that the economy was basically healthy. Therefore, the detailed work for which Bonn supplied all information the working group could think of, did actually no harm. In retrospect, this 'German striptease' turned out to be an ideal preparation for my later work in the German Economic Expert Council (1964–70).

After this year at the OEEC it became evident that work in an international organisation – despite an astronomical salary – was less attractive than academic freedom, except for short periods to sense urgent real world problems. On the other hand, after the first term of teaching at Münster University I asked myself whether, without continuous worries about economic life and public policy, my lectures would not become dull, running quickly into the diminishing returns of abstract theorising. There is, after all, only a limited set of interesting theorems one can derive from a few behavioural assumptions without engaging in a *jeu d'esprit* that pleases one's professional curiosity and pride but leads the student to believe that this world is full of paradoxes, anomalous reactions, and market failures waiting for a wise government. This is perhaps the appropriate place to apologise to my first students for having taught them economics without sufficient knowledge of the economy. My subsequent endeavours to bridge the gap were facilitated by the OEEC inviting me to work for them temporarily in 1952 and for another year in 1953, that time as head of a division to push what is still an unachieved task, i.e. the liberalisation of invisible trade.

After another year of teaching (both at Münster and, on a vacant chair, at Braunschweig's Technical University) I was appointed professor (of political economy) at the recently established University of the Saar in Saarbrücken, then part of the French economy. Still under the age of thirty-four every reason to praise the invisible hand. It had allowed me, despite Hitler's war and the fifteen months as a British prisoner of war, to achieve the professional goal of my life without a loss of that truly non-renewable resource called time. The signals given by the invisible hand had been opportunities: stimulating personalities to learn from, job openings to be considered as challenges. Some tempting opportunities that might have become blind alleys could be rejected: offers to join the German federal ministries of economic affairs and economic cooperation in 1950 and to accept an isolated chair at a Technical University in 1955. Of course, there had also been luck at work: in choosing a subject which turned out to benefit from a high income elasticity of demand and in gaining an undeserved terms of trade advantage from the heavy war losses of my age cohort. Even the fact that the place of my birth and my youth had become inaccessible was, in retrospect, a great advantage: being a refugee I had full freedom of choosing the location with the best long-run prospects. At least in my subjective accounting, the flow of income began to contain a substantial rent element. The problem was how to justify it in the coming years.

The Saar University's department of economics hardly existed at the time; and when the Referendum of October 1955 brought the Pro-German parties to power they uttered their intention to close down what they called an 'offspring of French cultural imperialism' and to give the country's daughters and sons comfortable scholarships for studying at some fine old established German universities. My career as a professor was close to becoming a non-starter. There were very few students around and none of them seemed to qualify for postgraduate work in economics. On the other hand, there was also no time for research and writing since everything seemed to depend on strengthening the institution by lobbying for money and co-opting colleagues, by agreeing on new rules and regulations, and by making tedious exercises in self-administration. Professors whom we offered a chair were asking for students, and the few students we had were deeply worried when the professors, usually after a short while of teaching, left for more reputable places. Nonetheless, we had Paul Senf after his term as minister of finance, we had Herbert Timm for more than two years, we got Wolfgang Stützel and Elisabeth Liefmann-Keil, we persuaded Egon Sohmen to join us and we enjoyed the intellectual company of two prominent professors of law, Ernst-Joachim Mestmäcker with his sharp mind on matters of antitrust law and competition policies, and Werner Maihofer who was specialising in social philosophy and later, in the seventies, became a cabinet minister in the Bonn government. Add to this Ralph Dahrendorf in the department of philosophy, and you may grasp the spirit of lively discussions on essential matters of liberalism. Around 1960 the Saar University was sufficiently settled, yet still so vivid that it took me no great pains to turn down tempting offers from German universities with long-established traditions.

My writings in the 1950s essentially consisted of articles on trade and business cycle policy, including a paper on the acceleration principle and the propensity to import[4] which had grown out of my OEEC experience, and an article on optimum trade[5] (both translated for the *International Economic Papers*) which came close to introducing monopolistic competition and effective tariff rates into considerations of trade and welfare but failed to make its points sufficiently clear and was also misunderstood by one critic as putting forward an argument for protection. From this time on I made it a habit to have everything intended for publication criticised by the best young scholars around me. Olaf Sievert did this perfectly for the first volume of my book on economic policy, and it sometimes happened that he urged me to rewrite long passages which had fully satisfied their author at first sight. He also deserves credit for having forced me to give up any natural author's pride which often makes team work an unpleasant affair. The intellectual atmosphere which gradually developed in this spirit attracted further competent scholars: Lutz Hoffmann, Klaus Stegemann, Manfred Streit, Gerhard Fels, Juergen B. Donges, and Wolfgang Kasper who all made their way – as did Sievert – to become full professors or find an even more attractive post.

Yale University which invited me as a visiting professor in 1962/63 – thanks to William Fellner, Jim Tobin, and Gustav Ranis – exhibited all the advantages and disadvantages of professional specialisation. The great names apart, it was surprising to learn how much everybody knew within the boundaries of his own field and how little interest he had in going beyond them. By contrast, I still remember an intensive discussion of philosophical and methodological issues, with Paul Streeten and Mike Montias, which made us suddenly aware that we all happened to be Europeans. Of course, this European accent could also be heard from Raymond Goldsmith, Henry Wallich, Robert Triffin, Bela Balassa, and Friedrich Lutz who was also a visitor. The students in my graduate course were hard working and – on the average – technically better than those at home, but they did not match the very best we had attracted to Saarbrücken. A short trip to give a paper in Gottfried Haberler's seminar made me feel that Harvard had a slightly more European touch. Anyway, the US, although fascinating in some respects and quite European in some locations in general, lacked the broad cultural background that made Europe a place to live for good. Moreover, as a professor there was no better place for a comfortable living than in Germany. Being determined to return, German rather than English was the language of the three articles on growth policy and on regional and structural policy produced and finished at Yale – without the incisive criticism they needed.

OPEN ADVICE

Back home, an important task seemed to be waiting. Numerous pages, perhaps too many, in my 1960 book[6] had been devoted to economic forecasting and to counselling on economic policy matters. As a follow-up, the 'Verein für Socialpolitik', the German Economic Association, had asked me to organise a workshop on economic diagnosing and forecasting (1962) and on normative economics and policy prescriptions (1963). This apparently made me a candidate for the newly established Council of Economic Experts, long favoured by

Erhard, the Minister of Economic Affairs, as an institutionalised ally against the business lobby that had direct access to Adenauer, the Federal Chancellor, but also supported by the social democratic opposition to the extent that they saw economics on their side. What made the Council attractive to me was its guaranteed independence of both organised interest groups and – contrary to the US – of the government administration. Other members of the profession who raised their voices on the preparatory stage (when I was at Yale) thought this independence to be unwise or unworkable. That apparently improved my position on the list of candidates for the five places to be filled: three by independent professionals and two by practitioners with links to business and labour. When those chosen for appointment met for the first time I came to the conclusion that I had to decline. It is true that the honorarium offered was attractive, but fearing that the two practitioners would at best offer only a small marginal product and considering that one of the other two professionals was not keen on playing an active role I felt incapable of providing the 50 per cent input that would fall upon me. And would the profession not attribute to me 100 per cent of the blame in the most likely case that the whole enterprise turned out to be a failure? For these reasons I wrote to the Minister of Economic Affairs (the successor to Erhard who in the meantime had become Chancellor) that I had to decline. After all, there was still Raymond Goldsmith in Paris waiting for my cooperation to build up the OECD Development Centre.

A ministerial envoy came to Paris (the person who had taken the job offered to me in 1950) to apply moral pressure for a whole evening. Flattered and depressed at the same time, I persuaded myself that I had to do the job, given my childhood's traumas and dreams and my understanding of economics as a public good. A renewed decision to decline might have proved good for the family but bad for my self-respect. If there was a rent element in my income, this was a good chance to compensate for it. But how would we avoid the disaster that others predicted, including Erich Schneider on the occasion of the 50th anniversary of the Kiel Institute in a private conversation on the very day when the names of the 'five wise men' were made public? Writing reports was a task not new to me; but giving them a profile and still getting them approved by the other four would be the real test. Years ago I had read Edwin Nourse's account of his time in the US Council of Economic Affairs under the programmatic title 'Economics in the Public Service'.[7] It would be on these lines that we could succeed: sticking to the objectives laid down in the law (price level stability, high employment, and balance of payments equilibrium to be achieved simultaneously with adequate growth) and adhering to the scientific norms prevailing in the profession. But something more would be needed. When the students assembled with torches in front of our home to appreciate my declining offers from other universities I summed up my mixed feelings in paraphrasing Alfred Marshall's dictum that one could not be a good economist and have the reputation of being a good patriot. The implication was: economics as a public good may not find popular support in the political arena.

So it happened. Supported by Olaf Sievert and Gerhard Fels we managed to produce the first Annual Report (by November 1964) roughly approximating our standards. Fortunately for the coherence of the group, we felt obliged to produce a short forerunner which was sent to the Government in June, calling for exchange rate adjustments to fight imported inflation, a message never acknowledged by the recipient and hence forcefully repeated in the Annual Report.[8] The latter (which was to be published and submitted to Parliament under the law) thus contained a substantial portion of dynamite given West Germany's loyalty to the Bretton Woods System and the fact that – after the introduction of convertibility on capital account – this system had become more and more rigid with respect to exchange rate adjustments. In these circumstances, the Government when publishing the Report heavily criticised the Council for exhibiting an unrealistic preference for exchange rate flexibility. The media and the business community shared the Government's judgement and the profession – with the exception of Karl Schiller and a few others – remained silent. It thus appeared that we had lost the battle. Chancellor Erhard remarked that we had given stones to a public in need of bread, and one of the leading commentators made the point that the economics of the ivory tower had turned out to be a disservice to the public. Unfortunately, Fritz Meyer of Bonn University gradually withdrew from the Council's work for health reasons so that I was becoming the only ivory tower economist in the group.

The ado about exchange rates distracted the public's attention from another important price variable which we also stressed in our first report: the wage rate. In long discussions the Council member close to organised labour could be convinced that maintaining both full employment and price level stability required wages rising roughly in proportion to labour productivity with due allowance to be made for changes (a) in the external terms of trade and (b) in unit capital costs. Adding the terms of trade argument to the popular but fiercely disputed rough wage guideline helped the spokesmen of organised labour (including Wilhelm Haferkamp, later a longtime EC Commissioner) to find themselves basically in agreement with representatives of employers' associations who in turn were strong proponents of the capital cost argument. On 17 June 1965, the Council reached a kind of tripartite agreement on this norm and submitted the rough outlines of a possible scheme for what the second report called 'stabilisation without stagnation'.[9] The idea was that an inflation rate slightly surpassing 3 per cent in 1965 could be brought down without losses in output and employment if the inflation component in nominal aggregates and prices, i.e. public expenditures, wage increases, interest rates, investment budgets, was simultaneously and gradually reduced by – say – one percentage point a year within a scheme that had been agreed upon by the government, unions, and employers' associations and thus should be credible to all of them. The time to implement such a policy framework of rational expectations was highly favourable since the economy could be viewed as being in an inflationary equilibrium. For obvious reasons we were careful not to raise the exchange rate issue at that time but we did not have any doubt that a parallel revaluation would be indispensable to curb inflationary pressures from abroad. In later reports, the focus shifted very much in this direction when we began to stress the point that the German inflation rate was largely determined by the external price level and the exchange rate and that pre-announced revaluations could serve the purpose of price level stabilisation without affecting the balance of payments.

In two conversations with Erhard – one in Saarbrücken before the submission of the Report and one in a special meeting in Bonn afterwards – we made the case for this policy of rational expectations by pointing out how much could be gained by behaving in a way that allowed relative prices in real terms to remain fairly constant in the process of fighting inflation. Unfortunately, these attempts at persuasion turned out to be in vain: Erhard, by temper not a gradualist anyhow, joined forces with Blessing, the President of the Bundesbank, and with the chairman of the Federation of Industries to decide in favour of what the then Minister of Economic Affairs later called 'die gewollte Rezession' (wanted recession), a fall in employment that eventually led to Erhard's resignation in late 1966.

With the second Report the Council had established itself as a 'pouvoir neutre' and with the nomination of a professional economist as Minister of Economic Affairs (Karl Schiller), its relationship with the government became as productive as one could hope for. The real test, however, was to come in 1968 when the Council (except Stützel who had been appointed to succeed Meyer) recognised and emphasised the need for a revaluation; in a letter to the Chancellor, the Council warned the Government about what it would have to spell out in greater detail in its forthcoming Annual Report. In a meeting in October with Chancellor Kiesinger, Blessing, Schiller and F.J. Strauß (then Finance Minister) it became obvious that the fear of losing farmers' votes to an extremist party on the right would lead the Grand Coalition Government to introduce import subsidies and export taxes as a substitute for a revaluation. It so happened, just at the time the Annual Report was published. When Schiller tried to defend this half-hearted move before the Advisory Council of his Ministry of Economic Affairs (of which I had become a member in 1961), he found himself confronted with a memorandum recommending an immediate revaluation. But the Christian Democrats, influenced by Hermann J. Abs, the most highly respected banker, and by Franz Josef Strauß were determined to defend the old parity at no matter what cost. My feeling was that the profession which had failed to raise its voice in the Great Depression, once again had a historical role to play; this encouraged me to initiate – together with Egon Sohmen – a telephone appeal to German university professors of economics, more than 100 of whom supported our resolution in favour of freeing the exchange rate. It took another five months and a general election (with a change of government) for the market forces to have their way, at least for the time being.

The six years in the Council taught me that economics as a public good makes little impact unless it is persuasively sold in the political arena in competition with the views expressed by organised interest groups. We were happy that this competition took place before the background of a broad political consensus on value judgements. Thus the arguments – at that time – concerned logic rather than ideology, consistency and expediency rather than basic political issues. Hostile criticism addressed to the Council strengthened the team spirit among the members and the small academic staff, except in the case of one member who held strong views about the exchange rate being a fundamental norm rather than the relative price of two monies and who eventually resigned. Whether the experiment of an independent

Council would have succeeded if it had begun in the subsequent period of political polarisation is open to doubt.

Apart from drafts for six annual reports and a few intermediate pronouncements of the Council I gave speeches on current issues of economic policy and wrote a few professional articles on wages and exchange rates, including a paper for the 1969 Bürgenstock conference on 'Greater Exchange Rate Flexibility' organised by Halm, Machlup, and Bergsten.[10] Exchange rate flexibility, so the paper's argument was meant to run, does not add to existing uncertainties even in a small country; if domestic monetary policy is aimed at price level stability exchange rate changes will merely reflect external disturbances relevant for the international sector and – by making import and export prices more flexible – help to stabilise domestic output in the face of cyclical movements of the world economy. This message was perhaps too strange to find attention and support; but I still happen to believe that even an individual firm can stabilise its output despite the ups and downs in its market if it raises and lowers its sales prices sufficiently and makes its employees accept what I am now calling their 'full employment terms of trade'. Would full price flexibility be more costly than fluctuations in output and employment? And is exchange rate flexibility not a useful substitute when prices are sticky? The argument, of course, can be generalised: if every country pursued a policy of monetary stability, the world economy would enjoy maximum stability since exchange rates would then merely reflect real disturbances requiring adjustments. Could monetary stability *cum* exchange rate flexibility not have prevented the Great Depression?

INTERNATIONAL ECONOMIC POLICY RESEARCH

In the 1960s I had declined several offers from other universities, including one from Berlin tailored to simultaneously becoming head of the German Institute for Economic Research. But when Eric Schneider asked me whether I would be a candidate to succeed him at Kiel I could simply not refuse in view of my old allegiance to the Institute and my persistent interest in international economics. As my closest associates and quite a few other junior economists from Saarbrücken were enthusiastically prepared to join me and to fill the vacancies Schneider had deliberately left open in the Institute, I could confidently accept the challenge. Fortunately, this decision was never regretted on my side. It involved leaving the Council after six years but did not change my view of economics and its role in society.

With the benefit of hindsight it appears that most of my previous work on growth and cycles, on structural and regional policy, on trade and exchange rates had been conceptual economics rather than empirical research, thus requiring or inviting complementary efforts in the form of a comprehensive research programme. This seemed to suit the Institute's purpose and facilities quite well. However, a conference in 1970, organised to enlist methodological advice from the best outside experts we knew, was not as encouraging as we had hoped. Thus Gerhard Fels had to become a pioneer in the research on structural change in advanced countries while Juergen B. Donges took the lead of a team to explore the challenges arising from the adoption of outward looking industrial strategies in LDCs.

The results soon became politically as exciting as the work in the Council. In 1972, while Helmut Schmidt was temporarily in charge of the Ministry of Economic Affairs succeeding Karl Schiller, we were prevented from publishing a publicly financed study on the industrial structure and the level and profile of protection in Germany simply because the leader of the textile union had intervened for reasons of job security. Some of the participants in the 1972 congress of the German Economic Association (which celebrated its 100th anniversary) had the occasion to witness a rather vivid conversation with Schmidt about freedom of thought and publication before and after 1945 and the importance of structural adjustment for the first and the third world. Shortly afterwards, the public could indeed take note of the research[11] financed by its taxpayers while the Institute – though government supported – could be confident of having asserted itself as intellectually independent.

This was but one additional example that economics – here information gained by research – is not universally welcome. Some textile firms actually complained that the Institute's findings had impaired their creditworthiness. This may be an exaggeration but, if true and viewed in due perspective, it demonstrates that information about trends in structural change has the potential social productivity of preventing a misallocation of investible resources. Similarly, we have testimony that an international cross-section analysis to assess the medium run prospects of Europe's steel industry had in fact a strong impact on a large firm's decision to change its output mix in anticipation of the steel crisis. But if privately so useful, why is such structural research not in demand as a private good? Part of the answer is: in contrast to the Chicago view, markets in some sense are always in a process of learning, often too slow for the impatient observers from Kiel. In the meantime, the German government has institutionalised tri-annual surveys on structural change to be competitively submitted by the five leading research institutes.

In the field of macroeconomic policy, the Institute carried some of the Council's thinking on the assignment problem to its logical conclusion, taking into account the new conditions of flexible exchange rates, inflation, and slow growth. Freed from the obligation to support the exchange rate and to care for balance-of-payments equilibrium, monetary policy could be held fully responsible for determining the domestic price level. With no money illusion left, the Central Bank had virtually no influence on the level of output and employment except in the case of a recession due to a declining income velocity of money. Therefore, the medium-run level of employment was seen to be essentially determined by the level and structure of real wages, a point that completely spoiled our relations with organised labour when early warning signals about the 'reprivatisation of the employment risk' emitted in 1972 were harshly dismissed by Helmut Schmidt and hence completely ignored by the trade unions in the wage rounds leading to the 1974 wage explosion. Having been publicly attacked as anti-labour in subsequent years I was glad to receive satisfaction from the EC Commission's 1985 economic report[12] which contained the message that wage moderation was a necessary condition for any strategy intended to substantially reduce Europe's unemployment before the end of the 1980s. In order to appreciate this message one should know that it was formulated under the responsibility of the German Commissioner who had previously been in charge of economic policy questions in the German Federation of Labour Unions (DGB).

Fiscal policy, in our solution to the assignment problem, is not considered instrumental in determining output and employment except under conditions of a Keynesian liquidity trap as it might develop in a recession as a 'secondary deflation' (to use Röpke's term). What fiscal policy really determines is the growth of potential output: (a) the aggregate supply of savings for (productive) capital formation via the budget surplus or deficit, the tax system, and the structure of public expenditures; (b) the marginal efficiency of autonomous (i.e. not demand-induced) private investments via the tax structure and the complementary character of public investments, and (c) the supply of labour and society's general motivation level via the level and rate structure of direct taxes. In a medium-run perspective, the Finance Minister is regarded as responsible for the population's economic mentality and the national economy's dynamism and attractiveness on world capital markets. Some commentators tend to view us as modernist supply siders whereas we ourselves simply see us rephrasing old fashioned classical truths, including the emphasis on long-run policies which are conducive to the growth of supply. This at least was behind my separate vote to the 1977 OECD Report 'Towards Full Employment and Price Stability',[13] prepared under the Chairmanship of Paul McCracken.

When inflation accelerated after 1973, I came out in favour of indexation that would allow long-term contracts to be concluded in real terms – on the labour market as well as on the capital market.[14] With respect to labour, this idea was complementary to assigning responsibility for employment to the partners at the bargaining table whereas the introduction of inflation-proof credit instruments was to lengthen the term structure of domestic and international debt and to prevent the flight into what I called 'Betongold' ('concrete gold'), i.e. houses and apartments built and bought as hedges against inflation. If there were no inflation-induced distortions and if elements of inflationary expectations in contracts were flexible in nominal terms (to be fixed only *ex post*), it would become easier to achieve 'stabilisation without stagnation', even in the absence of a concerted action of our 1965 vintage. We lost the argument in the public policy debate mainly because we failed to make it sufficiently clear that most wage indexation which was actually introduced in periods of accelerating inflation had a built-in time lag and thus made for over-indexation in the deceleration phase.

Once again, it was a point of economics rather than value judgements that led to failure. The smoke of the intellectual battle ground has long disappeared, but the concrete gold in the German landscape is still there, together with a structural crisis of the construction industry. Internationally, the debt problem of developing countries would almost certainly have been less severe had indexation warned the recipients of recycled petrodollars that there happens to be a real rate of interest which cannot possibly stay at zero (or even below!) before the world economy has attained the final stage of bliss. Next to the theory of comparative advantage, the indexation problem is perhaps the best test for understanding economics.

Depressed real rates of interest during periods of inflation – useful as a short run device for cushioning the cost push of excessive wages in a 'Phillips-Curve-Strategy' of fighting classical unemployment with inflation – became to me the clue for explaining why Europe has persistent unemployment despite high rates of capacity utilisation. In 1977, the Institute had convened a conference on 'Capital Shortage and Unemployment in the World Economy'[15] designed to draw attention to a – not so uncommon – anomaly which had become familiar to me in the early post-war years. Although we – again – failed to sell a theory, we saw it confirmed in the following years by direct observation at our doorstep: investible funds were diverted to constructing homes rather than plants and jobs, and those remaining funds which the productive sector was able to absorb were used for capital deepening rather than capital widening, for implementing labour saving process innovations rather than pushing product innovations. Years after, the EC Commission established the statistical series and presented the calculations to demonstrate how capital had been wasted all over Europe – to the detriment of the unemployed – under the impact of distorted factor prices. Some laymen attending my public lectures seemed to understand better than some professional economists from inside and outside Germany what I tried to make clear: classical unemployment, if fought by Keynesian policies, will merely be transformed into much worse diseases, i.e. capital shortage unemployment and, eventually, technological unemployment. The problem with experts is that their model is sometimes too much geared to what fits the facts of the American 'économie dominante'.

As to the international economy, we organised conferences to critically evaluate the attempts at cartelising supplies and coordinating economic policies, pursued under the temporarily fashionable heading of a New International Economic Order. In a paper for the 1976 F. Marcus Fleming Memorial Conference of the International Monetary Fund, I defended the position that exchange rate surveillance should concentrate on establishing rules for central banks requiring them to preannounce monetary targets and notify the Fund whenever they intervened in foreign exchange markets: 'no intervention without notification'.[16] When the dollar sharply fell after 1976 I strongly suspected that this was partly deliberate US policy inducing official and unofficial holders of dollar assets to change their portfolio, to 'emigrate from the dollar area', to let the 'dollar area implode'. In the same vein, the rise of the dollar after 1979 was considered as its re-emergence as a strong world currency supported by the home base of an economy which showed renewed dynamism. As to European monetary integration, we favoured either the monopoly approach (create a European central bank) or the competitive approach (let the most stable currency gradually gain dominance) over the old cartel approach so close to French thinking and to the heart of many officials and politicians that it was actually adopted in the form of the EMS. The best research in this field that I happen to know of is the work Roland Vaubel accomplished during his ten (or so) years as one of my closest associates and probably one of the sharpest minds the Institute has hosted since its beginning.

Schumpeter's spirit in the Institute and in my work became increasingly alive after the second period as a visiting professor at Yale (1977/78) which followed the completion of the second volume of my book on economic policy[17] (long delayed because of my Council involvement). The challenge came from Jim Tobin's article 'How Dead is Keynes',[18] which irritated me for what my European mind perceived as a misplaced emphasis. Attempts to formulate my position led to a paper on growth, structural change, and employment[19] later to be discussed in the 1979 Kiel Conference on 'Macroeconomic Policies for Growth and Stability – A European Perspective'. Instead of repeating the message it contained it seems better to mention the titles of the Kiel Conferences in the following years: 'Towards an Explanation of Economic Growth' (1980), 'Emerging Technologies: Consequences for Economic Growth, Structural Change, and Employment' (1981), 'Reassessing the Role of Government in the Mixed Economy' (1982), 'New Opportunities for Entrepreneurship' (1983), 'Economic Incentives' (1984). With this thrust we hoped to prepare the intellectual ground for a re-acceleration of Europe's growth later in the 1980s, assuming that courageous efforts at deregulation and improvement of the incentive system would cure Eurosclerosis and call forth more innovative activities at the frontiers of economic development.

Notes

1. Spiro J. Latsis, 'A Research Programme in Economics', in *Idem, Method and Appraisal in Economics* (Cambridge, New York, 1976) pp. 1–41.
2. Herbert Giersch, *Der Ausgletch der Kriegslasten vom Standpunkt sozialer Gerechtigkeit.* (Recklinghausen, 1948).

3. Herbert Giersch, 'Economic Union Between Nations and the Location of Industries', *Review of Economic Studies*. vol. XVII (1949/50).
4. Herbert Giersch, 'Akzelerationsprinzip und Importneigung', in *Weltwirtschaftliches Archiv*, vol. 70, no. 2, 1953, pp. 241–83 (trans. for *International Economic Papers*, no. 4, London, New York, 1954.)
5. Herbert Giersch, 'Das Handelsoptimum. Ein Beitrag zur Theorie der Wirtschaftspolitik', in *Weltwirtschaftliches Archiv*, vol. 76, no. 1, 1956, pp. 1–40. (trans. for *International Economic Papers*, no. 7, London, New York, 1957.)
6. Herbert Giersch, *Allgemeine Wirtschaftspolitik* (Erster Band: Grundlagen, Wiesbaden, 1960).
7. Edwin G. Nourse, *Economics in the Public Service* (New York, Harcourt Brace, 1953).
8. *Stabiles Geld Stetiges Wachstum*. Jahresgutachten 1964/65 des Sachverständigenrates zur Begutachtung der gesamtwirtschaftlichen Entwicklung. Mainz, Stuttgart, 1965.
9. *Stabilisierung ohne Stagnation*. Jahresgutachten 1965/66 des Sachverständigenrates zur Begutachtung der gesamtwirtschaftlichen Entwicklung. Mainz, Stuttgart, 1965.
10. Herbert Giersch and Kasper Wolfgang 'A Floating German Mark? An Essay in Speculative Economics'. In N. Halm (ed.), *Approaches to Greater Flexibility of Exchange Rates. The Bürgenstock Papers* (Princeton, N.J., 1970, pp. 345–55).
11. Juergen B. Donges *et al.* 'Protektion und Branchenstruktur der westdeutschen Wirtschatt', *Kieler Studie*, no. 123. Tübingen, 1973.
12. Commission of the European Communities. *Annual Economic Report 1985–1986.* (Brussels, 1985).
13. Paul McCracken *et al., Towards Full Employment and Price Stability*. A report to the OECD by a group of independent experts. Paris, 1977.
14. Herbert Giersch, 'Indexklauseln und Inflationsbekämpfung', *Kiel Discussion Papers*. no. 32, October 1973.
15. Herbert Giersch (ed.), *Capital Shortage and Unemployment in the World Economy* (Tübingen: J.C.B. Mohr (Paul Siebeck), 1978).
16. Herbert Giersch, 'Fund Surveillance over Exchange Rates – A Wider View'. Paper for the F. Marcus Fleming Memorial Conference of the IMF. Washington, November, 1976.
17. Herbert Giersch, *Allgemeine Wirtschaftspolitik*, Zweiter Band: 'Konjunktur- und Wachsumspolitik in der offenen Wirtschaft'. Wiesbaden, 1977.
18. James Tobin, 'How Dead is Keynes?', *Economic Inquiry*, no. 15, 1977, pp. 459–68.
19. Herbert Giersch, 'Aspects of Growth, Structural Change, and Employment – A Schumpeterian Perspective', *Weltwirtschaftliches Archiv*, vol. 115, no. 4, 1979, pp. 629–52.

12   Better than Ploughing
James M. Buchanan

FAMILY ORIGINS

My title's description of an academic career is taken directly from Frank H. Knight, from whom I take so much. Nonetheless, my origins in the rural agricultural poverty of the upper south (Tennessee) in the United States, along with the sometimes pretentious efforts of the middle-class poor to impose social distinctions, are surely explanatory elements in any narrative account of my own history.

My family was poor, but, in the county, it was important. My grandfather, John P. Buchanan, was the county's only Governor of the State of Tennessee. He was a one-term phenomenon, having been elected as the nominee of the Farmers' Alliance party, one of the several successful Populist electoral triumphs in 1891. By 1893, the Democratic Party had put its house in order, and the Populists had seen their best days. But Buchanan's governorship established the family in the community. The local public school which I attended for ten years was named 'Buchanan School'.

My father was the youngest of a large family, to whose lot fell the operation of the family farm after his siblings had departed. I grew up in a huge house on a hill, in varying states of disrepair, on a farm that had no owner. It was owned by 'the Buchanan estate', which was not divided until the farm was sold in 1944, and long after I had entered military service. My father had no incentive for effective maintenance. He was a jack of all trades, a farmer, a sometime carpenter, veterinarian, insulator, and equipment operator. He was locally political, a community Justice of the Peace during all of my childhood. A handsome man, he had been a fine athlete (two years varsity football at the University of Oklahoma); and with a fine sense of humour, he was a favourite with the ladies. He was possessed by intense personal courage; he made no pretence to intellectual interests.

My mother was the best and the brightest of a family of deputy sheriffs and Presbyterian preachers which had roughly the same class standing as my father's. As was general in rural Tennessee in the early years of this century, both families were pure Scots-Irish. My mother, Lila Scott, finished high school, took teacher training, and taught for a decade before meeting my father. Hers was the most curious mind I have known; she devoured anything she could find to read, and she was not discriminating, with interests ranging at least from Latin grammar through calculus through Zane Gray westerns. She, too, assumed easily a leadership role in the local community, organising the parent's association for the school, rising rapidly to county and regional offices. But, for this narrative, she was my teacher, and beyond the teacher that is in all mothers. She advanced me two grades by home instruction, and helped me in assignments through college years.

EARLY EDUCATION

From my early years, I was assigned the role as family successor to my grandfather. I was to be the lawyer-politician, and Vanderbilt University (pre-law, then law) was understood as the final rung on my educational ladder. There were early family misgivings about my personality; I did not exhibit the behaviour of the exaggerated extrovert required for any budding politician. But law remained my career focus, and I was trained in public speaking. Economic reality destroyed this dream; Vanderbilt moved beyond the possible as the Great Depression moved in. College was what I could afford, Middle Tennessee State Teacher's College in Murfreesboro, which allowed me to live at home and to earn enough for fees and books by milking dairy cows morning and night for four years.

My college education was non-systematic and stochastic. There was waste in the requirements in formal education, and poor instruction in biology, history, psychology, economics, and other subjects. But there was much of value in my exposure to Shakespeare, modern poetry, mathematics, and physics. When I finished, I had accumulated majors in three areas – mathematics, English literature, and social science, including economics. These college years were important as confidence builders; by the end of my second year my academic standing was the best in the college; the country boy more than held his own against the boys and girls from the towns.

Upon graduation in 1940, I faced three options – school teaching at

$65 per month; employment in a Nashville bank at $75 per month, and a $50 per month fellowship in Economics at the University of Tennessee. My career as an economist was settled by the dominance of the third opportunity, not by any desire to save the world. The 1940–41 graduate year in Knoxville, Tennessee helped me meet the world beyond. I learned no economics during that year, but I did learn about women and whiskey, which, after all, are important parts of an education. There were few good economists on the faculty, but I was exposed to a genuine scholar, a man whose work habits were important in shaping my own. Charles P. White became my example of the research economist, who took his position seriously and conveyed to me the notion that there is, after all, a moral element in academic employment. It was White also who, despite his own self-acknowledged limits in these respects, strongly advised me to stick with economic theory as the basis for all applications.

Plans were open beyond the one year until I secured a fellowship in Statistics at Columbia University for the 1941–2 academic year. But before I could take up this appointment, I was drafted into military service, and found myself in the United States Navy by August 1941.

I had an easy war. After officer training in New York, and a special stint at the Naval War college, I was assigned to the operations staff of Admiral C.W. Nimitz, Commander-in-Chief, Pacific Fleet. Aside from a six-weeks experience-gathering tour at sea during one of the island invasions, I worked throughout the war at Pearl Harbor and at Guam, at fleet headquarters control deep in the bowels of the earth. I enjoyed the military, the colleagues, the work and the setting; and I was good at the job. For the first and only time in my life, I worked closely with men who were important in shaping the lives and destinies of many others. I saw these military leaders as ordinary mortals, trying to do their job within the constraints they faced, and burdened with their own prejudices like everyone else. This experience has helped me throughout my academic career; I have been able to relegate to the third order of smalls the sometime petty quarrels that seem to motivate professors everywhere, both in their roles as instructors and as research scholars.

In one sense my only career choice involved the decision to leave the navy and to return to civilian life. This decision was not easy; I knew the important persons, who urged me to stay; I had enjoyed the four years. But I made the correct choice, and was discharged in late 1945. With the GI government subsidy for further schooling available, and with a new wife for partial support, I considered alternative graduate schools. Columbia University no longer beckoned because New York City had not made me want to return. I knew nothing about the competence or the ideological makeup of the University of Chicago economics faculty. But a teacher from my undergraduate days at Middle Tennessee, with a Chicago PhD in political science, conveyed to me the intellectual excitement of the place. Off to Chicago I went in late 1945, along with the many others who were just returning from military service.

CHICAGO, FRANK KNIGHT, AND KNUT WICKSELL

Had I known about the ideological character of the Chicago faculty I might have chosen to go elsewhere. I was not overtly political or ideological in my salad days; emerging from the family populist tradition, I grew up in a solidly Democratic setting, with Roosevelt emerging as the popular leader in the 1930s. I was basically populist and pacifist. But officer training school in New York radicalised me. Along with many others, I was subjected to overt discrimination based on favouritism for products of the eastern establishment universities. This sobering experience made me forever sympathetic to those who suffer discriminatory treatment, and it forestalled any desire to be a part of any eastern establishment institution.

When I reached the University of Chicago, I was what I now best describe as a libertarian socialist. I had always been anti-state, anti-government, anti-establishment. But this included the establishment that controlled the United States economy. I had grown up on a reading diet from my grandfather's attic piled high with the radical pamphlets of the 1890s. The robber barons were very real to me.

At Chicago, I found myself different from my graduate student colleagues, almost all of whom were socialist of one or another stripe. But within six weeks after enrolment in Frank Knight's course in price theory, I had been converted into a zealous advocate of the market order. Frank Knight was not an ideologue, and he made no attempt to convert anybody. But I was, somehow, ready for the understanding of economic process that his teaching offered. I was converted by the power of ideas, by an understanding of the model of the market. This experience shaped my attitude toward the use and purpose of economic instruction; if I could be converted so could others.

Frank Knight was *the* intellectual influence during my years at the

University of Chicago, and his influence increased over subsequent years, enhanced by the development of a close personal relationship. Knight became my role model, without which I wonder what turns I might have taken. The qualities of mind that Knight exhibited were, and remain, those that I seek to emulate: the willingness to question anything, and anybody, on any subject anytime; the categorical refusal to accept anything as sacred; the genuine openness to all ideas; and, finally, the basic conviction that most ideas peddled about are nonsense or worse when examined critically.

A second Chicago event profoundly affected my career. Having finished my work, including the German language examination, I had the leisure of a scholar without assignments in the Harper Library stacks during three months of the summer of 1948. By sheer chance, I pulled Knut Wicksell's 1896 dissertation on taxation from the shelves, a book that was untranslated and unknown. The effect on me was dramatic. Wicksell laid out before me a set of ideas that seemed to correspond precisely with those that I had already in my head, ideas that I could not have expressed and would not have dared to express in the public-finance mind-set of the time. Wicksell told us that if economists really want to apply the test of efficiency to the public sector, only the rule of unanimity for collective choice offers the procedural guarantee. If we seek reform in economic policy, we should change the rules under which political agents or representatives act. Economists should, once and for all, cease and desist proffering advice on non-existent benevolent despots. Wicksell's were heady words, and from that day, I was determined to translate Wicksell's contribution into English.[1]

Visitors to my office know that photographs of only two economists grace the walls, Frank Knight and Knut Wicksell. I consider them co-equals, Knight in his influence on my attitudes toward the world of ideas generally, and Wicksell in his influence on the specific ideas that have come to be associated with my work in public choice and constitutional economics. Both of these influences were embedded in my psyche when I left Chicago in mid-1948.

I entered the highly competitive world of American academia with no conscious sense of intellectual direction. In one of my first articles, based in part on the Wicksell exposure and, in part, by reading a translation of De Viti De Marco, I called for a tie-in between the theory of the state and norms for taxation. The point seemed so simple, indeed obvious, yet so locked in was the utilitarian mind-set of orthodox public finance that the article was widely cited as seminal. In 1951, Kenneth Arrow published his widely heralded book on the general impossibility theorem. For three years, I was bemused by the failure of reviewers and critics to make the obvious point that the whole Arrow construction was inappropriate for a democratic society. Why should the social ordering satisfy consistency norms if individual values and preferences generated inconsistencies? I published a review article in 1954 that few economists understood then, or understand now. Almost as a footnote, I published a second short article comparing individual choice in voting and in the market. Again, the points made seemed simple, but surprisingly no one had made such a basic comparison. In those two papers, there were elements of much that was later to be developed in my contributions to public choice.

The two 1954 papers were published in the *Journal of Political Economy*, under the editorship of Earl J. Hamilton, who deserves special mention in this narrative. I had not taken his courses at the University of Chicago, and only in my last few months there did I get to know him personally. But we did establish a friendship, and from him I got the advice that one major key to academic success was to 'keep the ass to the chair', a rule that I have followed and that I have passed along to several generations of students. But Hamilton's influence was not primarily in this piece of advice. Through his editorship of the journal, he encouraged rather than discouraged me as potential author; he was a tough editor, but his comments and reactions were never wholly negative, and it was only after several submissions that the two 1954 pieces were hammered into acceptable shape. Negation at that stage of my career might have been fatal.

THE ITALIAN YEAR

Hamilton was also influential in encouraging me to keep up with the languages, and I commenced to learn to read Italian. I wanted to go to Italy for a year's reading in the classical works in public finance theory. I got a Fulbright grant for the 1955–6 academic year, which I spent in Perugia and Rome. This Italian year was critical in the development of my ideas on the importance of the relationship between the political structure and the positive and normative theory of economic policy. The Italians had escaped the delusions of state omniscience and benevolence that had clouded the minds of England and German language social philosophers and scientists. The Italians had long since cut through the absurdities of Benthamite utilitarianism and Hegelian idealism. Real rather than idealised politics, with real persons as actors – these were the building blocks in the Italian constructions, whether those of the cooperative-democratic state or the ruling class-monopoly state. Exposure to this Italian conceptualisation of the state was necessary to enable me to break out of the idealistic-utilitarian mind-set that still imposes its intellectual straitjacket on many of my peers in social science. The Italian year was also important in the more general sense of offering insights into the distinctly non-American historical-cultural environment.

PUBLIC DEBT AND OPPORTUNITY COST

The Italian research year was indirectly responsible for one strand of my work that may seem to represent a side alley, namely, my work in the theory of public debt, which was less successful in convincing my economist peers than other work in public choice and public finance. At the very end of the Italian year, I suddenly 'saw the light'. I realised that the whole conventional wisdom on public debt was simply wrong, and that the time had come for a restoration of the classical theory, which was correct in all its essentials. I was as excited by this personal discovery as I had been by the discovery of the Wicksell book almost a decade earlier. Immediately on my return to America in 1956, I commenced my first singly-authored book, *Public Principles of Public Debt* (1958).

In my overall assessment, the work on public debt was not a digression. This work was simply another extension or application of what can be discerned as a central theme in my efforts from the very first papers written. I have been consistently reductionist in that I have insisted that analysis be factored down to the level of choices faced by individual actors. The orthodox theory of public debt that I challenged embodied a failure to treat relevant choice alternatives. My reasoning, once again, was simple. National economies, as such, cannot enjoy gains or suffer losses. The fact that making guns 'uses up' resources in years of war tells us nothing at all about *who* must pay for those guns, and *when*. The whole macroaggregation exercise that had captured the attention of post-Keynesian economists was called into question.

My work on public debt stirred up considerable controversy in the early 1960s, and I realised that the ambiguity stemmed, in part, from an absence of clarity in my initial challenge. Confusion centred around the conception of opportunity cost, and I laid my plans to write a short book, which I consider my best work in economic theory, narrowly defined. This book, *Cost and Choice* (1969), again emphasises my central theme, the reduction of analysis to individual choice settings which, in this extension, implies the necessity of defining cost in utility rather than commodity dimensions.

GORDON TULLOCK, *THE CALCULUS OF CONSENT*, AND PUBLIC CHOICE

I first encountered Gordon Tullock in 1958, when he came to the University of Virginia as a postdoctoral research fellow. I was impressed by his imagination and originality, and by his ability to recognise easily the elements of my own criticism of public debt orthodoxy. Tullock insisted not only that analysis be reduced to individual choice but, also, that individuals be modelled always as maximisers of self-interest, a step that I had sometimes been unwilling to take, despite my exposure to the Italians. Tullock wrote his seminal paper on the working of simple majority rule, and we decided to collaborate on a book that would examine the individual's choice among alternative political rules. We more or less explicitly considered our exercise to be an implicit defence of the Madisonian structure embodied in the United States Constitution.

The Calculus of Consent (1962) was the first work in what we now call 'constitutional economics', and it achieved the status of a 'classic' in public choice theory. In retrospect, it is interesting to me that there was no sense of 'discovery' at any point in that book's construction, no moment of excitement akin to those accompanying either the discovery of the Wicksell book or the insight into public debt theory. Tullock and I considered ourselves to be applying relatively simple economic analysis to the choice among alternative political decision rules, with more or less predictable results. We realised that no one had attempted to do precisely what we were doing, but the exercise was essentially one of 'writing out the obvious' rather than opening up wholly new areas for inquiry.

We were wrong. Public choice, as a subdiscipline in its own right, emerged in the early 1960s, in part from the reception of our book, in part from our own organisational-entrepreneurial efforts which later emerged in the Public Choice Society, in part from others works.

Once the whole complex web of political decision rules and procedures was opened up for economic analysis, the range of application seemed open ended. Public choice, in the 1960s was both exciting and easy; it is not surprising that graduate students in our programme at Virginia were highly successful and that budding economists and political scientists quickly latched onto the new subdiscipline.[2]

My own work does not exhibit a dramatic switching to public choice economics from standard public finance. As I have noted above, from my earliest papers I had emphasised the importance of political structure, a conviction that was strengthened by my exposure to the Italians. Immediately after my excursion into the theory of public debt and before collaboration with Tullock on *The Calculus of Consent*, I wrote a long survey essay on the Italian tradition in public finance and published this essay, along with other pieces in *Fiscal Theory and Political Economy* (1960). Considered as a package, my work over the decade, 1956–66, involved filling in gaps in the taxonomy of public goods theory along with various attempts to factor down familiar propositions in theoretical welfare economics into individualised choice settings. The paper, 'Externality' (1962), written jointly with W.C. Stubblebine was an amalgamation of strands of argument from Wicksell, Coase, and Pigou. The paper 'An Economic Theory of Clubs' (1965) was a filling in of an obvious gap in the theory of public goods.

During the early 1960s, my work specifically shifted toward an attempt to tie two quasi-independent strands of inquiry together, those of orthodox public finance and the theory of political decision structure. The result was a relatively neglected book, *Public Finance in Democratic Process* (1967), which contained implications for formative theory that remain unrecognised by modern research scholars.

The research programme embodied in elementary public choice theory developed almost naturally in a sequence of applications to the theory of economic policy. The whole of the Keynesian and post-Keynesian theory of macroeconomic management (including monetarism) depends critically on the presumption that political agents respond to considerations of 'public interest' rather than to the incentives imposed upon them by constituents. Once these agents are modelled as ordinary persons, the whole policy structure crumbles. This basic public-choice critique of the Keynesian theory of policy was presented in *Democracy in Deficit* (1977), written jointly with Richard E. Wagner. I have often used the central argument of this book as the clearest example of the applicability of elementary public choice theory, the implications of which have been corroborated in the accumulating evidence provided by the regime of quasi-permanent budget deficits.

BETWEEN ANARCHY AND LEVIATHAN

Through the middle 1960s, my analysis and interpretation of the workings of democratic politics were grounded in a relatively secure belief that, despite the many political failures that public choice theory allows us to identify, ultimately the governing authorities, as constrained by constitutional structure respond to and implement the values and preferences of individual citizens. This belief in the final efficacy of democratic process surely affected my analysis, even if unconsciously, and allowed me to defend the essential 'logic' of political institutions in being against the sometime naive proposals made by social reformers.

This foundational belief was changed by the events of the late 1960s. I lost my 'faith' in the effectiveness of government as I observed the explosive take-off in spending rates and new programmes, engineered by self-interested political agents and seemingly divorced from the interests of citizens. At the same time, I observed what seemed to me to be a failure of the institutional structure, at all levels, to respond effectively to mounting behavioural disorder. The United States government seemed to take on aspects of an agent-driven Leviathan simultaneously with the emergence of anarchy in civil society.

What was happening, and how could my explanatory model be applied to the modified reality of the late 1960s and early 1970s? I sensed the necessity of plunging much deeper into basic political philosophy than heretofore, and I found it useful to examine more closely the predicted operating properties of both anarchy and Leviathan. I was fortunate in that I located colleagues who assisted and greatly complemented my efforts in each case. Winston C. Bush formalised the anarchy of the Hobbesian jungle in terms of modern economic theory. Bush's independent and foundational analysis provided me with the starting point for the book that remains the most coherent single statement of my research programme, *The Limits of Liberty* (1975).

Although chapters in that book raised the threat of the Leviathan state, I had not worked out the formal analysis. Again I was lucky to be able to work with Geoffrey Brennan in pushing along this frontier of inquiry. We commenced the exciting project that emerged as *The Power to Tax* (1980). That book explored the implications of the hypothesis that government maximises revenues from any taxing authority constitutionally granted to it. Such analysis seems required for any informed constitutional calculus involving a grant of taxing power to government. As reviewers noted, the result of our analysis here was to stand much of the conventional wisdom in normative tax theory on its head.

CONSTITUTIONALISM AND THE SOCIAL CONTRACT

As I noted earlier, *The Calculus of Consent* (1962) was the first explicit contribution in the research programme that we now call 'constitutional economics' or 'constitutional political economy'. Gordon Tullock and I were analysing the individual's choice among alternative rules for reaching political decisions, rules to which he, along with others, would be subject in subsequent periods of operation. Such a choice setting is necessarily different in kind from that normally treated by economists, which is the choice among end objects within well-defined constraints. In a very real sense, the choice among rules becomes a choice among constraints, and, hence, involves a higher-state calculus of decision than that which most economists examine.

We were initially influenced to analyse the choice among political rules by at least two factors that I can now identify. First, we were dissatisfied by the apparent near-universal and unquestioned acceptance of majority rule as the ideal for collective decision processes. Secondly, we were influenced by our then colleague, Rutledge Vining, himself an early student of Frank Knight, who hammered home to all who would listen that economic policy choices are not made among allocations or distributions, but are, necessarily, among rules or institutions that generate patterns of allocations and distributions. Vining's emphasis was on the stochastic nature of these patterns of outcomes and on the necessity for an appreciation for and understanding of the elementary theory of probability.

How does a person choose among the rules to which he will be subject? Vining took from Knight, and passed along to me, a fully sympathetic listener, the analogy with the choice of rules in ordinary games, from poker to basketball. The chooser, at the rule-choosing or constitutional stage of deliberation cannot identify how any particular rule will precisely affect his own position in subsequent rounds of play. Who can know how the cards will fall? The choice among rules is, therefore, necessarily made under what we should now call a 'veil of uncertainty'. *The Calculus of Consent* was our straightforward extension of this nascent research programme to the game of politics.

In constitutional choice there is no well-defined maximand analogous to that which describes garden variety economic choice. The individual may still be modelled as a utility maximiser, but there is no readily available means of arraying alternatives. The formal properties of choice under uncertainty, properties that have been exhaustively explored during the middle decades of this century, did not concern us. But we did sense the positive value of the uncertainty setting in opening up the potential for agreement on rules. If an individual cannot know how specific rules will affect his own position, he will be led to choose among rules in accordance with some criterion of generality rather than particularity. And if all persons reason similarly, the prospects for some Wicksellian-like agreement on rules are much more favourable than prospects for agreement on political choices to be made within a defined rules structure. In my own interpretation, in *The Calculus of Consent*, Tullock and I were shifting the Wicksellian unanimity norm for efficiency in collective choice from the in-period level, where its limits are severe, to the constitutional level where no comparable limits are present.

This construction in *The Calculus of Consent* was essentially worked out independently of the comparable construction of John Rawls. But discovery of his early paper on 'Justice as Fairness' during the course of writing our book served to give us confidence that we were on a reasonable track. As early as the late 1950s, Rawls had spelled out his justice-as-fairness criterion and had introduced early versions of his veil of ignorance, which was to become universally familiar after the publication of his acclaimed treatise, *A Theory of Justice* (1971). The coincidence both in the timing of our initial work and in the basic similarity in analytical constructions has made me share an affinity with Rawls that has seemed mysterious to critics of both of us.

The subject matter of economics has always seemed to me to be the institution of exchange, embodying agreement between or among choosing parties. The Wicksellian extension of the exchange paradigm to the many-person collective has its most direct application in the theory of public finance, but when applied to the choices among political rules the analysis moves into areas of inquiry that are foreign to economists. At this research juncture, the disciplinary base merges into political philosophy, and the exchange paradigm becomes a natural component of a general contractarian theory of political interaction. Almost by definition, the economist who shifts his attention to political process while retaining his methodological individualism must be contractarian.

As noted earlier, my emphasis has been on factoring down complex interactions into individual choice components and, where possible, to explain and interpret such interactions in terms of cooperation rather than conflict models. Interpersonal, intergroup, and interparty conflict can scarcely be left out of consideration when we examine ordinary politics within defined constitutional structures. The contractarian or exchange programme must shift, almost by necessity, to the stage of choices among rules. The contractarian becomes a constitutionalist, and I have often classified my own position with both these terms.

I have continued to be surprised at the reluctance of my colleagues in the social sciences, and especially in economics, to share the contractarian-constitutionalist research programme and to understand the relevance of looking at politics and governance in terms of the two-stage decision process. A substantial share of my work over the decade, 1975–85, involved varying attempts to persuade my peers to adopt the constitutional attitude. In two volumes of collected essays, *Freedom in Constitutional Contract* (1978), and *Liberty, Market, and State* (1985), as well as in a book jointly with Geoffrey Brennan, *The Reason of Rules* (1985), I sought to defend the contractarian-constitutionalist methodology in many applications.

ACADEMIC EXIT AND VIRGINIA POLITICAL ECONOMY

Both in response to the demands of the series of autobiographical essays in which this paper appears and to my own preferences, I have, aside from the first two background sections, concentrated on the intellectual record, on the development of the ideas that have characterised my work, and on the persons and events that seem to have affected these ideas. I have deliberately left out of account the details of my personal, private experiences over the course of a long career. My essay would, however, be seriously incomplete if I should neglect totally the influences of the academic-intellectual environments within which I have been able to pursue my work, including the stimulation I have secured from colleagues, staff, and students, whose names are not entered in these accounts.

I cannot, of course, test what 'might have been' had I chosen academic settings other than I did select, I feel no acute sense of exceptional opportunities missed, nor do I classify any choices made as having been grossly mistaken. I have exercised the academic exit option that the competitive structure of the United States academy offers. In so doing, I have reduced the ability of those who might have sought to modify the direction of my research and teaching efforts, while, at the same time, I have secured the benefits from the unintended consequences that shifts in location always guarantee.

This much said, I would be remiss if I did not include some form of tribute to the three academic settings within Virginia that have provided me with professional breathing space for almost all of my career. Mr Jefferson's 'academical village', the University of Virginia, where I spent twelve years, 1956–68, allowed Warren Nutter and me full rein in establishing the Thomas Jefferson Center for Studies in Political Economy. This Center, as an institution, encouraged me, and others, to counter the increasing technical specialisation of economics and, for me, to keep the subject matter interesting when the discipline, in more orthodox hands, threatened to become boring in the extreme. Virginia Polytechnic Institute, or VPI, where I spent fourteen years, 1969–83, allowed Charles Goetz, Gordon Tullock, and me to organise the Center for Study of Public Choice, a Center that became, for a period in the 1970s and early 1980s, an international haven for research scholars who sought some exposure to the blossoming new subdiscipline of public choice. Finally, George Mason University, to which the whole Center shifted in 1983, insured a continuity in my research emphasis and tradition, even beyond that of my active career.

RETROSPECTIVE

Other contributors to this series have discussed the influences on their developments as 'economists'. I am not at all sure that I qualify for inclusion in terms of this professional or disciplinary classification. I am not, and have never been, an 'economist' in any narrowly defined meaning. My interests in understanding how the economic interaction process works has always been instrumental to the more inclusive purpose of understanding how we can learn to live with one another without engaging in Hobbesian war and without subjecting ourselves to the dictates of the state. The 'wealth of nations', as such, has never commanded my attention save as a valued by-product of an effectively free society. The ways and means through which the social order might be made more 'efficient' in the standard meaning – these orthodox guidelines have carried relatively little weight for me.

Neither have I considered myself a 'pure scientist' and my work as 'pure science'. I have not been engaged in some exciting quest for discovery of a reality that exists independently of our own making. I have sensed acutely the exhilaration in ideas that is shared by all scientists in the broader meaning, but the ideas that capture my attention are those that, directly or indirectly, explain how freely choosing individuals can secure jointly desired goals. The simple exchange of apples and oranges between two traders – this institutional model is the starting point for all that I have done. Contrast this with the choice between apples and oranges in the utility-maximising calculus of Robinson Crusoe. The second model is the starting point for most of what economists do.

If this difference between my foundational model and that of other economists is recognised, my work takes on an internal coherence and consistency that may not be apparent, absent such recognition. The coherence was not, of course, a deliberately chosen element of a research programme I have written largely in response to ideas that beckoned, ideas that offered some intellectual challenge and that had not, to my knowledge, been developed by others. I have rarely been teased by either the currency of policy topics or the fads of academic fashion, and when I have been so tempted my work has suffered. The coherence that the work does possess stems from the simple fact that I have worked from a single methodological perspective during the four decades that span my career to date, along with the fact that I have accepted the normative implications of this perspective. The methodological perspective and the normative stance are shared by few of my peers in modern social science. This location of my position outside the mainstream has the inestimable value of providing me with the continuing challenge to seek still other ideas and applications that may, ultimately, shift the frontier of effective agreement outward.

Notes

1. My translation of the centrally important part of the book was published in *Classics in the Theory of Public Finance* (1958).
2. For two volumes devoted largely to applications, see, Buchanan, James M., and Tollison, Robert (eds), *Theory of Public Choice* (1972), and *Theory of Public Choice*, II (1984).

References

Own Works

Buchanan, James M., *Fiscal Theory and Political Economy* (Chapel Hill, University of North Carolina Press, 1960).
Buchanan, James M., *Public Principles of Public Debt* (Homewood, Ill., Richard D. Irwin, 1958).
Buchanan, James M., *Cost and Choice* (Chicago: Markham, 1969) (Midway Reprint, University of Chicago Press, 1976).
Buchanan, James M., *Public Finance on Democratic Process* (Chapel Hill, University of North Carolina Press, 1966).
Buchanan, James M., *Freedom in Constitutional Contract* (College Station, Texas A & M University Press, 1978).
Buchanan, James M., *The Limits of Liberty* (Chicago, University of Chicago Press, 1975).
Buchanan, James M., *Liberty, Market and State* (New York University Press, 1985).
Buchanan, James M., 'An Economic Theory of Clubs', *Economica*, vol. 32 (February 1965), pp. 1–14.
Buchanan, James M., (with G. Tullock), *The Calculus of Consent* (Ann Arbor, University of Michigan Press, 1962).
Buchanan, James M., (with R. Wagner), *Democracy in Deficit* (New York, Academic Press, 1977).
Buchanan, James M., (with G. Brennan), *The Power to Tax* (Cambridge, Cambridge University Press, 1980).
Buchanan, James M., (with G. Brennan), *The Reason of Rules* (Cambridge, Cambridge University Press, 1985).
Buchanan, James M., (with C. Stubblebine), 'Externality', *Economica*, vol. 29 (November 1962), pp. 371–84.
Buchanan, James M., (edited with R. Tollison), *Theory of Public Choice: Political Applications of Economics* (Ann Arbor, University of Michigan Press, 1972).
Buchanan, James M., (edited with R. Tollison) *Theory of Public Choice, II* (Ann Arbor, University of Michigan Press, 1984).
Buchanan, James M., Translation of Knut Wicksell, 'A New Principle of Just Taxation', in *Classics in the Theory of Public Finance* (eds) Musgrave, R.A. and Peacock, A.T. (London, Macmillan, 1958), pp. 72–118.

Other works cited
Arrow, Kenneth, *Social Choice and Individual Values* (New York, Wiley, 1951).
De Viti De Marco, Antonio, *First Principles of Public Finance*. trans. by E.P. Marget (London, Jonathan Cape, 1936).
Rawls, John, *A Theory of Justice* (Cambridge, Harvard University Press, 1971).
Wicksell, Knut, *Finanztheoretische Untersuchungen* (Jena, Gustav Fischer, 1986).

13 The Challenge of Macroeconomic Understanding

Edmond Malinvaud

A PERMANENT AND MULTIFARIOUS QUEST

There was more unity in my professional activities than my academic colleagues seem to realise. No schizophrenia is revealed by the fact that I accepted work as an official statistician, and even to become head of a large government organisation, while at the same time planning to devote effort to research and teaching. My hope to improve understanding of macroeconomics provides the unifying concern behind these activities.

Improvement of knowledge of macroeconomic phenomena not only requires the success of many research projects, some quite fundamental, others dealing with the measure of specific effects, it also requires sensitiveness to problems that policy makers are trying to solve. It further requires appropriate teaching, i.e. transmission of proven methods of analysis and of the accompanying scientific corpus. It finally requires progress in the collection and analysis of data, as well as in the diffusion of the pertinent results to all users, including the general public.

None of these tasks is trivial. In their most delicate aspects, they all involve judgement as to what should be stressed and what the real needs are. This has two consequences, the one general, the other particular to this article. On the one hand, significant progress is not identified as easily in macroeconomic understanding as in the hard sciences or in microeconomic theory. On the other hand, I have long been reluctant to express myself in scientific journals about fundamental macroeconomic questions because this uncertainty may have influenced the orientation of my own research for the two decades of the 1950s and 1960s when my main publications dealt with microeconomic theory or econometric methods.

This article will, I hope, show how the concern for macroeconomic understanding came early in my life, and also how it incidentally led me to face some well-defined unsolved microeconomic or econometric analytical questions that I thought I could solve. As I got older, and microeconomics and econometrics progressed toward the consideration of what appeared to me as more and more special issues, my thoughts and writings progressively concentrated on macroeconomics. This does not mean that I now think the subject to be simpler, or my views about it to be necessarily right. But macroeconomic problems are important; my judgement was formed through years of thinking and experience; I no longer believe that other macroeconomic writers master the subject any better than I do.

Macroeconomics is indeed particularly difficult. Its theoretical construction must be firmly based on observation of complex phenomena. But these phenomena are changing as the technological, sociological and institutional context evolves, so that observation often is unconclusive. Interdependencies are as important as in microeconomic equilibrium theory but they occur within a less pure framework: industrial structures are partly oligopolistic and competition is partly monopolistic, adjustments are incomplete, markets do not always clear, anticipations matter and their formation obeys rules that are not easily detected. By necessity theoretical representations must be drastic simplifications. It is then a delicate question which representations will retain the most pertinent features of the phenomena and so be most useful.

While keenly aware of this fundamental difficulty of macroeconomic understanding throughout my life, it is noteworthy that I felt secure not only about the general structure within which macroeconomic analysis ought to take its place (national accounts, behavioural relations, market adjustment laws . . .) but also about the scientific way of proceeding in this field of knowledge. Since I am not really worried about the philosophy of science as applied to macroeconomics, I did not invest much time on it. But I feel at ease with what I understand to be Karl Popper's views on science in general and I do not think economics to be fundamentally special, even though its scientific achievements may be found meagre as a whole with respect to the questions to be solved.

INITIATION

During my school years I was somewhat exposed to economic facts but not at all to even the most rudimentary economic analysis. The classical French teaching did not then deal with socioeconomic realities, except indirectly by our study of French, Latin and Greek literatures and by our less stressed study of history or geography. My father, who was a lawyer in the provincial city of Limoges, had socialist ideas, which mainly meant a concern for the social situation in France; at the family table or beside the fireplace particular aspects of this situation were occasionally stated and commented on. Moreover, I could see in Limoges the impact of the depression on the traditional porcelain or shoe industries and on their workers.

I discovered economics at the age of 18 when studying law as a complement to my main studies in mathematics. I was attracted by the subject, which was probably aided by my increasing awareness of economic problems. But for some time I had no real teacher in the field. I first read manuals, then books, but without direction, as an autodidact discovering what was available in French in the early 1940s. It is hard for me to know what I really learned then: certainly the main basic concepts, the main historical facts and a sense of what writers were up to, probably a good knowledge of partial equilibrium price theory together with an understanding of the respective roles of observation and reflection in economics (I remember I was particularly interested in books where some data were discussed and that I found too few of them). But I did not gain then a proper and coherent analytical apparatus for the discussion of economic problems.

This came from 1946 on, when I entered the *Ecole Nationale de la Statistique et de l'Administration Economique* (ENSAE) of the *Institut National de la Statistique et des Etudes Economiques* (INSEE), thinking that it was the best place in which I might later work as an economist. I was then 23. The curriculum in economics was not so extensive but it brought to me what I was lacking, namely a structure for the organisation of knowledge and thought. The most significant event was my meeting Maurice Allais who became one of my teachers in 1947. After the initial surprise to be confronted with such an unusual man, I quickly understood I had much to learn from him. Not only was I a diligent student, but also, in 1948, at the same time I was beginning my career as an official statistician, I joined the informal group of young economists that was meeting around Allais at lunch time or in the late evening. The group included Marcel Boiteux, Gérard Debreu and others gifted with enthusiasm and imagination.

Besides an introduction to the Rockefeller Foundation, which gave me a fellowship to work in Chicago in 1950–51, I owe to Allais three important debts: my understanding of general equilibrium and capital theories, my access to the then modern literature available in English, and above all my association with someone who was doing real research (it is indeed a disgrace for the French educational system that I had had up to then no real opportunity to be exposed to active scientific research).

Arriving at the University of Chicago in June 1950, as a guest of the Cowles Commission for Research in Economics, I no longer had much to learn from teaching in economics. I was a bit annoyed because my fellowship stipulated that I should attend classes, but looking at the calendar I did not see any course in economics that I could usefully take; my problem was resolved when I discovered the mathematics section of the curriculum. My prior training in mathematics in school and at the *Ecole Polytechnique* had been quite good, but traditional; I still had to learn what was then called modern mathematics, which was precisely the backbone of the mathematics curriculum at Chicago.

The Cowles Commission was an ideal place for a 27 year-old mathematical economist and statistician, eager to learn. Jacob Marschak, Tjalling Koopmans, Gérard Debreu and others were deeply involved in fundamental research and always available for examination of a scientific point. The main work on the econometrics of simultaneous equations has recently been completed; but extensions, applications or better presentations were still looked for. Research on activity analysis and general equilibrium theory was in its most active phase. We could often see visitors involved in this joint effort, such as Kenneth Arrow or Leonid Hurwicz. Leonard Savage was at the statistics department and came often. From time to time Milton Friedman granted us the benefits of his criticism.

MICROECONOMIC THEORY

My list of publications begins in 1950 with three articles, two dealing with price indices and the estimation of price elasticities of imports and exports. But my entry into the circle of academic research workers was due to my work on theoretical questions of microeconomics.

The microeconomic theory of resource allocation is neat and clear. It poses well-defined problems of a purely logical nature. A young mathematical economist approaching them directly knows what the issues are. He has none of those doubts that macroeconomics inspires in a critical mind. In the early 1950s moreover, some of the main questions had not yet been solved and the recent development of mathematics was providing new and efficient tools to deal with them.

The preceding ten years I had spent studying economics had given me a better understanding of the existing theory than I realised. This is why I was able to point out to L. Metzler, then quite influential, a confusion in one of his articles on capital theory (see Metzler, 1951, p. 67). I was also able to give Samuelson the key to a problem in the axiomatics of the von Neumann-Morgenstern hypothesis that had been puzzling him (Malinvaud, 1952).

For all those reasons, including my earlier association with Maurice Allais, and my presence within the Cowles Commission group working on activity analysis, it was natural that I should work in microeconomic theory. My article on capital theory (Malinvaud, 1953) was the outcome of an effort to unify two approaches to resource allocation over time, the one extending the static neoclassical model, the other directly considering stationary states; the opposition between these approaches had been at the heart of a debate on capital theory in the 1930s, notably between F. Hayek and F. Knight (see in particular their papers in the A.E.A. *Readings in the Theory of Income Distribution*, 1950). The unification raised two mathematical problems: since it required the consideration of infinite time, generalisation of the results proved for the static model to the extended model was not trivial; on the other hand, one had to prove the stationarity of the price system supporting an efficient stationary rate. This work attracted attention and gave me the opportunity of discussions with many older economists. In particular I benefited in 1959 from a visit to Oxford at the invitation of Sir John Hicks.

If I later worked on other problems of microeconomic theory, it is because I had to teach a course on the subject and more importantly because of my association with French planning. As is well known, a few French engineers working on public utilities have contributed over several decades to the theory of resource allocation. In the 1960s some of them were particularly concerned with the logical problems raised by the determination of the interplay between their work, dealing with the choice of projects, and macroeconomic planning intended to give future growth prospects, a planning process to which INSEE contributed. P. Massé in particular, then 'Commissaire au Plan', was posing challenging questions. I thought that one way of enlightening these problems was to view them within the framework of the decentralised determination of an optimum resource allocation programme (Malinvaud, 1967). Such a vision is, of course, bold for one who is aware of the actual planning process; I believe, however, it helps to put ideas in order.

Its usefulness is not limited to providing a background for the choice of public projects. It provided microeconomic theory with a chapter that is too often forgotten after the three following ones: (1) existence and properties of a competitive equilibrium; (2) existence and properties of an optimal state; (3) definition and convergence of a process leading to a competitive equilibrium. The third of these chapters is notoriously less developed than the preceding two and less satisfactory than one should wish for a good understanding of the stability issue; but it exists in most books on microeconomic theory. On the contrary no chapter is usually found on the definition and convergence of a process leading to an optimal state. The subject has a definite interest; it was at the core of the debate about 'the economic theory of socialism' during the inter-war period; it becomes almost inescapable when one claims to deal with the optimal provision of public goods; what can be said about it today is at least as relevant as what can be said about the stability of the very idealised Walrasian *tâtonnement* process. In the 1960s my confidence in the relevance of the issue was strengthened by the discussions I had with L. Hurwicz and J. Kornai who were independently working on related issues.

Another question raised by the choice of public projects concerns the proper rules for risk-taking. Beyond my general interest about problems of resource allocation under uncertainty, I then had a particular problem motivation to consider the domain of validity of a property that had long been taken as intuitive: risk premia should not occur in economic calculations on public projects because, at the level of a whole nation, risks cancel due to the effect of the law of large numbers. Stating the property suffices to show that it abstracts from major common risks such as wars, but it deserves a theoretical investigation (Malinvaud, 1972 and 1973).

ECONOMETRIC THEORY

A training in mathematical statistics, participation in seminars at the Cowles Commission and work at INSEE, in particular for the setting up of French national accounts from 1951 to 1956, provided a background for my interest in econometric theory. But I was more deeply involved. I was going regularly to the European meetings of the Econometric Society and of the International Association for Research in Income and Wealth, which were then attended by fifty to one hundred people and were quite convivial, with such figures as R. Frisch, R. Stone, H. Wold and younger econometricians like H. Theil, J. Sargan, occasionally Durbin. From 1954 to 1964 I acted as co-editor of the journal *Econometrica* and in this capacity I had to read a large number of manuscripts in econometrics.

Above all, I was developing some teaching materials in econometric methods. I had initially been stimulated to do so by G. Darmois, the French mathematical statistician whose shrewdness and charm strongly influenced his students in my generation. I thought it was necessary to organise the subject on the basis of some fundamental theories; for so doing, I had to clear up some then unsolved problems. This led to my 1964 textbook, which was updated for later editions and widely used during twenty years.

MACROECONOMIC OBSERVATION

Turning back now to the main subject, macroeconomics, I shall consider it under its various aspects: (a) observation of the phenomena, (b) theory, (c) diagnosis and policy. Finally I should not forget: (d) teaching.

It is particularly noteworthy that nowadays problems raised by the observation of macroeconomic phenomena do not attract much academic attention, as if they were all satisfactorily solved. This situation is not very sound, since obviously some problems remain. It may reflect in part the complexity of these problems, which are not likely to have 'nice' solutions, but in part also a tendency to oversimplify the features of macroeconomic evolution when confronting them to theoretical constructs.

The situation was different during the first half of the century and even in the 1950s. The definitions of the basic concepts such as capital or income were seriously discussed; the aggregation problems, probably the main ones for macroeconomic observation, were considered within the theory of price and volume indices. Some of the best economists took an important part in the elaboration of these subjects, such as I. Fisher, J. Hicks and P. Samuelson.

During the 1950s the focus of the discussions often was the structure to be given to the system of national accounts. A group of French experts, with whom I collaborated, was advocating a structure that would be systematically built from the two basic notions of agents and operations, while other people tried to maintain the solution that had been chosen for systems previously introduced, i.e. an outgrowth of the balance between production of goods and its main uses: consumption, investment, net exports. Finally, reflection on the uses of national accounts, as well as the need of a common framework for the central system, for input-output tables and for financial flows tables, led to the acceptance of what had been the French position, R. Stone playing the main role in the evolution of ideas. (For French readers my 1957 book on national accounting may have helped to a softening of what had been an excessive dogmatism.)

I think that the most important problem that ought currently to be more widely discussed concerns the proper definitions that capital, income and profit rates should receive while prices and wage rates evolve. Clearly the figures given by business and national accounts are not adequate from this point of view. Macroeconomists need to make important corrections, for instance when they want to make inter-temporal or international comparisons. If the methodology for such corrections does not attract more attention beyond a narrow circle of specialists, it is probably because national capital accounting is everywhere underdeveloped and hence not often used.

Still close to observation stands the descriptive study of economic evolution, often seen in a historical perspective. This activity always involves some analysis and therefore has theoretical foundations; but the latter may often be taken for granted, at least by lack of better alternatives. My work within the French public administration dealing with economic problems, at INSEE, and from 1972 to 1974, as the head of the 'Direction de la Prévision', advising the minister of economics and finance, often required such descriptive study. Beyond what was required by this work, I have often spent time in looking more precisely into the quantitative assessment of a situation or of an aspect of observed evolution.

Considering how narrow our macroeconomic understanding is, I do believe that all macroeconomists, even those working on the most theoretical parts of the subject, should also spend some of their time on descriptive studies. In the absence of an intimate contact with the facts, one is all too easily tempted to make too much of a specific point on which one is working. This is why I never considered I was wasting my time by spending it on what some of my academic colleagues see as a trivial activity.

This may explain why I reacted positively in 1962 when I was asked by M. Abramovitz to take part in a joint project of parallel studies on modern economic growth in each one of the main developed countries. The project assumed acceptance of the quantitative and step-by-step methodology promoted by Kuznets, a part of which became known as growth accounting. Since it involved both judgement about some substantial issues and an important effort in data collection and processing, it seemed to require more than one person for each study. As for France I was fortunate to have the collaboration of three friends, one of which was not able to lead the project to completion and died just when our book was being published: P. Berthet, J.C. Carré and P. Dubois. Work on this project was a side activity for all of us, which in part explains why ten years passed before the book was published, in advance however of the studies dealing with the other countries. In our conclusion, speculating about the future, we did not exhibit perspicacity: writing in 1972, we did not forecast the turndown of world and French economic growth. We were not alone in making that mistake.

Much more recently, when approached in 1984 by R. Layard, I accepted responsibility for a study of France. This time the subject was for parallel national studies assessing the factors leading to the rise of unemployment during the last fifteen years. The outcome was an article in the special 1986 *Economica* supplement volume. Compared with others in the same volume, my contribution stays closer to observed facts and tries to avoid reliance on a specific model. This is revealing of my views about the respective roles of data analysis, judgement and econometrics when the purpose is explanation of a real complex phenomenon.

MACROECONOMIC THEORY

I am today considered as a proponent of disequilibrium theories and indeed I am. More precisely, for the correct elaboration of a theory the notion of disequilibrium must be clearly brought out wherever it is present; this is simply good axiomatics. Once this principle is accepted, one must recognise that disequilibria are involved in many more or less traditional ways of thinking about some important economic phenomena. Since these ways of thinking make sense, disequilibrium theories have a role to play in order to tighten up the rationale and help to the progress of our scientific understanding.

Such a position means neither that equilibrium theories have no role to play in macroeconomics, nor that I am satisfied with the existing disequilibrium theories. These two points will be considered here.

For the study of economic growth, a good part of the analysis relies on equilibrium theories; this is so for instance with growth accounting. Analysis will then benefit from improvement in the theories, which ought to be made more rigorous and more appropriate in their basic hypotheses.

In particular one must welcome the theoretical scrutiny of the validity of aggregate production functions and of the validity of the associated comparative statics properties linking changes in capital intensity with changes in real remuneration rates. This major example well shows the more general relevance of a systematic study of the aggregation leading from microeconomic relations to corresponding macroeconomic relations. The study is difficult since a purely theoretical search for perfect aggregation fails to lead to really positive results; one then has to take simultaneous account of specific features of the micro-relations and of the nature of the statistical distribution of the micro-units; the approach has been followed occasionally and is again the subject of attention; my 1956 methodological study of aggregation had already presented it as essential.

The purely theoretical scrutiny of the particular problem raised by macro-capital theory was the core of the well known dispute between the two Cambridges. This dispute resulted in a better understanding of the foundations of important macroeconomic issues. While I felt concerned by it because of my interest in macroeconomics and of my work in microeconomic capital theory, I avoided taking part because the dispute looked to me as misplaced: too much passion was involved in the exchange of arguments about purely abstract properties. The discussion too often seemed to imply that answers to the theoretical problems had far-reaching implications about capitalism, a claim that was absolutely unwarranted. I tried on various occasions, particularly in my Hicks Lecture (1986), to explain what I think has been learned from the dispute.

For the knowledge of the global operation of market economies, equilibrium theories have a different and more important role to play, namely exploring the stability or instability of sequences of temporary equilibria. The point was often made by F. Hahn with whom I had many stimulating discussions throughout the years. Stability depends on what are technological constraints, saving behaviour, modes of expectations formation and market structures. The issue then is so complex that one cannot hope to much improve insight about it by a microeconomic approach. Progress was usually made by the study of macroeconomic specifications chosen so as to exhibit what are thought to be the most relevant features of the problem.

But permanent market clearing, together with the required continuous full adaptation of the price system, rules out a number of phenomena that have long been considered as important in economic thinking. The most obvious one is provided by variations in involuntary unemployment. But positive or negative stimuli given by disparities in remuneration rates, in particular by the more or less strong leverage between profit rates in production and interest rates have long been considered major factors of economic evolution. Here, while discussing disequilibrium theories, I shall limit attention to those intended to deal with unemployment. I do think that disequilibrium growth theories also are relevant, as I tried to explain in various places, for instance in my Hicks Lecture (1986).

Already in the 1950s, while teaching or applying post-war Keynesian theory, I was well aware that the major discrepancy with microeconomic price theory lay in the notion that agents were facing quantitative market constraints: involuntarily unemployed workers had an unfilled labour supply while some firms could not sell as much as would have been profitable for them at prevailing prices. This is why I considered that building a general equilibrium fixed-price theory was a relevant fundamental achievement, on which young mathematical economists were fruitfully working in the early 1970s, notably in France. Stimulated by Y. Younes, and in collaboration with him, I tried to contribute to this theory. This was also one of the many subjects that gave me the opportunity of scientific discussions with J. Drèze.

At about the same time, when my main job was economic advising, I noted a new widespread concern among European government officials: it was no longer a problem with a too low or too high aggregate demand, but a disturbing trend in real wages, which were found to be increasing too rapidly, and in profit rates, which were deteriorating. The common diagnosis attributed to this trend part of the responsibility for the mounting unemployment. It became clear to me that the analysis then made by practitioners probably had some value but assumed a different hypothesis from the Keynesian one: a too low labour demand was related to an insufficient demand for goods. This could indeed occur, even within a very aggregated model, if the situation was considered as an example of a case that had previously been neglected in macroeconomic theory, namely classical unemployment.

Since I had been asked to deliver the Yrjö Jahnsson conferences in January 1976, I decided to devote them to presenting the newly elaborated theory of fixed price general equilibrium, to explain why it provided an adequate foundation for the macroeconomic theory of unemployment and to arguing that classical unemployment could have some relevance. The book, published a little later (1977), was my first production dealing with the heart of macroeconomic theory.

The book used a variant of the simple macroeconomic Barro-Grossman model. Ever since it was published, I have stressed that the study of this simple static model could only be a first step and I have tried to devote my research to what I thought to be important further steps. Those were first the dynamics of the static equilibrium, viewed as applying in the short run but as spontaneously evolving; second the specification of a model admitting existence of a full spectrum of cases from Keynesian to classical unemployment or to repressed inflation, the reason being the multiplicity of markets for the various goods and types of labour. Clearly, many others worked on these two important extensions of the theory, as well as on a third one concerning the macroeconomic equilibrium of an open economy.

After ten years some progress has been also made in understanding better what should be thought of the practitioners' view that real wages were too high in the 1970s and early 1980s. In particular macroeconometric modelling of the short-term equilibrium provided a test of the frequency of classical unemployment. Although this modelling work cannot be considered as complete, one of its conclusions is robust enough to be established, namely that classical unemployment, with its excess demand for goods, never proves to be the dominant feature of the short-term equilibrium, except at times of fast recovery from a depression when unemployment still exists and adjustment costs prevent production to keep pace with demand. Since the 1974 downturn, excess supply of goods seem to have prevailed almost permanently in Europe. This, however, occurred together with a growing discrepancy between full employment output and productive capacity, which increased much more slowly. I thus see the proper diagnosis as being that low profitability leads to an insufficient progress of domestic productive capacity, hence a tendency to foreign trade deficit, which forces governments to adopt depressive macroeconomic policies. Seen as a medium-run phenomenon, this situation has the same characteristics as classical unemployment since firms do not find it profitable to employ the full labour supply, which they would have employed under more favourable price conditions. Loosely speaking, one can then characterise the situation as medium-term classical unemployment, but short-term Keynesian unemployment.

A proper theory of this phenomenon ought in principle to be based on a dynamic model in which the evolving temporary equilibrium would present the two preceding features. This model ought in particular to correctly represent the productive sector and its decisions about expansion or contraction of productive capacities. It may be too complex for discussions in which the basic issues concern medium-term development. This is why I came to think that it would be useful to have a theory intended to directly deal with medium-term consequences: the comparative statics of the equilibrium defined by such a theory would provide a test of the logical validity of some properties to which practitioners believe but which are mainly based on their intuition. I intend to pursue work on the definition of such a theory, whose main building blocks seem to be now available.

While my reflections during these past fifteen years were concentrating on the research programme in disequilibrium macroeconomics, I witnessed with a good deal of dissatisfaction the main trends in macroeconomic theory that were occurring in American universities. My dissatisfaction was less concerned with research, which was exploring a number of often relevant questions, than what were said to be its implications about macroeconomic phenomena and what I imagined was then taught to good students coming from all over the world. Clearly, considering what I have written here, I have no *a priori* objection to the study of the supply side; but claims once made by the so called 'supply-siders' were distressing for anyone who consulted available econometric evidence; indeed they by now commonly appear as ridiculous. Similarly, the study of the rational expectations hypothesis is relevant as soon as one recognises, as I easily do, that dealing with expectations as exogenous, or even as adaptive, is not always realistic; but one should be aware of the extreme character of the hypothesis and of what is usually associated with it concerning the information of economic agents (one should even speak of credulity of economic agents, when they are assumed to hold as exact the theory one particular author is elaborating); in fact the claims of the rational expectations macroeconomists are usually not better founded on econometric evidence than the claims of supply siders. One sentence cannot do justice to monetarism, its many valuable contributions and its benign neglect of a number of considerations; I shall, however, note that it too easily tends to transpose to the short run, even to the medium run, properties that have good reasons to hold in the long run.

MACROECONOMISTS, POLITICIANS AND THE PUBLIC

In February 1972, Giscard d'Estaing, then minister of economics and finance, was looking for someone who would not be a conventional civil servant. He asked me to assume the responsibility of heading his 'Direction de la Prévision', the group in charge of advising him on economic policy. This assignment lasted up to the fall of 1974, when I became director of INSEE, which is best described as the central statistical office of France, but is also a *de facto* independent institute of economic and social analysis. After these three years, mainly devoted to economic advising, I am still occasionally called to take part in policy advising at the national or European level.

I shall not dwell at length on my experience in this capacity, since it is not very different from that of others. But a few comments may be in order. As an economic adviser who witnessed the downturn in European economic growth, and more particularly in French growth, I cannot help asking myself whether my advices were adequate. In retrospect I think they were not. My colleagues and I underestimated the difficulty of the change and gave too much weight to short term improvements that did not help, or even made matters more difficult, from a longer term viewpoint. We were, however, more far sighted than average informed public opinion, to which politicians always are very sensitive. This was obvious in particular in 1975–6 when at the *Commissariat du Plan*, a medium-term programme up to 1980 was being discussed, almost all partners agreed in thinking in terms of a quick return to past growth rates, against the advice of the technicians. Similarly the gloomy medium-term projections issued by INSEE in 1975, 1978 and 1979 were considered as almost scandalous. Governments repeatedly said these projections, which turned out to be too optimistic would not materialise because proper action would be taken. The whole society, except for some rare individuals, did not want to face the challenge. This was the second time in my life when such type of reaction could be observed, the first one having been the period immediately preceding the Second World War.

When they address others, macroeconomists should, it seems, limit their statements to what is sufficiently well established to be the object of a kind of consensus in the profession. Indeed, their statements are supposed to be objective, so that they can be accepted by people who are not able to judge of their validity by themselves. Acting in a country where the Marxist influence on intellectuals has been traditionally strong, I have been more constrained by this rule than my colleagues acting in some other countries. The rule, however, is imperative for anyone who considers economics as a science. It also implies that we should always resist the temptation of gaining easy success in the media by presenting as truth some of our personal views that are not yet shared by our professional colleagues.

Unfortunately what can objectively be said in macroeconomics is limited, while acting against macroeconomic difficulties may appear as urgent. The proper answer to this problem is, of course, that advisers should convey to decision makers some feeling about the likelihood of effects that are still imperfectly known. Politicians, however, typically interpret any probability assessment as leaving them the option to forget about the most unpleasant events. This difficulty of the division of roles between the advisers and politicians seems to have two consequences. The first one is to bias economic policy toward the short-term: politicians are naturally concerned by it and advisers can speak more confidently about short-term effects, most of which are by now well established, than about medium-term effects, many of which cannot be objectively assessed at present. The second consequence, which I noted in the behaviour of some high civil servants, is their inclination to take decisions themselves and then to find any kind of argument in order to talk politicians into endorsing the decisions; but this does not contribute in the long run to confidence in the civil service on the part of the political class.

An official statistician has to convey to the general public the result of his most important observations. This also requires confidence: the statistical tools must be commonly recognised as reliable. In my country in which most of the statistical system is of recent origin, in which economic and social education is insufficiently developed and in which the degree of political consensus is low, I have had to spend part of my time on this activity, notably when the matter measured by some statistics was the object of a public debate. I did it without reluctance and considered it as one aspect of my role as a teacher.

TEACHING MACROECONOMICS

Most of my readers share with me the vocation for teaching. This is why I shall not explain here how I always thought my time to be usefully spent when I was preparing a course or working on a textbook. By far the largest part of this teaching took place at the INSEE school, ENSAE (*Ecole Nationale de la Statistique et de l'Administration Economique*). Considering the length of their previous studies at university level, students are there at the graduate level. They typically have a good background in mathematics, but a weak one in economics. Hence the teaching of economics can rely on mathematical formalisation, but most devote time to place each question in its proper context.

My teaching materialised into three textbooks, respectively on econometrical methods (1964), on the microeconomic theory of prices and resource allocation (1969) and on macroeconomic theory (1980–81). The first one took almost ten years of preparation, as my teaching on econometrics was progressively taking a more satisfactory shape. The second one was very quickly produced: general competitive equilibrium theory was a well organised subject; I needed only to supplement it by a number of chapters, dealing for instance with imperfect competition or with public goods, and to find the appropriate level of rigour and generality for such a textbook.

The real challenge was teaching macroeconomics. I began in 1957 and went on giving a course in the field every year up to about the time when my textbook was sent to the editor. I long hesitated on the organisation of the subject and often changed the ordering of the main chapters and their contents. Above all, I was permanently concerned by how to choose the best way to show to the students the relevance of each piece of theory with respect to actual macroeconomic problems; I never found that easy and I do think that this difficulty reveals the weaknesses of present macroeconomic theory. This is why I shall comment here on the main aspects of the macroeconomic approach, as I think they fundamentally are and therefore ought to be taught.

The scope of macroeconomics covers both growth and fluctuations. The two dimensions, the long and the short run, must often be kept in mind simultaneously. An ideal theory would realistically deal with both; but it is out of reach. At least one must be aware of the assumption that short-term and long-term methods of analysis can deal consistently with the two dimensions that many macroeconomic problems actually have. This is why growth theory should be discussed as well as employment and inflation theories. On the contrary I do not insist on dealing with open economies in a general teaching of macroeconomics; depending on how small and open an economy is, its reactions to exogenous shocks will of course be different; but I think this can easily be understood as long as one has a good grasp of one theory of the closed economy. I grant, however, that one may disagree with this view and then be obliged to go into more elaborate theoretical constructions in order to avoid the closed-economy limitation.

National accounting has contributed to making students more familiar with the basic structure to be used in macroeconomic analysis. This structure, which distinguishes the various types of agents and operations is fully appropriate for theory, at least if it is understood to cover not only flows (incomes, output ...) but also stocks (wealth, productive capital ...). There are great advantages to introduce it systematically at the beginning of macroeconomic teaching. It deals with enterprises and households as independent units; the hypothesis looks to me as appropriate for almost all macroeconomic phenomena, even though enterprises are owned by the people, either directly or indirectly through public ownership; certainly the hypothesis is much preferable to the one that would lead to models in which enterprises would not appear, the idea then being that they would have no autonomy for their decisions. Macroeconomic phenomena depend so much on the behaviour of the production sector that it should always be recognised as playing the major role.

This raises the issue of the representation of market structures in theories dealing with the whole economy. This representation can only be very rough and neglect the great heterogeneity that exists in this respect. Many growth phenomena are properly approached with the perfect competition hypothesis, notwithstanding its extreme character. When the hypothesis cannot be fully satisfactory, for instance because full market clearing cannot be admitted, dealing with firms as pure price takers may still be sufficient. A better and still manageable hypothesis assumes imperfect competition, firms having market power for their output but acting as price takers for their inputs. The kinked demand curve hypothesis may be appropriate for the study of some phenomena; it is then almost tantamount to the assumption that firms face a quantitative constraint on their sales and that the price of their output is given.

Proper representation of behaviour plays a crucial role, the time dimensions being almost always essential. Since information is incomplete, since adjustment costs and even irreversibilities exist, modelling of behaviour raises many problems that are rightly considered in the literature. But aggregation does not usually receive the attention that it requires. Depending on what is assumed, for instance about market structures, it does not operate in the same way. It should be considered much more systematically and have its proper place in macroeconomic textbooks.

It is traditional to state that a macroeconomic model contains two types of equations: behavioural laws and accounting identities, the latter containing in particular equalities between supply and demand for markets that are assumed to be cleared. I prefer to speak of three types of equations and to qualify some of them as 'adjustment laws': they mostly describe the evolution of prices and wages when market clearing is incomplete; for instance a Phillips curve is an adjustment law. Using this denomination stresses the point that one has not fully clarified, in terms of behaviour, the rationale for the corresponding equation. There is no shame in recognising this situation and in stating that the justification lies in observed regularities. The wrong thing to do, when one cannot fully explain a complex phenomenon, is to pretend the phenomenon is different so as to be able to easily explain it by maximising behaviour.

Indeed, macroeconomics has two roots: theory and observation. Trying to forget about one of them is bound to fail, because one is then unable to prove specific conclusions of interest. This means in particular that our present macroeconomic knowledge embodies a lot that has been learned from statistics combined with reasoning. Hence, macroeconomic theory cannot be properly presented without its empirical base. I have long believed that some economists will never become macroeconomists precisely because they dislike too much the uncertainty attached to econometric results; this uncertainty exists but becomes bearable when enough replication of similar results has occurred. Combination of deductive theory and inductive econometrics within a textbook implies many imperfections that I shall not list; but elegance must not have precedence on transmission of a queerly shaped body of knowledge.

Any teaching of macroeconomics must contain a discussion of

policy formation. This implies a part taken from decision theory, the time and uncertainty dimensions both playing a role. But the teacher should have the sense of avoiding developments whose technical difficulty outweighs their relevance. To take just one example in order to make my point clear, I believe that any serious presentation of the time consistency issue in a macroeconomic textbook would today be premature; the distinction between fixed and discretionary rules can well be heuristically discussed without the recently developed formal apparatus. Actually the main difficulty in the parts discussing questions of economic policy lies in the choice of the underlying macroeconomic models. These must be very simple in order to permit an analytical treatment, but they should also be realistic from the point of view of the policy problem under examination. Simple Keynesian models can well illustrate short-term economic regulation; but simple monetarist models, which are meaningful only in the long run, cannot do. In any case the reader must be warned of the bias that reliance on a simple model necessarily implies. Presentation of a full macroeconomic model, actually used for the analysis of business trends, may help to make the point clear.

Such are the various challenges that I perceived in trying to understand macroeconomics. I have no doubt that our profession will eventually meet them better and better, notwithstanding their difficulty. Disputes of yesterday, today and tomorrow should not make us blind: slowly we are progressing in the right direction.

References

American Economic Association (1950), *Readings in the Theory of Income Distribution*, (London, Allen & Unwin).
Carré, J.-C., Dubois, P., and Malinvaud, et E. (1972), *Croissance Economique Française* (Paris, Le Seuil, translations in English and Polish).
Malinvaud, E. (1952), 'Note on the von Neumann-Morgenstern strong independence axiom', *Econometrica*, vol. 20, p. 679.
Malinvaud, E. (1953), 'Capital accumulation and efficient allocation of resources', *Econometrica*, vol. 21, p. 233–66.
Malinvaud, E. (1956), 'L'agrégation dans les modèles économiques', *Cahiers du séminaire d'économétrie*, no. 4.
Malinvaud, E. (1957), *Initiation à la comptabilité nationale*, Imprimerie Nationale, Paris.
Malinvaud, E. (1964), *Méthodes statistiques de l'économétrie*, (Paris, Dunod; translations in English, Spanish, Italian, Hungarian and Russian).

Malinvaud, E. (1967), 'Decentralized procedures for planning' in Malinvaud, E. and Bacharach, M.', (eds) *Activity Analysis for the Theory of Growth and Planning* (London, Macmillan).

Malinvaud, E. (1969), *Leçons de théorie microéconomique*, (Paris, Dunod; translations in English, Spanish, Japanese and Russian).

Malinvaud, E. (1972), 'The allocation of individual risks in large markets', *Journal of Economic Theory*, April.

Malinvaud, E. (1973), 'Markets for an exchange economy with individual risks', *Econometrica*, May.

Malinvaud, E. (1977), *The Theory of Unemployment Reconsidered* (Oxford, Basil Blackwell; translations in French and Spanish).

Malinvaud, E. (1980–81), *Théorie macroéconomique*, 2 vols, (Paris, Dunod; translation in Spanish and in process in English).

Malinvaud, E. (1986), 'The rise of unemployment in France', *Economica*, Supplement to vol. 53.

Malinvaud, E. (1986), 'Reflecting on the theory of capital and growth', Hicks Lecture, *Oxford Economic Papers*, vol. 38, pp. 367–85.

Metzler, L. (1951), 'The rate of interest and the marginal product of capital: a correction', *Journal of Political Economy*, February.

Name Index

Abason, Albert 105
Abramovitz, M. 305
Abs, Hermann J. 271
Adelman, Frank 131
Adenauer, K. 268
Adler, Alfred 76
Adler, Max 75
Aftalion, Albert 1, 110, 118
Aichhorn, August 77
Alchian, Armen A. 236, 243, 246
Alderson, Wroe 217, 219
Alejandro, Carlos Diaz 160
Alexander, Sidney 53–5
Allais, Maurice 5, 299, 301
Allen, Maurice 89–90
Allen, R.G.D. 127
Amoroso, Luigi 4
Angell, James 151–2
Antonelli, Etienne 1
Armack, Muller 262
Arrow, Kenneth 9, 210, 284, 300
Attali, J. 110
Aukrust, Odd 263

Bailey, Elizabeth 227–9, 231
Bain, Joe S. 217
Balassa, Bela 267
Balogh, Thomas xviii, 5, 51, 89–93, 95
Bamberger, Ludwig 20
Bandler, Poldi 73
Baran, Paul 133
Barber, Bill 92
Barber, Samuel 136
Barnett, Harold J. 157
Barone, E. 261
Barriol, Alfred 108, 111
Barro, R. 247
Bauer, Helene 77
Bauer, Otto 74, 91
Baumol, William xvi, xvii, 263
Becker, Gary 216
Beckhart, B. Haggott 152
Beecham, Thomas 93

Bergson, A. 116
Bergsten, C. Fred 272
Bernfeld, Siegfried 73
Berthet, P. 305
Bhagwati, Jagdish 96, 160
Bissell, Richard M. Jr. 150, 165
Black, John 92
Blaug, Mark 137
Blessing, K. 271
Blum, Leon 126
Bohm, Anne 215
Boiteux, Marcel 299
Bondi, Hermann 84
Borel, Emile 109–12, 119
Bowen, William G. 220–1, 223
Bowley, Arthur 116
Bradley, Omar N. 153, 157
Branscomb, Harvie 104
Branson, William 160
Brennan, Geoffrey 289
Brown, Radcliffe 81
Bruning, H. 259
Buchanan, James xvii, 213
Buchanan, John P. 279
Burchardt, Frank 5, 89–90
Burk, A. 116
Burns, Arthur and Evelyn 151
Bush, Winston C. 288
Busuioc, Otilia 106
Byrnes, J.F. 158

Cairncross, Alec 82, 150, 264
Carré, J.C. 305
Cassel, Gustav 20
Castle, Barbara 93
Ceriani, Luigi xiii
Chacholiades, Miltiades 160
Chamberlin, Edward 5, 210
Chandler, Lester 216, 223
Chenery, Hollis 96, 133, 142, 145, 176
Chipman, J. 36
Clark, John Maurice 150–1
Clayton, William L. 153, 158

Coase, R. 287
Coculescu, Nicolae 109
Coe, Frank 152
Cohen, Andrew 93
Corbett, Patrick 91
Cournot, A. 9
Cowles, Alfred (III) 120
Craig, C.C. 114, 120
Crosfield, Ned 90
Crossman, Richard 83
Crum, W. Leonard 117, 119

Dahrendorf, Ralph 266
Dalton, George 145
Darmois, Georges 111–12, 114, 116, 303
Davidoglu, Anton 105
Davies, William 81, 94
Davis, Harold 120
Day, Edmund 119
Debreu, Gerard 9, 263, 299–300
DeMarco, De Viti 4, 283
Demaria, Giovanni 4
Despres, Emile 152–5
Dewey, Davis R. 159
Dick, Marcus 91
Divisia, Francois 5, 110
Domar, Evsey 91, 264
Donges, Juergen B. 267, 273
Donovan, William J. 154
Dorfman, Robert 131, 217
Dorrance, Graeme 263
Dreyer, J.S. 36, 170
Drèze, J. 307
Durand, E. Dana 154
Durbin, E. 303
Dubois, P. 305
Dubourdieu, G. 5
Dumontier, Jacques 5

Eckstein, Otto 216
Einstein, Albert 99, 121
Ellis, Howard 217
Ellsworth, Paul 59
Erhard, L. 262, 268–70
Evans, Griffith C. 120
Evans, Herberton 91
Eyrault, M. 1

Faaland, Juist 264
Fabian, Tibor 236
Faulhaber, Gerald 227–30
Felix, Julienne 109
Fellner, William 267
Fels, Gerhard 267, 269, 273
Fels, R. 117
Fenichel, Otto 73
Finch, David 212
Findlay, Ronald 160
Fischer, Dietrich 227–8, 231
Fisher, Irving 121–2, 126, 303
Fisher, R.A. 114–15
Flanders, Alan 90
Flemming, Marcus 214
Florinsky, Michael 152
Foley, Duncan 225, 232
Fraser, Lindley 82
Frechet, Maurice 109
Fredholm, Erik Ivar 106
Frere, Maurice 33
Freud, Sigmund 3
Friedan, Betty 144
Friedman, Milton xvi, 92, 123, 150–1, 236, 243, 248, 251, 300
Frisch, Ragnar 123–4, 303
Froehlick, Walter 74
Fuchs, Klaus 84
Fyfe, William Hamilton 83

Gaitskell, Hugh 3
Gangemi, Lello 4
Gates, Noel 90
Geary, R.C. 115
Gellner, Ernest 90
Gerschenkron, A. 5
Gibbs, Willard J. 119
Gini, Corrado 4
Goetz, Charles 292
Gold, Tommy 84
Goldsmith, Raymond 267–8
Gonnard, René 1
Gordon, Aaron 152, 217
Goschen, George J. 20
Goulart, Joao 126
Gould, Julius 90, 209
Goursat, Eduard 108–9
Graaff, Jan de Villiers 91, 213
Graham, F. 158

Name Index

Griliches, Zvi 131

Haberler, Gottfried 2, 30, 34, 37, 64, 74, 263, 267
Haferkamp, Wilhelm 270
Hahn, Frank 212, 215, 307
Halm, G. 272
Hamilton, Alexander 184
Hamilton, Earl J. 284
Hankey, Beatrice 80
Hansen, Alvin 154
Harberger, Arnold 49
Hardy, Charles O. 42
Harris, Marshal 156
Harrod, Roy 5, 264
Hayek, Friedrich A. von 2, 5, 35, 74, 126, 212, 263, 301
Heilperin, Michael 151
Heller, Walter 150
Henderson, David 264
Henderson, Hubert 89
Hesse, Hermann 81
Heyn, Otto 20
Hicks, John R. 51–2, 90, 115, 149, 213, 261, 301, 303, 306–7
Hicks, Ursula 5, 127
Hilbert, D. 120
Hilgerdt, Folke 185, 187
Hirsch, Fred 86
Hirschman, Albert 77
Hoffmann, Walther 261–2, 264
Hoffmann, Lutz 267
Hollander, Samuel 214
Hoover, E.M. 118, 152
Hotelling, Harold 121
Hoyle, Fred 85
Huber, M. 111
Hughes, Jonathan 145
Hume, David 182–3, 185, 191
Huntington, Edward V. 119
Hurst, Leonard 112
Hurwicz, Leonid 300, 302
Hutchinson, Terence 263
Hutt, William 263
Hymer, Stephen 160

Isard, Walter 5

Jahnsson, Yrjo 308

Jahoda, Marie 73
Jacobsson, Per 154, 264
Jensen, Michael 253
Johnson, Harry 91–2, 110, 160
Jones, Ronald 160
Jordan, Jerry 236
Joskow, Jules 210
Julia, Gaston 109

Kahn, R.F. 90, 213
Kaldor, Nicholas xiii, 118, 123, 150, 212
Kalecki, Michał xviii, 5, 89
Karsten, Karl 110
Kasper, Wolfgang 267
Kaufman, Felix 3
Kelsen, Hans 78
Kendall, M.G. 117
Keynes, J.M. xix, 4–5, 30, 35, 114, 126, 210
Kindleberger, Charles xv, xvii–xviii, 59
Knight, Frank H. 279, 282–3, 289, 301
Knight, Rex 83
Koestler, Arthur 85
Kolm, Serge-Christophe 225
Koopmans, Tjalling 300
Koppelmann, Friederike 262, 264
Kornai, J. 302
Koyck, L.M. 263
Kris, Ernst 83
Krishna, Raj 95
Kuznets, George 131
Kuznets, Simon 91, 171–3, 192

Lachmann, L.M. 263
Lalescu, Traian 105–6, 109, 118
Lall, Sanjaya 92
Lange, Oskar 118–19, 261
Lapedatu, Al 107
Laski, Harold 212, 263
Latsis, S. 258
Layard, R. 305
Lazarsfeld, Paul 73, 216–17
Lebesgue, Henri 108–9
Lehmann, Lotte 3
Leibenstein, Harvey 216–17
Leinsdorf, Count 76

Name Index

Leontief, Wassily 5, 118, 263–4
Lerner, A. 35, 261
Lester, Richard 215, 223
Levy, Walter 155
Lewis, W. Arthur 90, 175, 192, 212, 223
Lewis, Arthur and Gladys 215
Leys, Colin 91
Liefmann-Keil, Elisabeth 266
Lieser, Berger 2
Linder, Staffman Burenstam 161
Lindsay, A.D. 90
Lingen, Count 84
Lipton, Michael 92
Long, Clarence 91
Losch, August 257, 261, 263
Lucas, Robert 246–7
Lutfalla, G. 5
Lutz, Friedrich 158, 215, 223, 263, 267

MacDougall, Donald 150
Machlup, Fritz xiv, xvii–xviii, 2, 74, 83, 91, 118, 151, 158, 223–4, 272
Mackinnon, Donald 89
Mackintosh, William 154
Magee, Stephen 160
Mahalanobis, P.C. 97
Maihofer, Werner 266
Mandelbaum, Kurt 96
Manoilescu, Mihail 107
March, Lucien 108, 111
Margolis, Julius 210
Marris, Robin 219
Marschak, Jacob 127, 300
Marshall, Alfred 114, 167, 185, 200, 202, 207, 269
Marshall, George C. 153, 157
Mason, Edward S. 155
Masse, P. 301
May, Stacy 117, 119
Mayer, Hans 2, 34
McCracken, Paul 275
McKenzie, Lionel 213
McLuhan, Marshall 94
McRae, Donald 90
Meade, James 46, 59, 150, 161, 212, 263

Mears, I. 133
Meckling, William 255
Meier, G.M. 91
Meinl, Julius 34
Meltzer, Allan H. 236, 238, 241, 243, 255
Mestmacker, Ernst-Joachim 266
Metzler, Lloyd 241, 301
Meyer, Fritz 269
Mill, John Stuart 150
Milligan, Martin 90
Millikan, Max 149
Minkes, Leonard 90
Mintoff, D. 96
Mises, Ludwig von 1, 3, 18, 34, 74
Mitchell, W.C. 151
Mitrany, David 121
Monahan, James 94
Monnet, Jean 188
Montias, Mike 267
Morgenstern, Oskar 2, 7, 34, 64, 127, 223–4
Morris, Cynthia Taft 133, 135, 140, 143, 145
Morrisson, Christian 136
Morse, Chandler 155
Mundell, Robert 160
Mundlak, Yair 131
Muth, Jack 246
Muth, Richard 91
Myrdal, Gunnar 4, 92, 96

Naipul, Shiva 178
Neisser, Hans 42
Neumark, Fritz 4
Neurath, Otto 73, 81
Nicolson, Harold 83
Nimitz, C.W. 281
Nourse, Edwin 268
Nurkse, Ragnar 59, 96
Nutter, Warren 292

Oates, Wallace 224
Ohkawa, K. 172–3, 194
Ohlin, Bertil 30
Ohlin, Goran 263
Olsen, Mancur 213
Onicescu, Octav 103
Orcutt, Guy 49

Name Index

Palomba, Giuseppe 4
Pant, Pitambar 97
Pantaleoni, Maffeo 4
Panzar, John 227–9
Papi, Ugo 4
Pareto, Vilfredo 7
Parkinson, Jack 264
Paterson, Alexander 85
Patinkin, Don 91, 216
Peacock, Alan 263
Pearson, Karl 112–16
Penrose, Edith 91
Pepelassis, A. 133
Perlman, Mark 91
Persons, Warren M. 110, 116–17
Phelps, E. 247
Planck, Max 126
Pigou, A.C. 13, 123, 225, 287
Poincare, H. 109–10, 116, 120
Popper, Karl xv, 73, 212, 263, 298

Quandt, Richard 216

Raa, Thijs ten 227
Radice, E.A. 151
Radulescu, Gheorghe 101, 106
Ramsey, Frank 230
Ranis, Gustav 267
Rasche, Robert 238
Rawls, John 290
Reddaway, B. 264
Reich, William xv, 73
Ricardo, D. 18, 20, 200
Rietz, H.L. 117
Rist, Charles 111
Robbins, Lionel xvi, 35, 212–14, 263
Robertson, Dennis 5, 55, 166, 213
Robinson, Joan 5, 59, 210, 213, 262
Robinson, Sherman 138–40
Rockefeller, John D. (III) 209, 220
Rosenstein-Rodan, Paul 96, 192
Roll, Erich (Lord) 264
Romanowsky, V. 114
Roos, Charles F. 120
Roosa, Robert V. 157
Rosovsky, H. 172–3, 194
Rossitter (alias P. Rosenthal) 261

Rostow, W.W. xv, xvii, 155, 157
Rowse, A.L. 81
Roy, Rene 5
Ruck, Berta 87
Rueff, Jacques 111

Salant, William A. 150, 155, 157
Samuelson, Paul 5, 124, 149–50, 159, 213–14, 242, 303
Sanielevici, Samuel 106
Sargan, J. 303
Sargent, T. 247
Savage, Leonard 300
Scarf, Herbert 138
Schacht, Hjalmar 27
Schiller, Karl 269, 271, 273
Schilpp, Paul 99
Schlick, Moritz 75
Schmeidler, David 225
Schmidt, Helmut 273–4
Schmitt, Carl 4
Schmolder, Gunter 260
Schneider, Erich 4, 268, 272
Schultz, Henry 120, 122
Schumacher, E.F. 151
Schumpeter, Joseph xv, 2, 5, 112, 116, 118, 125, 129, 227
Schuster, Arthur 112
Scitovsky, Tibor 144
Scott, Lila 280
Scott, Maurice 164
Scweinitz, Karl de 145
Seers, Dudley 95
Senf, Paul 266
Servien, Pius (Serban) 109
Shapiro, Eli 152
Shubik, Martin 216
Sievert, Olaf 266–7, 269
Simkovitch, Vladimir G. 152
Skelton, Alexander 154
Smith, Adam 12, 183–4, 249, 252, 254
Snow, Lord 100
Sohmen, Egon 160, 266, 271
Solow, Robert 149
Sombart, Werner 3
Southard, Frank 61
Spann, Othmar 2, 20, 77
Sproul, Allan 153

Name Index

Stackelberg, H. von 4
Staley, Eugene 185, 187
Stefani, Alberto de 4
Stegemann, Klaus 267
Steindl, J. 5
Stem, Paul 73
Stresemann, G. 259
Stewart, Frances 92
Stigler, George 150, 214
Stone, Richard 5, 303–4
Straub, F.J. 271
Streeten, Dorothy and Marjorie 80
Streeten, Paul xiv, xvii–xviii, 5, 59, 267
Streit, Manfred 267
Strigl, R. von 2
Strowski, Fortunat 109
Stubblebine, W.C. 287
Stutzel, Wolfgang 266
Sweezy, Paul 118
Szeliski, Victor von 120

Taussig, Frank 118–19, 123–4
Theil, H. 303
Timm, Herbert 262, 266
Tinbergen, J. 140, 142, 262
Tintner, Gerhard 118, 127
Titeica, George 105
Tobin, Jim 267, 277
Triffin, Robert 9, 267
Tullock, Gordon 213, 286, 289–90, 292
Turvey, Ralph 212, 263

Uri, Pierre 4

Vanek, Jaroslav 160
Vaubel, Roland 277
Vallarche, 2
Veblen, Thorstein 209
Villard, H.H. 151

Viner, Jacob xiv, 46, 154, 158, 215, 223, 232
Vining, Rutledge 289
Voegelin, Erich 75
Volterra, Vito 106, 120, 124

Wagemann, Ernst 127
Wagner, Richard E. 287
Wald, Abraham 127
Walker, Francis A. 159
Wallich, Henry 267
Wallis, Allen 151
Walras, Leon 1, 4–5, 261
Waugh, Frederick 211
Whalley, John 138
Wheeler, Donald 155
White, Charles P. 281
White, Harry Dexter 152, 154
Wicksell, Knut 4, 283, 285–7
Wilde, Johannes 85
Wilde, Oscar 77
Williams, John 35, 51, 149, 153, 214
Williamson, Oliver 219
Willig, Robert 227–9, 231
Willis, H. Parker 152
Wilson, E.B. 119
Wold, Herman 112, 124, 134–5, 140, 303
Wold, Svant 135
Wood, Ralph 61
Working, Holbrook 120
Worswick, G.D.N. 90

Younes, Y. 307
Young, Allyn xiii

Zellner, Arnold 131
Zilsel, Edgar 83
Zimmern, Alfred 150
Zuckerman, Solly 157